D0946474

The Myth of Market Failure

A World Bank Research Publication

The Myth of Market Failure

Employment and the Labor Market in Mexico

Peter Gregory

Published for The World Bank
THE JOHNS HOPKINS UNIVERSITY PRESS
Baltimore and London

Manufactured in the United States of America
First printing May 1986

The Johns Hopkins University Press
Baltimore, Maryland 21211, U.S.A.

Library of Congress Cataloging-in-Publication Data

Gregory, Peter.
The myth of market failure.

"Published for the World Bank."
Bibliography: p.
Includes index.
1. Labor supply—Mexico. 2. Wages—Mexico.
3. Migration, Internal—Mexico. 4. Mexico—Emigration and immigration. 5. United States—Emigration and immigration. I. World Bank. II. Title.
HD5731.A6G74 1986 331.12'0972 85-45927
ISBN 0-8018-3343-4

Contents

Preface

THIS BOOK is the outgrowth of research supported by the World Bank. The Bank has had a longstanding interest in the performance of labor markets in the developing countries. Over the past ten years, it has sponsored a series of inquiries into various aspects of labor market operation that has contributed greatly to our fund of knowledge and understanding of labor market phenomena. I feel fortunate to have been a participant in these inquiries for they have afforded me an opportunity to conduct research in greater depth than would have been possible with the resources available to most academic scholars. When I undertook this study of the Mexican labor market, I had no intention of writing a book-length manuscript. Rather, I expected to produce a report that would trace with broad strokes the changes that had occurred in the conditions of employment from about 1940 to 1980. My previous work on Mexico had partially prepared me for this task, and I expected that I would be able to complete it in expeditious fashion. Since I had been advised to base my study largely on published primary and secondary sources of information, I foresaw an effort constrained by a relative paucity of useful and reliable information.

I had long been aware of the assessment of employment conditions that prevailed in Mexico. It was one that stood in contradiction to a record of steady and relatively rapid growth. Employment conditions were held to be "bad" and even deteriorating. Virtually all of the literature dealing directly with employment was painted with the same brush. In view of the unanimity of Mexican and foreign observers, I was inclined to give some credence to this view, even though I detected elements in the picture that were not entirely consistent with it. Therefore, I welcomed the opportunity to examine the Mexican experience more closely, for Mexico seemed to me to pose a critical challenge to the hopes and aspirations of many developing countries. For, if Mexico, with its high and sustained rate of growth over a forty-year period, has been unable to realize an improvement in the general working conditions of most of its labor force, what hope could other countries with lesser rates of growth entertain of improving the lot of their people?

As I proceeded with my inquiry, I became increasingly dubious of the correctness of the common characterizations of current conditions in the labor market and of their evolution over time. Since my findings have proved to stand in such complete opposition to the established view, I felt that I could receive a hearing for my heretical notions only if I developed the case for them as carefully and as fully as I could. The result of that effort has grown into this book. I do not pretend that it addresses all of the questions that are of interest to students of labor markets and employment conditions. Limitations of both time and relevant information led me to pass over additional topics of interest. Rather, I have tried to focus on some of the elements that are critical to an evaluation of market performance, some of which are frequently cited as bases for conclusions that are sharply different from mine. Where I have found a traditional view wanting, I have attempted to make explicit the inadequacies of its conceptual or methodological underpinnings as I perceive them and then to set forth the evidence and reasoning leading to a different conclusion.

This work would have been much poorer but for the help and encouragement of many individuals and institutions. Without the material support of the World Bank, this study could not have been undertaken, and I gratefully acknowledge that support. Of equal importance has been the encouragement and critical comments of the several staff economists of the Bank who attended seminars on my research or who reviewed earlier drafts of my manuscript and offered many valuable suggestions. In particular, I am indebted to Mark Leiserson and Guy Pfeffermann for their careful readings and thoughtful comments. Although the Bank's support was critical to this undertaking, it could not have been accomplished without the cooperation and generous assistance of many individuals and institutions in Mexico. To all of them I extend my heartfelt thanks. A special note of thanks goes to Micha Gisser, my colleague at the University of New Mexico, who, during countless hours of jogging with me, served as a proving ground for many of the ideas and conclusions that appear in this book. I also thank Alice Scott and Patricia Gonzalez for typing various drafts of the manuscript. Finally, I wish to acknowledge the patience, understanding, and encouragement given me by my wife, Doris, and our children, Beate and Tom, during the seemingly endless process of producing this manuscript.

1. Introduction

THE DECADE OF THE 1970s witnessed the emergence of a widespread concern over employment conditions in developing countries. This development represented a significant shift in emphasis from the concerns that heretofore had dominated discussions of the problems of economic development. In the period shortly following World War II, economic development was viewed primarily as a problem of capital accumulation and growth of output. Implicit in this emphasis was the assumption that employment was simply a function of the rate of capital accumulation since capital–labor ratios were assumed to be fixed in most of the planning models of the times. Thus the emphasis in development planning rested on maximizing the rate of growth in the capital stock, and little explicit consideration was given to the implications of growth for employment. If anything, it was assumed that the developing countries of today would reproduce the patterns of labor force structure that the now-developed countries had manifested during successive stages of their earlier development.

That an employment "problem" might be a cause of concern followed the observation that the structure of employment in developing countries was evolving along a path that differed greatly from that followed during the industrialization of the developed countries. In particular, it was noted that, in developing countries, while accelerated development yielded early gains in employment in the "productive" sectors of industry and construction, these were soon surpassed by a rapid expansion of employment in the tertiary (service) sector. By contrast, today's industrialized nations did not experience rapid growth in tertiary sector employment until a much later stage in their development.[1] This unexpected growth was widely interpreted as unfavorable for the quality of employment. The tertiary sector came to be viewed as the sector of last resort, a sponge capable of absorbing, via jobs of very low productivity, all those unable to secure preferred employment in the "productive sectors." In view of the low absorptive capacity of the modern industrial sector and the rapidly increasing labor forces of most developing countries, an air of alarm replaced the complacency of the previous decades. Numerous comparative and country studies appeared, cataloguing the form and extent of underutilization of labor forces in developing countries. Invariably, the studies concluded that unemployment and underemployment affected a substantial proportion of labor forces in these countries, and that development strategies could no longer afford to ignore the implications for employment of alternative policy paths. This concern over employment was also heightened by an increasing interest in the social consequences of development and in the distribution of income.

The Employment Problem in Mexico

During the 1970s, Mexico began to mirror these same concerns. Several studies of employment conditions were spawned, all of which concluded that the labor force suffered from serious underutilization. Indeed, it was frequently stated that, not only were employment conditions currently unfavorable, but that they had actually deteriorated over time. During the regime of President López Portillo, finding a solution to the problem of employment was elevated to matter of high priority, and a national commission, the Comisión Consultiva del Empleo, was constituted to analyze the problem and propose policy measures for its amelioration. In 1979, the commission reaffirmed estimates that had been arrived at by other groups: an earlier national commission, the Grupo de Estudio sobre el Problema del Empleo, by the Regional Employment Program for Latin America and the Caribbean of the International Labour Office (PREALC), and by others. They agreed that approximately half of the labor force was either unemployed or underemployed and that the full-time equivalent of this underutilization amounted to an open unemployment rate approximating 25 percent of the labor force. The integration of the rapidly growing labor force and the backlogged stock of underemployed labor was viewed to be a herculean task that called for the maintenance of a high rate of overall growth as well as a series of policy measures calculated to increase the employability of labor.

Fortified by a rapidly swelling volume of revenues from petroleum exports and international credits, Mexico embarked on an expansionary course designed to stimulate growth and accelerate the rate of job creation. It was estimated that a growth rate of 7.5 percent was required to absorb increases in the labor force and to reverse the "deterioration in employment conditions" that accompanied the recession of 1976–77.[2] Beginning in 1978, the economy responded with annual growth rates of more than 8 percent that were to extend over four years. In view of the large volume of underutilized labor supposedly overhanging the labor market, one might reasonably have expected employers to be faced by ample supplies of labor. Yet, this did not prove to be the case. After only two years of growth at a rate of only about 2 percentage points above the long-run average growth rate of Mexico, unmistakable signs of labor shortages began to appear in many sectors and regions. Shortages were not limited only to skilled personnel—which would have been understandable—but extended to unskilled labor as well. "Help Wanted" signs could be seen posted at construction sites, and women began to appear in substantial numbers in construction crews. Although the legal minimum wage had customarily not been exceeded, by 1981 the wage for unskilled labor in construction was reported to have risen to one and one-half times the legal minimum in several cities around the country. The managers and owners of small and medium-size establishments in manufacturing whom I interviewed reported a ratio of only 2 to 3 applicants to every advertised vacancy of entry-level jobs, not all of whom were considered qualified for employment. The commercial agricultural sector, heavily dependent on seasonal labor, similarly reported difficulties in recruiting adequate labor forces.

The rapidity with which a condition of surplus labor had become one of shortage greatly surprised most Mexican observers, including government officials. How could the common perception have been so far off the mark? Was the fault to be found in the weakness of the empirical data on which these appraisals had been based? Were the underlying concepts adopted to characterize conditions in the labor market faulty? Or did the quality of analysis that had been applied to the problem leave something to be desired? These questions have more than a passing interest to economic policymakers. For example, had perceptions of the nature of the employment problem been different, would the López Portillo government have embarked on such an ambitious expansionary program that has proved, in retrospect, to have had disastrous consequences for Mexico?

I have concluded that the misreading of the nature of the employment problem derived not only from conceptual shortcomings but also from an incomplete or partial analysis, that is, a failure to include in the analysis more of the variables that are essential to an accurate appreciation of labor market operation. To be sure, labor market information is relatively scarce, particularly in a consistent form over time; data are scattered and often of dubious quality. But had labor market analyses been more systematic, had they been guided by a clear conceptualization of the market relationships that must hold if an internally consistent construct is to emerge, I believe that a very different perception of market conditions would have emerged.

Earlier Studies of the Mexican Labor Market

Throughout this book, I will refer to the conclusions of earlier studies of the Mexican labor market and will comment on the conceptual and empirical bases of those conclusions in some detail. As a backdrop to my study, however, it would be useful to review briefly the nature of those appraisals as well as some of their salient features.

By and large, Mexican studies of labor market conditions have focused on those prevailing at a moment in time, for example, as revealed by a population census. There have been intercensal comparisons made of measures such as labor force participation rates, unemployment, or the sectoral distribution of the labor force. Most of the analysis is static, however, and fails to address the determinants of change over time and thus does not explore fully the significance of observable changes. Consequently, one misses any sense of the dynamics of labor market operation and of the significant changes that have occurred in the welfare of the labor force over time. For example, it should come as no surprise to anyone that the employment conditions of a substantial proportion of the labor force are deplorable and that the income position of many households is precarious. Nevertheless, is the observation of such a state at a moment in time a sufficient basis for concluding that conditions in labor markets are deteriorating and that unemployment and underemployment are increasing in gravity?[3] Ordinarily, evidence of deterioration requires the comparison of observations at two points in time at the least in order to establish a trend, yet one looks in vain for a careful empirical documentation of trends that are supportive of such a strong and pessimistic conclusion.

The observations and their interpretation that underlie the pessimistic appraisal of Mexican labor market conditions before the economic crisis of 1982 and the recession that followed echo those that had become commonplace in much of the literature of the 1960s and early 1970s on employment conditions in developing countries. Most worrisome to observers was the "rapid" expansion of tertiary sector employment, a growth that was viewed as premature and indicative of a failure of the development process to create a sufficient number of preferred jobs at acceptably high levels of productivity. In the absence of significant barriers to entry, the tertiary sector could absorb unlimited quantities of labor in low-paying, low-productivity jobs, which would often be of a self-employed nature. Such activity was usually interpreted as seriously under-employing workers or as representing little more than disguised unemployment.[4] In more recent treatments of this theme, references to the absorptive role of this sector commonly use the word "informal" in place of "tertiary."[5]

Associated with the growth of tertiary sector employment was an acceleration of rural-urban migration. Rural poverty and limited land and employment opportunities were thought to be pushing the rural population toward the cities where, in view of the scarcity of job opportunities in the modern industrial sector, workers were forced to crowd into the tertiary or informal sector on unfavorable terms.[6] Migration came to be viewed as a process that simply transformed rural poverty into urban poverty. Hopes for increasing income by migrating were held to have been largely dashed.[7] A consequence of the rapid growth of the urban population under such unfavorable conditions has been the increasing "marginalization" of the population, groups divorced from the mainstream of economic, cultural, and political life.[8] By and large, this appreciation of employment conditions in Mexico has never been subjected to rigorous testing, although the conclusions drawn have given rise to empirically testable propositions. For example, consider the conclusion that the growth of tertiary sector employment has been "excessive"; rather than being seen as a response to demand, this growth is believed to be a consequence of an increase in the supply of labor. If, indeed, the surge has been supply determined, predictable consequences flowing from such growth should be observable. If the number of available workers is increasing more rapidly than is the quantity of labor demanded at the prevailing wage, then rates of earnings could be expected to show declines over time. If wages in the tertiary sector were above the subsistence level before the onset of accelerated growth in employment, these should have fallen toward the subsistence level. If wages had been at the subsistence level originally, then they could be expected to hover around the subsistence level, with declines below that level carrying with them increases in mortality rates, as a weakened and undernourished population succumbed to disease. Does evidence of such a deterioration in remuneration levels exist? If not, on what basis can it be argued that the growth of tertiary employment has been "excessive"? Unfortunately, any reference to empirical evidence of the secular course of wages is absent in these discussions.

Similar questions can be posed about the rate of rural-urban migration. What is an appropriate test of whether or not migration has been excessive and has increased poverty? From the point of view of the private welfare of migrants, migration becomes excessive if it is associated with a decline in income that is not expected to be offset by future increases. Stated more precisely, migration might be deemed to be excessive if the present value of the expected future stream of earnings and social services in the city (net of the costs of migration) is less than that of future earnings and social services in the countryside. Were this to describe accurately the fate of migrants, and migration were observed to continue at a high level, one would be led to the implausible conclusion that migrants are irrational in opting for an inferior material standard of living. If it is difficult to conclude that migrants are irrational, then the premise that migration leads to impoverishment should be reexamined. Certainly, what happens to migrants' incomes is an empirically verifiable phenomenon as is their perception of the change in their material welfare. Indeed, in Mexico substantial literature exists on empirical studies of migration and its economic consequences for the migrants. What is surprising is that the findings of such studies should be ignored in the various diagnostic studies of the employment problem of Mexico.

As indicated earlier, the conceptual and measurement aspects of underutilization of the labor force are open to question. Leaving these aspects aside for the moment, let us grant that underutilization has amounted to the equivalent of a 25 percent open unemployment rate, as has been concluded by the studies cited earlier. A further question still remains, however, that is particularly relevant for policymaking. What is the significance of this unemployment rate equivalent for the operation of the labor market? Is it correct to assume that it represents a supply of labor effectively available to certain expanding economic sectors, and, if so, at what wage rate? Essentially, this question addresses the elasticity of supply. Would employers in a rapidly expanding economy be faced with a perfectly elastic supply of labor as long as this "surplus" survived? While prediction is always difficult in economics, some helpful inferences might be derived from past experience. What has been the course of market-determined wages in the expanding employment sectors in the past? If real wages were found to have been rising coincident with annual rates of growth in the gross domestic product on the order of 6 percent, is there any reason to believe that a more rapid rate of growth could be accommodated without an even faster rate of increase in wages? Indeed, if past increases in employment were accompanied by increases in market-determined wages, what operational meaning does a labor surplus of 25 percent of the labor force really have? By contrast, if expansion of employment in the past has taken place at constant or even falling wages, this would support the view that the supply schedule of labor has been highly elastic and that an accelerated rate of growth could be accommodated without serious wage inflation. Again, however, this is an empirical question that can be resolved by reference to the past behavior of employment and wages.

Unfortunately, none of the diagnoses of Mexico's employment problem includes such a component.

Labor Market Models

The analysis and interpretation of labor market phenomena are likely to be most fruitful if they depart from a hypothesized statement of market relationships that can be empirically tested. Essentially, what a student of the Mexican labor market would like to establish is a model that most closely describes how that market functions. At least three models have been offered in the literature as descriptive of labor markets in developing countries. These include the neoclassical and dual labor market models; the latter is divided into those positing competitive market conditions in all sectors and those postulating the existence of barriers to entry and of institutional intervention in at least one segment of the labor market. Each model identifies the variables relevant to its operation and yields an observable outcome that flows from its underlying premises. Students of labor markets are thus provided with guidance in what to look for in their efforts to characterize any particular market. Let us consider these models and indicate how they might serve as useful guides to market analysis.

The neoclassical model provides the simplest descriptive statement of market operation. Competitive conditions prevail in all segments of the labor market, and mobility of labor is unhindered and serves an equilibrating function. In such a market, labor is fully employed, and open unemployment takes on the character of frictional unemployment. The existence of wage differentials in different parts of the labor market for a particular class of labor would be expected to give rise to movement of labor from low- to higher-wage employments, and, over time, differentials could be expected to shrink until they reflected only the monetary and nonmonetary costs of moving. An alternative scenario would be that, in order for an expanding sector to attract additional supplies of labor, a higher wage would have to be offered, which would open up a differential in the wages paid among sectors and stimulate mobility. In a dynamic and growing economy, equilibrium would be unlikely. Rather, the growth process would be characterized by successive movements away fom equilibrium as new focuses of growth emerged and by responses on the supply side that moved the market back toward a state of equilibrium. The empirical testing of such a model would focus on labor mobility and its correlates and on the course of wages in different segments of the labor market. Rapidly expanding sectors would be expected to face labor supply schedules that were upward sloping.

Another model of the labor market is offered by those who postulate the existence of a labor surplus in the rural sector that could be drawn upon for the expansion of the urban or industrial sectors.[9] Such models posit the existence of a dual labor market. In the rural sector, the marginal product of labor is negligible or zero; labor is compensated at a rate equal to its average product. As long as the condition of surplus labor survives in the rural sector, the supply of unskilled labor to the expanding urban sector will be perfectly elastic at a wage equal to the rural average product of labor plus a differential that compensates movers for the economic and noneconomic costs of movement. Only when the surplus has been absorbed, that is, when the marginal product of rural labor equals that of urban labor, will wages begin to rise in both sectors as the process of urban or industrial expansion continues.[10] The relevance of this model to any particular labor market can also be tested by focusing on the course of productivity of low-skilled labor in the rural and urban sectors and on the course of wages over time in the expanding urban sector. If the economy is characterized by the existence of surplus labor, one would expect to find the expansion of low-skilled employment in the urban sector to have occurred at a stable level of wages over time. Urban open unemployment would be expected to be negligible or of the frictional variety. If, at some point in time, the labor surplus has finally been absorbed, subsequent expansion of the urban sector would be expected to become possible only at successively higher wages, with wages in the rural sector following. At such a point, the surplus labor model ceases to serve as the appropriate model of the labor market and is supplanted instead by the neoclassical.

A third model, formulated by Michael Todaro, is a variant of the surplus labor model described aove.[11] The distinguishing feature of this model is the division of the urban labor market into two segments. The modern or industrial segment is noncompetitive, with wages established by institutional intervention (legal minimum wages, collective bargaining, and so on) at levels far above the opportunity cost of labor. Barriers to entry limit access to these preferred employments. Although the probabilities of immediate absorption in the high-wage sector are very low, the relative attractiveness of employment conditions in this sector nevertheless spurs rural–urban migration. The result is the formation of an urban queue as migrants wait for opportunities to materialize in the sectors of preferred employment; successful entry is a function of the length of time spent in the queue. The rate of migration to the urban sector will be governed by the relation between the present value of the expected streams of future net income from urban and rural employment. In turn, the present value of the future income stream that can be derived from urban employment will be heavily influenced by the probabilities assigned to successful entry to a preferred employment in successive time periods. Obviously, the shorter the urban queue, the more is that present value enhanced. Thus the equilibrating variable that regulates the flow of migrants is the length of the queue, for it is this that brings about the equality in the present values of the two streams of urban and rural future earnings. Those who are in place in the urban queue are not necessarily completely idle, although open urban unemployment may reasonably be expected to be high and durable. They may engage in activities with very low productivity and at very low wages. Indeed, they may be willing to accept wages below their opportunity cost in the short run in the expectation that these will be fully compensated by the high wages that will be forthcoming once accession to the high-wage sector has been realized.

The applicability of this model can likewise be tested by reference to the experience of migrants and the course of wage differentials within the urban market and between the informal, or competitive, segment of the urban labor market and the rural. Migrants to urban areas would be expected to experience great difficulties in finding gainful employment. In addition, high rates of unemployment would be found among unskilled workers in urban areas, and where wages are market determined they would appear to be depressed to levels approximating or even below those in rural occupations. The urban wage differential between the two segments would be very wide and would show no tendency toward narrowing until the rural surplus and the urban queue had been fully absorbed.

The views of the Mexican labor market that prevailed before 1980 would appear to approximate most closely the conditions posed by this third model. Rural–urban migration was seen as "excessive" and as surpassing the rate of job creation in the formal sector. Barriers to entry to the preferred sectors of employment forced workers to seek jobs in the informal sector at market-determined wages that were inferior and stagnating. In these characterizations, the labor supply schedule to the urban labor market seems to have been viewed as perfectly elastic. Also consistent with the third model is the belief that open unemployment and underemployment have been increasing over time. While one can frequently offer particular observations that seem to be consistent with a surplus labor model, it is not clear that the weight of the empirical evidence would lead to the conclusion that such a model represents the closest approximation of reality in Mexico. But whether it does or does not is empirically verifiable. In my opinion, it is not possible to test adequately the appropriateness of any of the models discussed on the basis of information pertaining to a moment in time. Since neither the Mexican economy nor the models themselves are static in nature, the performance of the labor market cannot be fully appreciated without an examination of its operation and responsiveness to dynamic elements in the economic environment.

Overview

In undertaking this study of the Mexican labor market, I therefore chose to adopt as a frame of reference a time interval of forty years, 1940–80. Over that time span, significant changes occurred in the structure and productivity of the Mexican economy that were paralleled by changes in the occupational structure and sectoral distribution of the labor force. It is the latter set of changes that forms the central concern of this study. Not only are these developments scrutinized, but an attempt is made to identify the forces that guided them and to evaluate the effect they have had on the material welfare of the labor force. At the conclusion of this exercise, the labor market model that most closely fits the Mexican experience should be discernible. These findings could help to clarify the "employment problem" that Mexico faced in the years up through the 1970s and the relevance of this characterization for public policy. Although recent labor market conditions have changed radically from those prevailing before 1982, this report might be helpful in suggesting how labor market information could be organized and analyzed fruitfully.

The work is organized in the following manner. Chapter 2 charts with broad strokes the structural changes that have occurred in the Mexican economy over time as well as the changes in the size and distribution of the labor force. Particular attention is devoted to the growth of tertiary sector employment and its correlates. An initial effort is made to determine whether its growth has been "excessive."

Chapter 3 examines the issue of the underutilization of the labor force and the conceptual and measurement problems associated with it. The question of whether the rate of underutilization of the labor force had been increasing before 1980 is also addressed.

Then follows an overview of the agricultural sector and its role as a source of labor for the rest of the economy. Essential to an understanding of this role is a knowledge of agricultural productivity, the trends in the distribution of land among the rural population, and the links between rural and urban labor markets. These factors are explored in Chapter 4.

As was indicated in the preceding brief review of labor market models, mobility of labor plays a pivotal role in each. The characterization of the flow of labor among different sectors or markets is vital to comprehending how the labor market has functioned. Chapter 5 is therefore devoted to an exploration of internal migration, largely rural–urban in character.

The following chapter extends the area of migration to include movement of labor across the border to the United States. Such migration has implications for the size of the labor force that must be accommodated in Mexico and may significantly affect the conditions of employment there.

The size of the migrant flow, however, has been a subject of intense debate, with various parties offering widely different estimates of the number of temporary migrants in the United States at a moment of time and of the number that "leak" into the U.S. labor force on a prolonged or permanent basis. In Chapter 6, I review and evaluate the available information on this phenomenon.

One of the key variables in understanding the character and functioning of labor markets is wages. Each of the models reviewed above posits a certain wage behavior for low-skill labor that follows from the underlying assumptions about supply and demand conditions and the institutional characteristics of labor markets. Chapter 7 brings together wage information from several sources to chart their course over time. In addition, the probable effect of institutional intervention on the course of wages is assessed.

The final chapter provides an integrated summary of the major findings of this study. It also compares the performance of the Mexican labor market with the outcomes predicted by the three labor market models outlined earlier in this introduction in order to determine which model offers the closest approximation of the Mexican experience. Some observations are offered regarding the relevance of my findings for employment policy. The chapter concludes with a brief review of recent developments associated with the economic crisis that erupted in 1982 and their implications for employment and real wage levels.

For the most part, the research on which this survey of the Mexican experience is based has relied on information culled from official statistical sources and from research reported by other scholars. Unfortunately, many of the basic statistical materials pose a serious challenge to anyone who wishes to use them. There are few data sources that provide consistency over time in the definition of variables or in coverage, and in the quality or reliability of the data. Even the population censuses, which might be expected to fulfill these conditions most closely, suffer from grave deficiencies. For some variables, information is available only for selected points in time. Thus, in order to fill in gaps, I have frequently had to resort to scattered information, frequently of a less than rigorous quality, and culled from a variety of sources. The difficulties posed by various data sources will be outlined in the text so that the reader will able to form an opinion on their significance. A more detailed description of data problems encountered in the measurement and sectoral distribution of the labor force has been relegated to an appendix to Chapter 2. The product of this investigation can best be described as a mosaic, a panorama pieced together from a wide variety of sources. Just as a mosaic must be characterized by form and order if it is to convey successfully a recognizable image, so must the outcome of this study present an internally consistent account of labor market relations over time if it is to be judged successful. Although there are gaps remaining in the mosaic, by and large the findings of this report provide a reasonably consistent and convincing account of the evolution of employment conditions in a substantial part of the Mexican labor market.

Notes

1. Colin Clark, *Conditions of Economic Progress*, 3d ed. (London: MacMillan 1957), chap. 9.

2. Leopoldo Solís M., "Reflexiones sobre el panaorama general de la economía mexicana," in *El sistema económico mexicano* (Mexico, D.F.: Premia Editora, 1982), p. 348; see also Jesús Reyes Heroles G. G., "Hacia una politica integral de ingresos, salarios, empleo e inflación," in the same volume, pp. 250–76.

3. Comisión Consultiva de Empleo, *Programa nacional de empleo 1980–82: Síntesis* (Mexico, D.F.: Secretaría del Trabajo y Previsión Social, 1979), p. 25.

4. Saul Trejo R., "El desempleo en México: characteristicas generales," *Comercio exterior*, vol. 24, no. 7 (July 1974), p. 732.

5. This is a broader concept that includes activities in other sectors similar in character to those formerly ascribed to only the tertiary sector. Informal sector jobs are characterized by small-scale productive or service activities that are not effectively governed by legal employment provisions. Handicraft production, many self-employed and unremunerated family workers, domestic servants, and petty commerce would make up the bulk of the urban informal sector. The rural informal sector comprises "small" or "traditional" farm units. Typically, the informal sector is viewed as having very limited capital resources and as suffering from low productivity and earnings.

6. Comisión Consultiva de Empleo, *Programa nacional de empleo*, pp. 16–17, 27; Grupo de Estudio del Problema del Empleo, "El problema ocupacional en México: magnitud y recomendaciones," versión preliminar (Mexico, D.F., n.d.), pp. 143–51; Donald B. Keesing, "Employment and Lack of Employment in Mexico, 1900–70," in *Quantitative Latin American Studies: Methods and Findings*, ed. James W. Wilkie and Kenneth Ruddle (Los Angeles: University of California, L.A., Latin American Center, 1977), pp.3–21.

7. Saul Trejo R., "Desempleo y subocupación en México," *Comercio exterior*, vol. 22, no. 5 (May 1972), p. 413.

8. Rodolfo Stavenhagen, "Marginalidad, participación y estructura agraria en America Latina," *Demografía y economía*, vol. 4, no. 3 (1970), pp. 267–91.

9. W. Arthur Lewis, "Development with Unlimited Supplies of Labour," *Manchester School of Economic and Social Studies*, vol. 22 (May 1954), pp. 139–91; John C. H. Fei and Gustav Ranis, *Development of the Labor Surplus Economy: Theory and Policy* (Homewood, Ill.: Irwin, 1964).

10. Stated more precisely, this constancy in the supply price of labor to the urban sector

depends on the constancy of the income per worker in agriculture. If the average product of labor rises as mobility draws down the quantity of labor applied to rural production and if this increase is not siphoned away by taxes or rent payments to a land-owning class, rural labor income will rise, thus raising the supply price of labor to the urban sector before equality is achieved in the marginal products of labor in the two sectors.

11. Michael P. Todaro, "A Model of Labor Migration and Urban Unemployment in Less Developed Countries," *American Economic Review*, vol. 59, no. 1 (March 1969), pp. 138–48.

2. Evolution of the Labor Force, 1940–80

THE PERIOD OF ACCELERATED growth and modernization in Mexico dates from about 1940. The groundwork had already been laid by the sweeping changes flowing from the preceding thirty years of revolutionary activity, which produced far-reaching social and institutional upheavals. The onset of World War II brought with it a disruption of traditional sources of supply for industrial goods and stimulated the expansion of manufacturing production for internal consumption. The large-scale land distribution program of the Cárdenas regime during the preceding decade led to a substantial increase in the land under cultivation and in agricultural output. Thus, the decade saw all of the principal sectors of the economy growing in tandem fashion. As is evidenced in table 2-1, the rates of growth of the three broad sectors showed only small differences.

Following the end of the war and a return to more competitive conditions in product markets, the government opted for a policy of fostering the further growth of domestic industry behind protective tariff walls and import controls. It also embarked on a large-scale investment program to provide infrastructure for an emerging modern commercial agricultural sector. Major irrigation and road-building projects in the sparsely populated north and northwestern provinces stimulated continued expansion of agricultural output for both domestic consumption and for export. With the exhaustion of "easy" import substitution, incentives were adopted for domestic production of consumer durable goods and then for intermediate and capital goods. Throughout most of the past four decades, Mexico has succeeded in maintaining a high and stable rate of growth, one that faltered significantly only during the mid-years of the past decade.

Although the achievements of the Mexican economy are surely impressive, there remain serious areas of concern. A rapidly growing population of labor-force age poses a formidable challenge to the economy's ability to absorb it in productive employment. The pattern of development, particularly in agriculture, has been uneven. While a highly productive commercial agricultural sector has developed, the bulk of the rural population is to be found in areas with scarce land and water resources, where increases in productivity have been modest. Rural poverty remains a serious problem; some students of Mexico hold that the incomes of a sizable rural population have not shared in the general increase that characterizes the country as a whole, or have shared only to an insignificant extent. The relative distribution of income continues to rank among the most unequal in Latin America and appears to be emerging as an acute social and political issue. The diverse character of agriculture is indicated by the large differences between the productivity of land and labor among the three classes of agricultural holdings. In 1970, the output per hectare on farm units employing "modern technology" was four times that of subsistence farm units (those in which only a small part of output was for market). The ratio of output per worker was even greater, on the order of 20:1.[1] These differences within the sector, moreover, have strong regional associations. In 1960, for example, the output per hectare was 20 times greater in Sonora than in Quintana Roo. In twelve other states, the productivity of land was no greater than one-fourth that of Sonora.[2] Large differences in the earnings of agricultural wage earners provide a further indication of regional differences in employment opportunities and productivity. In 1970 the average wage per worker was 14 times higher in Baja California Sur than in the more congested central state of Hidalgo.[3] These differences in employment conditions among regions may be presumed to provide at least a partial explanation for seasonal migrations of agricultural workers as well as for the tendency for many agricultural households to supplement incomes from agriculture with earnings from nonagricultural employment.

The agricultural sector is not the only one to evince large differences in productivity and earnings among productive units. The industrial sector also demonstrates such variance, although it is not as pronounced as that for agriculture. In 1975, value added and total remunerations per worker in establishments employing more than 750 workers were 3.8 and 2.1 times greater, respectively, than in small shops with 5 or fewer employees.[4] In the service sector, the differential in the rate of earnings between small (5 or fewer employees) and large (more than 50 employees) establishments was more modest, on the order of 2.1:1 in 1975. In the same year, the differential in earnings between small and large establishments in commerce was slightly narrower at 1.8:1.[5]

Equally impressive as the differences in productivity and earnings within each of the sectors enumerated here are the differences among them, especially those between the agricultural and nonagricultural sectors. In 1970, value added per worker in the latter sector was 5.2 times greater than in the former. The difference may have been even greater if (as I

Table 2-1. *Gross Domestic Product by Broad Sector, 1940–79*

	Gross domestic product									
	Millions of 1950 pesos				Millions of 1970 pesos		Annual rate of change (percent)			
Sector[a]	1940	1950	1960	1970	1970 revised[b]	1980	1940–50	1950–60	1960–70	1970–80
Primary										
Banco de México	n.a.	8,874	11,433	16,473	52,123	75,704	5.9	2.2	3.7	3.4
Unikel	5,221	9,242	13,917	17,607				4.2	2.4	
Secondary										
Banco de México	n.a.	13,329	20,956	48,727	145,070	296,046	6.3	5.3	8.8	7.4
Unikel	6,789	12,466	24,603	52,203				7.0	7.8	
Tertiary										
Banco de México	n.a.	22,183	39,404	76,278	250,474.	481,090	5.9	7.4	6.8	6.7
Unikel	10,931	19,352	35,696	82,431				6.3	8.7	

Total										
Banco de México	n.a.	44,106	71,793	141,478	444,271	841,855	6.0	5.7	7.0	6.6
Unikel	22,940	41,060	74,215	152,251				6.1	7.5	

Note: Throughout the tables, pesos are of course Mexican pesos.

n.a. Not available.

a. The sectors are defined as follows: primary—agriculture, cattle, forestry, and fishing; secondary—manufacturing, construction, mining, petroleum, and electricity; tertiary—transportation, communications, commerce and finance, government, and other services.

b. The 1970 revised and 1980 GDP figures are derived from the revised national product series based on the input-output matrix of 1970 and on the 1970 weights of the various economic divisions. In addition, several changes have been made in the industrial classification of several activities. Consequently, the revised 1970 GDP and that for subsequent years are not comparable to those of earlier years. As a result of the methodological changes, the revised 1970 product emerges 6.1 percent greater than the earlier measure. The totals for 1970 revised and for 1980 are not equal to the sum of the sectoral values because of an adjustment involving the imputed value of banking services included in the net value added of the respective user sectors as well as of the tertiary sector. The adjustment amounted to −5,395.5 and −10,985.1 million pesos in 1970 and 1980, respectively. In the accounts for the other entries, the adjustment was made by including in their tertiary sector total the value of banking services net of the amounts included in the primary and secondary sectors.

Sources: 1940–70—Luis Unikel, *El desarrollo urbano de México*, 2d ed. (Mexico, D.F.: El Colegio de México, 1978), tables VI-A5 to VI-A8. 1950–70—Banco de México. 1970 revised–1980—Secretaría de Programación y Presupuesto, *Sistema de cuentas nacionales de México*, vol. 1, *Resumen general* (Mexico, D.F., 1981), and *Sistema de cuentas nacionales de México, 1978–80*, vol. 1 (Mexico, D.F., 1982).

believe) the agricultural labor force was underestimated by the 1970 census. It is not surprising, therefore, that most of the poverty in Mexico is to be found in the rural areas. On the basis of the 1975 income and expenditures survey, it has been estimated that approximately 52 percent of the poor families were in the agricultural sector. Stated in other terms, 76 percent of all families in the sector lived in poverty.[6] The prevalence and durability of large urban-rural income differentials is likely to have served as one important underlying factor explaining the large rural–urban migration as well as the tendency of rural residents to seek seasonal employment in urban labor markets. Luis Unikel estimates that 1.5 million persons moved from rural to urban areas between 1950 and 1970.[7]

Thus, after four decades of rapid growth in Mexico, large income differences survive among households, giving rise to an income distribution that must be ranked among the least egalitarian among semi-industrialized countries. Before 1980, most studies concluded that the relative distribution of income had shown little change over the preceding twenty years or so. The share of the bottom deciles revealed only a modest increase. This gain, as well as that of some of the intermediate levels, came at the expense of the top decile.

While the discussion above has highlighted the large differences in productivity and income that exist among different groups, it does not depict the substantial changes that have occurred within the labor force over time. Nor does it give any impressions of how the labor market has evolved in the course of development, or of how it has responded to, and facilitated, the changing structure of demand and output. In the sections that follow, I will trace and evaluate some of the major developments in the Mexican labor market and relate these to the general pattern of growth.

Size of the Labor Force

Analyses of the Mexican labor force are based on two principal sources of information. The decennial population censuses provide the basis for charting historical changes over time. For the period since 1973, an additional source has appeared in the form of a quarterly labor force survey, the *Encuesta continua sobre ocupación* (ECSO).[8] But only the three major metropolitan areas of Mexico City, Guadalajara, and Monterrey have been continuously surveyed since its inception. As the decade progressed, more regions of the country were added; by 1979, coverage had been extended to the whole country. Unfortunately, only one report was issued that reflected the full national coverage and that pertained to the first quarter of 1979. Thereafter, the Secretaría de Programación y Presupuesto reverted to abbreviated reports for the three major metropolitan areas. As of mid-1983, a new survey instrument with coverage limited to urban areas is being tested as a replacement for ECSO.

Population censuses are generally relied upon to provide benchmark measures of various population components, including the labor force. Particularly in the absence of continual and systematic sample surveys of households, the censuses assume a primary importance as sources of information about the size and characteristics of the labor force. In the case of Mexico, the 1950 census has come to be regarded as one of the more reliable censuses and has served as a benchmark for various population measures. The 1960 census is acknowledged to have been distorted by processing errors that yielded an inflated measure of the labor force. Several efforts to correct the original published results have been made, and these are reviewed in some detail in the appendix at the end of this chapter. The data for 1960 that I have chosen to use and that are recorded in table 2-2 reflect the adjustments made by Altimir.[9] The 1970 census has not been subjected to the close scrutiny accorded the 1960 census in view of its greater apparent "reasonableness." Nevertheless, it appears to me that the 1970 census significantly underenumerated the male labor force, and I have adjusted the data reported by this census accordingly.

The 1980 census, by all general accounts, is a distinct disappointment. In particular, changes in the definition of the labor force and deficiencies in the enumeration process have rendered the labor force measures of dubious value and noncomparable with those of earlier censuses. Rather than adopt the implausible data of the 1980 census, I have chosen to estimate the labor force size in 1980 by applying to the census population of labor force age the labor force participation rates reported by the labor force survey (ECSO) for the first quarter of 1979. The details of these adjustment procedures employed are spelled out in the appendix to this chapter. As a consequence of the doubtful quality of the census results, there are limits placed on the confidence with which one can speak of the changes that have occurred in the size and distribution of the labor force. While the absolute values assigned to the various labor force measures are obviously subject to some error, I believe that they nonetheless reflect faithfully the broad sweep of changes that have occurred over time.

The size of the labor force is a function of the size of the population of labor force age (12 years and older in Mexico) and the participation rates of its components. In turn, the growth of the population of labor force age and the labor force follow with a lag the growth in the total population. Thus, as can be seen in table 2-2, the acceleration in growth of the population during the decades of the 1950s and 1960s leads that of the

Table 2-2. *Population, Labor Force, and Participation Rates by Sex, 1950–80*

Period	*Total population (thousands)*	*Population aged 12 years and over (thousands)*	*Labor force (thousands)*	*Labor force partic- ipation rate (percent)*	*Inter- censal rate of change (percent)*
June 1950					
Total	25,791.0	16,849.3	8,345.2	49.5	n.a.
Male	12,696.9	8,166.3	7,207.6	88.2	n.a.
Female	13,094.1	8,683.0	1,137.6	13.1	n.a.
June 1960					
Total	34,923.1	21,944.2	10,212.9	46.5	2.0
Male	17,415.3	10,796.7	8,496.2	78.7	1.7
Female	17,507.8	11,147.5	1,716.6	15.4	3.1
1969[a]					
Total	48,225.2	29,697.3	12,955.1	43.6	n.a.
Male	24,065.6	14,625.6	10,488.8	71.7	n.a.
Female	24,159.6	15,071.7	2,466.3	16.4	n.a.
January 1970[b]					
Total	48,225.2	29,697.3	13,328.5	44.9	2.8
Male	24,065.6	14,625.6	10,674.2	73.0	2.4
Female	24,159.6	15,071.7	2,654.3	17.6	4.7
June 1980[c]					
Total	67,382.6	43,618.4	20,041.0	45.9	4.0
Male	33,295.3	21,411.8	15,266.6	71.3	3.5
Female	34,087.3	22,206.5	4,774.4	21.5	5.8

n.a. Not available.

a. The 1970 census established the size of the labor force by reference to the entire year 1969. That is, anyone gainfully employed at any time in 1969 was included. This measure, therefore, does not correspond to the customary measure of the labor force at a moment in time.

b. The 1970 census also established the size of the labor force during the week preceding the census. This census datum is adjusted for underenumeration of male labor force members in the estimated amount of 419,000.

c. For 1980, the final version of the census reports a total population of only 66,846.8 thousand. Demographers in Mexico, however, believe this to be less accurate than the figure published in the preliminary census report. I have therefore relied on the latter source.

Sources: 1950—Secretaría de Industria y Comercio, Dirección General de Estadística, *VII Censo general de población, 1950* (Mexico, D.F., 1953); 1960—Oscar Altimir, "La medición de la población economicamente active de México 1950–70," *Demografía y economía*, vol. 8, no. 1 (1974), pp. 50–83; 1969 and 1970—Secretaría de Industria y Comercio, Dirreción General de Estadística, *VIII Censo de población, 1970* (Mexico, D.F., 1972); 1980—Secretaría de Programación y Presupuesto, *X Censo general de población y vivienda, 1980*, Resultados preliminares a nivel nacional y por entidad federativa (Mexico, D.F., n.d.).

population of labor force age and the labor force. The annual rate of increase in population peaked at 3.4 percent during the latter decade and began a gradual decline to 3.2 percent during the early 1970s and to 2.5 percent by 1980.[10] In contrast, the rate of increase in the population of labor force age peaked during the decade of the 1970s and can be expected to decline during the present decade. Finally, the rate of growth of the labor force lagged behind both of these broader population measures between 1950 and 1970. During the 1970s, however, the labor force expanded at an annual rate estimated at 4 percent, comfortably in excess of the 3.7 percent rate of increase in the population of labor force age.

The modest growth in the labor force before 1970 was attributable in part to a decline in the aggregate labor force participation rate, a decline that now appears to have run its course. Underlying this decline were changes in the participation rates of various age and sex subgroups, changes not unlike those that typically occur during the course of economic development. Participation rates of the male labor force declined continuously between 1950 and 1970; the declines were heavily concentrated in the very young and the very old age groups. In contrast, female participation rates increased in all age groups except for the over-65 group.[11] However, these increases did not suffice to offset completely the decline in male participation rates, so that the labor force as a proportion of the population 12 years and older declined from 49.5 to 44.9 percent between 1950 and 1970. The past decade has seen a deceleration in the decline in male participation rates while rates for women continued to increase. As a result, the decline in the aggregate participation rate appears to have been stemmed and even reversed.

In spite of the increasing incorporation of women in the labor force over the past three decades, the absolute rates still appear to be quite modest. The rates reported by the 1970 census were well below those of any of the more advanced countries of Latin America. The increases that have been recorded by ECSO over the 1970–79 interval now yield rates that more closely approximate those of 1970 in such countries as Chile, the Dominican Republic, Panama, Peru, and Venezuela.[12] The failure of these rates to rise more rapidly has been interpreted, not as unwillingness or lack of interest in employment among women, but as the absence of sufficient employment opportunities for the potential labor force. To enable a fuller employment of the male labor force, women's work aspirations have been sacrificed. Not only has discrimination based on strong cultural traditions limited the number of employed women, but it has also militated against the length of their participation in the labor force.[13] Thus, the female adult population has been held to represent a large repository of hidden unemployment, and the appeal to "traditional values" is the means society employs to avert the surfacing of this potential availability of women in the form of overt unemployment. To the extent that this is true, it becomes difficult to establish empirically the actual size of the potential female labor force and to distinguish the hidden unemployed from those who would truly not be available for employment even if the "cultural values" did not discourage it. What we do seem to be observing in Mexico, however, is the weakening of whatever cultural impediments there may have been to female labor force participation. The expansion of employment opportunities has brought with it an increase in female participation rates. Furthermore, it would appear that a potential exists in Mexico for substantial continued growth in the size of the female labor force. Special tabulations of data drawn from the 1977 survey of household incomes and expenditures indicate that higher labor force participation rates among women are associated with greater urbanization and higher levels of educational achievement. Since the trends in both of these correlates are positive, the secular increase that we have observed in female participation rates is likely to extend into the future.

The continuous decline in aggregate participation rates recorded between 1950 and 1970, as well as the similar decline for men, has frequently been interpreted as evidence of a failure of the Mexican economy to create enough jobs to absorb the increasing population of labor force age. It is thus concluded that disguised or hidden unemployment must have been on the increase. By contrast, a reasonable alternative interpretation of these declines can be advanced. For instance, the decline in participation rates among the old, particularly men, may be attributable to increasing longevity and to the extension of retirement benefits to a larger segment of the aging population that has facilitated an earlier voluntary withdrawal from the labor force. Among the very young, those aged between 12 and 19, small declines in participation have been associated with large increases in school attendance, whereas among those aged 20 to 24 both labor force participation and school attendance have risen. Among the population of labor force age, the secular increase in school attendance has been impressive. In 1940, the number of persons enrolled in schools above the primary level was only 69,000. It increased to 155,000 in 1950. Thereafter it expanded more rapidly, reaching 1.9 million in 1970 and approximately 4.1 million during the 1977–78 school year.[14] The proportion of the population 12 years and older that was enrolled in school increased from 6.5 to 12 percent between 1950 and 1970.

The continuing trend in school enrollment is clearly in evidence in the findings of the labor force surveys of the past decade. By 1979, the proportion of the population of labor force age that was enrolled in school had risen to 18.3 percent. Particularly notable has been the sharp increase in the enrollment of females. Traditionally, a significantly smaller proportion of women of school age had been in attendance than had been the case among men. However, considerable progress was made during the decade in closing the gap at all levels of schooling (see table 2-3).

An explanation of the notable expansion of school attendance can be offered that is based on demand and supply considerations rather than on labor market failure. On the demand side, there is ample evidence that the private returns to education must be substantial. A recent study based on the 1977 household survey of income and expenditures indicates that an additional year of schooling is associated with a 13.7 percent increase in income. In particular, significant income gains seem to follow from the successful completion of each schooling cycle—primary, secondary, or university. For example, completion of primary school yields almost a 50 percent increase in income over noncompletion. At the upper secondary and university levels, completion is associated with income increases of 37 and 79 percent, respectively.[15] Such differences in earnings associated with education would be expected to provide a powerful incentive for young people to extend their stay in school.

On the supply side, the Mexican government has made extraordinary efforts to expand educational opportunities. During the decade following 1970, the proportion of the gross domestic product devoted to education

Table 2-3. *Percentage of Labor Force Participation and School Enrollment Rates Among Young Men and Women, January 1970, and First Quarter 1979*

Sex and age groups	*Labor force participation rates*		*School enrollment rates*		*Sum of labor force participation and school enrollment rates*	
	1970	*1979*	*1970*	*1979*	*1970*	*1979*
Male						
12–19	36.2	35.4	41.6	57.7	77.8	93.1
20–24	78.3	82.5	6.9	12.5	85.2	95.0
Female						
12–19	16.6	15.4	32.0	52.2	48.6	67.6
20–24	25.0	33.4	2.5	6.8	27.5	40.2

Sources: Dirección General de Estadística, *IX Censo general de población, 1970: Resumen General* (Mexico, D.F., 1972); Secretaría de Programación y Presupuesto, *Encuesta continua sobre ocupación*, 1st quarter 1979 (Mexico, D.F., 1980).

almost doubled from 2.1 to 3.9 percent according to data provided by the education ministry. Between 1972 and 1980, the real per capita expenditure on education more than doubled. A notable expansion of secondary schools and universities made it possible to accommodate an increasing proportion of the school-age population. In 1980, almost 40 percent of the population of secondary school age was enrolled, and 15 percent of the group aged 20–24 was enrolled in institutions of higher learning. In 1960, the corresponding proportions were 11 and 3 percent, respectively.[16] Furthermore, as a rapid expansion of vocational schools was effected, the 1970s saw an increasing diversification in the types of available educational opportunities. From 281 vocational schools in 1970, the number increased to 1,573 by the 1979–80 academic year, and enrollment had increased fourfold.[17]

The significance of these increased enrollments is that they do not appear to have occurred at the expense of labor force participation. To be sure, a slight decline is recorded in labor force participation rates for the youngest age group of both sexes, although this may be understated if the 1970 census significantly underenumerated the labor force members of this group. If the decline was greatest among the 12–14 year age group, as would seem likely, the participation rate of the 15–19 age group may have even increased. (Unfortunately, the labor force survey does not separate the 12–19 age group into subgroups as do the censuses.) Clearer are the trends among the young adults 20–24 years of age. While large increases in school enrollment have been recorded, labor participation rates have also increased notably.[18] Thus, increases in school enrollment have not come at the expense of labor force participation. As enrollments have increased, so has the participation rate of the nonschool population. This can be seen if a comparison is made between the ratio of the labor force participation rate to the proportion of the population of labor force age *not* enrolled in school at different points in time as follows:

$$\frac{\text{Labor force participation rate}}{1-\text{Proportion of population of labor force age enrolled in school}} = \underset{1970}{\frac{0.449}{1-0.12}} = 0.510 \qquad \underset{1979}{\frac{0.455}{1-0.18}} = 0.555$$

Between 1970 and 1979 the ratio increased from 0.51 to 0.555, which indicates that an increase in school enrollment was more than offset by an increase in the participation rate of the nonenrollers.

In summary, it would appear that the secular intercensal decline in the aggregate labor force participation rate has run its course. Whereas the participation rates of the very young and the very old of both sexes can be expected to decline further, they are unlikely to have as large an effect on the aggregate rate as they have had in the past. Furthermore, it is reasonable to expect that such declines will be offset by continued increases in female participation in the labor force.

Sectoral Distribution

Ideally, the population censuses should provide an accurate portrayal of the evolution of the labor force in the process of industrialization and urbanization by charting faithfully the shifts that have occurred in employment among sectors. Unfortunately, the Mexican censuses do not provide an unambiguous basis for measuring the changes that have occurred. In part, this is the result of changing industrial classifications of the labor force over time or changing practices in the classification of certain population groups such as the *ejidatarios*.[19] A substantial problem is posed by errors in processing the 1960 census that exaggerated the size of the rural labor force. Difficulties in the 1970 census arose from an apparent underenumeration and from the very large number of individuals, almost 6 percent of the labor force, who could not be assigned to an economic sector of employment. A further complication is the long reference period adopted for defining most of the employment characteristics of the labor force. While the 1970 census did establish the status of the labor force in the week preceding the census, an alternative measure of the labor force was also applied to include all those who had worked at any time during 1969—a procedure that served to inflate the size of the labor force. All census tabulations of employment characteristics are based on this latter population; thus unknown biases are introduced into the data and the comparability of the data with the other censuses is possibly reduced. As indicated earlier, grave doubts about the accuracy of the labor force measures of the 1980 census limit the usefulness of the data.

Some of these issues have been addressed by Oscar Altimir in the process of carefully reworking the labor force data appearing in the 1950, 1960, and 1970 censuses.[20] The details of the adjustments made appear in the appendix to this chapter, along with a discussion of some of the problems of interpretation posed by the census data. Altimir succeeded in accounting for most of the changes in the industrial classification of the labor force. A resort to rather broad sectoral or industrial groupings became necessary because the data were not always available in sufficient detail to permit a consistent and detailed classification across the three censuses. He also devised a way of classifying according to sector a large proportion of those that had been left unassigned by the census. Although some problems with the data could not be resolved, Altimir's distributions are widely accepted as the most reliable for these years. I have adopted his estimates and present them in table 2-4.

As can be appreciated from the distributions in table 2-4, economic development in Mexico since 1940 has brought with it very substantial changes in the industrial structure of the labor force. The decade of the 1940s saw a rapid growth in the labor force as a whole and in employment in all sectors. During the following two decades, the industrial and construction sectors retained their role as "leading" sectors in the growth of employment, with rates well in excess of the growth of the labor force. During these three decades, the commercial sector showed declining rates of growth in each successive decade, while growth of the service sector oscillated within a narrow range. According to Altimir's adjusted census data, the growth of the agricultural labor force over the 1950–69 period amounted to less than one half of 1 percent per year. These intercensal rates of change are likely to be misleading, however, since problems of comparability and enumeration have not been fully and successfully resolved in my opinion.

The 1960 figure represents an attempt to adjust for the large errors incurred in the coding and processing of the census of that year. In addition, it reflects an attempt to improve the quality of the measurement of the agricultural labor force. In prior censuses, all ejidatarios were automatically presumed to be engaged in agriculture and were so classified for census purposes. Recognizing that many ejidatarios did not work the land themselves but rather rented out their plots while they sought employment in other sectors, the census authorities attempted to identify the sector of principal activity in the course of the 1960 census. But the order of the questions probably resulted in only a limited success in properly identifying the principal sector of employment.[21] Alterations made in the 1970 census questionnaire, however, are quite likely to have avoided the earlier difficulties. The importance of this change is that the agricultural labor force for 1950 and earlier is overestimated compared with that of subsequent censuses and reduces the observed rate of growth in the agricultural labor force between 1950 and 1960. Alternatively, the greater accuracy in distinguishing the principal activity of ejidatarios in 1970 would tend to bias the size of the agricultural labor force downward compared with earlier years. An additional bias in the same direction stems from the underenumeration of the male labor force in 1970. Since the participation rates of prime-age men appeared to be particularly low in some of the predominantly rural states of Mexico, I am led to surmise that most of those who escaped enumeration were actually engaged in agriculture. The fact that, in contrast to the June 1960 census, the 1970 census was taken in January, a month of low agricultural activity, may also have contributed to this underenumeration. The long reference period of a full year should have offset this possible source of bias, however. In any event, although the precise size of the agricultural labor force is arguable, there can be no doubt that it has grown at a much slower rate than the labor force as a whole.

As for the evolution of the sectoral distribution of the labor force between 1970 and 1980, I can offer only a tentative estimate. As was pointed out above, the 1970 census provided a measure of the labor force in the week prior to the census but no other information about its employment characteristics. In the case of the 1980 census, the sector of employment could not be specified for 30 percent of the labor force. I have therefore resorted to the following procedure for distributing the labor forces in the two years. From the total labor force, as estimated in table 2-2, I first subtracted the number of unemployed. For 1970, this datum was given by the census; for 1980, it had to be estimated. For the first quarter of 1979, the national unemployment rate was reported to be 3.3 percent by the household labor force survey ECSO. Since the period from the second quarter of 1979 up to the census date of June 1980 saw a rapid expansion of employment (estimated by the Banco de México to have been at an annual rate of approximately 6 percent), it is reasonable to suppose that the rate of unemployment had declined. I have arbitrarily assumed it to have reached 3 percent in June 1980. I then distributed the 1970 employed labor force over the various sectors in the same proportions as reported for the population that had been employed at any time during 1969. For 1980, I applied to the employed labor force the same proportional relationships among sectors that appear in ECSO's survey results for the first quarter of 1979, the last such nationwide distribution available.[22] The results of this procedure are presented in table 2-5. It should be noted that these distributions are not comparable to those presented for the years prior to 1970 in table 2-5, because the classification of various activities was changed, and the 1979 data are not presented in sufficient detail to permit consistency with the pre-1970 period.

The distributions yielded by these procedures identify construction and the tertiary sector as the leading generators of employment during the decade. Within the tertiary sector, commerce and government recorded the largest relative gains. Agricultural employment expanded only slightly. The precise rate remains in question, however, because of the suspected underenumeration of the agricultural labor force by the 1970 census and the questionable accuracy of the ECSO survey's estimate of the size and distribution of the rural labor force. Within the extractive sector, employment gains in petroleum extraction were partly offset by declines in mining

Table 2-4. *Sectoral Distribution of the Labor Force and Rates of Change, 1940–69*

Sector	*Labor force (thousands)*				*Average annual rates of change (percent)*			
	1940	*1950*	*1960*	*1969*	*1940–50*	*1950–60*	*1960–69*	*1940–69*
Agriculture, forestry, and fishing	3,832.4	4,864.9	5,048.3	5,292.7	2.4	0.4	0.5	1.1
Manufacturing, electricity, and extractive	709.7	1,237.5	1,760.3	2,829.1	5.7	3.6	5.4	4.9
Construction	115.9	263.8	414.2	609.8	8.6	4.6	4.4	5.9
Commerce and finance	413.7	732.6	1,083.4	1,397.0	5.9	4.0	2.9	4.3
Other services[a]	786.7	1,246.4	1,906.7	2,826.5	4.7	4.3	4.5	4.5
Total	5,858.5	8,345.2	10,212.9	12,955.1	3.6	2.0	2.7	2.8

a. Includes transportation, communications, government, and personal and other services.

Sources: 1940—Luis Unikel, *El desarrollo urbano de México*, 2d ed. (Mexico, D.F.: El Colegio de México, 1978), table VI-A9; 1950–1969—Oscar Altimir, "La medición de la población economicamente activa de México, 1950–1970," *Demografía y economía*, vol. 8, no. 1 (1974), table 16. The observations drawn from the 1970 census refer to activity in 1969. Altimir's distribution of the labor force includes his redistribution of the unclassified workers over the several sectors.

activity and thus yielded only a small net increase. Intermediate rates of growth were evidenced by manufacturing and transport. The estimates presented here should be treated with caution. As noted earlier, there are no actual measures of employment for either year, and the bases from which I derived these estimates are far from robust. At best, they provide only a rough indication of change in the distribution of employment over the decade.

The changes that have occurred in the sectoral distribution of the labor force over the entire forty-year interval are considerable. In 1940, agriculture predominated as a source of employment and accounted for almost two-thirds of the total. Currently it employs less than 30 percent of the labor force. In contrast, the tertiary sector has doubled in its relative importance, from 20 to more than 40 percent of total employment. Employment in manufacturing and construction activities also doubled in relative importance and comprised more than 25 percent of the total by 1980.

These structural changes in the labor force indicate parallel changes in the structure of output of the Mexican economy. The two sets of changes can be related to show trends in sectoral productivity over time (tables 2-6 and 2-7). The 1940–69 interval recorded broadly based increases in

Table 2-5. *Estimated Sectoral Distribution of the Labor Force, 1970 and 1980*

Sector	*Labor force (thousands)*		*Annual rate of change (percent)*
	January 1970	*June 1980*	
Agriculture, forestry, and fishing	5,362.7	5,645.3	0.5
Manufacturing, mining, and electricity	2,524.6	4,141.9	4.8
Construction	600.0	1,250.4	7.2
Commerce and finance	1,257.7	2,696.2	7.5
Services	3,082.6	5,704.9	6.0
Total employment	12,827.6	19,439.8	4.0
Unemployment	500.9	601.2	1.8
Total labor force	13,328.5	20,041.0	4.0

Note: Figures for the labor force are based on those in table 2-2.

Sources: Secretaría de Industria y Comercio, Dirección General de Estadística, *IX Censo general de población, 1970* (Mexico, D.F., 1972); Secretaría de Programación y Presupuesto, *Encuesta continua sobre ocupación*, 1st quarter 1979 (Mexico, D.F., February 1980).

Table 2-6. *Output, Employment, and Output per Worker in Mexico, 1940–69*
(output in 1960 pesos)

Sector	*1940*	*1950*	*1960*	*1969*	*Average annual rate of change (percent)* 1940–50	1950–60	1960–69
Primary[a]							
Output (millions)	8,543	15,442	23,970	32,912	6.1	4.5	3.6
Labor force (thousands)	3,832	4,867	5,048	5,293	2.4	0.4	0.5
Output per worker (pesos)	2,229	3,173	4,748	6,218	3.6	4.1	3.0
Secondary[b]							
Output (millions)	12,447	23,467	43,933	94,362	6.5	6.5	8.9
Labor force (thousands)	826	1,490	2,175	3,439	6.1	3.9	5.2
Output per worker (pesos)	15,069	15,750	20,199	27,439	0.4	2.5	3.5
Tertiary[c]							
Output (millions)	27,663	48,061	84,127	153,469	5.7	5.8	6.9
Labor force (thousands)	1,200	1,988	2,990	4,223	5.2	4.2	3.9
Output per worker (pesos)	23,053	24,176	28,136	36,341	0.5	1.5	2.9
Total gross domestic product[d]							
Output (millions)	48,653	86,973	150,511	277,400	6.0	5.6	7.0
Labor force (thousands)	5,858	8,345	10,213	12,955	3.6	2.0	2.7
Output per worker (pesos)	8,305	10,422	14,737	21,413	2.3	3.5	4.2

a. The primary sector includes agriculture, livestock, forestry, and fishing.
b. Includes mining, petroleum, manufacturing, construction, and electric power generation.
c. Includes commerce, finance, transportation, communications, government, and other services.
d. Since the totals have been adjusted for the value of interindustry financial transactions, they may be less than the sum of the sectoral products.

Sources: Output data for 1940 and 1950—Luis Unikel, *El desarrollo urbano de México*, 2d ed. (Mexico, D.F.: El Colegio de México, 1978), tables VI-A5 and VI-A6; for 1960—Banco de México, *Producto interno bruto y gasto, 1970–78* (Mexico, D.F., 1979), p. 61; for 1969—Banco de México, *Informe anual 1977* (Mexico, D.F., 1978), statistical appendix, table 3. Labor force data refer to the adjusted data of O. Altimir, "La medición de la población economicamente activa," *Demografía y economía*, vol. 8, no. 1 (1974), pp. 50–83.

output and productivity (table 2-6). All the principal sectors participated in the developmental process, although to varying degrees in each decade. The 1940s and 1950s featured impressive increases in total output and output per worker in the agricultural sector as the large investments made in rural infrastructure began to yield returns. During the 1960s, this sector demonstrated less dynamism as the limits of cultivatable land were reached and the more obvious or easy investment opportunities in rural infrastructure (large-scale irrigation projects, trunk roads, and the like) were exhausted. Gains in both output and output per worker were only modest. That these gains may not have been evenly distributed over the sector, however, is suggested by the interregional differences (referred to above) in the productivity of agriculture.[23]

During the 1940s, the secondary sector expanded its output by 89

Table 2-7. *Output, Employment, and Output Per Worker by Sector, 1970 and 1980*
(output in 1970 pesos)

Sector	*1970*	*1980*	*Annual rate of change (percent)*
Primary			
Output (millions)	54,123	75,704	3.4
Labor force (thousands)	5,377	5,503	0.2
Output per worker (pesos)	10,065	13,756	3.1
Secondary			
Output (millions)	145,070	296,046	7.4
Labor force (thousands)	3,133	5,244	5.3
Output per worker (pesos)	46,305	56,457	2.0
Tertiary			
Output (millions)	250,474	481,090	6.7
Labor force (thousands)	4,352	8,204	6.5
Output per worker (pesos)	57,555	58,641	0.2
Total gross domestic product			
Output (millions)	444,271	841,855	6.6
Labor force (thousands)	12,862	18,951	4.0
Output per worker (pesos)	35,541	44,422	2.5

Note: See notes to table 2-6.

Sources: 1970—Secretaría de Programación y Presupuesto, *Sistema de cuentas nacionales de México*, vol. 1, *Resumen general* (Mexico, D.F., 1981), table 2.2–2.5; 1980—Secretaría de Programación Presupuesto, *Sistema de cuentas nacionales de México, 1978–80*, vol. 1 (Mexico, D.F., 1982).

percent; this was accompanied by an almost equally large increase in employment. Since access to capital goods from abroad was limited during World War II, the growth of output was apparently achieved with little or no deepening of capital. Also encouraging the expansion of the sector's employment may have been real minimum wages that were either stable or declining from their highly inflated levels of 1940, and apparently declining real wages in the modern industrial segment.[24] The following decade produced an equally large increase in output as Mexico actively pursued policies of import substitution. In contrast with the 1940s, however, employment growth lagged that of output. With the restoration of normal access to capital goods from abroad, capital deepening must have been a factor contributing to the sharp rise in output per worker of 28 percent over the decade. The rate of growth of the secondary sector's labor force declined in comparison with the previous decade but still managed to increase by 46 percent. The 1960s saw an acceleration in the rates of growth of sectoral output, employment, and productivity.

The tertiary sector proved to be a full participant in, and contributor to, growth. Output increases in each decade closely approximated the growth of GDP. This sector persistently reported the highest absolute levels of productivity in the economy, and the rate of increase in productivity accelerated in each decade. The recorded growth in productivity might be expected to follow from an increasing weight of highly skilled employment within the sector, as well as from increments in physical productivity that occurred in some subsectors such as transport and communications. Obviously, any expansion in marginal activities that may have occurred within this sector was too small to offset the effect of these more favorable developments.

In short, the broad sectoral data indicate a shift in employment from the sector with the lowest productivity, agriculture, to those of higher productivity. Moreover, this shift did not depress the rate of increase in productivity to inconsequential levels in those sectors undergoing the most rapid growth in employment. In fact, the rate of increase in output per worker accelerated over the twenty-nine-year period.[25] Furthermore, a significant narrowing occurred in the spread among the sectoral rates of increase in productivity over the three decades. By the 1960–69 period, the annual rates of increase had become clustered between 2.9 and 3.5 percent. Relative differences in output per worker between the sectors characterized by the highest and lowest productivity levels also narrowed, although the absolute difference increased markedly. In the decade of the 1940s, output per worker in the tertiary sector was more than ten times that in the primary. Although this ratio declined to 5.8 in the 1960s, the absolute difference increased from 20,824 to 30,123 pesos of 1960. The same pattern of change is observable in the productivity differences between the primary and secondary sectors.

Changes over the most recent decade have been estimated and are recorded in table 2-7. The output data employed for this purpose are based on the input-output matrix of that year and on data from the 1975 economic censuses and thus are not comparable with measures for earlier years. While the output data can be regarded as reasonably reliable, the employment data must be considered more tentative for the reasons outlined above. The employment data are taken from table 2-5 with an adjustment made to the 1980 data. Since the 1970 census measure of the employed labor force corresponded to January of that year I have adjusted the June 1980 measure of the labor force to its estimated January level but maintained its relative distribution.[26] It should be pointed out that there is not a complete correspondence between the sectoral assignment of productive activity by the national accounts and that of the labor force by the population census of 1970 and ECSO. Although this may result in some distortion in sectoral measures of output per worker, I consider it to be a lesser probable source of error than that originating in my estimates of the absolute size of the labor force and its distribution over sectors. In light of these qualifications regarding the quality of the labor force measures, the employment and productivity data must be viewed with caution.

The resulting estimates yield rates of growth in output per worker that are well below those recorded during the two preceding decades and bear a greater resemblance to the pattern recorded for the 1940s. As in that earlier decade, agriculture emerges with the highest rate of increase in productivity, a rather unexpected result because of the relative stagnation characterizing the sector over much of the decade. This major increment may be unduly influenced by the very large increase in agricultural output in 1980, an atypical year blessed with excellent weather and particularly favorable price incentives. The decline in the rate of increase of output per worker yielded for the secondary and tertiary sectors is not out of line with the productivity trends derived from the economic censuses for the first half of the 1970s. If my estimates for the decade as a whole prove to be reasonably correct, they would indicate that no significant recovery in the rate of productivity increase occurred during the second half of the decade. For the economy as a whole over the decade, my estimates yield an annual increase of output per worker of 2.5 percent. In view of the very rapid rate of growth of the total labor force by 4 percent per year, the achievement of even this rate of increase in productivity could be viewed as a positive development. Also encouraging would be the apparent continuation of the past trend of declining relative differences in output per worker among sectors.

Growth in Tertiary Sector Employment

Although the broad picture of the evolution of the labor force highlights the relative shift of labor from low- to high-productivity sectors, this has not relieved a longstanding concern about the implications of growth of tertiary sector employment. The conventional view of this sector tends to characterize it as an infinitely expandable sponge ready to absorb a burgeoning labor force that is incapable of finding satisfactory wage employment. Thus, workers are "forced" into a marginal employment and productive status in the subsectors of easy entry in commerce and services, often in the status of self-employed or unremunerated family worker.[27] Essentially, this view would seem to hold that employment growth in certain sectors has been largely determined by supply rather than a response to shifts in demand. An important inference that is drawn from this explanation of the growth of tertiary sector employment is that the quality of employment has deteriorated over time.

Unfortunately, the criteria employed for deciding that tertiary sector growth has been "excessive" are not explicitly set forth and verified empirically. Even a cursory look at the sectoral rates of growth, however, would not seem to indicate an "explosive" growth of marginal employments. Until 1970, at least, both the commerce and service sectors, for example, expanded at rates below those of the "productive" sectors of industry and construction. Furthermore, much of the expansion of the service sector has been in technical and professional occupation categories. Government employment expanded at approximately the same rate as total service employment and accounted for just under one-fourth of the total in 1969. Finally, the growth of both services and commerce is likely to be closely related to that of urban population; the growth in the latter would be expected to shift the demand for labor in the former.[28] In the case of Mexico, the urban population, defined in the census as those residing in communities with a population in excess of 2,500, grew at a rate of 4.8 percent per year between 1940 and 1970, a rate that exceeded the growth of tertiary employment.

Yet one cannot judge whether the growth of the tertiary sector has been "excessive" merely by looking at its absolute size. An examination of productivity and incomes generated in the sector over time would be more instructive and would also provide a test of the widespread notion that employment expansion in this sector had been "supply-determined" and, therefore, "excessive." Consider the implications of the "labor surplus" and "overcrowding" characterizations of growth of tertiary employment. If the wages of the unskilled and unorganized labor force had been at the subsistence level at the beginning of the period under observation, then we should observe the expansion of employment in the sector at a constant level of real wages, or, in the short run, at wages falling below subsistence. If wages began at a level above the subsistence level, then one should observe a decline in wages toward the subsistence level. If one could observe declines in real wages, this would provide support for the deterioration hypothesis, at least within the sector.[29] Alternatively, one could examine the distribution of employment within the service sector to see if a large concentration of marginal employment could be detected. Let us first consider this latter course.

Table 2-8 presents the distribution of employment in the service sector in detailed form according to the classification employed by the census in 1970. The various subsectors are grouped in ascending order according to the ease of entry, the latter being a function of labor skill or capital requirements. The largest single category of service workers are domestic servants, who account for just one-fourth of the total. Other subsectors employing relatively large proportions of low-skill or low-wage workers are hotels, restaurants, and providers of cleaning and repair services.[30] Together with domestic servants, these categories account for 54 percent of service sector employment. It can be presumed that, if overcrowding were to characterize the service sector, this is the subsector in which one would expect to find it; all of the other subsectors would appear to pose various barriers to entry. Yet, within these low-skill subsectors, there does not seem to be the overconcentration of workers in the categories of the unpaid family worker or the self-employed that is supposed to be the hallmark of "overcrowding." At 4.1 percent, unpaid family workers are no more prevalent here than in the nonagricultural sector of the economy as a whole, and only slightly more prevalent than within the service sector. The proportion of the Group I work force that is self-employed, 19.3 percent, does diverge from that characterizing either the service sector (15.9 percent) or the nonagricultural sector as a whole (16.6 percent), but not by a great deal. Indeed, other evidence is available that suggests the growth of service employment has not been increasingly "excessive." One comprehensive study of employment found that, in 1970, for every nine urban inhabitants, there was one person employed in services—a relationship that was similar to that held in 1950.[31]

Commerce is the other sector that is believed to harbor many of the marginally employed. On the surface it may seem to do so, for the proportion of unpaid family workers (8 percent) is twice as high as that for the nonagricultural sector as a whole, as is the ratio of the self-employed (32 percent). However, employment in the commerce sector lagged the growth of urban population, 4.3 to 4.8 percent a year between 1940 and 1969. Expansion of service employment, 4.5 percent a year, was also less than urban growth. Since service and commercial employment is predominantly urban, these lags behind increases in urban population would not seem to indicate patently "excessive" growth in the former.

The persistently high and rising level of output per worker employed in the tertiary sector over time can be observed in tables 2-6 and 2-7. It suggests that this sector has not simply served the passive role of absorbing

Table 2-8. *Service Sector Employment by Employment Status, 1970*
(number)

Service sector	*Total employment*	*Self-employed*	*Unpaid family workers*
Group I			
Hotels, restaurants, and bars	259,206	43,072	12,631
Cleaning and personal services	129,347	43,589	5,156
Household domestics	541,063	87,049	21,705
Repair services	236,126	50,904	8,866
Subtotal	1,166,742	224,614	48,358
As percentage of Group I employment		19.3	4.1
Group II			
Radio, television, and communications	33,538	1,065	383
Entertainment and cultural	90,831	24,874	2,424
Business agents, rental services	78,313	16,473	1,986
Credit, insurance, finance	105,671	3,323	1,212
Subtotal	309,353	45,735	6,005
As percentage of Group II employment		14.8	1.9
Group III			
Education	319,574	16,656	10,313
Scientific research	7,073	303	82
Medical services (social)	168,252	6,635	2,839
Professional services	84,735	25,547	1,883
Subtotal	579,634	49,141	15,112
As percentage of Group III employment		8.4	2.6
Group IV			
Miscellaneous services	80,291	19,299	2,590
Religious services	16,577	2,183	1,052
Inadequately specified	7,578	1,187	382
Subtotal	104,446	23,669	4,024
As percentage of Group IV employment		22.7	3.8
Sector total	2,158,175	343,159	73,504
As percentage of sector total employment		15.9	3.4

Source: Secretaría de Industria y Comercio, Dirección General de Estadística, *Censo de población, 1970: Resumen general* (Mexico, D.F., 1972), table 44.

large numbers of workers unable to find remunerative employment in more productive activities. A clearer test of the relationship between supply and demand in these labor markets is provided by the course of earnings. This is carefully and extensively documented in Chapter 7. The weight of the evidence reviewed reveals that real remunerations of low-skill sectors in services and commerce, as well as in manufacturing, have shown steady increases at least since 1960. These increases would suggest that the growth of employment in the two sectors has reflected a response to greater shifts in demand relative to supply rather than the reverse.

Domestic Service

It may be instructive to examine more closely one market that is conspicuous in its importance to developing societies—the market for domestic servants. As was noted above, the 1970 census recorded more than a half million persons in this occupational category. It is a market with no barriers to entry and often serves as a port of entry to the urban labor market for women of rural origin. Since domestic service is frequently viewed as "an employment of last resort," this market should offer a sensitive indicator of the relative existence of alternative employment and wage opportunities. Focusing on this market may determine whether domestic employment growth can be viewed primarily as a function of an expanding supply of labor rather than as a response to shifting schedules of both supply and demand.

While domestics formed the largest single category of employment within the service sector in 1970, their relative importance within the sector has been declining over time. From 1950 to 1969, the number so employed grew at an annual rate of just under 3 percent, while the service sector, as defined and recorded in table 2-4, expanded at a rate of 4.4 percent. As a result, domestic employment as a proportion of total employment in "other services" declined from 25 to 19 percent. This category of employment also lagged well behind the 5.6 percent annual increase in the population of larger urban centers (which provide the principal market for such services) as well as behind the increase in the urban labor force.[32] It cannot be argued convincingly that pressures of labor supply have led to a deterioration of employment conditions for domestics. As is documented in Chapter 7, the real cash wage of domestic servants in Mexico City is estimated to have increased on the order of 25 to 35 percent between 1963 and the early 1970s. While real wages dropped during the inflationary surge of the mid-1970s, they recovered and advanced rapidly toward the end of the decade.

The observed increase in real wages would suggest that the growth in employment in domestic service reflected a response to greater demand for such services. One might reasonably expect that changes in the demand for domestic services would be a function of changes in income and in the proportion of the population residing in urban centers, since domestic employment is very largely an urban phenomenon. Support for the presumption of a relationship between income and the demand for domestic services is provided by the 1968 income and expenditures study, reported in a study of the market for domestic services in Mexico City.[33] Cross-sectional data contained therein revealed that the size of family expenditures on domestic services was associated with the level of family income. The income elasticity of demand calculated from these data proved to be particularly high for families in the middle income categories. The arc elasticities ranged from almost three to just over one. Thus the rapid increases in real incomes that have occurred in Mexico over the past three decades can be expected to have been reflected in an increasing demand for domestics.

I have tried to quantify the relationship between changes in income, urbanization, and domestic employment by applying the following procedure. On the basis of cross-sectional data for 1970 on the 32 states in Mexico, I have estimated a regression of domestic servants per thousand population (*DS*) on per capita gross domestic product (GDP) and the proportion of the state's population residing in urban centers of 15,000 or more inhabitants (*UP*):

$$DS = a + b_1\text{GDP} + b_2 UP.$$

The employment date originate with the 1970 population census; income and urbanization data are from Unikel. The solution of the regression equation yields the following:

$$DS = 2.03 + \underset{(0.0007)}{0.00063\text{GDP}} + \underset{(0.0561)}{0.1308UP}$$

In this formulation the degree of urbanization proves significant at the 5 percent level while the income variable fails of significance. The presence of multicollinearity renders the standard error of the income term larger than the coefficient. (GDP and *UP* are significantly correlated with an $r = 0.88$.) The proportion of the variance explained by these two variables, the adjusted R^2, is 0.595, about the same proportion that is explained by either of the two variables alone. Substituting 1950 values for income and urban population, the equation estimates the 1950 employment of domestics as 7.75 per thousand population for a total of 205,088, well below the actual level of 310,165. However, this estimate is derived under the implicit assumption that the 1969 ratio of the price of domestic service to other prices also held in 1950. If the price of domestic service, in fact, rose relative to other prices over this time interval, then the application of the 1969 coefficients should result in an underestimation of the 1950 employment level.

Unfortunately, I do not have data regarding the change in relative prices over the entire time interval, nor do I have a measure of the price elasticity of demand. There are wage data available for the decade of the 1960s that record a sharp increase in the wages of domestic servants in Mexico City relative to the general consumer price index. If it is reasonable to assume that the same annual rate of increase of 2.11 percent in the relative price of domestic service held over the entire nineteen-year period, 1950–69, and that the price elasticity of demand approximates unity, then the estimating equation can be amended. It can now include a term that reflects the relative price change over the entire period, P, times the assumed price elasticity times the 1970 employment of domestics per thousand population DS_{1970}:

$$DS_{1950} = 2.03 + 0.00063\text{GDP} + 0.1308UP + (-1)(-P)(DS_{1970}).$$

The substitution of the values for the independent variables of the equation yields an estimated level of employment in 1950 of 348,139, or 12 percent greater than the actual level. Given the tenuousness of the assumptions made with respect to relative price changes and elasticity of demand, this estimate is not unreasonable. If the actual rate of change in relative prices was slower during the decade of the 1950s than it was during the 1960s, or if the price elasticity of demand were, in fact, less than unity, then the estimated level of employment for 1950 would have more closely approximated the actual.[34]

Although this exercise may be lacking in precision, it does serve the useful purpose of supporting the view that the increase in domestic employment has been associated with a shift in demand for such services rather than a response simply to the availability of a greater number of individuals seeking employment. Expressed in terms of a formal supply and demand apparatus, the observation of both an expansion of employment and a rising real wage must have involved both a rightward shift in the demand for domestics and a movement upward along a demand schedule. Clearly, the shift in demand must have been greater than the shift in supply. In contrast, had the growth of employment been supply-led, it would have involved a rightward shift in the supply of domestics that outran the shift in demand, with the unavoidable consequence of a decline in the real wage.

There is every reason to believe that the past trends observable in this market will extend into the future, that the relative (if not the absolute) importance of domestics in the labor force will decline, and that their wage will rise. In the past, this source of employment has provided a haven for women with disproportionately low levels of education. Almost 40 percent of the domestics surveyed in Mexico City by a study in 1970 proved to be illiterate; another 46 percent reported less than a primary school education.[35] By contrast, 56 percent of the female labor force had achieved an education beyond the primary level. As educational levels of the female population continue to rise and approach those of males, it is reasonable to expect that the range of employment opportunities open to women will expand, and their willingness to accept employment as domestics will wane. Furthermore, domestic service has represented an important point of entry into the metropolitan labor market for women migrating from rural or small urban communities. Over 60 percent of the domestics encountered by this same study originated in such communities, and 80 percent of these reported that their first employment in the capital was as a domestic. As the relative size of the rural population continues to shrink, this source of domestics will likewise lose importance. Thus, the supply of women to this market may be expected to continue to decline in relation to total female labor supply even in the face of increasing labor force participation rates. Indeed, in an expanding economy, rising education levels among women that lead to greater participation and to higher wage employment opportunities will tend to reinforce the influence of increasing incomes and urbanization on the demand for domestic services. Demand schedules will thus shift further to the right and produce further gains in relative wages. This appears to have been occurring between 1979 and the onset of the economic crisis in mid-1982 (see Chapter 7).

Food and Beverage Services

In contrast to the domestic service category of employment, the others included in Group I appear to have grown at rates that exceeded the rate of growth of the total labor force or of urban population. For example, employment in the preparation and sale of food and beverages more than tripled over the 1950–69 interval, with an annual growth rate of 6.5 percent. This expansion and the substantial proportion of total employment in the categories of the self-employed and unpaid family workers (about one-fourth of the total) may be misleading. It might appear that this sector represents one of those frequently characterized as harboring the marginally employed, those unable to find employment at the "going" wage who are then reduced to self-employment at levels of productivity and income well below those of wage labor. However, a careful analysis of data reported in the service sector census of 1971 is not consistent with such a pessimistic interpretation of the observed growth in employment. The *Censo de servicios* presenting data for 1970 reports a coverage of 51.8 and 19.6 thousand establishments in the food preparation and beverage industries, respectively. Within both of these subsectors, establishments that employ no remunerated labor are in the majority, although they do not account for a majority of the covered employment.

Some of the key data for such establishments are presented in table 2-9. A sharp contrast can be observed in the measures of capital employed and net value added per person employed between those establishments without and with paid employees. With the exception of one of the eight subsectors that compose the food and beverage industry—restaurants—establishments with no paid employees rather uniformly report net value added per worker as well as gross sales per worker (not shown in the table) equal to about one-half those in establishments with paid help. Indeed, the net value added per worker in the former class of establishments in six of the eight four-digit classifications was less than the wages paid in the establishments with paid employees. In the other two subsectors, net value added per worker in the former class of establishment barely exceeded the average wage in the latter.

These comparisons would serve to confirm the suspicion that the industry harbors a substantial number of workers who are "marginally employed." However, a comparison of the returns to labor in the two types of establishments suggests that these are not as different as may have been expected. For the establishments with paid employees, the census provides the sum of the wages and salaries paid as well as the number of paid employees, thus making it feasible to calculate the average annual earnings of this class of workers. In the case of the establishments with unremunerated labor, it was necessary to estimate the return to labor. This was done by imputing a return to the capital employed and subtracting this from net value added with the balance thus derived assigned to labor.[36] As can be observed, the returns to labor of the self-employed and unremunerated workers, shown in parentheses, do not depart very far from the wages paid to hired labor. To the extent that unremunerated workers are more likely than hired labor to be part-time workers, as the evidence seems to show, the actual differences in average rates of remuneration per time unit may be even narrower than those suggested by these data.[37]

A further observation that does not correspond to a commonly held notion about the quality of employment concerns the level of earnings of labor in very small establishments. Table 2-9 presents data for all establishments with no paid employees followed by a similar set of data for all establishments with hired labor but limited to those with total employment of one or two persons. It is commonly thought that very small

Table 2-9. *Employment, Productivity, and Earnings in Food and Beverage Services, 1970*
(pesos)

Subdivision	*Employment (number)*	*Net capital investment per worker*	*Net value added per worker*	*Average annual wages and salaries*	*Average annual total remunerations*[a]
Restaurants and cafes					
No paid employees	21,112	5,597	7,697	—	7,246
Paid employees	62,071	20,103	27,137	14,499	16,340
One or two workers	4,803	12,646	19,667	10,966	11,791
Food and taco stands					
No paid employees	14,594	5,795	9,226	—	8,768
Paid employees	13,410	7,239	17,545	8,566	9,549
One or two workers	3,271	7,758	21,091	8,018	8,831
Ice cream parlors and soda fountains					
No paid employees	10,725	3,989	6,944	—	6,606
Paid employees	3,781	11,480	17,132	7,492	8,337
One or two workers	1,412	11,732	19,071	6,458	7,134
Oyster bars					
No paid employees	2,382	5,490	11,167	—	10,807
Paid employees	2,568	8,304	21,269	12,272	13,446
One or two workers	558	8,608	23,701	12,535	13,403
Shops for preparation and sale of posole and tamales and similar establishments					
No paid employees	7,784	3,053	7,551	—	7,307
Paid employees	2,678	8,046	15,290	8,505	9,217
One or two workers	840	7,907	16,548	9,120	9,541
Taverns and bars					
No paid employees	6,986	9,617	12,500	—	7,328
Paid employees	14,769	16,566	25,662	11,699	13,191
One or two workers	5,689	19,107	28,667	12,056	13,249

— Not applicable.

a. Figures for service establishments with no paid employees are imputed values.

Source: Secretaría de Industria y Comercio, Dirección General de Estadística, *VI Censo de servicios, 1971* (Mexico, D.F., 1974), tables 8 and 16.

establishments form part of the "informal" sector and are characterized by wage conditions and productivities significantly inferior to those found in larger establishments. The census data, however, reveal no such differences within each of the subsectors except for restaurants, a sector in which differences in the quality of services and labor employed are most likely to span a very wide range. In all other subsectors, net value added (as well as gross sales) per worker and remunerations per employee in establishments with no more than two persons employed either exceeded the average for all establishments with paid employees or were not far removed from the average. The relationship of the average earnings to the legal minimum wage may be of interest . In 1970, the unweighted average of the urban minimum wage rates for all zones amounted to 9,092 pesos (Mex$) per year; the urban rates weighted by the labor force of each zone yielded a national average of Mex$9,851.[38] Only in the ice cream parlor and soda fountain sector did reported average earnings depart significantly from the legal minimum.

It is reasonable to expect that employment in the food and beverage service industry would expand in the course of economic development and rising incomes. Data from household income and expenditures studies in Mexico provide strong support for a hypothesis that the demand for such services is income elastic.[39] Growth of employment in the industry would also be expected to accompany the growth of the urban population. As in the case of domestic service employment, I tried to see whether the growth in employment could be explained by changes in income and urbanization. I proceeded to fit a linear regression of employment in this industry per thousand population (*FB*), on the gross domestic product per capita (GDP), and the proportion of the population residing in urban centers with 15,000 population or more (*UP*) in 1970 across the 32 states. The form of the regression was as follows:

$$FB = a + b_1 \text{ GDP} + b_2 \; UP.$$

Solving the equation for the coefficients of the independent variables yielded

$$FB = 0.434 + \underset{(0.00025)}{0.0005}\text{GDP} + \underset{(0.0199)}{0.0547}UP.$$

Both coefficients proved to be significant, at the 5 and 1 percent levels, respectively, and the adjusted R^2 was 0.765. Substituting the 1950 values for GDP and *UP* and solving for the 1950 level of *FB*, I obtained a value of 2.227 per thousand population. Multiplying the estimated employment per thousand by population (in thousands) for 1950 yielded a predicted employment for 1950 of 58,933. The actual level of employment in this industry was 60,145. Given the very close approximation of the predicted to the actual level of employment, the hypothesis that the growth of employment is largely a response to shifts in demand is again supported.[40]

Other Services

Another subgroup of Group I in table 2-8, cleaning and personal services, unfortunately, does not lend itself to further decomposition, and its precise content cannot be determined in a way that would permit extensive comparisons with earlier population censuses. Nevertheless, some information about the quality of employment in this subsector of services can be gleaned from the census of services for 1970. Five kinds of establishments are reviewed in table 2-10. As in the case of the other subgroups of the service sector we have reviewed, there is a sharp difference to be noted in the net value added per worker in establishments with and without paid employees. However, the earnings per worker reveal much narrower differences. As before, the earnings of paid employees in the smallest establishments, those with two or fewer workers, could not have compared unfavorably with those in larger establishments. In several cases, they actually exceeded the average wage payments made in all establishments with paid employees. Wage payments in all but one of the subgroups, shoeshine parlors, exceed the legal minimum wage. Shoeshine establishments yielded recorded earnings of paid employees which were, on average, only 77 percent of the weighted average legal minimum wage, although the estimated return to labor in establishments with no paid employeees was estimated to fall short of the minimum by only about 9 percent. Recorded payments to labor, however, may understate actual earnings of workers since establishment data do not include a consideration of any tips received in this category of establishment or any of the others that provide personal services directly to consumers.

Finally, the remaining subsector from Group I of table 2-8 is examined in table 2-11. While one would normally expect workers employed in repair service activities to possess skills that would limit easy entry, it is also likely that the quality of such services would be characterized by wide variance and that only rudimentary skill would be evidenced by many practitioners, particularly in small establishments. The data in table 2-11 suggest that skill levels in this sector must be quite low, for productivity and wage levels appear to be low by comparison with the other subsectors of Group I. Annual wage payments below the weighted legal minimum wage appear in all but one of the strata of wage-paying establishments. This subsector resembles the others in Group I in the small differences in the earnings of workers in the smallest establishments as compared with the average of all paid employees. Yet the imputed returns to unremunerated labor are higher here relative to payments made to wage labor.

If one could accept the data presented here as representative of generally low-skill service employments, it would not appear that "overcrowding" exists or that productivities and earnings have been pushed down to very low levels. It could be argued, however, that the establishments that are likely to be enumerated in a census are unlikely to be the repository of the

Table 2-10. *Employment, Productivity, and Earnings in Personal and Cleaning Services, 1970*
(pesos)

Subdivision	*Employment (number)*	*Net capital investment per worker*	*Net value added per worker*	*Average annual wages and salaries*	*Average annual total remunerations*[a]
Barber shops					
No paid employees	12,091	4,794	8,689	—	8,305
Paid employees	8,653	5,039	16,274	9,598	10,420
One or two workers	4,141	5,479	15,236	9,041	9,671
Beauty shops					
No paid employees	5,364	6,809	9,992	—	9,447
Paid employees	7,898	9,436	18,748	10,417	11,678
One or two workers	3,211	9,661	18,525	10,377	11,497
Laundries and dry cleaners					
No paid employees	5,104	6,419	10,440	—	9,926
Paid employees	13,349	33,003	27,211	11,326	12,975
One or two workers	2,706	48,181	44,310	12,465	14,359
Shoeshine parlors					
No paid employees	478	1,826	9,182	—	9,036
Paid employees	247	2,381	13,441	7,396	7,610
One or two workers	98	2,867	13,204	7,545	7,764
Car washes and lubrication shops					
No paid employees	259	20,888	13,185	—	11,514
Paid employees	4,243	29,254	27,435	9,981	11,575
One or two workers	591	51,589	35,096	12,677	14,908

— Not applicable.

a. Figures for service establishments with no paid employees are imputed values.

Source: Secretaría de Industria y Comercio, Dirección General de Estadística, *VI Censo de servicios, 1971* (Mexico, D.F., 1974), tables 8 and 16.

"marginal" adherents of the sector. The latter may be expected to be self-employed individuals with no establishment or business premises. As "unregistered" enterprises, they could not be expected to find their way into the universe from which the census observations are drawn. Thus, those who are presumed to be the most disadvantaged workers in the sector simply escape detection.

Although this may appear to be a persuasive observation, I would not wish to discount the relevance of the census data. Of particular significance would be the data for the smallest establishments with paid employment, those with *total* (remunerated and unremunerated) employment of two or fewer workers. Such tiny establishments are frequently judged to be part of the "informal" sector and, therefore, free of the legal constraints

Table 2-11. *Employment, Productivity, and Earnings in Repair Services, 1970*
(pesos)

Subdivision	*Employment (number)*	*Net capital investment per worker*	*Net value added per worker*	*Average annual wages and salaries*	*Average annual total remunerations*[a]
Domestic electric appliance repair and installation					
No paid employees	6,615	4,707	11,069	—	10,692
Paid employees	5,766	17,016	22,314	9,480	11,072
One or two workers	1,948	7,347	17,138	8,349	9,349
Automobile repair					
No paid employees	11,774	11,698	9,586	—	8,650
Paid employees	36,236	21,583	26,183	10,238	11,969
One or two workers	7,013	14,235	20,715	9,039	10,258
Motorcycle and bicycle repair					
No paid employees	2,658	5,156	10,109	—	9,697
Paid employees	920	13,328	17,716	8,076	8,732
One or two workers	565	14,050	19,326	8,078	8,645
Plumbing and soldering					
No paid employees	1,805	5,032	9,648	—	9,245
Paid employees	1,956	10,037	16,984	8,678	8,678
One or two workers	590	10,075	16,756	8,737	9,588

— Not applicable.
a. Figures for service establishments with no paid employees are imputed values.
Source: Secretaría de Industria y Comercio, Dirección General de Estadística, *VI Censo de servicios, 1971* (Mexico, D.F., 1974), tables 8 and 16.

that govern employment conditions in large, modern employing units. Thus, one would expect remunerations in such establishments to reflect more closely the opportunity cost of labor rather than the legal minimum wage. Indeed, we have observed that *average* remunerations frequently either barely approximated or actually fell below the legal minimum wage. These facts suggest that an important proportion of paid employees received less than the legal minimum and that the wage payments do respond to labor market conditions.[41] Since the opportunity cost of workers employed in such small establishments is the earnings that would be forthcoming in a self-employed status, the remunerations paid may not be a poor approximation of the former. On the contrary, if the imputed returns to labor in establishments with no paid labor can be accepted at face value, these returns are even more likely to approximate the opportunity cost of such labor. They would thus be representative of returns to self-employed labor in similar activities in the informal sector.

Commerce

I mentioned earlier that, like the service sector, commerce is also frequently singled out as a sector that serves as an absorptive sponge for labor in "excess supply." References to the ubiquitous street peddler are legion in the literature, as are those to tiny retail establishments with limited inventories and "underemployed" labor. Drawing on data for 1970 contained in the 1971 census of the commerce sector, I conducted exercises similar to those reviewed above for the service sector.[42] Since the findings were similar to those reported for the low-skill service sector, I will not present the findings in detail. Suffice it to say that even the imputed earnings of workers in establishments with no paid employees exceeded the legal minimum wage for 1970, as did those in the smallest establishments with paid employees but employing no more than a total of two persons.

While the observation of remunerations at a moment in time—in this case, 1970—may lead to a conclusion that employment conditions in the small establishment strata of the commerce and service sectors were not as depressed as might have been expected, this might not be as important as the trend in conditions over time. If these sectors are viewed as flexible, accommodating, and expanding repositories for "excess" labor, then the true significance of expanding employment can be gauged only if account can be taken of secular changes in earnings. This is undertaken in some detail in Chapter 7. The findings reported there provide evidence that the wage conditions of employment improved steadily in all sizes of establishments in both of these sectors, at least over the interval 1960–75. Indeed, earnings in the smallest sized units appear to have gained relative to larger sized units. Therefore, I would view the evolution of the labor force and the structure of employment as having had favorable implications for the lot of the Mexican worker. The shift of labor from the agricultural sector to others has occurred without causing a depression in earnings in the recorded parts of the "informal" labor market and has resulted in a steady improvement in wage conditions.

A final observation that casts doubt on the view that labor market conditions have deteriorated over time is drawn from income distribution data for 1963, 1968, and 1977.[43] If the economy were developing in such a manner that increases in productivity and wages in some sectors were being partially offset by declines in others, then one would expect this to be reflected in a sharp drop in the share of income accruing to the lowest income deciles. In fact, there has been great stability in that share. The share accruing to the bottom 40 percent of the households has varied within the narrow range of 10.5 to 10.9 percent.[44] This implies that the incomes of these households have increased at approximately the same rate as has the average per capita income. Nevertheless, it is quite likely that some households, particularly in the agricultural subsistence sector, have had stagnant incomes and have not shared in the general increase in prosperity. The bottom decile, for example, has suffered a decline in its relative share of total income, from 1.69 to 1.08 percent. However, given the strong growth in per capita income, this still allows for an increase in real income for this decile of approximately 13 percent. For the most part, the lowest incomes in Mexico are to be found in remote stagnating agricultural regions of the country that often have large, partially assimilated indigenous populations—not in the expanding urban sectors. The other three deciles of the bottom four must have enjoyed substantial increases in real income, a phenomenon that would not ordinarily be consistent with a widespread depresssion of urban wages at the lower end of the wage structure. This conclusion will be seen to be consistent with the earnings data reviewed in Chapter 7.

Summary

Concerns regarding the secular trend in the quality of employment in Mexico have been based on, among other things, observed declines in aggregate rates of labor force participation and a rapid growth in tertiary sector employment. Both have been interpreted as indicative of a failure of the Mexican process of economic development to create sufficient amounts of productive employment. Although these changes are empirically verifiable, they can be interpreted to be reflections of positive forces rather than indicators of a deterioration in the availability and quality of employment. The declines in participation rates of teenagers and young adults have gone hand in hand with increases in school enrollments. Only if school attendance can be shown to be an unproductive use of time might one be led to hypothesize that schools were mere repositories of frustrated job seekers. Since there is clear evidence that investment in education carries with it generous rewards in the form of higher earnings, it is reasonable to hypothesize that a decision to substitute schooling for labor force participation represents a rational choice, especially among young teenagers. Furthermore, the willingness of families to forego the potential incomes of their children may reflect a continuing improvement in household incomes which permits an increasing consumption of normal goods, including education. The decline in the participation rates of the elderly population parallels trends observable in more highly industrialized societies and may simply reflect the effects of the extension of social security pension coverage as well as rising household incomes that permit the purchase of the elderly's leisure time.

Nor does the expansion of tertiary sector employment appear to have as ominous a character as has been generally supposed. Until recently, it has expended at a rate below that of the growth of the urban population, the primary consumer of services. When the determinants of the demand for some of the low-skill services—the growth of the urban population and increases in per capita income—are taken into account, much of the growth in employment can be explained. Furthermore, the observation that the real remunerations of those engaged in establishments most likely to be paying market-determined wages have risen over time suggests that the demand for such services has been increasing more rapidly than their supply. In short, the concurrent increases in employment, productivity, and earnings in the major sectors of the economy would seem to point to a more optimistic appraisal of the course of employment conditions than that generally held by observers of the Mexican scene. Optimism at so early a point in this exposition derives from a rather narrow empirical base; the chapters that follow will provide further evidence that reinforces this appraisal.

Appendix: Technical Notes on Labor Force Measurements

In the course of Chapter 2, several references were made to shortcomings in the available published labor force data. All of the population censuses since 1950 have been characterized by problems that have greatly inhibited the charting of changes in the size and distribution of the labor force over time. This appendix examines the various procedures adopted by students of the Mexican labor force for adjusting the published data that refer to labor force participation rates and to the industrial distribution of the labor force.

Labor Force Participation Rates

While the trend in rates of labor force participation is not in question, the precise amount of change is. Unfortunately, the population censuses since 1950 do not provide an unambiguous basis for measuring change. In part, this is attributable to variations in the concept of labor force participation that is applied from one census to another. One analysis of the evolution of the labor force holds that some of the decline in male participation rates observable in the 1970 census stems from changes in the criteria applied.[45] The 1960 census poses a particularly severe problem. Processing errors resulted in gross distortions of participation rates, which necessitated a later revision of the published data. However, even the corrected data proved unconvincing. As a result, greater reliance has come to be placed on the adjustments made by the Colegio de México and on the work of Oscar Altimir.[46] Yet, in light of the basic deficiencies of the census tabulations, even the adjusted data must be approached with care and not a little skepticism. Unfortunately, these two approaches to the adjustment of the census lead to different conclusions with respect to the size of the labor force and to the internal structure of age-specific participation rates for the two sexes. Table 2-12 presents participation rates by age and sex derived from the population censuses and, for 1960, the adjusted data of the census, the Colegio, and Altimir.

The difficulties posed by the data for 1960 immediately come to light. Although the male participation rates seem plausible in the 30–60 age groups, they seem higher than one might expect, relative to the 1950 rates, at the two extremes of the distribution. The female rates appear quite implausible, given the continuous increases in participation rates for each age group from age 25 on. Altimir's adjustments result in lower participation rates in all age groups for both sexes. However, they also yield wider variations in the rates among the prime-age groups than one would normally expect to find. The Colegio's estimates for men fall somewhere between the census and Altimir estimates except for the two oldest age groupings; these show lower participation rates than Altimir's. Regarding the female rates, the Colegio's estimates lie above the other two for the young and below for the older women. In short, no one of the distributions is entirely satisfactory, that is, has a form that meets expectations based on international comparisons. Nevertheless, the literature on the Mexican labor force seems to have adopted the Altimir estimates more widely than the others. I will do the same, although I retain some reservations.

One obvious result of the different sets of participation rates is the different estimates of the size of the labor force for 1960. Whereas the census yielded a labor force of 11.253 million, the Colegio and Altimir adjustments yielded 10.631 million and 10.213 million, respectively. Obviously, the rate of intercensal changes in the labor force will vary depending on which of these numbers for 1960 is adopted.

Less controversy surrounds the 1970 census results—perhaps because they have not been subjected to the same close scrutiny as that accorded the census for 1960. However, there are grounds for believing that this census underenumerated the labor force. Note, for example, the participation rates for males in the prime age groups. These show significant declines from past levels and are lower than international comparisons would lead us to expect. In the case of women, the rates would suggest a decline in participation rates of most age groups in comparison with any of the three distributions for 1960. Again, in line with past trends in Mexico and with international experience, one might reasonably have expected female rates to rise. Indeed, an interesting paradox of the 1970 rates for females comes to light in the two measures that were made of the labor force. One was based on activity during 1969: anyone who had been employed at any time in 1969 was counted as a member of the labor force. The other measure was more conventional and referred to activity during a reference week prior to the census. One would normally expect the measure based on activity during 1969 to yield a larger labor force than that of a one-week reference period during the first month of 1970. Yet, in the case of women, the 1970 reference week yielded the larger labor force.

Support for the hypothesis that the 1970 census underenumerated the labor force is provided by the quarterly labor force surveys which were initiated in 1973.[47] It is possible to compare the participation rates of men and women in the Federal District as reported by the census with the survey's rates for 1973 (see table 2-13). For men, the survey participation rate amounted to 75.1 percent, expressed as an average of the four quarterly rates, as compared with the census rate of 71.7 percent for 1969 and 70.6 percent for January 1980. For women, the absolute and relative differences are even greater. Whereas the survey yielded an average rate of 35.0 percent, the two census measures were reported as 29.7 percent and 28.8 percent. Although one would expect a labor force survey to capture a larger and closer approximation of the actual labor force than a popula-

Table 2-12. *Labor Force Participation Rates by Sex and Age Group, 1950–79*

Age group	1950	1960 Revised	1960 Colegio de México	1960 Adjusted by Altimir	1969	1970 January	1979 January–March
Male							
10–11	25.8	—	—	—	—	—	
12–14		32.2	22.4	15.3	12.8	15.5	35.4
15–19	79.0	77.6	68.2	61.6	49.9	52.2	
20–24	93.3	94.7	91.8	86.8	79.6	78.3	82.5
25–29	97.3	96.7	94.7	92.5	90.6	88.2	95.9
30–34	98.5	97.1	95.9	94.8	93.2	89.6	
35–39	98.8	97.4	96.6	96.0	94.3	90.2	96.7
40–44	98.7	97.3	96.6	96.9	93.9	89.8	
45–49	98.6	97.3	96.3	97.2	93.9	89.6	93.4
50–54	98.3	96.6	95.4	94.4	92.3	88.0	
55–59	98.1	96.3	94.0	96.4	90.6	86.2	85.1
60–64	97.8	96.0	91.8	95.4	86.1	81.5	
65–69	97.1	94.4	88.8	94.6	81.1	76.7	53.2
70+	95.6	90.2	81.0	85.2	63.2	60.7	
Female							
10–11	5.9	—	—	—	—	—	
12–14		4.8	7.0	4.4	5.1	7.6	15.4
15–19	15.2	16.7	20.8	15.4	20.9	23.1	
20–24	11.2	19.4	23.0	17.8	24.1	25.0	33.4
25–29	13.3	15.6	16.9	14.4	17.4	18.6	27.3
30–34	13.4	16.0	16.1	14.7	15.7	16.8	

35–39	13.6	17.5	17.1	16.1	15.8	16.6	24.5
40–44	13.7	20.4	18.3	17.6	16.2	16.7	
45–49	13.8	22.3	18.3	18.2	16.4	16.8	21.1
50–54	13.7	25.2	18.1	19.4	15.9	16.2	
55–59	13.9	26.1	17.7	19.1	15.1	15.4	16.3
60–64	13.5	30.8	17.0	21.4	14.1	14.4	
65–69	13.8	30.2	15.6	20.0	12.9	13.5	9.3
70+	12.9	29.2	11.7	18.6	9.7	10.7	
Total labor force (thousands)	8,345.2	11,253.3	10,631.2	10,212.9	12,955.1	12,909.5	19,839.2
Male	7,207.6	9,235.0	8,732.0	8,496.2	10,488.8	10,255.2	14,976.2
Female	1,137.6	2,018.3	1,899.2	1,716.6	2,466.3	2,654.3	4,863.0
Total population 12 years and over	16,849.3	n.a.	n.a.	21,944.2	29,697.3	29,697.3	43,639.0
Male	8,166.3	n.a.	n.a.	10,797.1	14,625.6	14,625.6	20,966.2
Female	8,683.0	n.a.	n.a.	11,147.1	15,071.7	15,071.7	22,642.7
Total labor force participation rate	49.5	51.1	48.3	46.5	43.6	43.5	45.5
Male	88.2	85.1	80.5	78.7	71.7	70.1	71.3
Female	13.1	18.0	16.9	15.4	16.4	17.6	21.5

n.a. Not available.

— Not applicable.

Sources: 1950—Secretaría de Industria y Comercio, Dirección General de Estadística, *VII Censo de población, 1950* (Mexico, D.F., 1953). 1960—Secretaría de Industria y Comercio, Dirección General de Estadística, *VIII Censo general de población, 1960: Poblacion economicamente activa*, Rectificación de los cuadros 25, 26 y 27 del *Resumen general* ya publicado (Mexico, D.F., 1964). 1960—El Colegio de México, *Dinámica de la población de México* (Mexico, D.F., 1970). 1960—Oscar Altimir, "La medición de la población economicamente activa de México 1950–1970," *Demografía y economía*, vol. 8, no. 1 (1974), pp. 50–83. 1969 and 1970—Secretaría de Industria y Comercio, Dirección General de Estadística, *IX Censo de población, 1970* (Mexico, D.F., 1972), unadjusted for underenumeration. 1979—Secretaría de Programación y Presupuesto, *Encuesta continua sobre ocupación*, vol. 7, 1st quarter 1979 (Mexico, D.F., February 1980).

Table 2-13. *Labor Force Participation Rates in the Federal District by Sex and Age Group, 1969, 1970, and 1973*

Sex and year	Total	Age group: 12–19	20–24	25–34	35–44	45–54	55–64	65 and over
Male								
1969	71.7	28.0	80.0	94.9	96.4	94.5	85.9	57.9
1970, January	70.6	29.9	78.9	92.9	94.2	92.3	83.2	55.1
1973, average	75.1	37.9	85.9	98.1	98.2	95.8	80.8	51.0
Female								
1969	29.7	23.8	44.2	33.0	31.2	29.2	23.6	13.8
1970, January	28.8	24.7	42.0	31.6	29.7	27.6	22.0	12.8
1973, average	35.0	29.6	50.7	39.5	39.0	34.0	24.7	12.0

Sources: Secretaría de Industria y Comercio, Dirección General de Estadística, *IX Censo general de población: Resumen general* (Mexico, D.F., 1972); Secretaría de Programación y Presupuesto, *Encuesta continua de mano de obra*, vol. 1, 1st–4th quarter 1973 (Mexico, D.F., 1977).

tion census, these differences would seem to be unusually large, particularly in view of the fact that one of the census definitions of labor force participation used the entire year 1969 as the reference period.

Further support for the hypothesis that undercounting occurred in the 1970 census is provided by the labor force surveys for the other regions. Since the surveys were not extended to all regions of the country until 1979, the data for the first quarter of 1979 provide a basis of comparison with the 1970 census. It should be kept in mind, however, that this is not an ideal basis for checking the accuracy of the census. Since the long-term trend of participation rates for men has been downward, some reduction in participation rates may reasonably be expected to have occurred between 1969 and 1979. Yet, if only the prime age male groups are considered—those between the ages of 25 and 55—one would not expect significant changes to have occurred. Table 2-14 presents the participation rates of the 1970 census for the week preceding the census in January 1970 and those of the labor force survey for the first quarter of 1979. As can be seen, six of the ten regions reported labor participation rates below 90 percent; the other four reported rates in the low 90s. The survey rates for 1979 lie well above these. Applying the survey rates to the census population in these age groups, one derives a male labor force in the prime-age groups that is 7.3 percent greater than the force reported by the census. In absolute terms, therefore, an estimate of the underenumeration of the

Table 2-14. *Labor Force Participation Rates of Men in Prime-Age Groups by Region, January 1970 and First Quarter 1979*

	Age group		
Region	*25–34*	*35–44*	*45–54*
Federal District			
1970	92.9	94.2	92.3
1979	96.7	97.9	94.4
North			
1970	87.0	89.3	88.1
1979	93.3	94.3	87.3
Northeast			
1970	90.3	91.7	89.9
1979	96.9	97.5	94.2
Northwest			
1970	90.5	89.2	88.2
1979	95.2	97.1	93.8
North Central			
1970	86.9	89.1	88.5
1979	90.0	97.1	97.8
Peninsular			
1970	90.1	91.8	91.7
1979	98.1	98.5	96.3
Central Pacific			
1970	85.4	86.2	85.3
1979	95.9	96.2	92.5
Central[a]			
1970	87.4	88.7	87.6
1979	95.9	96.2	92.5
South Pacific			
1970	85.0	87.3	87.0
1979	96.1	97.3	94.6
Central Gulf			
1970	89.5	91.1	90.4
1979	96.9	99.1	99.0
All Mexico			
1970	88.5	90.0	89.0
1979	95.9	96.7	93.4

Note: See table 3-2 for definitions of the regions.

a. Includes those municipios that form part of the Mexico City metropolitan area but that lie outside the Federal District.

Sources: Secretaría de Industria y Comercio, Dirección General de Estadística, *IX Censo de población, 1970* (Mexico, D.F., 1972); and Secretaría de Programación y Presupuesto, *Encuesta continua sobre ocupación*, vol. 7, no. 1 (1979), table 2A.

census amounts to approximately 419,000 males in the prime-age groups. Rather than a measured labor force participation rate of 89.1 percent for this group, as given by the census, the surveys yield a rate of 95.6 percent—much closer to the figure one would be led to expect from international comparisons.

It is likely that the 1970 census also underestimated the size of the female labor force. One could reasonably have expected the secular trend suggested by the change from 1950 to 1960 to have continued to 1970.[48] The female participation rate increased from 13.1 percent in 1950 to 15.2 percent in 1960 after the adjustments made by Altimir. Over the next decade, it increased by just over one percentage point to 16.4 (based on 1969 labor force experience). For the week prior to the census, however, a higher rate of 17.6 is reported. Nevertheless, even the latter rate may represent undercounting. The labor force surveys suggest that female participation may have been greater than that reported by the census. For example, the first survey, in the first quarter of 1973, reported a rate of 33.8 percent for the Federal District, more than a third greater than the census figure for January 1970.

This difference, however, is not likely to be typical of the degree of underreporting that may have characterized the census as a whole. This can be inferred from the participation rates reported by the quarterly surveys for the first quarter of 1979 (see table 2-15). There, the January 1970 census rate is presented, along with the rates for the more recent quarter, for each region. The recent national participation rate can be seen to be 22 percent higher than the census rate. Of course, the entire difference cannot be ascribed to underreporting in 1970; secular tendencies may well account for some of the intervening increase. Over the decade of the 1970s, the largest increases in participation rates appear to have occurred in those regions in which expanding urban centers exert a heavy weight. These areas include the Federal District, Central Pacific (which includes Guadalajara), Central (parts of metropolitan Mexico City), and North (Juarez). The apparent decline in participation in the Northwest region would seem to be misleading. This region includes the rapidly expanding border region of northern Baja California, an area in which light border industries have offered expanding employment opportunities to women. The surveys report unusually wide fluctuations in the female participation rates for this region, possibly a consequence of the sample design. The one for the first quarter of 1979 is among the lowest to be reported for recent quarters. For example, the rates for the first quarters of 1977 and 1978 were 17.9 and 18.7 percent, respectively. Therefore, skepticism about the reported decline in female participation in that region would be warranted.

While the data suggest that the 1970 census underenumerated the female labor force, they do not provide a basis for estimating the extent of the underenumeration—that part of the difference between the 1979 and 1970 participations which reflects the secular increase in participation cannot be extracted. Thus, no attempt is made here to adjust the female labor force for 1970; the figures given are simply accepted. The participation rates of men in the prime age groups of the labor force are less subject to significant secular trends. I have therefore adjusted the census labor force measures for 1970 (presented earlier in this chapter) by the 419,000 men whom I have estimated above as having been overlooked.

The 1980 census results offer grounds for continued uncertainty about the accuracy of census measures of the labor force. The reported labor force appears to be larger than expected. For example, the aggregate labor force participation rate of 50.9 percent is considerably greater than the 1970 census rate of 44.9 percent and the household survey rate of 45.5 percent for the first quarter of 1979. The absolute size of the labor force is given as 22.066 million in June 1980, the month of the census, whereas the estimated size of the labor force during the first quarter of 1979 was 19.839 million. Even if one allows for a generous 6 percent growth over the ensuing year and a quarter, the labor force in June 1980 would still have measured only 21 million.

A possible explanation of the larger-than-expected measure may lie in the change in the definition of the labor force. In previous censuses and in the household labor force surveys unremunerated family workers were included in the labor force only if they had been occupied fifteen or more

Table 2-15. *Labor Force Participation Rates of Women by Region, January 1970 and First Quarter 1979*

Region	*January 1970*	*First quarter 1979*
Federal District	24.7	34.1
North	15.5	20.9
Northeast	17.0	19.0
Northwest	17.4	16.1
North Central	14.2	14.1
Peninsular	13.3	15.3
Central Pacific	16.5	22.7
Central[a]	15.6	26.7
South Pacific	14.5	18.2
Central Gulf	13.2	15.8
All Mexico	17.6	21.5

a. Includes those municipios that form part of the Mexico City metropolitan area but that lie outside the Federal District.

Sources: Same as table 2-14.

hours during the reference week. The 1980 census removed this qualification so that all such workers were included regardless of the hours worked. Such a definitional change could account for the large increase in the participation rates of both sexes. Unfortunately, it is not possible to determine whether this definitional change is a sufficient explanation. No information has yet been published on the numbers of hours worked during a reference week. In one table the labor force is classified according to employment status, and one category is unremunerated family workers. Although the proportion of the labor force of each sex in this category in 1980 is very similar to that of the 1970 census, a very large proportion (21.5 percent of the total labor force and 24.4 percent of the females) is not classified according to status. Even larger proportions of the labor force are not assigned to a sector of economic activity (26.9 percent of the men and 36.9 percent of the women). Thus, I cannot observe whether there are unusually large concentrations of workers in sectors, such as agriculture and commerce, that often employ large numbers of unremunerated family workers.

Classification of the Labor Force by Sector of Employment

The second problem noted in Chapter 2 related to the difficulties that are encountered in relying on census data to trace the evolution of the sectoral distribution of employment over time. Among the obstacles mentioned were changes in the industrial classification of individual activities, the shifting treatment of *ejidatarios*, the overenumeration of the labor force by the 1960 census, and the large number of labor force members who could not be assigned to a sector of employment. The discussion that follows is restricted to the last issue. Different treatment of the unclassified workers can yield sharply different perceptions regarding the secular changes in the quality of employment in Mexico.

Let us examine first the sectoral distributions offered by Earl L. McFarland. Table 2-16 presents the distribution of the labor force as reported by the censuses of 1950, 1960, and 1970, with adjustments McFarland made in the 1970 census to account for changes in the classification of subsectors. The 1960 census data are presented as reported, without any adjustment for the apparent overenumeration of that year. Included in the last column, however, is a revised sectoral distribution of the labor force for 1969. This adjustment reflects his reallocation of a major portion of the unclassified group among most of the other sectors. The reallocation conforms to the sectoral distribution yielded by a 1969–70 sample survey of family income and expenditures.[49] Results of this survey led to the assignment of the bulk of the unclassified workers to the service and

Table 2-16. *Economically Active Population of Mexico by Sector, 1950, 1960, and 1969*
(thousands)

Sector	*1950*	*1960*	*1969*	*Estimated 1969*
Agriculture, livestock, forestry, and fishing	4,823.9	6,084.1	5,103.5	5,103.5
Mining and petroleum	97.1	141.1	180.2	178.7
Manufacturing	972.5	1,550.2	2,169.1	2,405.2
Construction	224.5	407.2	571.0	571.0
Electricity, gas, and water	25.0	41.3	53.3	93.4
Transportation and communication	210.6	356.1	368.8	456.9
Commerce	684.1	1,071.9	1,196.9	1,498.0
Services	600.6	1,048.9	2,158.2	1,792.7–1,903.1
Government	278.8	470.2	406.6	763.3–652.9
Insufficiently specified	355.0	81.6	747.5	92.3
Total	8,345.2	11,253.3	12,955.1	12,955.1

Source: Earl L. McFarland, Jr., "Employment Growth in Services: Mexico 1950–1969," Ph.D. dissertation, Columbia University, 1974, tables 1.2 and 1.4.

government sectors (for these two sectors, he provides a range of possible numbers rather than a single figure). From these distributions, McFarland concluded that there has been an alarmingly rapid rate of increase in the labor force employed in the service sector and that it must represent an influx of persons unable to find satisfactory remunerated employment. Thus, the sector is seen as becoming a repository of labor employed in marginal activities at very low levels of productivity.

A very different impression of the evolution of the labor force by sector of employment is gained from Altimir's approach.[50] His treatment involves the distribution of the unassigned labor force for all three censuses. In the cases of the 1950 and 1960 censuses, he is able to reallocate to agriculture and mining a substantial number of workers by cross-reference with the tables of the occupational groupings of these same people. The balance is distributed over the sectors in the same proportion as the measured employment. The assumption is made that the failure to specify sector was randomly distributed with respect to sector. Altimir's adjustment for 1960 also includes a reduction in the size of the agricultural labor force to correct for the overenumeration of this group, an adjustment that McFarland does not make. The problem for the 1970 census is considerably more complex than for the others. First, the size of the unclassified group is much larger. Second, the occupational designation does not lend itself to reclassification since the bulk of those who could not be classified with respect to sector also defy classification by occupational group. Altimir attributes these failures to the long reference period to which the occupational questions referred. The enumerators were expected to record the individuals according to their principal occupation during the whole of 1969 rather than as of a specific date (such as the week prior to the census). He concludes that the shifting of many individuals among sectors during the year complicated their assignment and yielded the large unclassifiable residual. This conclusion leads Altimir to conjecture that, in these circumstances, it is reasonable to assume that the inability to specify a sector is dominated by random elements rather than by a systematic bias that fails to identify correctly persons who are employed in one or more particular sectors. Therefore, he proceeds to distribute the unclassified persons over the sectors in the same proportions as the measured specified labor force. It is the distribution so derived that is included in table 2-4.

A comparison of the Altimir and McFarland distributions reveals substantial differences. These differences affect the perception of both productivity growth by sector and the "healthfulness" of the employment increases associated with Mexico's model of development. Therefore, it is necessary to offer some judgments about the relative merits of the conflicting estimates.

I find it difficult to accept McFarland's assignment to the service sector of most of the unclassified workers of the 1970 census. His reliance on the sectoral distribution yielded by a sample survey of income and expenditures as the basis for adjusting the census seems to me to be misplaced. I have found that most Mexican surveys that have as their primary objective the collection of information relating to other subjects produce labor market information of dubious quality. Further reservations stem from an examination of the census and the character of the unclassified. Service sector employment is closely associated with urbanization. Indeed, the common characterization of the service sector as a "sponge" absorbing the "excess" workers who cannot gain employment in preferred jobs is offered as typical of large urban areas. In addition, as might be expected, measured employment in Mexico's service sector is heavily urban. For example, although only 30.1 percent of the labor force is found in localities with populations of over 50,000, fully 55.1 percent of measured service sector employment is found there.[51] If McFarland's conjecture were correct, it should follow that the unclassified workers should be heavily concentrated in the more urbanized areas. Yet, this does not appear to be the case. Whereas 30.1 percent of the labor force is to be found in localities with populations in excess of 50,000, only a slightly larger proportion of the unclassified—32.5 percent is found there. At the other end of the spectrum, 39.1 percent of the labor force is in localities with fewer than 2,500 inhabitants while 34.8 percent of the unclassified are reported there. The data for Mexico City also cast doubt on McFarland's thesis. If disguised service employment exists anywhere, one would suppose that Mexico City would harbor a disproportionate part of it. Yet, while the Federal District is reported to hold 17.2 percent of the labor force, it has only 11.7 percent of the unclassified workers.

If the data are broken down by sex, a confused picture emerges. Among males, there is a slightly disproportionate share of the unclassified in larger urban areas: 27.2 percent of the male labor force and 33.5 percent of the unclassified males are found there. Among females, however, the disproportionate share of the unclassified is in the rural areas: whereas 21.4 percent of the labor force is in localities with fewer than 2,500 inhabitants, fully 39.7 percent of the unclassified is there. Conversely, in the most urbanized localities, the two proportions are 46.0 and 30.3 percent, respectively. The heavier incidence of unclassified workers in less urbanized areas would seen to offer a rationale for Altimir's treatment. To the extent that rural workers divide their time between agricultural and nonagricultural activities, the specification of a "principal" activity may have posed real difficulties for the enumerators and respondents.

Two others aspects of the unclassified labor force may be noteworthy. Over half (56.2 percent) of the unclassified workers report that they were employed in a wage- or salary-earning capacity. One could reasonably expect that, if the unclassified workers were primarily those forced into marginal employment in the service sector, a disproportionately large number would be found in the categories of the self-employed or unpaid family workers. Yet, the proportions of the unclassified (by sector) workers in these two employment categories were only a little larger than those for the classified portion of the labor force. For example, 18.8 percent of the classified labor force is listed as self-employed as compared with 23.9 percent for the unclassified. The proportions for the unremunerated family workers are 6.5 and 7.1 percent, respectively.[52]

Finally, there is a slightly higher incidence of nonclassification among the youngest and the oldest members of the labor force. These may be rationalized as follows.[53] To the extent that the youngest workers "shop" around for a desirable employment, they will tend to shift jobs over an interval of a year, subsequently making identification of the principal activity more difficult. Similarly, the oldest age groups may be active only intermittently and may show no permanent attachment to any single sector of activity.[54]

These observations on the characteristics of the unclassified workers may imply a less pessimistic appraisal of their employment situation than that offered by McFarland and may provide some justification for Altimir's procedure for distributing them over the various sectors. It should be recognized, however, that Altimir's figures are also subject to an error of unknown dimension. Nevertheless, the rationale underlying his approach and the ensuing distribution seem sufficiently convincing to lead me to prefer his allocation to that of McFarland. Therefore, I have relied heavily on Altimir's work in the text.

Notes

1. Enrique Hernández Laos and Jorge Córdova Chavez, "Estructura de la distribución de ingreso en México," *Comercio exterior*, vol. 29, no. 5 (May 1979), p. 506.
2. Luis Unikel, *El desarrollo urbano de México*, 2d ed. (Mexico, D.F.: El Colegio de México, 1978), table VI-A15.
3. Luis Gómez Oliver, "Crisis agrícola, crisis de los campesinos," *Comercio exterior*, vol. 28, no. 6 (June 1978), p. 719. The average wage was estimated by dividing total wage payments to permanent workers by the number of wage earners in the census.
4. Secretaría de Programación y Presupuesto, *X Censo industrial 1976* (Mexico, D.F., 1979), table 8.
5. Secretaría de Programación y Presupuesto, *VIII Censo de comercio 1976* (Mexico, D.F., 1979), table 17; *VII Censo de servicios 1976* (Mexico, D.F., 1979), table 17.
6. Poor families are defined as those households with incomes equal to less than one-half the estimated national mean. The proportions presented in the text should be taken only as rough approximations. The 1975 survey appears to have underestimated severely the incomes of some groups, largely in the form of income in kind. The results of the 1977 survey, which are thought to be of better quality, are not available for employment of the head of household by sector.
7. Unikel, *El desarrollo urbano de México*, p. 213.
8. The labor force survey report was originally entitled *Encuesta continua de mano de obra*. Beginning with the third quarter of 1978, the publication was renamed *Encuesta continua sobre ocupación* and is commonly referred to by its acronym, ECSO. I refer to both the original and the subsequent publication by this acronym. Both were published by the Secretaría de Programación y Presupuesto in Mexico, D.F.
9. Oscar Altimir, "La medición de la población economicamente activa de México 1950–70," *Demografía y economía*, vol. 8, no. 1 (1974), pp. 50–83.
10. Consejo Nacional de Población, Secretaría de Programación y Presupuesto, Centro Latinoamericano de Demografía, *México: estimaciones y proyecciones de población 1950–2000* (Mexico, D.F., September 1982), pp. 17–18. The population figures appearing in table 2-2 are taken from the official census publications. Revised estimates of total population appearing in this publication purport to adjust the census count for the underreporting of population, particularly of infants and children under 5 years of age. The revised estimates increase the total population by about 1.5 million in 1950 and 1970 and by about 2 million in 1960 and 1980. The intercensal rates of growth, however, are only slightly different from those yielded by the official censuses.
11. Detailed data on sex- and age-specific participation rates are presented in the appendix.
12. Organization of American States, *América en cifras 1977* (Washington, D.C., 1979), vol. 3, pp. 52–56. The low recorded participation rates for women probably understate their true participation in productive activity. Their rates are particularly low in the rural states of

Mexico. It is likely that many rural women view their contribution to agricultural production as part of their household duties and not as a separate activity that would qualify them as members of the labor force.

13. Donald B. Keesing, "Employment and Lack of Employment in Mexico, 1900–70," in *Quantitative Latin American Studies: Methods and Findings*, ed. James W. Wilkie and Kenneth Ruddle (Los Angeles: University of California, L.A., Latin American Center, 1977), pp. 3–21.

14. Secretaría de Industria y Comercio, Dirección General de Estadística, *VII Censo general de población 6 de junio 1950, Resumen general* (Mexico, D.F., 1953); *IX Censo general de población 1970, Resumen general* (Mexico, D.F., 1972); Carlos Muñoz Izquierdo, "Educación, estado y sociedad en México (1930–76)," *Revista de la educación superior*, no. 34 (1980), pp. 5–56.

15. Juan Díez-Canedo and Gabriel Vera, "La importancia de la escolaridad en la determinación del ingreso en México," in *Distribución del ingreso en México*, vol. 2, ed. Carlos Bazdresch Parada, Jesús Reyes Heroles G. G., and Gabriel Vera Ferrer (Mexico, D.F.: Banco de México, November 1982), pp. 480, 502–08.

16. World Bank, *World Development Report 1983* (New York: Oxford University Press, 1983), pp. 196–99.

17. Secretaría de Educación Pública, *Estadísticas básicas del sistema nacional de educación tecnológica 1979–80 (preliminar)* (Mexico, D.F., August 1980), pp. 9–10.

18. In fact, the recorded data understate the proportion of the population enrolled in school. The labor force survey gives precedence to the employed status over school enrollment of individuals in classifying the population of labor force age. Thus, those who are both employed and attending school are recorded only as employed.

19. *Ejidatarios* are members of communities, or *ejidos*, that were granted land by the land reform process to be held in common. The ejidatario receives rights to use the land but does not have title to it.

20. Altimir, "La medición de la población economicamente activa."

21. In 1960, the question designed to determine the status of the respondent as an ejidatario or otherwise was asked first. The sector of principal activity was left to be determined later in the interview. However, many of the census takers, in spite of instructions to the contrary, apparently accepted the status of ejidatario as indicative of agricultural employment and did not pursue the occupational questions further. In 1970, the order of the questions was reversed, so that the sector of employment was established prior to determining the status as ejidatario.

22. For purposes of this exercise, the respondents who did not specify a sector of employment, 0.5 percent of the total, were distributed over the several sectors in the same proportions as measured employment.

23. The distribution of the gains of agricultural productivity will be explored in Chapter 4.

24. Stylianos Perrakis, "The Surplus Labor Model and Wage Behavior in Mexico," *Industrial Relations*, vol. 11, no. 1 (February 1972), pp. 80–95;Clark W. Reynolds, *The Mexican Economy* (New Haven, Conn.: Yale University Press, 1970), pp. 84–88; Timothy King, *Mexico: Industrialization and Trade Policies since 1940* (London: Oxford University Press, 1971), pp. 26–27.

25. It is possible that the changes in output and productivity recorded for the 1960s understate the actual rates of increase. The revised national accounts, which extend back to 1970, have resulted in an increase of 6.1 percent in the 1970 GDP over earlier measures. If the 1969 GNP has been understated by a similar order of magnitude, the rates of change in output and productivity appearing in the last column of table 2-6 would prove to be conservative.

26. Employment during 1980 was estimated to have grown by 6.3 percent, or by 0.51

percent a month compounded. Therefore, I reduced the June 1980 estimated labor force by 2.57 percent. Secretaría de Programación y Presupuesto, *Sistema de cuentas nacionales de México, 1978–80*, vol. 1 (Mexico, D.F., 1982), p. 58.

27. Earl L. McFarland, Jr., "Employment Growth in Services: Mexico 1950–69," Ph.D. dissertation, Columbia University, 1974, chap. 1; Saul Trejo R., "Desempleo y subocupación en México," *Comercio exterior*, vol. 24, no. 7 (August 1974), pp. 411–16; Comisión Consultiva del Empleo, *Programa nacional de empleo 1980/82, Síntesis* (Mexico, D.F.: Dirección del Empleo, November 1979), pp. 16–27.

28. Those who subscribe to the view that employment in the tertiary sector is supply determined emphasize the impact on labor *supply* of the rapid growth of the urban population.

29. A decline in wages within the tertiary sector would not provide sufficient grounds for concluding that average employment conditions had deteriorated if the growth of the tertiary sector occurred at the expense of an even lower wage agricultural sector.

30. While one might normally expect repair services to be heavily weighted by skilled labor, data to be reviewed below indicate the prevalence of wages that are too low to be consistent with high-skill levels.

31. Grupo de Estudio del Problema del Empleo, "El problema ocupacional en México: magnitud y recomendaciones," versión preliminar (México, D.F., n.d.), p. 162.

32. The urban population considered here is that in communities with 15,000 or more residents. A sharper decline in the relative importance of domestic employment can be noted for the Federal District. In 1930, it accounted for 16.3 percent of the labor force. Over the following three population censuses, this proportion declined to 14.3, 10.8, and 8.8 percent. "Análisis del mercado de los servicios domesticos en México," *Cuadernos de empleo*, no. 1 (Mexico, D.F.: Secretaría del Trabajo y Previsión Social, 1976), p. 64.

33. Ibid., p. 79.

34. In view of the multicollinearity present in the multiple regression equation, I also estimated the 1950 employment with a regression equation that omits the income term, but includes the relative price change term. The estimate of 1950 employment yielded a closer approximation of the actual level. A simple regression of employment per thousand population on the proportion of the population in urban centers took the following form: $DS = 1.938 + 0.1761UP$, with the coefficient of UP significant at the 1 percent level and an adjusted R^2 of 0.597. This equation yields an estimate of only 181,219 domestic servants in 1950. However, the addition of the relative price change term raises the estimate to 324,468, only 4.6 percent greater than the actual level.

35. "Análisis del mercado de los servicios domesticos," p. 76.

36. The procedures followed in this exercise are described in some detail in Chapter 7.

37. Empirical evidence indicates that almost half of the unremunerated family workers in the large metropolitan urban labor markets of Mexico City, Guadalajara, and Monterrey work only part-time, that is, fewer than forty hours a week. In contrast, among hired workers, no more than 20 percent are so employed. Secretaría de Programación y Presupuesto, *Información basica sobre la estructura y caracteristicas del empleo y el desempleo en las areas metropolitanas de las ciudades de México, Guadalajara y Monterrey* (Mexico, D.F., 1979), table 32.

38. Comisión Nacional de los Salarios Minimos, *Memoria de los trabajos 1972 y 1973* (Mexico, D.F., 1975), p. 358.

39. The 1977 study permitted the calculation of an income elasticity of demand on a cross-sectional basis over fourteen income groups. A regression equation in log form of semiannual expenditures on food and beverages consumed outside the home on semiannual income was run; it yielded an income elasticity of 1.163. Secretaría de Presupuesto y

Programación, *Encuesta nacional de ingresos y gastos de los hogares 1977* (Mexico, D.F., n.d.), table P3.1.

40. The estimating procedure followed here omits a price variable since no data are available regarding the price movements of food and beverages served in commercial establishments. The sources of the data used in these calculations are the same as those reported for the estimating equations for domestic service.

41. In the absence of wage distributions by minimum wage zones, it is hazardous to make strong statements about the quantitative importance of wage payments below the legal minimum on the basis of the national average minimum and the national average wage. Many rates of wage payment that lie below the national average minimum wage may either equal or exceed the minimum wage of their particular zone (and the reverse may hold for earnings rates that lie above the national average minimum wage). However, if the national average wage were to fall "substantially" below the national average minimum wage, it would be likely to reflect payment of subminimum wages within zones, unless there is reason to believe that low-minimum wage zones are "overrepresented" in the census enumeration.

42. Although the years in which the economic censuses are taken always end in 1 or 6, the data reported refer to the year preceding the census, that is, 0 or 5.

43. Hernández and Córdova, "Estructura de la distribución de ingreso en México."

44. All of the estimates of income distribution for Mexico are derived on the basis of assumptions that, by necessity, involve a high degree of arbitrariness. This arises from the large discrepancy, which has increased over time, between the estimates of national income based on the household income and expenditures studies and those derived from the national income accounts. Since the former serve as the basis of estimating the distribution of income, it is necessary to distribute this discrepancy over households in some manner. Different scholars have adopted their own method of distributing the discrepancy with rather significantly different results for the shares of particular deciles. A thorough review of these studies is available in Joel Bergsman, *Income Distribution and Poverty in Mexico,* World Bank Staff Working Paper no. 395 (Washington, D.C., June 1980).

45. Brigida García, "La participación de la población en la actividad económica," *Demografía y economía,* vol. 9, no. 1 (1975), pp. 14–15.

46. Oscar Altimir, "La medición de la población economicamente activa de México 1950–70," *Demografía y economía,* vol. 8, no. 1 (1974), pp. 50–83; Colegio de México, *Dinámica de la población de México* (Mexico, D.F., 1970).

47. Secretaría de Programación y Presupuesto, *Encuesta continua de mano de obra.*

48. For a discussion of the difficulties involved in fully and accurately accounting for the labor force participation of women, see Mercedes Pedrero, *La participación femenina en la actividad económica y su presupuesto de tiempo,* Serie Avances de Investigación no. 3 (Mexico, D.F.: Centro Nacional de Información y Estadisticas del Trabajo, 1977).

49. Secretaría de Industria y Comercio, Dirección General de Muestreo, *Ingresos y egresos de las familias en la republica mexicana, 1969–1970* (Mexico, D.F., n.d.).

50. Altimir, "La medición de la población economicamente activa."

51. Secretaría de Industria y Comercio, Dirección General de Estadística, *IX Censo general de población, 1970* (Mexico, D.F., 1972), table 37.

52. Ibid., table 40.

53. Ibid., table 35.

54. The census offers information for three age groups over 65 years of age, and it is for these that the incidence of nonclassification is greatest. In absolute terms, however, the numbers involved in these age groups are rather small.

3. The Underutilization of Labor: Unemployment and Underemployment

As was previously mentioned, two critical issues for students of Mexican economic development have been the degree to which the existing labor resources have been utilized productively and the quality of the employment available to an expanding labor force. The empirical foundations upon which these concerns rest include the following elements: (1) the observed decline in the labor force participation rates of males and the persistence of low female rates, trends that could mask high and increasing levels of hidden or discouraged unemployment; (2) the secular increase in rates of open unemployment reported by population censuses; and (3) the existence of underemployment as evidenced by the prevalence of less than full-time employment or of low earnings, or both, among a substantial proportion of the employed labor force. Chapter 2 dealt with the first of these elements. It was argued that the trends in male and female participation rates could be interpreted as positive responses to higher incomes and expanded educational opportunities rather than as reflections of deteriorating conditions of employment. Nevertheless, that analysis does not suffice to preclude the possibility that hidden unemployment characterizes a significant proportion of the population of labor force age. Therefore, certain empirical data that permit an assessment of the prevalence of this phenomenon will be examined. This issue will be explored after a consideration of the most obvious form of underutilization of labor resources—open unemployment. The final form of underutilization—underemployment, in several of its presumed manifestations—will be discussed in the final sections of the chapter.

Open Unemployment

An analysis of secular trends in unemployment in Mexico faces severe obstacles. Reliable data are simply not available on a consistent basis prior to 1973. The censuses since 1940 have presented measures of unemployment, but the concept has varied from one census to another, as have the questions designed to explore the unemployed status of the labor force. Table 3-1 presents a summary of census measures of unemployment from 1940 to 1970, along with two noncensus measures for 1940 and 1979. The census reports yield an upward trend in measured unemployment, although even the highest rate of 3.8 percent reported for 1970 can hardly be considered a troublesome level. Normally, such a rate would not be viewed as departing far from the frictional level of unemployment.

The problem of interpreting the historical data is illustrated by the appearance of two measures of unemployment for 1940. The census of that year is the first to have included a clear reference to an unemployed status of labor force members. This category was limited to those who had been unemployed for at least a month—in this census, 1 percent of the labor force. An alternative measure of unemployment for that year was published in a series of annual unemployment rates for 1931–40 attributed by James Wilkie to the Dirección General de Estadística.[1] The origin of the rates is unknown, however, and some doubts have been expressed about the capacity of the agency to have obtained a reliable measure of unemployment.[2] If the "longer term" unemployment of over one month's duration was accurately recorded by the census, then the

Table 3-1. *Unemployment Rates in Mexico, 1940–79*
(percent)

	Unemployment rate		
Year	*Total*	*Male*	*Female*
1940[a]	1.0	1.0	0.7
1940[a]	3.1	n.a.	n.a.
1950	1.3	1.3	1.2
1960[b]	1.8	1.9	1.3
1970	3.8	2.8	7.5
1979–1st quarter	3.3	2.8	5.0

n.a. Not available.

a. Census includes only those unemployed for at least a month at the time of the census.

b. The measure of the labor force used here includes the adjustments to the census made by Oscar Altimir.

Sources: Secretaría de Industria y Comercio, Dirección General de Estadística, *Censo general de población*, 1940, 1950, 1960, 1970; Secretaría de Programación y Presupuesto, *Encuesta continua sobre ocupación*, 1st quarter 1979; James W. Wilkie, "New Hypotheses for Statistical Research in Recent Mexican History," *Latin American Research Review*, vol. 6, no. 2 (Summer 1971), table 4; Oscar Altimir, "La medición de la población economicamente activa de México 1950–70," *Demografía y economía*, vol. 8, no. 1 (1974), pp. 50–83.

Dirección's measure of 3.1 percent might very well represent a reasonable estimate of total open unemployment for the year. It would yield a 2.1 percent level of unemployment of a short-term, or frictional, character. If the Dirección's rate is thus accepted as a more likely and all-inclusive measure of unemployment for 1940, the onset of the upward trend in the census measures is moved forward to 1950.

An interpretation of the census measures for 1950 and 1960 is complicated by the lack of precision in specifying the reference period and the conditions defining an unemployed status. It is quite possible that persons who were in fact unemployed may have been classified as not in the labor force. In addition, of course, the 1960 census is plagued by enumeration and processing errors (see the appendix to Chapter 2). The 1970 census is the first to adopt a precise definition of unemployment as inclusive of those who, in the week prior to the census, were without work and had actively sought employment.

Perhaps the most striking change that appears in the census data is the emergence in 1970 of an abrupt increase in the female unemployment rate. In prior census years, unemployment among women appeared to be at insignificant levels and always below the male rate. Suddenly, in 1970, it emerges at a level 2.7 times that of males. Is this indicative of the failure of earlier censuses to properly capture the full incidence of female labor force participation and unemployment? Or does it represent a new phenomenon associated with the accumulated changes in labor market conditions and attitudes of women toward employment? In either case, it does not appear that this census measure was a temporary aberration. Throughout the decade of the 1970s, ECSO[3] has reported a consistent and clear tendency for female unemployment rates to lie significantly above those of males, not only in the aggregate (see table 3-1 for 1979), but also in virtually all the surveyed regions of the country.

A consistent feature of the existing measures of unemployment is the relatively low incidence of long-term unemployment. We noted above that the 1940 census found that only 1 percent of the labor force had been unemployed for more than one month. In subsequent censuses, the unemployed were divided into those who had been so for twelve or fewer weeks and those who had been seeking work for thirteen or more weeks. In 1950, more than two-thirds of the unemployed were in the latter category, equivalent to about 1 percent of the labor force. In 1960 and 1970, however, this proportion shrank sharply to 16.3 and 13.4 percent of the unemployed, respectively; as a proportion of the total labor force, the long-term unemployed represented 0.3 and 0.5 percent in the two years, respectively. The 1970 census provided a more detailed breakdown of the duration of unemployment among those currently unemployed who had held a job during 1969. Fully three-fourths of these had been unemployed for four weeks or less, and an additional 15 percent had been unemployed between five and twelve weeks. The relative paucity of long-term unemployment suggests that an absolute scarcity of employment opportunities has not been a chronic affliction of the Mexican economy. Although existing opportunities may frequently have offered wages that may not have appeared particularly attractive, the absence of unemployment insurance would be expected to render the prospect of continuing unemployment an even less attractive alternative.

Beginning in 1973, measures of unemployment became available on a quarterly basis with the initiation of the household labor force survey (ECSO). While the first of these surveys was limited to only the three major metropolitan areas of Mexico City, Guadalajara, and Monterrey, the area covered was gradually extended until, by 1979, the whole country was included. The initial impression gained from the surveys is that the 1973 unemployment rates were significantly higher than those reported by the 1970 census. For example, the census reported the rate of unemployment in the Federal District to be on the order of 5 percent in the week preceding the census in January 1970. Yet the first survey of the labor force undertaken by ECSO during the first quarter of 1973 yielded a rate of 7.2 percent, a level around which several subsequent surveys hovered. It is possible that the unemployment rate had increased in the interval since the population census. However, I consider it more likely that most of the increase is attributable to the greater thoroughness with which labor force surveys determine the status of the population. It has commonly been found that such specialized surveys are more efficient in identifying labor force members and the unemployed than are censuses. In addition, an important difference in the definition of unemployment probably played a role in raising the survey rate above that of the census—the census classified the population in accordance with its activity during the week immediately preceding the census. In contrast, the surveys extended the reference period to two full months. Thus, anyone who was not working but had looked for employment at any time during this prolonged interval was counted as unemployed. I believe that these two factors suffice to account for the major part of the difference between the census and survey measures.

Certainly, the subsequent surveys do not evince any secular tendency for unemployment to rise (see table 3-2). The economic recession that followed the devaluation of 1976 and the pursuit of increased economic stability by the new administration of President López Portillo was reflected in a cyclical increase in recorded unemployment in the three major metropolitan regions. But, with the resumption of rapid growth in

Table 3-2. *Annual Average Unemployment Rates by Region, 1973–79*
(percent)

Region	*1970*	*1973*	*1974*	*1975*	*1976*	*1977*	*1978*	*1979 January–March*
1. Federal District	7.1	7.6	7.4	7.3	6.7	8.1	7.1	6.3
2. Metropolitan Guadalajara	n.a.	6.6	5.8	6.2	6.2	7.4	6.0	6.2
3. Metropolitan Monterrey	n.a.	7.5	7.1	7.9	7.6	9.0	7.6	5.7
4. All large urban centers	n.a.				5.6	5.5	4.8	3.5
5. Northeast	3.9				6.8[a]	5.7	4.5	3.9
6. Northwest	3.4				7.5[a]	5.7	3.7	2.5
7. North	4.0				7.2	4.3	3.7	3.8
8. North Central	2.9				2.6	1.8	1.9	2.1
9. Peninsular	2.0					2.2	1.7[c]	1.2
10. Central Pacific	3.3					4.3	3.4	3.2
11. Central	2.4					2.8[b]	2.9	2.3
12. Central Gulf	2.7						1.8[a]	1.5
13. South Pacific	1.5							0.9
All Mexico	3.8							3.3

n.a. Not available from 1970 census.

Note: The regions listed comprise the following: (4) All 42 municipios with a population of 100,000 or more in 1970; (5) Tamaulipas, Nuevo León, and Coahuila; (6) Northern and Southern Baja California, Sonora, Sinaloa, and Nayarit; (7) Chihuahua and Durango; (8) Aguascalientes, San Luis Potosí, and Zacatecas; (9) Yucatán, Quintana Roo, Tabasco, and Campeche; (10) Colima, Jalisco, and Michoacán; (11) Querétaro, Guanajuato, Hidalgo, Morelos, Puebla, Tlaxcala, and México; not included are those portions of the state of Mexico that form a part of the Metropolitan Mexico City area; (12) Veracruz; (13) Chiapas, Oaxaca, and Guerrero.

a. October-December.

b. July-December.

c. January-September.

Sources: 1970—Secretaría de Industria y Comercio, Dirección General de Estadística, *IX Censo general de población, 1970: Resumen general* (Mexico, D.F., 1972), table 32. 1973–77—Dirección de Programación y Presupuesto, *Encuesta continua de mano de obra.* 1978–79—Dirección de Programación y Presupuesto, *Encuesta continua sobre ocupación.*

1978, the unemployment rate declined throughout the country. By the first quarter of 1979, it had fallen to 3.3 percent, a rate below even that of the 1970 census. Clearly, the level of unemployment and degree of change since 1970 has varied by regions. The more highly urbanized regions tend to report higher rates of unemployment than do the more rural, poorer regions. For example, the Federal District unemployment rate seems to hover at a level about twice the national average. The other two major metropolitan areas also report much higher rates in 1979 than the average. The average of the 42 municipalities with populations of 100,000 or more report rates intermediate to those of the large metropolitan areas and the less urbanized regions. Significantly, not a single region for which a comparison could be made reported a higher unemployment rate in 1979 than in 1970. In view of the much more liberal definition of unemployment adopted by the survey, the real improvement in employment conditions over the decade is likely to be understated by the decline in unemployment rates observed here. Incidentally, the entire reduction in the national rate is attributable to a significant decline in the unemployment rate among women from 7.5 to 5 percent (see table 3-1).The rate for men remained constant at what must be close to the frictional rate.

A decline in unemployment rates, of course, may appear to be less encouraging if it is accompanied by a decline in labor force participation rates. In other words, if the unemployed despair of findings jobs and withdraw from the labor force to join the ranks of the discouraged unemployed the measured rate of unemployment would decline, but so would the labor force participation rate. It is reassuring to note that in Mexico this has not been the case. Table 3-3 is a summary of changes in labor force participation and unemployment rates by region and sex between the census date January 1970 and the first quarter of 1979. Note that for this purpose, unemployment has been measured as a proportion of the population 12 years and older rather than as a proportion of the labor force in order to preserve a common denominator for the two measures. For the country as a whole, the labor force participation rate increased by 2.1 percent, while the unemployment rate declined by 0.1 percent. The increase in participation was markedly greater among women; nevertheless, the unemployment rate registered a decline.

Regional differences in the rates of change would appear to be considerable. Three regions, the North, Northwest, and North Central, appear with declines in the aggregate labor force participation rates which exceed the declines in the rate of unemployment, a relationship that could be interpreted as an unfavorable development. However, for the latter two regions, the 1979 first quarter observations seem to be sharply out of line with those for the immediately preceding quarters. For example, a com-

Table 3-3. *Summary of Percentage Point Changes in Labor Force Participation (LFP) and Unemployment (U) Rates between January 1970 and First Quarter 1979*

	Total		*Male*		*Female*	
Region	*LFP*	*U*	*LFP*	*U*	*LFP*	*U*
Federal District	3.8	0.8	−3.0	0.9	5.3	0.6
North	−0.5	−0.2	−3.6	−0.3	4.4	−0.2
Northeast	0.4	0	0.1	0	2.0	0
Northwest	−1.7	−0.9	−0.5	−0.9	−1.3	−1.0
North Central	−2.4	−0.8	−3.0	−0.4	−0.1	−1.0
Peninsular	1.2	−0.8	2.4	−0.7	2.1	−0.8
Central Pacific	4.4	0.1	4.9	0.3	6.2	0.2
Central	2.9	−0.1	1.2	0.1	5.9	−0.7
Central Gulf	5.2	−0.4	7.6	−0.3	2.6	−0.9
South Pacific	2.1	−0.6	0.9	−0.1	3.7	−0.6
All Mexico	2.1	−0.1	1.2	0	3.9	−0.2

Sources: Secretaría de Industria y Comercio, Dirección General de Estadística, *IX Censo general de población, 1971: Resumen general* (Mexico, D.F., 1972), table 32; Secretaría de Programación y Presupuesto, *Encuesta continua sobre ocupación*, vol. 7, 1st quarter 1979, table 2.

parison of the first quarter 1978 with the census measures would have yielded an increase in the participation rates of 1.3 and 1.7 percentage points, respectively, and 0.2 and −1.1 percentage point changes in unemployment, changes that are more closely in line with those of the other regions. Thus, it may well be that the 1979 observations are the product of a sampling or processing aberration. In all the other regions, the labor force participation rate increased more rapidly than did the unemployment rate, or increased while the latter declined. In either case, the findings would not be consistent with a hypothesis that the decline in the unemployment rate merely disguises an increase in hidden or discouraged unemployment.

Women appear to have experienced a very substantial improvement in labor market conditions. Participation rates were up in almost all regions, sharply in several. In spite of this, unemployment rates either declined or showed little change. The exceptions were, again, the Northwest and North Central regions. As in the totals for these regions, female participation rates showed declines in contrast to other recent sampling periods. The first quarter of 1978, for example, reported increases in participation rates of 1.3 and 1.1 points over 1970 and declines in unemployment of 0.3 and 1.1 points, respectively. In short, employment opportunities for women during the decade appear to have expanded more rapidly than have their participation rates; this occasioned the decline in measured unemployment.

In the aggregate among men, employment opportunities and labor force expanded at the same rate, netting out to no change in the measured unemployment rate. However, there were rather substantial differences among the various regions. The least favorable evolution in employment conditions would appear to have occurred in the Federal District. There, a small decline in the participation rate was accompanied by an increase in the unemployment rate. Otherwise, participation rates increased and unemployment rates either declined or increased by less than the participation rates. The Northwest and North Central regions again present a divergent pattern from other recent observations. Survey results for the first quarter of 1978 yielded an increase in participation of 3.1 and 2.5 percentage points and changes in unemployment of 0.7 and −1.1 over 1970 for these two regions. In brief, then, the data do not lend broad and consistent support to a hypothesis that open unemployment has been converted into a more disguised form. If anything, employment opportunities would appear to have improved. Indeed, given the more liberal definition of unemployment embodied in the 1979 survey data, the improvement evident in these intertemporal comparisons was more likely to have been understated than overstated.

The accelerated growth rates of 1978–81 would be expected to have brought about a further improvement in employment conditions. Unfortunately, the national coverage of ECSO was suspended following the first quarter of 1979; labor force information for subsequent quarters is limited to only the three major metropolitan regions of the country. The expansion of employment in those areas was accommodated by increases in labor participation rates of both sexes and declines in open unemployment. Participation rates for men increased between 1 and 2 percentage points, those for women increased by a full 2 percentage points. Unemployment rates, defined here in the conventional manner as a proportion of the labor force, fell by approximately one-third below the 1979 first-quarter level. If the national rate of unemployment declined in the same proportion, a rate of about 2.1 percent at the end of 1981 and early 1982 would be implied. Unfortunately, the onset of an economic crisis in mid-1982 carried with it a rapid deterioration in employment conditions. At the end of the year, open unemployment characterized about 8 percent of the metropolitan labor force.

As in most countries, the incidence of unemployment proves to be greater among young people of both sexes than among the more mature adult population. Table 3-4 provides unemployment rates by sex and age

Table 3-4. *Unemployment Rates by Sex and Age, January 1970 and First Quarter 1979*
(percent)

Age	*Men*		*Women*	
	1970	*1979*	*1970*	*1979*
12–19	5.1	6.5	7.8	10.9
20–24	3.5	4.7	6.5	6.4
25–34	2.2	2.2	7.3	3.4
35–44	2.0	1.4	7.8	2.2
45–54	2.1	1.2	7.6	1.8
55–64	2.2	1.2	7.6	1.0
65 and over	2.1	0.7	8.4	0.7
Total	2.8	2.8	7.5	5.0

Sources: Secretaría de Industria y Comercio, Dirección General de Estadística, *IX Censo general de población, 1970: Resumen general* (Mexico, D.F., 1972), table 32; Secretaría de Programación y Presupuesto, *Encuesta continua sobre ocupación*, vol. 7, 1st quarter 1979, table 2A.

as reported by the 1970 census and by ECSO for the first quarter of 1979. Teenage unemployment rates are more than double the average in the more recent survey; they remain above average for the 20–24-year-old group and then taper off to very low levels. The rates yielded by the census reveal a smaller variance than that of the labor force surveys, although the pattern for men is generally similar to that for the more recent period. The census data for women, however, are quite curious. On the one hand, the unemployment rate seems to be invariant over the several age groups. On the other hand, the 1979 pattern exhibited by women in table 3-4 holds consistently both over time and across regions in the surveys. Unfortunately, there are no earlier census distributions of female unemployment by age group against which to compare these more recent distributions.

The unemployment rates of the youngest labor force members tend to be quite volatile over time and show large variations over the several regions of the country. Teenage unemployment is highest in the large urban metropolitan areas. For example, in the ECSO survey for the first quarter of 1979, Mexico City reported unemployment rates for this youthful group of almost 18 percent. Guadalajara reported rates in the 12–15 percent range, while Monterrey's teenage unemployment rate was in the 15–17 percent range. These rates are in sharp contrast to those prevailing in the rest of the country. In virtually all the other areas, the male teenage rate lies below 10 percent; it dips as low as 2 percent in a few regions. Female rates in most regions lie above the male rates. The male rates are lowest in those regions that are more rural and in which agricultural activity predominates. The labor force participation rates of the teenage males also tend to be higher in these regions. The relationship between the two rates is an inverse one, yielding a simple correlation coefficient of -0.6 that is significant at the 5 percent level. The female unemployment rates are also lower in the more rural regions. However, the labor force participation rates also tend to be lower; thus a positive correlation coefficient of 0.76, significant at the 1 percent level, results.

The pattern of teenage unemployment rates across regions is therefore similar to that for the total labor force. Unemployment rates tend to be directly related to the degree of urbanization. A probable consequence of this relationship is that, as the population continues to shift from rural to urban areas and the weight of the latter increases in the national averages, the national unemployment rate, total and teenage, will be higher than if constant weights were employed. Thus, the secular trend in unemployment may be obscured unless the data are decomposed by region or by the degree of urbanization.

Some further useful insights into the characteristics of the unemployed can be gained from a set of special tabulations prepared by the Secretaría de Programación y Presupuesto, based on the ECSO survey for the second quarter of 1978.[4] These tabulations were limited to the three major metropolitan areas of the country. While the coverage is thus limited, it does include the regions with the highest rates of unemployment. These data confirm my earlier observation that unemployment is disproportionately heavy among the young. Of the unemployed with previous work experience, between 50 and 60 percent are between the ages of 15 and 24. In the absence of more detailed information about this group, it is difficult to assess the significance of this unemployment. In more highly developed countries like the United States, higher-than-average unemployment rates among young people are often attributed to their search for "desirable" jobs—jobs to which they are willing to make a permanent commitment. When these workers know little about the characteristics of the available jobs, the search becomes a process of trial and error or movement among jobs. It is quite possible that at least part of this higher incidence of unemployment among Mexican youth is of a similar nature. Among those unemployed with no previous work experience, the young again predominate, as might be expected. Between two-thirds and three-fourths are teenagers; the bulk of the remainder is aged between 20 and 24.

It has frequently been observed that the unemployed in developing countries tend to have attained higher levels of education than the employed or the labor force as a whole. In part, this has been explained in terms of the higher income levels of families with more highly educated members, a condition that permits the luxury of unemployment and a more leisurely search for the "ideal" job. The survey data for Mexico, however, depart from such a pattern: there appear to be no consistent and significant differences in the educational levels of the unemployed and the employed.

Information about the length of time that elapsed since the last previous employment is also provided by this special report.[5] Unfortunately, this time interval is not synonymous with the duration of unemployment; thus, we have no information more recent than that provided by the 1970 census. As a rough indicator of duration, it may be noted that the majority of the unemployed had been separated from their previous employment within the past six months. The proportions ranged from 55 percent of the unemployed with previous work experience in Monterrey, to 62 percent in Mexico City, and 75 percent in Guadalajara. The presence of numerous individuals who had not held a job for more than two years (or over five), especially among women, suggests that many of these were simply re-entering the labor force after a period of withdrawal. Indeed, among those reporting the longest interval since the last employment, the predominant reason offered for separation from that employment was "personal."[6] The interval of time since the previous employment seems to be directly related to the level of skill of the respondent as indicated by the occupational classification of his or her last employment.[7] For everyone who reported their previous status as an agricultural laborer, the interval between jobs was less than six months; this was also the case for about three-fourths of the nonagricultural laborers. At the other extreme, only 42 percent of the professional and technical occupational group in Mexico City and 25 percent of that in Monterrey reported so short an interval. Within the managerial occupational group, 60 and 50 percent did so in these two regions, respectively. It is difficult to believe that prolonged absence of employment in the last two occupational groups could be ascribed to other than voluntary reasons, especially since a substantial number of these individuals had not been employed for over two years.

Among the unemployed with previous work experience, the predominant reasons for separation from their last jobs were either personal or attributable to the end of seasonal employment. The former accounted for almost half of the responses, the latter for about one-third. The more detailed information for Mexico City indicates that personal reasons are offered by women twice as often as by men, while men offer seasonal employment as a reason for termination twice as often as do women. The data suggest that close to one-half of the separations were voluntary in all three regions. From this observation—and the one made previously about the short duration of unemployment—it would seem that workers do not view the labor market as offering very limited employment alternatives. If workers assigned a low probability to the chances of finding another job, one would not expect them to abandon so readily a job they already had.

Hidden or Discouraged Unemployment

Early in this chapter, the possibility was mentioned that labor force participation and open unemployment rates may not provide accurate measures of the quantity of available labor resources. This may hold true especially among women. To the extent that individuals of labor force age believe that employment opportunities are nonexistent, they will neither search for work nor report themselves as being unemployed. Some may have actually searched for work but given up after an unsuccessful effort. These individuals constitute the pool of the hidden or discouraged unemployed. It is presumed that they are available for employment and would accept it, were it offered.

The labor force surveys have made an attempt to determine the importance of this category of individuals. All people of labor force age who were neither employed nor actively searching for work were asked, "Would you be willing to accept immediately either a paid part-time or full-time job?" Those who responded in the affirmative were classified as hidden unemployed. As an indication of the size of the group that responded in the affirmative, the first quarterly survey for 1979 yields a figure of almost 950,000, or 2.2 percent of the population of labor force age. If this number were added to both the labor force and the open unemployed, an "unemployment rate" of 7.8 percent would result, a rate more than twice the measured national open unemployment rate of 3.3 percent. Table 3-5 is concerned with the incidence of this hidden unemployment by sex and region. It would appear to be more prevalent among women than among men: the female national rate was about 25 percent greater than the male. In only three of the thirteen regions does the male rate exceed the female. Moreover, there are substantial differences in the reported rates among regions. These range from 0.5 to 3.1 percent of the population of labor force age. Differences among regions do not appear to be related to any obvious regional characteristics. The hidden unemployment rate might be expected to vary directly with the open rate of unemployment since the prospects of finding jobs might be perceived as poorer, the higher the visible unemployment. Yet this does not seem to be the case.

The correlation across regions between the rate of open unemployment and the proportion of the population classified as hidden unemployed is positive at 0.24 but proves to be statistically insignificant.

A closer examination of the data for metropolitan Mexico City from 1975 through the middle of 1979 reveals that the hidden unemployed have remained within the range of 1.7 to 2.5 percent of the population. However, fifteen of the eighteen quarterly observations fall within the much narrower range of 1.9–2.2 percent. Rates among males are concentrated within 1.7–1.9 percent of the population. Those for women show a somewhat greater variance, although the bulk of the latter are in the 2.2–2.6 percent range. As in the case of the regional cross section, there seems to be no consistent relationship between changes in the open unemployment rate and the hidden rate over time. Neither the cyclical increase in unemployment in 1977 nor its subsequent sharp decline into 1979 seems to have been accompanied by paralled movements in hidden unemployment. Yet the economic boom that endured through the first half of

Table 3-5. *Incidence of Measured "Hidden" Unemployment by Sex and Region, First Quarter 1979*

Region	*Unemployment rate (percentage of labor force)*	*Hidden unemployment (percentage of) population of labor force age*		
		Men	*Women*	*Total*
North	3.8	4.1	1.0	3.1
Northeast	3.9	1.6	2.0	1.8
Northwest	2.5	0.9	2.6	1.7
North Central	2.1	3.5	1.6	2.6
Peninsular	1.2	0.3	0.9	0.5
Central Pacific	3.2	1.8	3.1	2.5
Central	2.1	2.0	3.5	2.8
Central Gulf	1.5	0.7	1.0	0.8
South Pacific	0.9	2.3	2.0	2.2
Metropolitan Mexico City	6.1	2.1	2.5	2.3
Metropolitan Guadalajara	6.2	1.9	2.4	2.2
Metropolitan Monterrey	5.7	1.3	1.7	1.5
All other large urban areas	3.5	1.4	1.5	1.4
All Mexico	3.3	1.9	2.4	2.2

Source: Secretaría de Programación y Presupuesto, *Encuesta continua sobre ocupación*, vol. 7, 1st quarter 1979, table 2.

1982 did appear to have reduced the measured rates slightly in Mexico City and Guadalajara and moderately in Monterrey.

The lack of a consistent responsiveness in this measure to differences or changes in open unemployment raises some question about what in fact is being measured. One would expect that changes in the objective conditions of the labor market would lead individuals to reevaluate the probability of finding employment, with predictable consequences for the rate of hidden unemployment. Of course, a behavioral change would depend on a widespread perception of a change in labor market conditions. If actual changes are not perceived or are too small to be taken seriously, then the expected behavioral response might not occur. The issue then revolves around the question of what constitutes a significant or perceptible change. For example, between the first quarters of 1977 and 1979, the open unemployment rate for the Mexico City metropolitan region declined from 8.3 to 6.1 percent. The rates for both sexes fell by about the same proportion, one-fourth. Yet the hidden unemployment rate moved in the opposite direction from 1.9 to 2.3 percent of the population of labor force age, an increase of over 20 percent.

One possible explanation for the lack of conformity to the "expected" relationship between open and hidden unemployment may be that the latter is an imperfect measure of the phenomenon it purports to represent. It may be argued, for example, that the responses to such a hypothetical question about availability for employment are likely to be misleading, that many more persons are likely to answer in the affirmative than are actually available. Indeed, this would seem to be the case in Mexico, just as it has been shown to be commonly true of other countries.[8] The special tabulations based on ECSO's second quarterly survey of 1978 illustrate that, of those who initially indicated that they were available for employment, only a small minority actually proved to be so.[9] In the three metropolitan areas of Mexico City, Guadalajara, and Monterrey, only 4.1, 6.7, and 7.4 percent, respectively, of the populations were actually available for immediate employment. If one were to add these to both the labor force and to the ranks of the open unemployed, their impact would be minimal. The unemployment rate would be increased on the order of 1 percentage point.

Clearly, the vast majority of those classified as hidden unemployed were only conditionally available. The special report does not identify the conditions placed on the respondents' availability nor the reasons for not having actively sought employment. However, it does report the current activity of the respondents so classified. Among men, the overwhelming majority, over three-fourths, were students, a status that effectively precludes an active labor force status except on a part-time basis. Among women, involvement in household duties was by far the most frequent current activity. It was cited by over 75 percent of those classified as hidden unemployed; school attendance ranked second. Together, these groups accounted for virtually all of the respondents. It is noteworthy that between one-third and one-half of the respondents had had no previous work experience, and an additional 20–25 percent had not been employed for over five years. Over 40 percent were teenagers. These characteristics suggest that those classified as hidden unemployed had only a weak attachment to the labor market. Thus, it is unlikely that the measured rate of hidden unemployment can be considered an accurate indicator of the number of discouraged workers currently available for employment.

It would seem that if the concept of hidden or discouraged unemployment were to have any operational meaning, the true status of those professing their availability for employment would need to be established in a more precise manner. Such persons should also be asked why they have not actively sought employment. Only if they respond that they did not do so out of a conviction that no jobs were available should they be eligible for consideration as hidden unemployed. Another condition that would have to be satisfied if individuals were to qualify would be that their reservation price (the minimum pay for which they are willing to work) not be above the current market price for the class of services they could offer. Only then could an individual be considered to be involuntarily excluded from employment. The practical difficulties of relating a reservation price to the appropriate wage in the market, however, are overwhelming; consequently, it is rarely, if ever, attempted. The resulting ambiguity in measures of hidden unemployment thus impedes any assessment of its true significance.

Nevertheless, it is also clear that the appearance of job opportunities may induce individuals who had not previously contemplated employment to enter the labor force. Given time, some of those who are not currently available for employment might be able to make arrangements that would permit them to seek and accept employment. This would be particularly true of women engaged in household activities (for example, effective substitutes could be found in the form of hired domestic help or a relative who would release a woman for employment purposes). It would seem that the large expansion in output and employment during 1979–81 was effected by an increase in active participation rates, particularly in those for women. It is tempting to point to this response as evidence that hidden unemployment must have been present in significant amounts. However, it does not seem to me that this necessarily follows. As noted above, the observed increases in participation rates did not necessarily come about by the incorporation into the labor force of people who had previously been classified as hidden unemployed. The proportion of the population of labor force age classified as such declined only slightly, by considerably less than the increase in the participation rate. Furthermore, to the extent that the expansion of employment opportunities materialized at levels of remuneration higher than those previously available, a supply response would be expected from those whose reservation price had exceeded the previously prevailing and available wage. The conclusion to be drawn from these observations is that the procedures currently available and used for measuring the size of the potentially available labor force are quite inadequate to the task. Data professing to offer such measures should be viewed with great care, if not with skepticism.

Underemployment

Since open unemployment in Mexico appears to be low in comparison with that reported for many other developing countries, concern with the underutilization of labor resources has centered much more heavily on the presumed high level of underemployment. Unfortunately, most discussions of underemployment of labor in Mexico reflect the same problems of concept and measurement that prevail generally. No single criterion for the definition of underemployment is generally accepted as an ideal, nor do the available data conform to the requirements of most of the abstract definitions. In spite of the different definitions adopted by various labor market studies, a striking feature of their estimates of underemployment in Mexico during the 1970s is their concentration within a relatively narrow range. Estimates of the proportion of the labor force that is underemployed range from about 45 to 52 percent. It would be premature, however, to conclude that the convergence of the estimates confirms the correctness of these measures. Rather, their similarity may be due to the inclusion of some common elements or to their derivation from related distributions.

A common component of most measures of underemployment is that portion of the labor force that is employed on a part-time basis during some reference period, for example, a week, a year, or both. Once a normal work week or work year has been defined in terms of "normal" hours or days, it is no difficult task to identify those who have worked fewer hours or days than "normal." The difference between a full-time or "normal" work period and the time actually worked provides a measure of underemployment. This may be expressed either as a proportion of the labor force or in terms of an equivalent rate of open unemployment.[10] This is frequently referred to as "visible" underemployment since it is so readily amenable to measurement.

If a measure of underemployment is to have any operational value (for example, for determining the employment objectives of a development program), it should relate to the volume of labor services that are potentially available to the labor market. In other words, the conversion of all short-time work into unemployment equivalents implicitly assumes that all part-time employment is involuntary. If, on the other hand, some part of such employment is voluntary, and the workers so employed prefer not to work longer hours or more days, the measured underemployment will exaggerate the seriousness of the employment problem.

Until recently, only scattered data have been available from census reports about the time intensity of employment of the labor force. Unfortunately, different bases of measurement were adopted by the various sources. Therefore, no consistent basis exists for making intertemporal comparisons of the degree of utilization of the labor force. The 1950 population census reported that 7.5 percent of the labor force had worked four or fewer days during the week preceding the census. It appears, however, that this proportion includes the 0.4 percent of the labor force that had been unemployed for more than thirteen weeks as well.[11] The 1970 census offered a different basis for determining underutilization, the number of months in 1969 during which each labor force member worked. A substantial proportion of the labor force, 12.6 percent, is recorded as having worked fewer than six months; another 6.5 percent reported six to nine months of employment.

The distribution of men and women over these classes was not very dissimilar, although the incidence of shorter-term employment was somewhat greater among women.[12] As might be expected, the seasonality of employment in the agricultural sector gave rise to a greater incidence of employment of fewer than ten months. Fully 56.6 percent of all men working fewer than ten months had held their major employment in that sector. As a proportion of the men employed principally in agriculture, this group accounted for 23.1 percent.[13] After agriculture, the manufacturing sector gave rise to the largest volume of male employment for fewer than ten months. Here, however, the incidence was lower than that in construction, which ranged from 14.8 to 29.2 percent. Among women, the incidence of short-year employment was greatest in the agricultural, service, and manufacturing sectors. About 21 percent of the labor force in each of these sectors reported employment of nine months or less.

Since the censuses make no attempt to distinguish voluntary part-time employment from involuntary, these data are likely to lead to an overestimation of the true extent of underemployment attributable to part-time work. Another shortcoming of the 1970 census data as a measure of underemployment is that they are not related to the number of months during which respondents participated in the labor force. New entrants to the labor force appear throughout each year who will not have been available for employment during the entire year. There are also others who retire from the labor force during the year. In the 1970 census, both of these types of groups will have been registered as having been part of the labor force in 1969 and their duration of employment duly recorded. If the labor force is growing at about 3 percent per year, the sum of retirees and new entrants could amount to as much as 5 percent of the labor force. Thus, factoring in these entrants and retirees could reduce the volume of "measured underemployment" by approximately one-fourth. The elimination of workers who may have been voluntarily employed for only part of a year would further reduce the volume of those who were truly underemployed.

An alternative approach to the measurement of underemployment is pursued by the quarterly labor force surveys. The employed labor force is classified according to the number of hours worked during the week preceding the survey. While the normal work week in Mexico generally consists of forty-four hours, for purposes of ESCO, those employed for fewer than forty hours are considered as having worked less than full time and are further divided according to whether they are voluntarily or involuntarily so employed. The survey publication for the first quarter of 1979 provides a summary table for the national labor force.[14] Fully 15.7 percent of the employed labor force worked fewer than forty hours during the reference week. Women were three times as likely as men to have worked a short week (32.6 to 10.3 percent). It is surprising that the agricultural sector did not report the highest incidence of part-time employment, in spite of the fact that the first quarter of the year is the trough of the agricultural cycle; only 9.9 percent of sector employment proved to be part-time. The significance of this finding, however, is open to question in view of the survey sample's underrepresentation of the rural labor force. The highest incidence of part-time work was found among professional and technical occupational groups, 39.5 percent of which worked fewer than forty hours.

These surveys underline the problems that occur from classifying all people who work a short week as underemployed. Fully two-thirds were found to be voluntarily so employed. Voluntary part-time employment was more prevalent among the women working a short work week than among men, but not by a very large margin: 73 to 62 percent. Even among the men in agriculture, 63 percent of those working fewer than forty hours were recorded as doing so voluntarily. Taken as a proportion of the employed labor force, workers who were involuntarily employed for fewer than forty hours amounted to only 5.1 percent. Obviously, if this were to be reduced to full-time unemployment equivalents, the unutilized proportion of the labor force would amount to only a fraction of this percentage.

Disaggregation by region shows some variation in the prevalence of part-time employment. The highest incidence occurs in the metropolitan areas of the capital and Guadalajara, on the order of 20 percent of the employed labor force. Yet these regions also report the next to the lowest incidence of involuntary short-week work: around 29 percent. Most of the other observations of part-time workers as a proportion of the labor force cluster closely around the national average of almost 16 percent. The Northwest and South Pacific regions presented the largest departures on the low side, with 10.3 and 11.9 percent, respectively, of their employed labor forces working part-time. While the latter also reports the least amount of involuntary underemployment—19 percent of those working short hours—the Northwest records one of the highest incidences at 43.5 percent. Note that these two regions provide a sharp contrast in their characteristics. The Northwest, which combines a highly productive agricultural sector with important urban concentrations, enjoys one of the highest levels of per capita incomes in the country; the latter is largely rural and very poor. Indeed, it is difficult to observe any systematic relationship between the recorded levels of part-time employment and regional characteristics.

The more detailed tabulations based on the second quarterly survey of 1979 provide one further basis for disaggregating the part-time workers in the three major metropolitan regions.[15] The employed labor force is classified according to employment status and hours worked. As is usually assumed, a short week is more characteristic of a self-employed status and of unremunerated family workers than of others. In the Mexico City and Monterrey metropolitan regions, the incidence of part-time employment among the self-employed was about 1.5 times the average for the labor force as a whole; in Guadalajara, it was only 1.17 times greater. Among unremunerated family workers, approximately half in each region was employed part-time. Unfortunately, ECSO does not use employment status to distinguish further between those who were voluntarily working short work weeks and those who were involuntarily so employed. The self-employed, however, are also more likely to work significantly beyond a normal week of forty to forty-eight hours. Whereas the proportion of the employed labor force working over forty-eight hours ranged fell between 26 and 31 percent in the three metropolitan areas, the proportion among the self-employed ranged between 39 and 46 percent. Among the unremunerated family workers, the incidence of "overemployment" was slightly greater than average in Mexico City, but well below the average for all employed persons in the other two large urban areas.

Most of the measures of underemployment include workers who earn an income below some arbitrary level. A recent estimate for Mexico of 47 percent underemployment adopted the legal minimum wage of each zone as the dividing line between the fully employed and the underemployed.[16] A 1976 estimate by the Regional Employment Program for Latin America and the Caribbean (PREALC) adopted the average income of the modal interval in the household income distribution as the socially determined minimum income level. It is this application of an income criterion to the determination of the status of workers that results in the large proportions of the labor force deemed to be underemployed. The rationale underlying the inclusion of all low-income workers within the ranks of the underemployed derives from the presumption that their low productivity is evidence that they are not employed in a way that makes full use of their productive capacities. Included among these workers are those whose earnings are low because of part-time employment and those whose productivity and incomes are very low in spite of full-time employment. One can presume that it is this last category of individuals that makes up the bulk of the group considered to be underemployed.

Although an income criterion is widely used for identifying the underemployed, the usefulness of this characterization depends on the use to which it is put. Generally, it is used to derive an estimate of the number of new jobs that must be created in order to absorb fully the labor force at "satisfactory" levels of productivity. The underemployed are first converted into unemployment equivalents, which then are used to define the number of new jobs required to eliminate underemployment. Adding this number to the expected growth of the labor force and to the number of open unemployed provides a measure of the total expansion required to achieve full employment. The Grupo de Estudio del Problema del Empleo followed this procedure in 1974. They estimated that just keeping unemployment and underemployment at 1969 levels would require an increase of 6.8 million new jobs between 1970 and 1980. For full employment to be achieved, jobs would have to be created to address the needs of an additional 5.8 million individuals who were underemployed and who represented the equivalent of 3 million unemployed.[17] The estimated intercensal increase in employment of about 6.6 million might lead one to conclude that employment conditions could not have improved significantly and might even have deteriorated slightly. Yet, in light of the course of wages during the 1970s for various groups reviewed in Chapter 7 and the tightness of the labor market during 1980–82 visible evidence of deterioration is not at hand.

The use of the earnings criterion as the basis for an estimate of the new job requirements for the economy is very likely to lead to a substantial overestimate of those requirements. In the first place, part of those low earnings are the result of a voluntary decision to limit the amount of time devoted to market employment. Recall that the bulk of part-time employment was found above to be voluntary. These workers are probably individuals who are not available for "fuller" employment. Furthermore, an unspecified proportion of the low-income earners is already fully employed in a time dimension and may not consider itself available for other jobs. Nor can it be taken for granted that those whose current earnings are low have the skills or education necessary to qualify for new, high-productivity employments. Most of the recipients of low earnings have corresponding low levels of formal education, or they are likely to be either very young or beyond an age at which an adaptation to new employment opportunities is likely to be possible.

These observations receive considerable substantiation from a profile of the urban labor force employed at low earnings drawn from the data in a special supplement to the labor force survey ECSO for the last calendar quarter of 1976.[18] The supplement was designed to investigate the character of "informal" sector employment. This was defined as employment with earnings no greater than 10 percent above the legal minimum wage of the included urban areas (the three major metropolitan areas plus a grouping of 43 municipalities with populations of 100,000 or more in 1970). In addition to low earnings, all those grouped in the informal sector had jobs that lacked at least two of the following attributes: access to prepaid medical services; fringe benefits such as paid vacations, retirement benefits, or life insurance; employment stability defined by reference to the contractual relationship of the worker to his place of employment; and unionization of the work force. All unremunerated family workers were also included. Since low or zero earnings served as the common denominator of this population, it qualifies for inclusion in the category of the urban underemployed as this group is generally defined.[19]

The findings of the ECSO survey point to some of the difficulties inherent in any attempt to characterize the "employment problem" by reference to the level of earnings of labor force members at a moment in time. A review of some of the distinguishing demographic features of the recipients of low earnings follows. An attempt will be made to identify some of the conditions in the workers' relationship to their employment that seem to be associated with those earnings. One possible interpretation of the data will be offered as will a comment on their significance for the phenomenon of underemployment.

The ECSO supplement's rough breakdown of the labor force by sex reveals a higher incidence of low earnings among women than among men. Whereas 45.5 percent of all employed women reported low earnings, 35 percent of the men did so. The probability of being counted among the low-earnings recipients is also greater the fewer hours worked, as might be expected. One-third of the low-earnings recipients worked fewer than forty hours; only one-fifth of those with higher earnings did so. Among part-time workers, roughly half of both sexes reported low earnings. For men working more than forty hours, this proportion falls to 32 percent; among women, it declines modestly to 42.5 percent.[20]

Unfortunately, the survey does not distinguish between voluntary and involuntary part-time employment. It may be presumed, however, that the distribution of these two conditions is similar to that regularly reported by ECSO. As was mentioned above, two-thirds of part-time workers were voluntarily so employed. If earnings had been converted to an hourly basis, the incidence of low wages would surely have been reduced significantly. For example, the survey reports that almost one-tenth of the low earners were drawn from the occupational ranks of professionals, managerial or supervisory personnel, and clerical workers, all of whom should normally expect rates of earnings well above the legal minimum wage.[21] As noted earlier, however, these are occupational groups among which the incidence of part-time employment is highest, a factor that may account for their inclusion in the informal sector. Surely, one would not usually expect to find these occupational groups contributing to a general problem of underemployment.

Among the demographic characteristics that distinguish the low earners from the rest of the labor force are their relative youth and low level of formal schooling or technical training. The incidence of low earnings is clearly a declining function of age. Ninety-three percent of those in the labor force under 15 years of age qualify as informally employed, as do 66 percent of those 15 to 19 years old and 35 percent of those 20 to 24 years old. Thereafter, the incidence declines, only to turn up again among workers 55 years and older. If viewed in a different light, fully half of the informally employed are either under 25 or over 55 years of age. These same age groups form 38 percent of the total urban labor force.[22] With respect to the educational attainments of the low-earnings population, the following associations emerge: the highest incidence of low earnings, 66 percent, is to be found among those with no formal education, followed by a 55 percent incidence among those with incomplete primary school education. Expressed in other terms: although workers with an incomplete primary school education formed 38 percent of the total urban employed labor force, they made up 57 percent of the informal labor force.[23] Related to these findings is another: the younger the age of entry into the labor force, the greater the probability that the individual will realize low earnings. Whereas almost half of those entering before age 16 received low earnings at the time of the survey, only one-quarter of those beginning work between ages 18 and 29 did so. An apparent anomaly appears in the statistic showing that over half of those entering the labor force after age 30 received low earnings. Almost all of these individuals were women, but nothing can be inferred about their personal or job characteristics.

Unfortunately, the findings of the ECSO study are presented in the form of simple bivariate distributions of the population. No multivariate analysis was undertaken that might have enhanced our understanding of the phenomenon of low earnings, and this limits our ability to speak with authority on its significance. Nevertheless, the information does at least provide a basis for a tentative interpretation of this phenomenon that stands in sharp contrast to the explanation based on market failure. The relative youth and poor education of the low earners suggest that they possess only modest endowments of human capital. To the extent that these workers are employed in occupations utilizing general skills—a likely event—the low earnings may simply reflect the incidence of the costs of training. Human capital theory holds that the costs of acquiring general skills will be borne by the individual. They will be financed either by out-of-pocket payments for institutionally provided training or by the acceptance of a wage during the training period that reflects the low marginal product of an inexperienced worker.[24] Particularly among those with very little or no formal education, the concept of "general skills" may be extended to include the development of attitudes and personal discipline that are prerequisites to the finding and holding of a well-remunerated employment.

What the data suggest is that, with the passage of time and an increase in work experience, workers do improve their earnings. The cross-section data for males indicate that the chances of holding a job that pays at least 110 percent of the minimum wage vary with age. They are only one in twenty for teenagers between the ages of 12 and 14; three in ten for those aged 15 through 19; two out of three for workers 20 through 24 years; and three out of four for those in the prime labor force age groups.[25] Further support for this human capital interpretation of low earnings is supplied by the finding that wages are an increasing function of tenure in the current employment. Whereas 56 percent of workers holding their current jobs for less than one year reported low earnings, this proportion falls to one-third of those with two years' tenure, one-fifth of those with four to ten years', and 14 percent of those with longer tenure.[26]

Formal education or technical training appears to serve as a partial substitute for experience, although to what extent this may be so cannot be determined from this survey without more detailed cross-tabulations or multivariate analysis. The data suggest that low earnings are by no means a permanent condition for the bulk of the male wage earners in the labor market. Rather, there appears to be considerable mobility up the earnings ladder in the urban labor market. In short, for most male entrants to the labor market, low earnings appear to be only a temporary phenomenon and hardly indicative of a chronic condition over a working life. If viewed in this light, the measures of underemployment based on an earnings criterion appear to include a substantial number of individuals in the process of acquiring general skills and bearing the costs of training.

The earnings situation for women exhibits features similar to those for men but in a less definitive form. The earnings data for females are muddied by the greater incidence of part-time employment and the absence of tables relating earnings to hours worked. This problem was present among males as well but to a lesser extent. Whereas only 20 percent of men reported fewer than forty hours of work, over 36 percent of the females did so. Nevertheless, the incidence of low earnings among women drops very sharply as age increases, up to the age of 30; this closely resembles the findings for men reported above. After age 30, the number of low earners increases to around half of the remaining age groups. Since these are the ages during which most women are likely to bear substantial domestic responsibilities, the increased incidence of low earnings may be heavily influenced by the frequency of part-time employment. Furthermore, the female data are heavily weighted by the preponderance of women with very short tenures in their current employment. In fact, if the incidence of low earnings among women is related to tenure, their situation matches very closely that for men in this respect. Thus, tenure may be the principal factor accounting for the larger concentration of women in the low-earnings category.

In view of these observations, the use of an earnings criterion for defining underemployment would seem to lead to an exaggeration of the extent of an employment problem and to a misspecification of its nature. The fact that low earnings prevail within a segment of the labor force does little by itself to advance our understanding either of the workers' relationship to the labor market or of the appropriate policies required to ameliorate employment conditions. Indeed, the consistent use of income as a criterion in defining underemployment would permanently consign a large portion of the employed labor force to that status—regardless of the country's stage of economic development or its current level of income. In the absence of complete wage equality, even the most highly developed country will have a substantial body of workers employed at earnings below some modal or other arbitrary level. Alternatively, the incidence of low earnings might be considered as indicative of the extent of poverty. Even for this purpose, however, earnings of individuals are likely to be an imperfect guide to the incidence of poverty; poverty is more appropriately defined on the basis of household incomes. From the demographic characteristics of this sample of low earners—most of whom are youths and women—one may surmise that a signficant proportion of these were secondary wage earners rather than the sole sources of household support.

A brief review of the various estimates of underemployment advanced for Mexico illustrates the difficulties confronting attempts to measure the phenomenon. In 1976 PREALC published an estimate of Mexican underemployment rates that prevailed in 1970.[27] Different methods were used to estimate rural and urban underemployment. In the case of the agricultural sector, the extent of underemployment was calculated by subtracting from the man-days of labor available to the sector the number of man-days required to produce the sector's output. The latter requirement was derived from estimates of the production functions for different crops and different size farm units. The labor input coefficients of these models serve to define the labor requirements of the sector. The available supply of labor was taken to include all male adults. It was further assumed that "the work of women and children is available according to labor demand."[28] This method yields an estimate of the agricultural labor force that is underemployed equal to 46 percent of the total, a proportion that includes rural open unemployment as well.

One of the difficulties associated with the estimation of labor requirements in this way, however, is that it may not capture all of the productive activities undertaken by household members. Labor time devoted to home production or to activities ancillary to agricultural production (such as marketing) is quite likely to escape detection and inclusion in these estimates. Furthermore, what appears to be a surplus of labor to the agricultural sector may not prove to be a surplus to the economy as a whole. Since seasonal movements of labor from the agricultural to the nonagricultural sector are a common phenomenon in Mexico, it cannot be assumed that the agricultural labor "surplus" is idle when not directly employed in agricultural production. Finally, some of the labor force that is available for peak season employment in agriculture may not be available for work at other times. The reported resistance of small farmers to technological changes that would require increased labor may be a further indication that farm families do not view themselves as repositories of surplus labor.[29]

There is some precedent for the belief that the application of technical coefficients to an estimate of labor requirements is likely to lead to an overestimation of the amount of nonproductive time of agricultural workers that might be available for application elsewhere in the economy. A pair of studies of the agricultural sector of Guatemala illustrates the point. Based on alternative measures of labor supply and on the technological labor input requirements of the sector, one study concluded that, about 1970, the proportion of available labor actually utilized ranged from 48 to 70 percent.[30] A reasonable implication that might be drawn from these estimates is that a substantial body of manpower resources is available for other productive purposes. However, another study undertaken in the middle 1960s by the Comité Interamericano de Desarrollo Agricola found that, once all the various tasks and obligations of typical *minifundistas* were taken into account, including market and home production as well as community services, only 13 percent of their time was unoccupied. An unexpected finding was that the highland minifundistas who would ordinarily be considered underemployed actually hired outside workers for up to 35 percent of the labor required on their plots.[31] It should not be surprising to find in Mexico, as well, a much smaller surplus of labor time than that yielded by production models of the agricultural sector. Indeed, the evidence presented in Chapter 4, which deals in greater detail with that sector, would appear to confirm this expectation.

In the PREALC estimate of underemployment in Mexico, a different methodology was applied to the urban sector. The source of the estimates was the household survey of income and expenditures for 1968. Underemployment was defined exclusively by reference to income. Since the income data referred to household rather than individual worker incomes, an adjustment had to be made according to the presumed number of employed members per household. This study chose to assume that the number of labor force members per household was inversely related to household income.[32] Unfortunately, the basis for this choice is not discussed. A contrary assumption would seem more reasonable, namely, that a larger number of labor force participants is more likely to yield a higher level of household income rather than a lower one. This was clearly revealed to be the case by a household income and expenditure study of urban households in Costa Rica.[33] The number of employed persons per household increased progressively, from 0.87 in households with monthly incomes of under 500 Costa Rican colones to about two workers at an income level of 2,500 Costa Rican colones. At higher income levels, the number of workers stabilized at about two. To the extent that household incomes in Mexico are likewise directly related to the number of employed members, PREALC's assumption would have the effect of understating the earnings of workers and overstating the extent of underemployment. A further bias in the same direction is the result of the inclusion of an unknown number of household members whose low incomes were not the product of earnings, but of low nonlabor incomes such as retirement pensions.

As indicated above, the income level by which underemployment was to be estimated was the average income of the modal interval in the urban household income distribution. One-third of the workers in the modal income group and all of those in the still lower income groups were then deemed to be underemployed. To be sure, the choice of an income level is bound to be quite arbitrary; there is no obvious choice. In this case, the selection of the modal group is an accident of the choice of the limits of each income class. Altering these limits could generate a whole family of modal income intervals. Choosing the appropriate interval from such a set of intervals would pose a severe challenge.

The application of this procedure to the urban sector yielded a figure of 27.9 percent of the labor force as underemployed. In terms of open unemployment equivalents, this amounted to an unemployment rate of 11.8 percent. For the rural sector, the open unemployment equivalent was 35 percent; the weighted average for the Mexican labor force as a whole amounted to 25.4 percent.[34]

The vagaries of measures for underutilization of labor are illustrated by PREALC's later estimate for 1970, the same year of the estimate given immediately above. The criteria employed in this later study are quite different from those applied earlier, and the extent of underutilization of the labor force assumes different proportions.[35] The openly employed form an obvious component of the underutilized labor force. Underemployment is defined differently for the rural and urban sectors.[36] Rural underemployment includes all workers who are self-employed in traditional agriculture, as well as all unpaid family members (adjustment is made for an imputed additional participation of women and minors). The urban informal sector, the repository of the urban underemployed, includes the self-employed and unremunerated family members, but not people in professional and technical occupational groups who report these same two employment statuses. Nor are salaried workers with low earnings included in this characterization of the underemployed. The portions of the labor force thus deemed to be underemployed are 53 percent of the rural and 35 percent of the urban, figures significantly greater than those given in the earlier study. However, the method used to convert the underemployed into open unemployment equivalents yielded a measure below the 25.4 percent of the earlier study. The open unemployment equivalent of the underemployed is given as 15.3 percent of the labor force. When the rate of measured open unemployment is added, a total open unemployment equivalent of 19.1 percent results. This study charts the changes in the degree of underutilization from 1950 to 1980 and concludes that it has declined from 23.7 to 17.0 percent over that period for the labor force as a whole.[37] However, the average conceals two divergent trends. A sharp decline in rural underemployment has been partially offset by an increase in urban.

The Grupo de Estudio del Problema del Empleo concluded that in the early 1970s underemployment characterized about 44.8 percent of the national labor force.[38] Regional variations were considerable and ranged from 33.4 percent in central Mexico to 61.5 percent in the southern peninsula. Rural rates were higher than those for urban. The underemployed were defined to include all part-time workers plus those earning less than the legal minimum wage. Since no distinction could be made between those workers who were voluntarily working part-time and those who were not, the measure is upward biased. Using the legal minimum wage to distinguish between the underemployed and fully employed is again arbitrary. The application of this criterion guarantees that the degree of underemployment will fluctuate with the current relationship of the minimum wage to the market price of unskilled labor. For example, in the late 1930s, when the legal minimum wage was far above the market price of labor, the measured underemployment would have encompassed an overwhelming proportion of the labor force. That proportion would have fallen dramatically over the following decade as the real value of the legal minimum wage declined and the market price of unskilled labor surpassed the legal minimum. Therefore, the utility of such a criterion is in question. It could yield widely different perceptions of the employment problem even though the objective conditions of the labor force might have changed very little.

Dr. Saul Trejo's estimate of underemployment in 1972 was derived from the proportion of the labor force that was employed at a capital–labor ratio below the average for the economy as a whole. This method yielded an estimate of 52 percent of the labor force.[39] No attempt was made to convert this proportion into its open unemployment equivalent. Since the amount of capital with which labor is combined tends to be directly related to the productivity and income of labor, it is not surprising that this method should yield an underemployment ratio that departs only modestly from those based on an income criterion. However, this measure can only account for the quantity of physical capital combined with labor and ignores the human capital endowment of workers. It may be this omission that accounts for the larger rate of underemployment yielded. Would underemployment be eliminated if all workers were provided with an amount of physical capital equal to the average for the economy? Clearly not, if the criterion were applied consistently. In fact, this would only increase the proportion of the labor force that would have to be considered underemployed—the remedy would have had the effect of raising the average capital–labor ratio, and a larger number of workers would now lie below the average.

The supplement to the ECSO survey cited above yielded an underemployment figure of 38.2 percent of the labor force (for urban centers with populations of 100,000 or more).[40] This proves to be significantly larger than PREALC's estimate of 27.9 percent for the urban labor force and may simply reflect ECSO's choice of a higher income standard. No basis is provided for the conversion of this percentage into open unemployment equivalents.

The object of this discussion has not been to belittle previous attempts to characterize or quantify the employment problem. Rather, it has been to illustrate the difficulties of developing a meaningful measure that is not subject to variations unrelated to actual conditions in the labor market. For example, the use of an earnings criterion that is tied to a certain concept of average income could lead to a paradoxical conclusion—that employment conditions were deteriorating and underemployment increasing, even though real wages of all workers were actually increasing steadily. This would be the case if a rising general wage level were accompanied by widening skill or income differentials. Even if the relative distribution remained constant as wages rose generally, no improvement in the condition of underemployment would be apparent. Surely, a procedure that ignores absolute changes in the well-being of workers leaves something to be desired. This method, if applied consistently, would preclude the attainment of full employment. How *will* we know when underemployment has been eliminated?

Disguised Unemployment

One of the components of underemployment that merits separate attention is disguised unemployment. This refers to a phenomenon that might be categorized as "make-work" employment. It is presumed to exist in a labor market that offers so few salaried employment opportunities that individuals are forced to create their own jobs. These are usually of a casual nature and presumably at very low levels of productivity and remuneration. Itinerant vendors, street entertainers, bootblacks, parking guards, and an assortment of other offerers of goods or services are frequently assumed to constitute this category. Unremunerated family workers are also sometimes included here. An essential element in the characterization of the disguised unemployed is the assumption that the activity performed is not the product of a voluntary choice but rather one of last resort. Relatively little empirical evidence is available for testing the validity of the assumptions regarding this component of the labor force. Therefore, it is of interest to review the findings of a recent survey of self-employed casual workers in several areas of metropolitan Mexico City.[41]

The study undertaken by the Department of Social Studies of Banamex, one of the leading banks in the country, was directed toward "those persons with the following characteristics: self-employed, unattached in any formal way to a firm or any other identifiable establishment, and whose earnings from work are unstable" (translation mine).[42] Two separate surveys were undertaken: one in January 1982 when economic activity and employment were at very high levels, the other in September of the same year during an economic crisis characterized by a sharp contraction of the economy and rapidly rising unemployment. One hundred and fifty individuals were interviewed in the first survey and an additional hundred in the second. Those interviewed did not constitute a scientifically random sample of the designated population. Rather they were selected at random on the streets in various sections of the city by the interviewers. While the nonrandom nature of the sample becomes evident in the sharp contrasts in personal characteristics of the two sampled groups, much less variation is evidenced in the responses to most of the questions posed.

The interviewees exhibited a certain degree of ambivalence toward their current labor market status. On the one hand, a majority indicated that they would like to hold paid employment for its greater security, fringe benefits, and training opportunities. On the other hand, these workers professed an overwhelming preference for self-employment because the work hours were flexible and they were free of supervision.[43] Indeed, virtually all of those interviewed liked their current occupations.[44] Nor can it be said that those surveyed labored for long hours at low rates of remuneration. In both samples, the median hours worked were between seven and eight per day; 40 percent of the workers in each sample averred that they were not available for full-time employment.[45] An examination of the reported earnings reveals that the remunerations can hardly be considered marginal. Only 17 percent of each of the two samples indicated monthly earnings of less than Mex$5,000 at a time when the legal minimum wage was Mex$6,720. In view of the large number of part-time workers, however, this rate of earnings probably exceeded the minimum wage in most cases. The median rate of earnings for the January sample approximated Mex$8,800. By September it had risen to Mex$10,000, while the legal minimum had been increased to Mex$8,730 pesos. Fourteen and 21 percent of the two samples reported monthly earnings of more than Mex$15,000. The average daily earnings of virtually every occupational group exceeded the legal minimum wage. Only the "fire-eaters," a small group of very young teenage street entertainers, reported earnings well below the legal minimum. Casual observation suggests, however, that they work only a few hours a day during the heaviest commuter traffic. Even bootblacks and those dependent on gratuities—for example, auto watchers and organ grinders—reported daily earnings in excess of the legal minimum.[46] An interesting finding was a lack of a close correspondence between educational and earnings levels in this particular labor market.

Nor can one characterize the sampled individuals as coming from impoverished households. The incidence of additional workers in the households of the sampled workers was quite high. In the households of the 150 workers sampled in January, there were eighty-two other employed persons; in the 100 households of the September sample, there were eighty. The earnings distribution of employed household members in the January survey resembled closely that for the interviewed workers. The corresponding distribution from the later survey generally revealed higher earnings among household members than among the interviewed. However, the interviewed group was unable to specify the earnings of approximately one-fourth of the employed household members.[47]

In short, the results of the Banamex survey do not lend support to the classification of casual workers as truly marginally employed or as disguised unemployed. On the contrary, they appear to have a strong attachment to their present employment, either because their earnings exceed their opportunity cost or because they value highly the freedom and flexibility that self-employment allows them. Although these findings may be challenged on the grounds that they are not the product of a scientific sampling process and thus may be suspect, there is a sufficient degree of consistency in the respondents' replies to warrant questioning the more conventional view of the casual self-employed worker. This is clearly a segment of the labor force deserving of greater empirical investigation.[48]

Summary

My findings for Mexico indicate an absence of a serious problem of open unemployment. Unemployment rates for the mature adult labor force have approximated frictional levels, and no secular trend in the average rate is discernable. There appears to be no real shortage of employment opportunities. Periods of unemployment tend to be very short, and workers seem to have sufficient confidence in a high probability of reemployment that they are not loath to quit jobs voluntarily.

Underemployment has been held to be the greater problem as evidenced by the incidence of less-than-full-time employment and low earnings. Other studies have set the degree of underutilization of the labor force at an open unemployment equivalent rate of 25 percent. I have offered reasons for believing that this greatly exaggerates the degree of underutilization and also fails to provide a reliable measure of the potential supply of labor that is readily available to new sources of employment.

Within the urban labor force, too little attention is given to the possible reasons for low earnings and to the personal characteristics of those receiving them. A proper consideration of these factors might lead to a very different appreciation of the significance of the observed low earnings. Given the youth of many urban low earners, the state of "underemployment" may reflect a transitory phenomenon—a stage in the working lives of young people during which they acquire general skills and bear the cost of doing so. The prevalence of individuals with very low educational levels speaks of human capital deficiencies. These may be overcome with age and increased work experience in many cases but, in others, may permanently disqualify workers from significant improvements in employment status.

Underutilization among the rural population is usually estimated with arbitrary criteria that cannot fully account for the whole of the productive activity of the agricultural labor force. While one may be certain that low earnings are more prevalent in rural than in urban areas, it does not follow that low earners are either immediately available or qualified for employment in newly created jobs at high levels of productivity and earnings. Chapter 4 deals exclusively with the agricultural labor force and includes a discussion of the reliability of conventional measures of underemployment as applied to this sector.

The limited usefulness of current measures of labor force underutilization for predicting the effective availability of labor was clearly demonstrated by Mexico's experience during the recent economic boom. As noted in Chapter 1, the acceleration of the growth process that got under way in 1978 led to widespread labor shortages by 1980. Clearly, the large labor surplus that was thought to exist failed to materialize. Rather than providing a reliable measure of the labor available for employment, the commonly applied earnings criteria for measuring underemployment may be more appropriate for the identification of the population in poverty. The shortcomings in using individual earnings for this purpose, however, have already been indicated. Little can be gained from reclassifying the phenomenon of low earnings or poverty as underemployment. It contributes nothing to an understanding either of an individual's relationship to the labor market or of the appropriate policies for the alleviation of poverty.

Notes

1. See James W. Wilkie, "New Hypotheses for Statistical Research in Recent History," *Latin American Research Review*, vol. 6, no. 2 (Summer 1971), table 4.

2. Donald B. Keesing, "Employment and Lack of Employment in Mexico, 1900–70," in *Quantitative Latin American Studies: Methods and Findings*, ed. James W. Wilkie and Kenneth Ruddle (Los Angeles: University of California, L.A., Latin American Center, 1977), p. 5. Keesing observes that the trend in the unemployment series for the 1930s does follow the recorded changes in output of the economy. However, he was unable to venture a judgment regarding the accuracy of the recorded levels of unemployment.

3. ECSO is the acronym for both *Encuesta continua de mano de obra* and *Encuesta continua sobre ocupación*; see Chapter 2, note 8.

4. *Información basica sobre la estructura y caracteristicas del empleo y el desempleo en las areas metropolitanas de las ciudades de México, Guadalajara y Monterrey* (Mexico, D.F., n.d.), table 46. Cited hereafter as *Información basica.*

5. Ibid., table 58.

6. Ibid., table 49.

7. Ibid., table 50.

8. Regional Employment Program for Latin America and the Caribbean (PREALC), *Employment in Latin America* (New York: Praeger, 1978). The authors conclude that, "as for hidden unemployment, most recent investigations tend to show that its quantitative significance is relatively slight" (p. 1).

9. *Información basica*, table 59.

10. On the basis of the work week, this conversion is made by first summing up over the employed labor force the number of hours by which workers fall short of the normal work week. That sum is then divided by the length of the normal work week. The dividend would represent the equivalent of some number of fully employed persons.

11. Secretaría de Industria y Comercio, Dirección General de Estadística, *VII Censo general de población, 1950* (Mexico, D.F., 1952), p. 240.

12. *IX Censo general de población, 1970*, p. 723.

13. While respondents were classified by the sector of their principal employment, the duration of employment was intended to apply to all jobs held, irrespective of sector.

14. ECSO, vol. 7, 1st quarter (1979), table 10.

15. *Información basica*, table 10.

16. Comisión Consultiva del Empleo, *Programa nacional de empleo 1980/82*, vol. 1 (Mexico, D.F., 1979), p. 42.

17. Grupo de Estudio del Problema del Empleo, "El problema ocupacional en México: magnitud y recomendaciones," versión preliminar (Mexico, D.F., n.d.), p. 41.

18. Secretaría de Programación y Presupuesto (SPP) and Secretaría del Trabajo y Previsión Social (STPS), *La ocupación informal en areas urbanas, 1976* (Mexico, D.F., 1979).

19. The adequacy of the attributes selected by the survey authors for defining the informal

sector or, for that matter, the usefulness of the concept of an informal labor market is not a matter of concern here. The relevance of the study for my purposes rests on the inclusion of that segment of the labor force employed at low rates of earnings.

20. SPP and STPS, *La ocupación informal en areas urbanas*, p. 191.

21. Ibid., p. 170.

22. Ibid., pp. 126–31.

23. Ibid., pp. 137–45.

24. Gary S. Becker, *Human Capital* (New York: Columbia University Press, 1964), chap. 2.

25. SPP and STPS, *La ocupación informal en areas urbanas*, p. 127.

26. Ibid., p. 233.

27. PREALC, *Employment in Latin America*, chap. 1.

28. Ibid., app. A.

29. Teresa Rendón, "Utilización de mano de obra en la agricultura mexicana, 1940–73," *Demografía y economía*, vol. 10, no. 3 (1976), p. 353. However, this resistance may simply be indicative of the perceived marginal product of that additional labor input applied to the family plot. If the marginal product is "small," it may not be viewed as compensating adequately for the disutility of the extra effort required.

30. Erik Thorbecke and Everardus J. Stoutjesdijk, *Employment and Output: a Methodology Applied to Peru and Guatemala* (Paris: Organisation for Economic Co-operation and Development, 1971), pp. 104–10.

31. Comité Interamericano de Desarrollo Agricola, *Tenencia de la tierra y desarrollo socioeconómico del sector agricola: Guatemala* (Washington, D.C.: Pan American Union, 1965), pp. 100–02 and 159–61. The term *minifundista* can be translated loosely as "small subsistence farmer."

32. PREALC, *Employment in Latin America*, p. 20.

33. Peter Gregory, "Legal Minimum Wages as an Instrument of Social Policy in Less Developed Countries, with Special Reference to Costa Rica," in *The Economics of Legal Minimum Wages*, ed. Simon Rottenberg (Washington, D.C.: American Enterprise Institute, 1981), pp. 398–99.

34. PREALC, *Employment in Latin America*, p. 25.

35. PREALC, *Dinámica del subempleo en American Latina*, Estudios e Informes de la CEPAL, no. 10 (Santiago: United Nations/International Labour Office, 1981), pp. 29–30, 81–101.

36. For purposes of this study, the so-called urban sector actually encompasses the entire nonagricultural sector.

37. PREALC, *Dinámica del subempleo*, p. 26.

38. Grupo de Estudio, *El problema ocupacional en México*, p. 37.

39. Saul Trejo R., "Desempleo y subocupación en México," *Comercio exterior*, vol. 24, no. 7 (August 1974), pp. 411–16.

40. SPP and STPA, *La ocupación informal*, p. 126

41. Departamento de Estudios Sociales, Banamex, *Encuesta de subempleados* (Mexico, D.F., May 1983).

42. Ibid., p. 1.

43. Ibid., pp. 30, 31.

44. Ibid., p. 40.

45. Ibid., pp. 44, 49.

46. Ibid., pp. 18, 52.

47. Ibid., pp. 54–56.

48. The only other reference I have found to the economic status of ambulatory peddlers is

drawn from a survey of households in Mexico City as part of a study of migration by social scientists from the Colegio de México. That study recorded the occupational status and earnings of the labor force members of the sampled households. Two percent of the labor force was found to be employed in this capacity. Average earnings in 1969–70 of this group were reported to be Mex$1,113, or 31 percent greater than the legal minimum wage (48 percent for men and 7 percent for women). Since no information about work hours is provided, however, earnings per time unit cannot be determined. The only other datum provided that characterizes this group is the average level of schooling completed: a low 3.2 years. Humberto Muñoz García, Orlandina de Oliveira, and Claudio Stern, "Migración y marginalidad ocupacional en la Ciudad de México," *El perfil de México en 1980*, vol. 3, 6th ed. (Mexico, D.F.: Siglo Veintiuno, 1979), pp. 354–57, 345

4. Agriculture and the Labor Market

WHEN DEVELOPING COUNTRIES are at an early stage of modernization, the agricultural sector is the dominant area of employment. As the country develops, labor shifts from agriculture into the expanding secondary and tertiary sectors. During this process, closer links are forged between the agricultural and nonagricultural labor markets. In 1940, when Mexico was at the beginning of the period of accelerated growth and modernization of its economy, about two-thirds of the labor force were still employed in the primary sector of the economy. A vast pool of labor services was thus potentially available to the other sectors as they expanded. However, the manner in which labor resources shift and the rate at which they do so is determined not only by the rate at which new employment opportunities appear in the economy but also by the economic and institutional conditions prevailing in the countryside. This chapter reviews the evolution of the agricultural sector over recent decades and the implications this has had for the supply of labor to the rest of the economy. Also addressed is the degree to which available labor resources are involuntarily underutilized.

The antecedents of the revolution that reformed the sector earlier in this century date back to the latter half of the nineteenth century. A major reorganization of the agricultural sector began during the 1850s with the expropriation of extensive church holdings and their redistribution in large units to private landholders. This was followed by a series of "reforms." In 1885, the Porfirian administration began seizing communal lands and private holdings with uncertain titles and giving them, along with federal lands, to land development companies and favored individuals. Justifications for this reform were that agricultural output was stagnant and that the indigenous and mestizo rural population was too stupid and lazy to increase output. These events occurred at a time when the government was emphasizing the rapid development of the domestic economy and an expansion of exports.[1] The effect of this reform was to deprive 90 percent of the villages in the central plateau of all of their common lands. In the country as a whole, 90 percent of all rural families were left landless, while 50 percent of the rural population became integrated into the hacienda system.[2]

One result of this upheaval was the creation of a large force of wage labor. Stimulated by expanding export opportunities and favorable prices, output expanded and, between 1885 and 1898, the real daily minimum market-determined wage for agricultural laborers rose by about 37 percent. The increase was abetted by the expansion of urban production and employment. At the turn of the century, the terms of trade for agricultural exports had begun to decline, mechanization of industrial production proceeded to displace artisans, and urban labor began to drift back to the rural areas. By 1911, the real daily wage in agriculture had fallen back to the level of 1885, or by 27 percent from the peak reached around 1897. The combination of a decline in the demand for labor and falling wages gave rise to increasing pressures for the return of the communal and private lands that had been distributed to the large commercial agricultural enterprises. The mounting demands erupted in a violent revolution, which was again to change the face of the agricultural sector.

Land Distribution

For about ten years, anarchy prevailed in the countryside. Forcible seizures of land and armed struggles for the control of the land took their toll in lives and lost output.[3] Beginning in the early 1920s, new land reforms were directed by government decree. The state, however, did not possess effective centralized powers of enforcement, and the titling of transfers proceeded very slowly. In the face of uncertain tenure, neither investment nor productivity responded. Not until the administration of Lázaro Cárdenas (1934–40) did the reform process become thoroughly institutionalized, orderly, and enforceable. By the end of Cárdenas's term, some 25.5 million hectares had been redistributed, 70 percent of this total during his administration alone. At the end of 1969, the total land transferred amounted to 75.6 million hectares. Although large amounts of land were redistributed during the 1960s during the terms of López Mateos and Díaz Ordaz, most of this was pastureland or of low productivity. For example, of the 18.1 million hectares distributed between 1965 and 1969, only 8.7 percent was arable cropland.[4]

Approximately half of the redistributed land was assigned to ejidos in an effort to recreate the communal system of landholding that characterized precolonial Mexico. Under the land reform law, the land is entrusted to a village or community, which then assigns usage rights to its members on an egalitarian basis. Frequently, haciendas were expropriated and simply reconstituted as ejidos. The original intention was to provide each family with a ten-hectare plot, but this goal was not achieved in the majority of cases. During the 1920s and early 1930s, the average plot consisted of two to three hectares, five to seven during the rest of the 1930s, and seven to eight hectares through the mid-1940s.[5] While most of the ejidos assigned usage rights to individual members, some were constituted as cooperative agricultural enterprises, especially in the northwestern region, with the land cultivated as a single unit under a formal managerial system.

Farm output failed to increase as quickly as expected, however. It was therefore necessary to reconsider the desirability of continuing a pattern of reform that would lead to the fragmentation of farmland and create disincentives for investment among the remaining larger units still in private hands.[6] Greater domestic and foreign demand for cash crops resulted in changes governing the distribution of lands in areas in which large-scale irrigation projects had been undertaken. Land was distributed in the form of private holdings rather than as communal property to ejidos, and the size of the units was considerably larger than the typical plot in the latter. From 1925 through the 1940s, the combination of large-scale irrigation projects and heavy investment in rural infrastructure created very favorable conditions for large private farmers, particularly in the arid northwestern and coastal regions. Technologically progressive and highly motivated to save and invest, the new agricultural entrepreneurs spearheaded a sharp increase in the sector's production, which appeared to "solve" the perceived problem of deficient output.[7] However, a disproportionately small share of government investment in rural infrastructure and credit has been directed toward small private farmers and ejidatarios. As a result, large disparities in productivity and incomes were created between the smaller beneficiaries of land reform and the larger private commercial farmers.

While the land reform satisfied the immediate demands for land of many rural workers, it could not do so in units of sufficient size to assure an adequate level of living. Particularly in the crowded regions of central Mexico, where distributions to ejidos predominated, the individual family plots were especially limited in size. As of 1960, 10 percent of the ejidatarios had no more than one hectare at their disposal for cultivation; 44 percent had no more than four hectares. Only 16 percent held plots with over ten hectares of cropland, and these held 45 percent of all the cropland assigned to ejidos. Since approximately a third of the cultivatable land is left fallow in any crop year, the income-producing area is still further reduced. In the private sector, there was an even greater preponderance of small plots. Minifundistas with fewer than five hectares of cropland accounted for 77 percent of the 1.2 million private farmers. Among them, they held less than 11 percent of the land in private hands. At the other end of the distribution were 3.1 percent of the private farmers with fifty hectares or more, accounting for 63 percent of the cropland.[8]

A consequence of so many small plots is a yield per farm unit (in terms of the value of output) that is insufficient to provide even a subsistence level of income. Fully half of the plots have been classified as "sub-subsistence" units on the basis of 1960 output levels. The annual value of crops produced on these units was estimated to average Mex$500 annually, or US$40 at the 1960 exchange rate. The addition of the value of livestock and forest products would increase the figure by no more than 50 percent. These small plots accounted for only 4 percent of the total agricultural output of Mexico. Furthermore, over the decade 1950–60, no change occurred in the value of output per farm unit in this class.[9] Typically, these small plots cannot fully employ a household's available labor resources. It has been estimated that during the mid-1960s they required only between 75 and 150 man-days per year for direct cultivation.[10]

Another one-third of the units falls into the category of subfamily farms, units that employ fewer than two man-years of labor. In 1960, they accounted for 17 percent of total farm output. Between 1950 and 1960, the average value of harvested crops per farm unit increased in real terms by 24 percent and reached a level of Mex$3,101, or US$240, in the latter year. If the value of livestock and forestry production is added, total value of output per unit would be increased by an estimated 50 percent. It is considered unlikely that the average income per unit exceeded Mex$5,000, or US$400, per year. These plots could barely employ fully a single individual for a year; annual labor inputs were estimated to average 250 to 350 days.[11] In view of this, it is reasonable to expect that a large number of families in this and the sub-subsistence categories would have to supplement farm income with earnings from other sources.[12] For many regions dependent on rain-fed agriculture, the uncertainty surrounding the amount of rainfall—and subsequently the size of harvests—has lent even greater urgency to the pursuit of supplementary sources of income.[13]

The remaining 16 percent of the farm units may be considered to have achieved levels of output adequate for the maintenance of a family. They accounted for 79 percent of Mexico's agricultural output in 1960 and for most of the growth in the sector's output between 1950 and 1960. Indeed, fully 45 percent of the increase in total output was achieved by the largest farm stratum, which employed more than twelve man-years of labor or produced output valued at more than 100,000 pesos in 1960. These units represented only 0.5 percent of all farm units but accounted for one-third of total sector output. The next stratum, that of units employing four to twelve man-years of labor or producing output valued at Mex$25,000–100,000 a year, accounted for 3 percent of all farm units—22 percent of sector output in 1960, and 35 percent of the total increase in agricultural output over the decade.[14] In short, the picture of the agricultural sector that emerges from these data is one of a majority of subsistence units with stagnant output levels on the one hand, and, on the other, a minority of commercial farms that account for the bulk of total output and for the increase in output over time. On average, the largest farms produce an output approximately 513 times greater than that produced on the smallest plots.

Data from the 1970 agricultural census confirm the reduced incomes obtainable from small landholdings. Private farms of less than five hectares yielded an average net income of only Mex$918, or about US$75. Those over five hectares yielded net incomes twenty times greater. Among ejidatarios, annual net incomes from holdings of all sizes averaged Mex$4,426, or about US$350, an income substantially unchanged from that reported for 1960. Within the ejido sector, however, the same large differences among different-size holdings can be noted as among the private sector units. Plots up to one hectare in size yielded net incomes of only Mex$875, or US$70, while those with more than twenty hectares yielded almost thirty times more.[15] P. Lamartine Yates's interpretation of the agricultural censuses, however, suggests a less static picture of overall productivity levels than that gained from observation of only the tiniest plots. He holds that, between 1950 and 1970, for example, output per hectare on private farms of over five hectares increased by 147 percent, while increasing by 73 percent on smaller units. For ejidos of all sizes, output per hectare increased by 113 percent. These figures suggest that output, even on relatively small plots, must have recorded significant increases.[16]

As indicated above, disparities in the size of cultivated plots lead to very large differences in incomes from the land. Differences in productivity per hectare, however, are much narrower but apparently have been widening over time. For example, although the output per hectare of private holdings of five hectares or more was only 6 percent greater than that on smaller private plots in 1940, the margin increased to 40 percent in 1960. In 1940, output per hectare on ejido plots actually exceeded that on the larger private farms; in 1960, the latter reported output levels per land unit 25 percent greater than that for ejidos.[17] These data imply that somewhat narrower differences exist in productivity of land than might have been expected from more aggregated data available on a regional basis.

The distribution of land and irrigation over the rural population is very uneven. Moreover, these disparities have strong regional associations. The Northwest and Northeast, which enjoy greater access to irrigation facilities and in which larger farm units predominate, report significantly higher levels of output per hectare and per worker than do the Peninsular and the heavily populated Central regions. In 1970, the value of output per hectare in the Northwest and Northeast was Mex$3,435 and Mex$2,002, respectively, but only Mex$1,397 and Mex$1,436, respectively, in the Peninsular and Central sections. The differences in output per worker were even greater: Mex$16,603, Mex$10,723, Mex$4,201, and Mex$2,778, respectively. In the Central region, the paucity of agricultural resources other than labor is particularly striking. The region contains a third of the national agricultural labor force but only 11 percent of the cultivated land. Less than 20 percent of the land is irrigated. The average amount of cultivated land per member of the agricultural labor force is reported to be no more than 1.3 hectares.[18] Indeed, fully 70 percent of the smallest private plots are located in four of the states comprising this region (Hidalgo, México, Tlaxcala, and Puebla), plus Oaxaca in the South. Given the small size of so many plots and the limited incomes it is possible to wrest from them, it should come as no surprise to observe a reduction in their numbers as their owners have either sold out or abandoned their holdings. Between 1940 and 1970, there has actually been a decline in the number of private smallholdings and in the total land area they occupy.[19]

Since ejidatarios do not possess title to their holdings, they cannot sell them. Nor can they retain the right to use this land if they do not cultivate it. Nevertheless, these farmers have found ways of avoiding active cultivation of their land so that they are free to seek off-farm employment. The practice of sharecropping is becoming more widespread.[20] A certain amount of renting of ejido land is also believed to be taking place; however, since the practice is illegal, it is impossible to obtain estimates of its incidence.

In retrospect, the initial impact of the land reform was to provide a floor under the incomes of the recipients of land. In the process, it created a more permanent tie to the land for the majority of recipients who received land through ejidos. Indeed, the prospect of receiving land induced some farm workers who had migrated to urban areas to return to their villages so that they might exercise their right to land. Yet the land reform fell far short of its objective, for it failed to provide its beneficiaries with enough land and other resources from which to achieve incomes adequate for subsistence, much less keep those earnings rising over time in tandem with wages in other sectors of the economy. Furthermore, the increasing pressures of population on the available land supply have meant a narrowing margin for satisfying the demands for land. One of the ironies of the land reform has been that, in spite of its being one of the most sweeping of its kind in the world, so many agricultural workers remain landless. Indeed, in 1960, the number of such workers exceeded by an estimated 15 percent that which existed in 1940. The 1963 household survey of income and expenditures of the Banco de México reported that half of all heads of households in the agricultural labor force were landless. According to the population censuses, agricultural wage laborers formed the fastest growing component of the sectoral labor force and, by 1970, accounted for just half of the total. An increase of almost 16 percent in their number occurred between 1960 and 1970 even as the number of self-employed producers was declining. Over this same interval, the number of unremunerated family members showed a marginal increase.

Further distribution to landless people is obviously constrained by the limited availability of suitable land. The possibilities have already been exhausted for making vast new arid areas cultivatable through large-scale irrigation projects. However, some scope remains for increasing arable lands in rain-fed areas with small-scale irrigation projects that tap local supplies of underground and surface water. Colonization projects in the south are proceeding, but they require large expenditures on reclamation projects to make the land arable and will result in distributions to the local population rather than to the workers of the congested Central region. Some lands may become available as individual farm holdings are discovered to exceed legal size limits. The Sistema Alimentario Mexicano, introduced in 1980, provided for the expropriation and distribution to ejidos of those cattle ranches deemed suitable for crop production by the Ministry of Agriculture.[21] As yet, the extent to which those provisions have yielded a significant amount of land for redistribution cannot be determined.

The other remaining source of arable land is the larger private holdings that survived the land reform process in the older agricultural regions, or those larger holdings that were created in the northern regions of the country. Since these units have been the most dynamic sources of growth of agricultural output over the past thirty years, a decision to expropriate and redistribute them would be a difficult one for the Mexican government. Should it satisfy the continuing demands of the landless for land, or maintain the high and growing levels of agricultural output? As recent Mexican governments have espoused the goal of greater self-sufficiency in food supply, the risks inherent in breaking up efficient production units may appear too great to be assumed. In short, the prospects of converting much of the landless labor force into an independent peasantry appear to be quite remote.

Rural Workers

There is a large number of landless households and of landowners with plots too small to employ fully their households' available labor resources. This implies a potential supply of labor for employment within the sector on those larger units that are net buyers of labor services as well as on those smaller units whose households are net sellers of services. In fact, the sector has long had an active wage market. In the older agricultural regions the large haciendas—survivors of the land reform process—provide employment for workers drawn from the surrounding countryside. Large farm units created by the reform, located mostly in the North and Northwest, depend on wage labor for the bulk of their labor requirements. The diversity of climatic conditions and cropping patterns in different parts of the country gives rise to different planting and harvesting seasons. This provides employment opportunities that do not conflict with the requirements of the smallholders' own plots.

Migrant Labor

The prevalence of migrant farm labor within Mexico has long been established. In 1940, it was estimated that 200,000 farm workers made up a migrant labor force available for the harvest of various crops. In Chiapas alone, some 35,000 indigenous peasants would descend from the mountains to harvest coffee on farms situated along the Guatemalan border.[22] Peasants from Puebla and other states of central Mexico had well-established contacts with sugar-growing areas along the Gulf coast; migrations during the cane-cutting season were an annual phenomenon.[23] The tobacco growers of the state of Nayarit rely on migrant workers from within the state as well as from neighboring states for the harvesting and processing of their crop.[24] Ejidatarios and their families annually desert entire villages in northeastern San Luis Potosí for the sugar and cotton harvest in Tamaulipas.[25] The large commercial farms of the Northwest also depend heavily on migrant labor for the harvest of crops requiring large labor inputs, such as cotton and vegetables. Since the population density of the region is relatively low, active recruitment of farm migrants is undertaken by roving recruiters in the largely rural states of the Central region. The wages paid for such labor are effectively governed by the high legal minimum wages prevailing in that area. Although employers are responsible for the housing of migrants, the facilities provided are frequently very primitive and lack adequate sanitary conditions.[26]

A high incidence of short-term migration of rural workers has been recorded by numerous studies of rural communities by social scientists. For example, Balan, Browning, and Jelin report that approximately 59 percent of the ejidatarios of a poor ejido near Cedral, Nuevo León, had been short-term migrants.[27] Foster found that half of the men in the village of Toxi had been to the United States, many of them ten or more times.[28] Even more remote villages, such as Tilatongo in Oaxaca, are characterized by internal migration of a temporary or permanent kind. About one-third of the male population had migrated either temporarily or on a more extended basis, while another third had become permanently established in other places.[29] DeWalt found both temporary and permanent migration to be a common phenomenon in his study of the ejido of Puerto de las Piedras in the state of México, especially among the landless. Even those with land were participants in the process.[30]

An alternative source of farm employment was provided by the bracero program of the United States during World War II and the two succeeding decades. During this interval, some 5 million Mexicans were contracted for employment in the United States. Concomitant with the formal contracting of farm workers was a substantial flow of illegal migrants to the United States, many of whom also found employment in agriculture but without the contractual protection provided by the formal bracero program. The end of the bracero program, of course, did not put an end to this movement of workers but rather converted a larger proportion of it to illegal migration. This phenomenon will be discussed in greater detail in Chapter 6.

Off-Farm Employment

While much of the migration involved movement between jobs within the agricultural sector, the prevalence of employment opportunities in nonagricultural activities should not be overlooked. At least over the past forty years or so, agricultural workers have sought and found temporary employment outside the sector. During the 1940s for example, the widespread construction of feeder roads in rural areas provided off-season employment opportunities. With the completion of these projects, workers increasingly turned to urban areas for employment. The construction industry in the larger urban centers has long provided an important source of seasonal employment. In Mexico City, the large central market district provides another source of temporary employment for stevedores or materials handlers. Street vending of newspapers, fruits, vegetables, candy, and so forth is also held to offer employment opportunities to temporary migrants. Women seeking temporary employment enter domestic service, street vending, or work as helpers or dishwashers in food service establishments.[31]

With the exception of construction jobs, these occupational opportunities are relatively unaffected by cyclical variations in economic activity. Apparently, short-term migrants seeking temporary employment have relatively little difficulty in finding casual jobs that pose no entry requirements or long-term commitment. For example, one study of agricultural communities in the valley of Toluca in the state of México reported minimal time spent in search of off-farm employment. While 4,423,600 days were so employed, only 113,300 were spent in job searches—a ratio of 39 days worked to each day of search.[32] To be sure, the earnings yielded by such employments are typically low, no higher than the legal minimum wage and frequently below it. Nevertheless, given the low opportunity cost of the labor so occupied, even these wages must appear attractive.

While these descriptive accounts indicate that substantial numbers of rural workers are involved in labor market activity, they do not convey an appreciation of the full importance to farm households of off-farm employment. Fortunately, such an appreciation can be gained from studies undertaken at the household level over the past twenty years. Viewed as a whole, they provide a picture of the farm household that departs substantially from the conventional one of subsistence farmers and their families eking out an existence on undersized plots and facing few options in the disposition of the labor resources available to their households. What emerges is a much more complex set of alternatives for such households. The mix of opportunities ranges from own-account employment (on one's own land), to wage labor within the agricultural sector, wage labor in nonagricultural productive activities, and nonagricultural production in a self-employed capacity—not only for the head of the household but also for other members of the unit. Most of the household studies to be found, however, limit their attention to workers who have access to land either as ejidatarios or as private owners. Very little information is available on the sources of income and employment of landless farm households.

A study of 100 ejidos dispersed through six distinct regions in the state of San Luis Potosí during the mid-1960s highlights the importance of employment off the family plot for the majority of the sampled population. Given the small size of the average landholding, two to five hectares, the average number of work days devoted to its cultivation generally averaged less than fifty a year. Only where irrigation was available and double cropping prevailed did the family plot require more than a hundred work days. Most households provided wage labor for various activities outside the ejido; the proportion of total income derived from such sources generally exceeded by a considerable margin that generated on the ejidatario's own plot.

The highest proportion of outside income was reported by the ejidos located in an arid zone close to the capital city of the state. There, the ejidatarios reported that 87 percent of their income originated from wages earned outside the ejidos. Of the remaining 13 percent, most income reportedly came from irrigated plots. Although the largest single source of off-farm employment was wage labor within the agricultural sector, the majority of workers were employed in a variety of rural and urban nonagricultural activities ranging from construction and mining to commerce and the gathering of wood for sale. Only 9 percent of the sampled ejidatarios declared that they were either not interested in outside employment or were unable to find work.[33]

In three other districts, similarly small proportions indicated an absence of off-farm employment. On average, earnings from off-plot activities constituted more than half of household income, ranging from 56 to 70 percent. Since these districts were farther from urban centers, however, nonagricultural work accounted for less than half of off-farm income. Daily wages varied widely, even within agriculture. In general, the daily rate for agricultural day labor on small holdings averaged less than half the applicable legal minimum wage. By contrast, large farms were reported as offering wages two to three times those paid by smallholders.[34] Earnings rates in nonagricultural activities were considerably greater than those available from most agricultural employments.

The monumental study of the agricultural sector by Sergio Reyes Osorio and his associates, undertaken during 1966–68, confirms the importance to farm households of employment off their own lands. Among the private producers, 6 percent also held jobs as wage laborers in agriculture in addition to cultivating their own land. Another 38 percent had held employment in nonagricultural activities during the reference year. Among ejidatarios, the proportion was 23 percent in each type of outside activity.[35]

The nonagricultural employments were distributed over several sectors. The principal sector of off-farm employment was in commerce, in which 35 percent of the jobs were to be found. At 15 percent, a distant second sector was formed by the sum of unskilled jobs held in manufacturing, construction, mining, and transport activities. Another 13 percent were in services. Included in this listing of off-farm employment were those involving the rental and operation of farm machinery; these accounted for 13 percent of the total. Another 13 percent of the sampled workers held skilled jobs without reference to sector; handicraft production occupied less than 10 percent. However, there were sharp differences in the distribution of employments among sectors in the sampled areas. Proximity to urban areas appears to have been associated with a greater concentration in commerce and in industrial-type jobs (the second category above). More isolated areas reported a greatear incidence of handicraft production and employment in skilled jobs.[36]

As might be expected, the incidence of employment off the family farm was greater among those with subsistence-size or smaller plots. Indeed, for these groups, the great bulk of individual and family income derived from sources other than the family plot. But even among those producers with family-size units, outside employment occupied significant proportions of total days worked and contributed as much as a third of family income.[37] Although the incidence of outside employment was greater among peasants with rain-fed lands, those holding irrigated plots, which yield higher returns and might be expected to offer more days of employment, were not far behind in the frequency with which they sought off-farm jobs.

A study of El Bajío, a fertile but densely populated region in the state of Guanajuato, offers further confirmation of the importance of off-farm employment.[38] The data have been ordered according to the status of the producer, ejidatario, or private farmer; by size of plot; and by rain-fed or irrigated agriculture. In general, farmers in rain-fed areas or with small plots spend fewer days per year working on their own plots and are thus available for more off-farm employment. For example, among producers with infrasubsistence plots in rain-fed areas, the proportion of days worked off-farm to total days worked was 39 percent for ejidatarios and 62 percent for private farmers. Other small-scale farmers spent from 15 to 25 percent of their working days at off-farm labor. While these jobs included day labor in agriculture, they were far less numerous than those devoted to nonagricultural activity. Among ejidatarios, days spent in nonagricultural activity were more than three times as numerous, and among private cultivators almost seven times as numerous, as the days spent as farm laborers. Since wages are higher in nonagricultural jobs, the importance of earnings from this work relative to farm day labor is even greater. In most strata, earnings from hiring out within the farm sector bordered on the insignificant.

The importance of wage employment as a supplement to self-employment for cultivators and their families has also been extensively documented in the six regional studies undertaken during the decade of the 1970s by A. René Barbosa-Ramírez and the Centro de Investigaciones Agrarias.[39] The prevalence of small plots, too small to provide either full-time employment or an adequate income, implies the existence of strong incentives to enter the wage employment market. Indeed, more days were occupied in wage labor than in self-employment in most of the regions studied. For example, the region of Valsequillo in the state of Puebla is one in which small farms, averaging only 2.5 hectares, predominate. Almost 80 percent of the land was irrigated, and "modern" techniques of production, as evidenced by the nature of inputs, prevailed. Yet outside employment occupied the majority of days worked by both the cultivator and his family members. Only 30 and 13 percent, respectively, of his and his family's work days were spent on the family plot.[40] Even in the much poorer and more isolated region of Mixteca Baja in the state of Oaxaca, 60 percent of the days worked by the family unit were off-farm.[41] A region in the Toluca valley of the state of México revealed a strong inverse relationship between the size of the family plot and the proportion of days worked in off-farm employment. Cultivators with less than one hectare of land devoted almost seventeen times more days to off-farm than to own-account employment. It is not until the average plot size approaches approximately eight hectares that days of on-farm employment exceed those for off-farm.[42] For the region as a whole, 84 percent of all days worked were off-farm.

A recent study, undertaken in the Mixteca region of Oaxaca, illustrates the wide range of productive alternatives available to the rural population. In this very poor and relatively isolated region, the importance of off-plot activity is striking. Although the study does not account for the distribution of days worked, it does provide information on the sources of income. For example, in the case of producers on rain-fed lands, almost 64 percent of their incomes originated in off-plot employment, while an additional 4 percent was derived from artisan production. For the region as a whole, the value of artisan production amounted to 32 percent of all household production, exceeding the 19 percent originating in the value of crop output on rain-fed lands. Furthermore, between a third and a half of the labor force migrates to other regions of the country and to the United States in search of temporary employment. The importance of these activities can be gauged from the size of the remittances that flow from both domestic and foreign destinations of the migrants: more than Mex$2 billion in a recent but unspecified year (probably 1982 or 1983), an amount well in excess of the value of all agricultural and livestock production of the region.[43]

It is thus amply clear that, in virtually all of the regions that have been studied, regions with very different quantitative and qualitative endowments of land, off-farm employment has accounted for a substantial, if not dominant, proportion of the total for both cultivators and their families.

The Demand for Labor and the Evolution of Employment Conditions

As was discussed in Chapter 3, there is a widely held view in Mexico that the countryside shelters a large mass of underemployed labor. Furthermore, it is believed that employment conditions for the agricultural labor force have been deteriorating over time. The lack of growth in output for much of the small-farm sector is held to be a contributing factor. But more important for the recent deterioration has been an agricultural labor force that is alleged to be growing in the face of stagnating, or possibly even declining, labor input requirements for the sector as a whole.

One recently published study of the sector by the Centro de Estudios en Planeación Agropecuaria (CESPA), an agency within the agricultural ministry, points to a steady reduction in labor inputs over time as agricultural technology and cropping patterns have changed. It offers the following estimates of the rates of change in the total number of days of direct labor that are required by cropping and livestock activities:

	Crop production	*Livestock*	*Total*
1946–48 to 1964–66	5.0	5.2	5.1
1964–66 to 1976–78	−2.9	2.8	−1.3

Until the mid-1960s, the rapid expansion of cultivated lands carried with it a great increase in labor requirements. Since then, the rate of expansion in cultivated hectarage has declined substantially and has provided an inadequate offset to the employment effects of technological and cropping changes. According to this view, shrinking labor requirements in the context of a growing rural population have implied a deterioration in job opportunities for the actual and potential agricultural labor force. This decline has motivated the large movement of population from rural areas to the cities, where workers are destined to suffer conditions of underemployment in an overcrowded tertiary sector.[44]

A less pessimistic appraisal of the course of the demand for labor is offered by Teresa Rendón over an interval that overlaps the more recent years of the CESPA study. Over the 1960–73 interval, Rendón calculates the total labor requirements of the annual crop sector to have increased by about 15 percent, and by almost 20 percent for the agricultural sector as a whole.[45] Her contrasting findings are apparently due to the use of technical coefficients that differ from those applied by the CESPA researchers. In addition, her interval includes several years of the early 1960s, during which the sector enjoyed a considerable expansion in the area under cultivation and growth in output; the beginning of the recent CESPA interval corresponds to a period of significantly slower growth in both.

Changes in Technology and Cropping Patterns

As indicated above, secular changes in labor input requirements are generally ascribed to changes in agricultural technology and in cropping patterns. By all indications, the degree of mechanization has been increasing. For example, the use of tractors has shown a significant expansion over the past two decades (see table 4-1). Until 1970, the irrigated districts, with only 15 percent of the cultivated land, employed over half of the tractors. This, however, is not surprising in view of the fact that the irrigated districts contain farm units that are considerably larger than the average in the rain-fed-areas. What is striking, however, is the rapid extension of tractors in the rest of the agricultural sector since 1970. (I will return to a discussion of the possible significance of this increase at a later point in this chapter.)

Broader measures of mechanization provide further evidence of changing technological coefficients. The value of machinery used by each agricultural worker increased from an average of Mex$142,600 in 1940 to Mex$380,500 and Mex$709,900 in 1950 and 1960, respectively, all in 1960 pesos.[46] The rate of increase was much greater on the large private farms, which are also the principal employers of wage labor. The increase on these large units was more than sevenfold over this interval, from Mex$216,700 to Mex$1,506,000 in 1940 and 1960. Over the same interval, little mechanization was reported among private smallholders, while in the ejido sector use of machinery more than tripled. However, these data may understate significantly the use of mechanical traction

Table 4-1. *Number of Tractors by Type of Agricultural Area*

Year	*Total*	*Irrigated districts*	*Rain-fed areas*
1963	63,184	34,553	28,631
1970	89,720	48,506	41,214
1975	119,318	48,174	71,144
1976	134,346	51,342	83,004
1977	148,412	50,020	98,392
1978	158,247	54,442	103,805

Source: CESPA, *El desarrollo agropecuario de México*, vol. 6, *El empleo de mano de obra en las actividades productivas agropecuarias* (Mexico, D.F., 1982), p. 76.

among smallholders, particularly for certain tasks such as plowing. Mechanized services are available for hire, and various regional studies reveal that these are widely utilized by small farmers.[47] Finally, the proportion of land subject to mechanization has increased sharply from 3.9 percent in 1950 to 8.2 and 21.5 percent, respectively, in 1960 and 1970.[48]

Within the irrigated sector, a 25 percent increase occurred in the mechanized hectarage during the 1960–70 decade. This boosted the proportion of land employing mechanical traction to over 50 percent for the first time; another 39 percent of irrigated land was reported to be partially mechanized. The trend was carried forward during the 1970s. For the crop year 1972–73, the mechanized part of the irrigated districts encompassed 57 percent of the total area, while the proportion partially mechanized declined slightly to 35 percent. For the sector as a whole, the rapid extension of mechanization between 1960 and 1978 can be seen in the growth of the depreciated stock of farm machinery at an annual rate of 7.1 percent.[49] The labor displacement effects of mechanization have been estimated by Rendón to have been on the order of an annual reduction of 0.3 percent in sectoral labor input requirements between 1960 and 1973.[50] The CESPA study, however, calculates a much greater displacement effect: 3.2 percent a year from 1964–66 to 1976–78.[51] An alternative measure of displacement holds that each tractor serves to replace from ten to twelve workers.[52]

Changes in cropping patterns have also tended to reduce labor requirements on each unit of cultivated land. Table 4-2 illustrates the changes in cropping patterns according to the degree of labor intensity of production and the associated changes in labor requirements. During the twenty years 1946–66, when the harvested area expanded rapidly in association with the land redistribution process, most of the growth occurred in crops classified as semi-intensive in their use of labor. The crops accounting for most of this increase were corn and beans, traditional subsistence crops, and sugarcane. Significant relative increases also occurred in hectarage and labor devoted to labor-intensive crops, although their absolute importance is overshadowed by the semi-intensive crops. A similar change occurred in the area and labor devoted to extensive crops. Thus, during this period of dynamic expansion of the sector, all three classes of production grew in step with each other.

The more recent 1964–78 period provided a sharp contrast. The area on which semi-intensive crops were grown declined. This was largely attributable to a reduction in the planting of subsistence crops, beans and corn. The increase in hectares used for extensive crops more than offset the decline in the semi-intensive cropping area, as the production of safflower, sorghum, barley, and soybeans expanded. There was a moderate increase

Table 4-2. *Harvested Area and Labor Input Requirements by Degree of Labor Intensity of Land Use, 1946–48 to 1976–78*

	Hectares in crops[a] *(thousands)*				*Labor input required (millions of work days)*			
Crop year	*Intensive*	*Semi-intensive*	*Extensive*	*Total*	*Intensive*	*Semi-intensive*	*Extensive*	*Total*
1946–48	752	4,631	820	6,664[b]	62	159	12	264[c]
1964–66	1,701	10,954	1,779	14,434	145	459	34	638
1976–78	2,171	9,704	3,275	15,150	169	264	33	466
	Annual percentage rate of change							
1946–48 to 1964–66	4.6	4.8	4.4	4.6	4.8	6.1	6.0	5.0
1964–66 to 1976–78	2.1	−1.0	5.2	0.4	1.3	−4.5	−0.2	−2.6

a. Extensive crops require 15 or fewer work days for each cultivated hectare, semi-intensive crops 16–40 days, and intensive crops 41 or more days.

b. The total includes 441,000 unclassified hectares.

c. The total includes 31 million unclassified days.

Sources: CESPA, *El desarrollo agropecuario de México*, vol. 6, *El empleo de mano de obro en las actividades productivas agropecuarias* (México, D.F., 1982), pp. 65–66.

in land devoted to labor-intensive crops, but there was a shift within this sector away from cotton toward alfalfa and some vegetable crops.

The employment effects of these shifts are held to be considerable. The 42 percent decline in labor requirements for the semi-intensive sector far outweighed the expansion of the intensive, and requirements in the extensive sector remained virtually unchanged despite the large increase in hectarage. Thus, the annual net decline in the sector's labor requirements is estimated at 2.6 percent. Within the annual crop subsector, cropping changes are estimated to have reduced labor requirements at an annual rate of 0.5 percent, not much different from the 0.6 percent annual rate offered by Rendón.[53]

Table 4-3 is a summary of the effects that various developments have had on the labor requirements of the sector as calculated by CESPA and Rendón. Rendón's estimates refer to an annual crop sector composed of thirty-one commodities; CESPA's figures refer to groups of eighteen and twenty-one crops, respectively, in the two intervals cited. These selected crops, however, account for the overwhelming proportion of the hectarage dedicated to annual crops, 97.9 and 93.3 percent in the two time

Table 4-3. *Factors Accounting for Changes in Labor Requirements for the Principal Agricultural Crops*
(annual percentage change)

Factor	CESPA[a] 1946–48 to 1964–66	CESPA[a] 1964–66 to 1967–78	Rendón[b] 1960–73
Area harvested	4.7	0.0	0.6
Mechanization	0.8	−3.2	−0.3
Cropping changes	0.1	−0.5	−0.6
Increased yields	n.a.	n.a.	0.5
Total	5.6	−3.7	0.2

n.a. Not available.
a. Includes the twenty-one most important annual crops.
b. Refers to the annual or "short-cycle" crop subsector.
Sources: CESPA, *El empleo de mano de obra*, p. 62; Rendón, "Utilizacion de mano de obra," p. 369.

intervals, 1946–48 to 1964–66 and 1964–66 to 1976–78, respectively. Note that, in Rendón's calculations, the negative impact of mechanization and cropping changes is offset by increases in labor requirements associated with increasing yields per hectare. In addition, Rendón observes that increases in the area cultivated also added to the labor requirements of the sector. The CESPA calculations, however, show a zero contribution from this source during the more recent interval even though more land was reported harvested; this expansion amounted to 3.5 million and 0.965 million hectares between 1960–70 and 1970–77, respectively.[54] Another indicator of the declining labor requirements of the sector is the number of days employed on each cultivated hectare. Rendón estimates that, in the subsector comprising the most important annual crops, labor inputs per hectare declined by 5 percent between 1960 and 1973.[55] For the agricultural sector as a whole, CESPA offers a much sharper decline of 36.7 percent between 1964–66 and 1976–78.[56]

Both of these analyses concur that an increase in the production of perennial crops, largely high-value fruits, has had a favorable impact on employment. Between 1960 and 1973, the hectarage devoted to perennials grew by about one-half, and labor requirements by 40 percent. By and large, the labor input for each hectare cultivated is large—an average of 112 days in 1973.[57] Finally, more labor has been required in the rapidly expanding livestock sector. Given the low labor intensity of the sector, however, its contribution to total employment has remained modest.[58]

Measures of Labor Requirements

The CESPA study offers an estimate of the total direct and indirect labor needs of the agricultural and livestock sector for 1977. The direct requirements amounted to 692.4 million days, of which almost 70 percent were occupied in agricultural crop production. Direct requirements, in turn, represented almost 85 percent of total labor requirements. The indirect labor requirements refer to those tasks ancillary to cropping activities, such as administration, maintenance, and repair of machinery. Labor needs for this type of work were estimated at 103.1 million days, or 14 percent of the total. Finally, 23.3 million days were occupied in construction and other investment activities. The sum total of days required was 818.8 million.[59] Of course, given the seasonality of agricultural production, the demand for workers is not evenly distributed over the year. Peak months of employment are associated with planting and harvesting seasons: June through August for planting and cultivation, and October and November for harvesting. The months of lowest activity are January and February. The peak month of July in 1977 required 84.4 million days, 69 percent more than the trough month of February.[60]

On the basis of field studies undertaken in 1977 by two other government agencies, the CESPA study reports the duration of employment, in months, of the agricultural labor force (table 4-4). As can be observed, the two sets of findings show considerable divergence in the distribution of individuals by duration of agricultural employment. The CESPA authors indicate their belief that the FEDA/BANRURAL results represent a more faithful portrayal of rural reality, although the reasons for this conclusion are not spelled out. In both data sets, approximately 0.5 million members of the estimated agricultural labor force remain unaccounted for. These workers are presumed to represent those who stand in the most precarious position in the labor market and are the most underemployed. Although more than half of the labor force appears to be employed at least eight months of the year, the number of days worked in each month is estimated to have averaged only fifteen. The implication is that even this relatively "permanent" portion of the agricultural labor force is not "fully employed." Beyond identifying the above-mentioned half million workers as marginal, however, the study makes no atempt to quantify the degree of underutilization of the labor force. It is presumed to be self-evident that the available labor resources are seriously underemployed and will continue to be so in the near to intermediate future.

The regional case studies by René Barbosa-Ramírez during the middle of the 1970s did make an effort to measure the volume of unutilized labor resources in five of the six regions studied. These crude estimates suggested

Table 4-4. *Agricultural Labor Force by Number of Months Worked in 1977*

Months worked	Reported by PROCAP		Reported by FEDA/BANRURAL	
	Number	Percent	Number	Percent
1–3	192,660	2.9	797,297	12.2
3–6	488,785	7.5	985,398	15.0
6–8	33,387	0.5	620,886	9.5
8	2,874,700	43.8	n.a.	n.a.
8 or more	n.a.	n.a.	3,726,730	56.8
12	2,340,746	35.7	n.a.	n.a.
Unaccounted	626,722	9.6	426,689	6.5
Total	6,557,000	100.0	6,557,000	100.0

n.a. Not available.
Source: CESPA, *El empleo de mano de obra*, p. 158.

that the proportion of the "available" labor time that was actually used ranged between 32.8 and 57.2 percent; only one of the five surveyed regions recorded a proportion greater than 50 percent.[61] The study acknowledged that the time not occupied in production on or off the family plot could not be equated with the conventional concept of unemployment, since the actual availability of time for employment was not universally determined. Nevertheless, it was held in most of the regional accounts that these crude estimates sufficed to indicate the seriousness of the employment problem. (I will return to a discussion of some interesting aspects of this study below.)

A set of measures for labor utilization provided by the CESPA study suggests that rural underemployment has increased in recent years as a result of declining labor input requirements and growth of the agricultural labor force. These measures take the form of an estimate of the average number of days of annual employment for each agricultural worker at three points in time and is derived from the corresponding technical coefficients of labor inputs. According to these estimates, the average number of days worked increased sharply from 77 to 168 during two decades of dynamic growth, 1946–48 to 1964–66. Subsequently, the trend was reversed; by 1976–78, the days worked had declined to only 120. This number is probably understated, however, because the size of the agricultural labor force was substantially overestimated.[62] A more realistic labor force size would yield an average work year of 132 days. However, these estimates are limited to days of direct labor. They omit days spent in indirect or investment activities that account for about twenty-three additional working days.

Another widely cited source would place the deterioration of employment opportunities for landless wage earners even earlier than does the CESPA study. Reyes Osorio concluded that the number of days worked by wage laborers declined from 190 in 1950 to only 100 in 1960.[63] This estimate was based on agricultural census reports of total wages paid divided by the average agricultural legal minimum wage. The total number of utilized days thus obtained was then divided by the number of agricultural laborers to derive the average number of days worked by each.

There are plausible reasons for believing that this procedure yields a decline that is exaggerated. The legal minimum wage is not a reliable guide to the wages actually paid at all points in time. Particularly when it departs substantially from the market price of labor, the legal minimum is likely to be widely ignored by employers, and especially by small farmers.[64] With respect to the two years employed in Reyes Osorio's estimate, the legal minimum wage in 1950 reflected a decade-long decline in real terms and probably was close to the market wage. In contrast, the real legal minimum was increased substantially during the 1950s; it reached a level 40 percent above the 1950 minimum by 1960.[65] To the extent that the market wage lagged behind the legal minimum, the procedure used by Reyes Osorio would understate the days of employment in 1960. Indeed, a preliminary version of this same study explicitly acknowledges a divergence between the legal minimum and the actual prevailing wage and suggests that use of the former results in an underestimation of days worked of from 10 to 20 percent.[66]

Although one might quibble over details of the various statistical measures enumerated here, they all seem to point to a growing gap between days of labor required by the agricultural sector and the available labor supply. It is virtually unanimously concluded that these trends reflect a deterioration of employment conditions for the rural labor force and that the sector faces an increasing volume of surplus labor. The CESPA report summarizes its finding as follows:[67]

> [As a result of technological changes that have been enumerated] an important part of the total mandays available to the sector were not employed. . . . Agricultural workers were afforded limited opportunities for year-round employment. This signifies that there have accumulated very high levels of visible underemployment and unemployment among those persons who found it impossible to be employed over the entire productive process. The scarcity of employment opportunities was aggravated by the agricultural crisis faced by the country [that is,

the relative stagnation of the sector since the mid-1960s; translation mine].

One of the most important government agricultural planning documents of recent years also views the principal goal of the agricultural sector as that of increasing the demand for labor in order to alleviate the underutilization of the existing labor force.[68]

> During the past ten years, agriculture has lost some of its dynamism and a number of problems have arisen. The chief symptoms of this decline include the need to import large quantities of grains during the last two years, a fall in exports, an increase in rural unemployment, and the existence of unsatisfactory rural living conditions. . . . A review of employment in the sector reveals that: (1) during the 1950s employment opportunities increased, generally speaking, as rapidly as the working-age population, so that there was no increase in either unemployment or underemployment; (2) during the 1960s available jobs increased more slowly than the working-age population; and (3) at the present time about 40 percent of the potential work force is not being used effectively. A number of studies have yielded the same conclusion with regard to the rate of agricultural underemployment. . . . The challenge at the present time is how to increase manpower absorption and at the same time narrow the income gap between [the large commercial farmers and poorest segments of the agricultural labor force].

Employment and Underutilization

In view of the overwhelming consensus among Mexican observers in their assessment of the gravity of the employment problem within the agricultural sector, it may appear foolhardy for me to offer one that runs counter to the prevailing view. Yet I cannot help but feel that the analyses of the employment conditions of the rural population on which the somber conclusions are based have been too narrowly focused and have tended to overlook considerations that might lead to a less distressing set of conclusions. Two major weaknesses of these analyses can be identified. One derives from estimates of the supply of labor available to the sector. The other is the general omission from consideration of that part of the rural supply of labor that is diverted to nonagricultural labor markets. This diversion reduces the number of workers who are idle and available for employment within agriculture.

Estimates of the Agricultural Labor Force

The measurement of the agricultural labor force poses formidable difficulties. A large part of the difficulty stems from the seasonal nature of production. As noted above, the number of persons employed and the number of days expended vary sharply over the year. One can presume that those individuals employed during the trough month of the year represent a sort of core, or permanent, part of the agricultural labor force. But what about the remainder—what is the nature of their attachment to the agricultural labor force?

Consider the CESPA estimates of monthly employment. During the trough months, an estimated 3.7 million workers are employed and may be assumed to work throughout most of the year. In table 4-4, this number corresponds to those laborers employed at least eight months of the year according to the FEDA/BANRURAL source. Supplementing this core are workers employed for shorter periods. In the months of peak employment, their numbers rise by 2.4 million and yield a total employed labor force of approximately 6.1 million.[69] This supplementary labor force thus represents about 40 percent of the total in the peak months. If the seasonally employed persons in agriculture are considered to be available for year-round employment within—and only within—the sector, then the conclusion that has been reached by various observers (that 40 percent of the agricultural labor force is underemployed) would clearly follow. However, can the assumption that the peak labor force is available for employment throughout the year be considered valid? No representative data are offered that permit us to reach definitive conclusions, but I consider it unlikely that this assumption is a realistic one.

The difficulties involved in estimating the size of the agricultural labor force in terms of the work days available are illustrated by the series of regional studies undertaken by René Barbosa-Ramírez. In the first of the regions reviewed, the valley of Toluca in the state of México, the available days were defined as 252 days in the year times the number of family members between the ages of 15 and 55 without regard to sex.[70] In the second, the Mixteca Baja in Oaxaca, the age group was extended to include all those between 12 and 55 while the work year remained fixed at 252 days.[71] In the third region, Valsequillo in Puebla, this same age group was taken, but the work year was extended to 300 days.[72] The study of Los Tuxtlas, Veracruz, adopted still another criterion for calculating the available labor supply; it included all those who, during the nine-month reference period, had worked for at least ten days with or without remuneration.[73] The work year again was defined as 300 days. Finally, in the study of Las Huastecas, San Luis Potosí, the labor force was defined simply as consisting of those who had worked at least thirty days during the reference period.[74] Obviously, the absence of a universally accepted definition of the labor force is bound to give rise to different and noncomparable measures of unemployment or underemployment.

It is interesting to note the evolution of perceptions of Ramírez-Barbosa with respect to the size of the rural labor surplus. By the second phase of the study, which coincided with the Valsequillo study, he began to harbor some doubts about the legitimacy of the measurement procedures followed, particularly after the publication of a pilot study done for a national household survey of incomes and expenditures. That study found that "a surprisingly low proportion of the idle population was willing to work" (translation mine).[75] The author then resolved to undertake a much more careful investigation of the availability for employment of the population of labor force age. The change in procedure was not implemented fully until the final regional study was undertaken. While the findings are clearly limited to the region of Las Huastecas, they serve to raise strong cautionary signals about the usefulness of the traditional methods of estimating rural labor surpluses.

As indicated above, the available labor force was originally estimated in an arbitrary manner by assuming that everyone of labor force age was available for employment for a full year. How far this assumption falls short of reality was illustrated in Las Huastecas when various subgroups of this population were subjected to more careful examination. For example, the population of labor force age that had not been actively employed for at least thirty days during the reference period included 9,258 individuals. Of these, 92.8 percent stated they were not available for employment. Of the remainder, 587 individuals expressed an interest in full-time employment and 78 in only occasional employment. Instead of 2.8 million work days available fom this population, no more than 190,000 were actually available.[76]

In the case of individuals who are employed, there is a common procedure for estimating the days available for additional employment. The normal work year is defined as consisting of a number of days (300, for example); from that is subtracted the number of days required for the cultivation of the family plot. Sometimes the days of employment off the plot may also be deducted. For either case, the remainder is defined as time available for employment. In Las Huastecas, the head of the family, as well as the other family members who were employed on the family plot, were asked to enumerate the number of work days lost from productive activities on the plot during the year. In the stratum comprising nuclear families, the average family head reported an average of sixty-seven such days. Of these, twenty-six days were occupied in ritualistic or civic obligations and on personal errands; thirteen days were lost because of illness, eighteen to inclement weather, and only ten to a lack of work. All other employed family members reported an average of twenty-four days for each household not spent in productive activity on the family plot, of which five were attributed to a lack of work to be done. While the number of days lost by the producer and the members of extended family and other forms of household organization did vary somewhat, the distribution of days lost for various reasons was quite similar.[77]

About one-third of those individuals who worked on the family plot also reported off-plot employment. These workers were asked why they sought outside employment as well as why they did not seek more such employment. The most frequently offered response to the first question was a desire for more money. Over half of the family heads and 40 percent of family members so responded. A related reason of "necessity" was given by an additional 12 to 15 percent of the respondents. Lack of work on the family plot or insufficiency of land together accounted for most of the remaining answers. Of greater interest, however, are the reasons cited for not seeking more outside employment. Seventy-eight percent of the household heads and 64 percent of other employed household members cited the time-consuming cultivation of their plots as limiting their availability for additional employment. Only 14 percent of the family heads and 17.5 percent of the members found the absence of employment opportunities to be a limiting factor.[78]

Estimates of Unemployment

The study concluded by estimating the volume of available and unemployed labor time. The total days available numbered 4.939 million. After deducting the number of days worked and those voluntarily dedicated to nonwork activities, 1.120 million days of involuntary unemployment were left. This total was composed of three separate components. The first—459,900—was derived from the "registered" or reported days lost from on-plot employment mentioned above. These days of "involuntary unemployment" included days lost to illness or inclement weather and amounted to 71 percent of the total. Only 29 percent of this measure of involuntary unemployment consisted of days when no work was available on the plot. One may question whether days lost to illness or inclement weather represent a measure of open unemployment in the sense that workers are then available for employment in the labor market.

The second major component of estimated "unemployment" came from family workers (other than the head of the household) who had blocks of unaccounted time. Those who had been established as "workers" were assumed to have 300 days of available time for employment just as did the family heads. But household members could not account fully for the disposition of time between employment and registered days of voluntary and "involuntary" unemployment (as defined above); there remained 60 days per household for which an accounting could not be made. The authors of the study did not establish the actual availability for employment of these days but adopted the normative assumption that the behavior of these individuals should match that of household heads, for whom all time was successfully allocated. The total unemployed days yielded by this procedure amounted to 584,522. This is obviously an outside or maximum figure, for it may be questioned whether all of the unaccounted days were actually available for employment.

Finally, the remaining 73,400 days of available time were ascribed to the 587 individuals who were not currently working but who indicated they were available for immediate employment.[79] The sum of the "unemployed days" over the several household subgroups amounted to 23.8 percent of the estimated total available work days. This figure can be compared with a 63.2 percent unemployment rate that would result from the crude procedure followed in the earlier regional studies. (According to that method, the available labor resources were defined in terms of the product of all the household members of labor force age times 300 days.)

Even this lower estimate overstates the quantity of surplus labor available for employment outside the household's own farm unit. As noted above, work days lost because of illness are not available for employment anywhere. Neither are those lost to inclement weather since such days are not predictable events or of sufficient duration to permit or justify a job search. Over half of the total days of "open unemployment" have been so designated because they were not worked by household members and could not otherwise be explained. Of course, there is no way of determining the extent to which such idleness was voluntary or involuntary. The fact that only a modest minority reported that it did not seek more off-plot employment because of an absence of job opportunities suggests that at least some of this idleness was intentional. But, even if it was not voluntary, whether it was time that could have been made available for employment elsewhere depends on the frequency and duration of the idle periods. Unless idleness occurs in blocks of time uninterrupted by on-plot work obligations, the days not worked may not effectively be "marketable." Another factor is that the costs of job search may loom too high relative to the earnings that can be anticipated from a brief period of outside employment. This would seem to be the case particularly when available job opportunities lie beyond a commuting radius of home.

A more meaningful estimate of the rate of open unemployment can be achieved with a few adjustments. For example, one procedure would alter the size of the pool of "available" work days by excluding those days lost to voluntary causes, illness, and inclement weather. Unemployed days would then include those days idle from lack of work on the family plot plus the available days of workers not currently employed but desirous of employment. To these days one might add some proportion (such as one-half) of the days of family workers for which no accounting can be offered. Calculated in this way, the unemployment rate is reduced to only 11.5 percent. While this may either understate or overstate somewhat the actual rate, depending on how one wishes to treat the unaccounted time of family workers, the absolute value of this ratio would still prove to be far lower than that generally assumed to hold in the countryside. It would also come closer to approximating the volume of labor services likely to be available in the labor market.

A more recent survey of employment and underemployment in agriculture was undertaken on a state-by-state basis by the Banco Nacional de Crédito Rural (BANRURAL) during 1980–82.[80] The study attempted to account for all days worked as well as for those not worked by all those employed on the sampled plots at the time of the survey. The study adopted 300 days worked as a measure of full employment. Multiplying the number of interviewed workers by 300 thus yielded the total number of work days assumed to be available for employment. Of this total 20.5 percent were not worked, but almost half of all days not worked were voluntarily forgone. Although 10.4 percent of all the available days were involuntarily idled, not all were available for alternative employment. Almost a fourth of the days lost from work involuntarily were attributable to illness or inclement weather. Only those idle days associated with the seasonality of agricultural production might be considered available. In the eighteen states for which the research reports were available, such days represented only 8.1 percent of the days in a fully employed year.

Hired Labor

Other observations support the view that households harbor limited amounts of surplus labor that is readily available for employment. For example, one of the features of peasant agriculture that is strikingly documented by the Barbosa-Ramírez study is the prevalence of hired labor on even the smallest of plots in most parts of the country. Given the size of rural households and the number of family members of productive ages, one would have expected that the labor requirements of family plots could and would be satisfied by the household unit itself. Yet, this does not seem to be the case. For example, in the region of Valsequillo, Puebla, workers were hired for more than half the days expended on both the private and ejido plots. On average, the cultivator provided 27 percent of the total days expended, other family members another 17 percent, while hired labor accounted for 56 percent of the total.[81] As noted earlier, only a small proportion of the total days worked by the cultivator and other family members was devoted to the family plot. Farm households clearly preferred to hire themselves out in rural or urban labor markets and to substitute hired labor for their own. Apparently, there was still no shortage of household labor time available for cultivating the plot. The study estimated that no more than 30 percent of the total days potentially available from household members of labor force age was actually engaged productively.

In the region of Mixteca Baja, Oaxaca, one-fourth of all the labor was hired, in spite of estimates that only 18 percent of the time of available household workers was employed on family plots, and less than half of the available days was occupied productively either on or off the family holding. In this case, too, a majority of employed days was off the family plot.[82] In the Toluca valley, half of the labor requirements were met by hired labor, while family households allocated over 80 percent of their productive time to off-farm employment. According to the study, the number of family members in the sampled households who were idle (other than heads of households) amounted to twice the volume of actually employed labor.[83] In view of this potentially available labor, the decision to hire seems incongruous unless those "idle" labor resources do not really consider themselves available for employment of any kind.

Several possible explanations have been advanced for the prevalence of so much hired labor in spite of the presumably large surpluses of family labor. In some regions, the growing season is so short that labor inputs must be concentrated in large amounts within brief intervals. At such times, these requirements exceed the supply of family labor. This explanation would be more convincing were it not for the large quantities of household labor that are potentially available and probably could be pressed into service for short periods of time.

Another explanation offered for areas such as Mixteca Baja with large indigenous population concentrations points to the breakdown of traditional practices of labor exchange within the community. Given the survival of traditional production techniques, the size and timing of labor requirements have remained unaltered. The increasing monetization of economic activity, however, renders an exchange of free services unacceptable. Wage labor has come to replace bartered labor even though no change has occurred in the patterns of family and nonfamily inputs of labor.[84] Although some part of the hired labor may be attributed to this change, it is not likely to account for a large part of the hiring. If hired labor reflected merely a monetization of a traditional exchange of labor services, then one would expect the landholders to report a figure for the time they worked as farm day laborers that was comparable to the number of days they used hired labor. Yet very few days are so reported. Indeed, several strata of farm households in the Reyes Osorio study reported no days at all in farm wage employment for their members even though they were employers of wage laborers.

Alternatively, the prevalence of a large amount of hired labor in some heavily populated regions has been attributed to payments made to family members, primarily adult sons who had little or no land of their own.[85] While this may provide a partial explanation, it is unlikely to explain a significant part of the hired input. For example, on the basis of his six regional studies, Barbosa-Ramírez concluded that family labor is unremunerated almost in its entirety.[86] Finally, some interviewed observers attributed the prevalence of so much wage labor to a concern of the rural communities for the economic status of the landless. In order to avoid extreme deprivation, the landless are hired as a way of effecting an income redistribution within the community. Thus, even the poor are willing to share with those who are poorer still. In addition, there is status attached to being an employer of labor, so that this form of charity is viewed as yielding some psychic rewards.

Perhaps more persuasive than these explanations is one that views the hiring of labor as a rational decision arrived at by a comparison of the cost of hiring labor with the opportunity cost of the time of landholders and their families. The field studies of rural Mexican communities report a very sensitive perception of the opportunity cost of time and household responses leading to an allocation of labor that most efficiently realizes the desired level of family income.[87] To the extent that the rural labor force is not homogeneous, individuals will have different opportunity costs. Many landholders may find it more profitable to accept employment off-farm and hire lower-wage laborers to cultivate their plot. A not unreasonable assumption is that, as a class, landholders are likely to possess greater endowments of human capital and labor market connections then the landless rural labor force. Thus, the existence of an active market for wage labor suggests that labor is a scarce resource even in poor rural communities. This conclusion would be consistent with studies of some resident field researchers who have observed relatively little involuntary underemployment. It also jibes with the experience of the Plan Puebla program which encountered resistance among subsistence farmers to technological changes that would increase labor requirements.[88]

To be sure, most of the literature concentrates on households cultivating their own land and ignores the plight of landless laborers. If one were to accept the observation of Reyes Osorio, cited earlier in this chapter, that the number of days of annual employment had declined to only 100 by 1960, this would indeed be indicative of a precarious situation. However, those estimates were limited to days of agricultural employment and ignored all others. Another study suggests that the number of days of annual employment increases substantially if account is taken of all work sources. For example, in the mid-1960s, landless laborers reported total number of days worked annually ranging from 177 in Laguna, to 226 in several zones of Michoacán, and 238 in Tlaxcala.[89] Although this would still leave a significant number of days potentially available for employment, there is no way of knowing what proportion of these would actually have been made available.

Evaluation of the Findings

If one takes an objective view of the economic conditions of the agricultural population at a moment in time, there is much reason for concern. A more encouraging assessment might emerge, however, if one places the changes observable in the agricultural sector in a secular perspective. It is generally accepted that these changes add up to a gradual process of modernization of Mexican agriculture. I would add to this that they are also indicative of a greater degree of integration of agricultural and nonagricultural labor markets. What I find interesting about the assessments made of these developments is that they are held to be intensifying the "employment problem" of the rural sector. The increase in mechanization is seen as causing a reduction in labor utilization. Analytically, this is treated as an autonomously determined independent variable that expands the ranks of the openly unemployed. One could legitimately ask, however, whether the line of causation does indeed run from technological change to unemployment. In the case of mechanization, for example, one might instead hypothesize that the recent acceleration is a response to changes in the availability of labor and to a changing price ratio of labor to machinery. This hypothesis has not been posed and so remains untested as far as I know.

Yet there is a recognition that relative factor prices can determine how much labor and machinery will be employed, even though no effort has been made to explore the actual contribution of changing prices to past changes in the factor proportions employed.[90] Some authors attribute the extension of mechanization to government encouragement and to the subsidization of capital purchases by low-interest loans and tariff-free imports.[91] Although such support may have played a role, to be decisive it would have to be shown that the price of machinery was falling continually relative to that of labor as the pace of mechanization accelerated. Unfortunately, the prices of farm machinery and of farm wage labor are not available over time; therefore, relative price trends cannot be established. And, of course, since all observers of the agricultural sector have harbored the conviction that it is endowed with a large surplus of labor, the possibility that an absolute or relative scarcity of labor could have motivated the increase in mechanization has never even been considered. Yet this possibility should not be so lightly discarded.

Similarly, cropping changes in the direction of less labor-intensive crops are viewed as autonomous developments that reduce labor requirements and contribute to the underutilization of agricultural labor. There are straws in the wind, however, that suggest that the cropping changes may reflect the rational response of output to changing demand for different food commodities as well as to the opportunity cost of labor to the agricultural sector.

One of the striking findings of a recent study of this sector is the importance of livestock and poultry as a source of income to small farmers, those with fewer than four hectares of land.[92] In twelve of the twenty-five states surveyed, the income from these sources exceeded that from crop sales, usually by a substantial margin; the addition to crop sales of the value of home consumption would not change this relationship. In several of the other states, livestock and poultry sales were significant in size even though they were outweighed by the value of crop production. Earlier in this chapter, it was noted that surveys of the sector during the 1960s valued livestock and poultry output at no more than 50 percent of the value of crops. If that was an accurate estimate of small farm output, then it would appear that even such plots, which one might expect to be devoted to subsistence production and cultivated in a labor-intensive fashion, are increasingly being devoted to animal and poultry production. Hence an increased demand for forage crops would follow, and an expansion of production of such crops and of livestock could be expected to displace that of the traditional subsistence crops of the small farm sector.

Still remaining, however, is the question of why these changes have occurred, especially at the level of the small farm unit. Unfortunately, it is impossible to offer definitive explanations. But it is possible to advance some plausible propositions for which some support can be found in many of the empirical studies of the sector that have been cited.

The following is one scenario that might reasonably be expected to unfold in an economy that has been undergoing a high and steady rate of economic growth and that has been characterized by large disparities in earnings between agriculture and nonagricultural employment. As will be demonstrated more clearly in Chapter 7, urban wages, even in the low-skill labor market, appear to have been rising steadily since 1940 and have thus increased the opportunity cost of agricultural labor. Those rural residents with the demographic characteristics required for successful employment in the nonagricultural sector will have strong incentives to seek employment there. They will work first on a seasonal basis and later, once the probability of success is perceived to have exceeded a certain level, perhaps on a permanent basis. To the extent that the value of output of the vast majority of small plots had stagnated at very low levels between 1950 and 1970 (as indicated by some of the studies cited earlier in this chapter), the gap between farm earnings and potential nonfarm earnings would have increased and thus created a greater incentive to shift from agricultural to other employment. Such a shift might then precipitate changes in the organization of agricultural production. Plots yielding very low returns could simply be abandoned or consolidated with other plots into larger, more economic units either through sale or rental. During a transition period, cultivators could devote increasing proportions of their time to nonagricultural work while continuing to cultivate their land by using wage labor or that of family members. Alternatively, the labor requirements of production on smallholdings could be reduced by changes in cropping patterns toward less labor-intensive products; forage crops and livestock or poultry production would so qualify. Such a shift in output would also be motivated by the high income elasticity of demand for meat products in the face of rising average family incomes in the country as a whole.

Intersectoral mobility of labor forestalls an increase in the size of the agricultural labor force even as the harvested area continues to expand. Indeed, the effective supply of labor to the sector may actually be declining if a numerically stable labor force allocated a shrinking proportion of its available working days to agricultural production in favor of nonfarm employment. In such a context, a rising land-labor ratio also serves as a stimulus to the adoption of technological and cropping changes that are labor-saving. The use of farm machinery would be encouraged as would a shift to less labor-intensive crops. Increases in output per unit of labor employed would follow. In view of the rising opportunity cost of labor to the agricultural sector and its increasing relative scarcity, it would be reasonable to expect the price of agricultural labor to rise. An added stimulus to this process would thus be provided, especially if this price rises relative to that of farm machinery services. Gradually, the flow of labor out of the sector would be expected to lead to an intensification of the land consolidation process. This would continue until units were formed that could yield incomes competitive with those available in other sectors. Clearly, this process of adjustment is likely to be a gradual one, but one could argue that it has already been under way for some three decades and that it accelerated during the decade of the 1970s.

Consider the data presented in table 4-5. Up until 1970, there was a steady expansion in the area harvested and in the number of plots, expansion that outran the growth of the agricultural labor force. This resulted in a gradual increase in the land-labor ratio until, in 1970, it stood 67 percent above the 1940 level. One of the striking features of the table is that, in spite of the increased number of agricultural plots, the number of self-employed farmers has been declining since 1950. This has been particularly sharp among private farmers since the absolute number of such plots declined visibly by almost 30 percent between 1950 and 1970. However, the table masks the probability that, in spite of a notable increase in the number of ejido plots (804,000, or 58 percent), the number of self-employed ejidatarios has also declined, perhaps significantly. By 1970, the number of plots outnumbered the number of self-employed farmers by 1.1 million.

Underlying these observable changes may be any or all of the hypothetical adjustments that were described above as possible concomitants of dynamic economic growth. For example, small private farmers are reported to be abandoning the cultivation of their holdings completely in favor of nonagricultural employment. If they sell their holdings to other surviving farmers, the land and potential incomes of the latter should increase. If they retain their land, they may continue to cultivate it with hired labor and family members. This would be profitable as long as the owner's wage in off-farm employment exceeds the wage of rural day labor and the reservation price of family labor. Ejidatarios, of course, cannot sell their land and may forfeit their usufruct if the land is not cultivated. They

Table 4-5. *Number of Harvested Hectares, Cultivated Plots, and Agricultural Workers, 1940–70*
(thousands)

Year	Area harvested (hectares)	Plots			Labor force			
		Private	*Ejidos*	*Total*	*Self-employed*	*Laborers*	*Family workers*	*Total*
1940	6,637.15	1,211	1,223	2,434	1,726	1,913	192	3,831
1950	8,528.00	1,366	1,378	2,744	2,905	1,567	340	4,812
1960	11,297.00	1,346	1,532	2,869	2,340	2,204	504	5,048
1970	14,840.00	997	2,182	3,179	2,076	2,499	528	5,103

Source: CESPA, *El empleo de mano de obra*, tables 14 and 15.

therefore have less incentive to abandon the land, and one would not expect to find the number of ejido plots declining. The plots may continue to be cultivated with hired and family labor, however, even as the ejidatario himself shifts to off-farm employment.

Therefore, some part of the increased discrepancy between the number of agricultural plots and that of self-employed farmers may reflect an increase in the average number of plots cultivated by each individual farmer. Part may also be ascribed to the substitution of hired and family labor on lands that are retained even though the head of household is no longer actively engaged in exploiting them. Unfortunately, the agricultural censuses do not permit us to delineate the contribution of each of these factors—plots are recorded individually even though several may belong to or be cultivated by a single individual. Thus, any changes that may be occurring in the pattern of land ownership or usage are obscured.

The presumption that farm households have been heavily involved in off-farm employment has, of course, been substantiated by numerous studies, some of which have already been cited above. There is no way of establishing empirically the secular trend in the proportion of available work time devoted to off-farm employment. One can estimate the rate at which entire rural households have abandoned the countryside in favor of urban residence (internal migration is the subject of Chapter 5). We can also observe the considerable importance attributable to sources of income other than own-plot production for the current farm population, especially households with plots of under four hectares. In several states, the average income received from off-farm employment and family remittances exceeds that from the sale of farm produce.[93] On the one hand, this should facilitate a shift from subsistence to market-oriented production. On the other, it may reflect a state of transition for rural households as their status shifts from agricultural to nonagricultural producers.

It is reasonable to expect that this process will continue into the future if the overall growth rate of the Mexican economy can be restored to levels approximating the past secular rate. The relative attractiveness of nonagricultural wages should continue to stimulate mobility out of agriculture. Viewed from the opposite perspective, in order for agricultural production to be worthwhile, it will have to yield an increased return to labor and at least keep pace with returns in alternative occupations. This is likely to be possible only as the agricultural sector undergoes an increasing commercialization, with a progressive consolidation of smallholdings into larger units capable of providing an income competitive with that obtainable from without the sector.

This process seems to be well under way. I have noted the increasing land-labor ratio with its likely consequences for labor productivity. I can also point to earnings data reported by the 1970 and 1980 population censuses; they suggest that earnings in agriculture have increased significantly relative to those in other sectors. I have compared the changes in the median monthly earnings derived from agricultural employment with those originating in the nonagricultural sectors from 1970 to 1980 by state. Although some questions may be raised about the quality of the reported earnings data, these do seem to evince a large and reassuring measure of internal consistency.[94]

As can be seen from table 4-6, median agricultural earnings in twenty-six of the thirty-two states increased considerably more rapidly than those originating in the rest of the economy. In four other states (Colima, Quintana Roo, Sinaloa, and Sonora), three of which were relatively high-earnings states, income in the two sectors advanced at roughly the same rate. In only two, Nayarit and Baja California Sur, which boasted relatively high agricultural earnings in 1970, did agricultural income lag nonagricultural over the decade. Equally significant is the observation that the largest relative increases in reported agricultural earnings occurred in states such as Durango, Querétaro, Zacatecas, and San Luis Potosí, in which the absolute levels of farm earnings were lowest in 1970.

In other words, a process of narrowing differentials in income from agricultural and nonagricultural employment appears to have occurred within states during the decade as well as a narrowing between rich and poor states. The latter tendency is confirmed by the strong negative correlation between the income level in 1970 and the percentage change in the median income between 1970 and 1980. The correlation coefficients for the agricultural and nonagricultural sectors are -0.51 and -0.63, respectively, both significant at the 1 percent level. Furthermore, the degree of dispersion, among states, as measured by the coefficient of variation also declined, from 49.9 to 41.1 percent in agriculture and from 24.5 to 18.9 percent in the nonagricultural sectors. The intrasectoral and intersectoral narrowing that appears to have occurred would be expected to occur only as labor supply conditions generally become "tighter." Certainly the observable narrowing trend would not be expected to occur in a rural environment characterized by "surplus labor" readily available for employment. To the extent that the relatively rapid increases in incomes of labor force members reflect increasing prices of labor services, these might represent contributory explanations for the accelerated pace of mechanization and cropping changes.

Table 4-6. *Median Monthly Earnings by State*
(pesos)

	Total			*Agricultural*			*Nonagricultural*		
State	*1970*	*1980*	*Percent change*	*1970*	*1980*	*Percent change*	*1970*	*1980*	*Percent change*
Aguascalientes	492.8	3,422.4	594.46	359.3	2,612.8	627.27	670.0	3,734.3	457.39
Baja California N.	1,332.8	5,917.7	344.00	929.6	4,816.7	418.13	1,414.3	6,104.6	331.62
Baja California S.	899.0	5,957.9	562.69	692.7	4,129.0	496.09	1,050.6	6,508.2	519.47
Campeche	451.8	3,608.4	698.74	340.5	2,560.5	651.91	659.3	4,376.0	563.72
Coahuila	685.1	4,348.1	534.63	377.9	2,323.3	514.71	858.7	4,769.8	455.48
Colima	581.6	4,269.7	634.18	531.2	3,383.6	537.01	768.4	4,878.8	534.92
Chiapas	247.0	2,671.6	981.50	215.1	1,919.0	792.17	506.5	3,601.3	611.00
Chihuahua	719.1	4,532.1	530.27	402.9	3,233.2	702.53	896.5	4,788.8	434.17
Durango	426.8	3,522.5	725.36	292.3	2,366.0	709.30	703.6	4,193.6	496.05
Federal District	1,027.8	5,843.1	468.47	598.9	5,637.4	841.23	1,053.4	5,599.3	431.53
Guanajuato	405.5	3,258.8	703.60	259.5	2,135.1	742.00	682.2	3,726.3	446.21
Guerrero	270.9	3,160.0	1,066.36	171.7	1,592.1	827.42	733.9	3,917.0	433.73
Hidalgo	272.2	2,395.4	780.06	194.1	1,213.8	525.18	675.3	3,641.0	439.13
Jalisco	614.7	4,427.8	620.34	422.6	2,829.5	569.51	803.2	4,771.7	494.10

México	421.5	4,124.9	878.54	265.7	1,981.2	645.72	753.3	4,741.7	529.48
Michoacán	381.1	3,127.6	720.64	291.7	2,446.4	738.57	606.9	3,744.0	516.91
Morelos	492.1	3,623.9	636.48	382.3	2,386.8	524.40	790.3	4,256.4	438.61
Nayarit	554.8	3,398.1	512.46	531.7	2,960.3	456.81	740.7	4,213.7	468.86
Nuevo León	883.3	5,354.9	506.22	391.8	2,818.9	619.41	970.6	5,636.5	480.69
Oaxaca	187.6	2,291.9	1,121.69	159.8	1,261.7	689.53	426.7	3,300.8	673.55
Puebla	287.5	2,693.1	836.65	198.6	1,325.3	567.16	687.9	3,920.1	469.88
Querétaro	391.2	3,618.6	825.03	230.2	2,083.2	804.90	689.0	4,330.2	528.47
Quintana Roo	507.5	4,507.4	788.23	332.8	1,979.8	494.82	893.1	5,322.9	495.98
San Luis Potosí	307.0	2,771.0	802.58	213.1	1,524.4	615.33	637.7	3,702.3	480.58
Sinaloa	742.8	4.496.5	505.35	615.4	3,533.3	474.12	904.2	5,210.1	467.23
Sonora	883.5	4,946.0	459.84	753.6	4,142.9	449.78	998.6	5,535.1	454.28
Tabasco	406.9	3,879.1	853.36	308.6	2,428.7	686.95	804.3	5,398.8	571.23
Tamaulipas	720.7	4,499.1	524.25	414.1	2,783.1	572.00	904.4	4,865.7	438.01
Tlaxcala	367.9	2,925.8	695.29	263.4	1,739.3	560.43	630.9	3,520.7	458.04
Veracruz	424.0	3,157.7	644.69	292.6	1,971.2	573.67	833.9	4,480.4	437.26
Yucatán	272.0	2,609.3	859.26	189.7	1,129.2	495.21	602.0	3,528.5	486.13
Zacatecas	312.4	2,785.2	791.43	233.5	2,147.7	819.79	553.2	3,353.4	506.13

Sources: Secretaría de Industria y Comercio, Dirección General de Estadística, *IX Censo de población, 1970* (Mexico, D.F., 1972); and Secretaría de Programación y Presupuesto, *X Censo de población y vivienda, 1980* (Mexico, D.F., 1983, 1984), 32 vols.

Summary

Although it has been popular to describe the agricultural sector as the repository of considerable open unemployment and underemployment, the evidence seems to suggest that this perception is not entirely correct. It is true that earnings derivable from agriculture have been low. This has been largely the result of a disproportionately great number of very small farm units, many of which lack adequate supplies of cooperating factors of production, especially a reliable source of water. The sector has been undergoing a gradual process of change, however, and an appreciation of the full significance of that change cannot be gained if the sector is viewed in isolation from the rest of the economy. The farm sector households have long been integrated into regional and national labor markets. Income from off-farm sources has been significant in most regions for which we have information, even those seemingly most isolated from large urban areas. The process of modernization of the sector is evident in the rising land-labor ratio and the increasing mechanization of production. It is also reflected by the shift in cropping patterns away from traditional staples and labor-intensive crops to oilseed, grain, or forage crops and livestock and poultry production. Rather than viewing these as changes contributing to an aggravation of the rural employment problem, one should treat them as possible responses to a tightening rural labor market in which the cost of labor is rising and in which absolute scarcities may be occurring at critical times in the cropping cycle.

Clearly, the traditional methods of estimating the degree of underemployment of the agricultural population need to be reconsidered. The assumption that all adults in farm households or that all those working in agriculture for any length of time during the year are interested in, and available for, full-time employment represents an untenable simplification of the determinants of labor force participation. A careful investigation of the supply of labor effectively available for employment is likely to conclude that farm households make as full use of that supply as they deem desirable and that involuntary unemployment or underemployment characterizes only a relatively small proportion of the rural population. Furthermore, the practice of measuring underemployment by deducting from the presumed size of the agricultural labor force the number of work days required for recorded levels of output overlooks the importance of employment outside the agricultural sector.

By treating the agricultural sector in isolation, one can uncover a huge surplus of labor. However, what may appear to be a surplus to the agricultural sector may not be surplus to the economy as a whole. To the extent that agricultural households divide their time between intra- and extrasector employment, the latter cannot be ignored. Nor is off-farm work to be viewed as an act of desperation on the part of impoverished farm households. All the evidence points to a much more careful consideration by households of the returns to labor from different employments. In addition, household labor resources are allocated in a way that is most likely to minimize the resource costs of gaining the income target established for the household. When the opportunity cost of the household head or other members of the unit exceeds the returns to own-account employment, these workers seek off-farm employment and substitute less costly hired or other family labor. As links to the nonagricultural labor market become firmly established, it is reasonable to expect that the process of mobility from a farm to a permanent nonfarm status will be facilitated.

In short, a case can be made that Mexico is undergoing a process similar to that observed during the process of modernization and industrialization of the now more highly developed economies. Labor resources, responding to differences in potential earnings, gradually are redirected from agriculture to employments characterized by higher productivity. As the rural labor force shrinks, changes in the structure of agricultural production occur, the productivity of rural labor increases, and the returns to farm labor also increase. The maintenance of sustained growth of the national economy may then be expected to lead to a narrowing in some of the extreme intersectoral differentials in earnings.

Notes

1. Clark W. Reynolds, *The Mexican Economy* (New Haven, Conn.: Yale University Press, 1970), p. 136.
2. World Bank data.
3. The cost in human life of the revolution must have been very high; the census of 1921 reported a decline in the population from 15.2 million in 1910 to 14.8 million. During the preceding decade, the population had increased by 1.4 million, or 11 percent.
4. U.S. Agency for International Development (USAID), *Spring Review of Land Reform, June 1970*, 2d ed., vol. 7 (Washington, D.C., 1970), pp. 19–20; Sergio Reyes Osorio, Rodolfo Stavenhagen, Salomon Eckstein, and Jaun Ballesteros, *Estructura agraria y desarollo agricola en México* (Mexico, D.F.: Fondo de Cultura Económica, 1974), pp. 43–52.
5. Reynolds, *Mexican Economy*, p. 141. Reynolds' figures apparently refer to the size of arable plots assigned to each family. If the total area of the ejido is divided by the number of recipients of land, the average area for each member is considerably larger—the total area includes pasture or other common lands as well as that deemed unsuitable for purposes of cultivation. Measures of total area are available in James W. Wilkie, *The Mexican Revolution: Federal Expenditures and Social Change since 1910* (Berkeley: University of California Press, 1968).

6. Hacendados were permitted to retain for their own use 100 hectares of irrigated land or 300 hectares of rain-fed land. In addition, under provisions of nineteenth-century laws governing "colonization," it was possible for large landowners to divide their estates into smaller units. These were thus ineligible for expropriation and could be distributed among family members. The several units could then continue to be cultivated as a single entity. This practice was outlawed by legislation in 1962. USAID, *Spring Review*, pp. 20–22.

7. Reynolds, *Mexican Economy*, pp. 142–44; USAID, *Spring Review*, pp. 29–30.

8. Reyes Osorio and others, *Estructura agraria*, pp. 56–58.

9. Ibid., pp. 197–98. It should be noted, however, that these output figures may understate the production accruing to cultivators of minifundia. The census records each plot separately, while some small farmers may cultivate more than one unit. It is not unusual, for example, to find ejidatarios who also own private plots. It is of interest to note that over 60 percent of even these small units marketed at least part of their output.

10. Ibid., p. 349.

11. Ibid.

12. The value terms employed here are gross value of output, not net income. For the smallest category of farm units, there are probably few purchased inputs, and the amortization of capital equipment is likely to be minimal. Thus, the difference between gross and net incomes is probably minor. The importance of these factors and of hired labor, however, may be expected to increase with farm size; therefore, the difference between gross and net income for larger units would also increase.

13. An account by Alemán illustrates the uncertainty posed by climatic conditions in rain-fed agriculture. A study of sixteen ejidos located in the state of San Luis Potosí found that 37 percent of the ejidatarios lose their entire crop as a general rule. In 1965, some ejidatarios were reported to have gone five consecutive years without a harvest, in spite of which they persisted in annual plantings in hopes that rainfall would prove adequate. Farmers who successfully harvested a crop reported very low yields. Eloisa Aleman, *Investigación socioeconomica directa de los ejidos de San Luis Potosí* (Mexico, D.F.: Instituto Mexicano de Investigaciones Económicas, 1966), p. 68.

14. Reyes Osorio and others, *Estructura agraria*, pp. 199–201.

15. P. Lamartine Yates, *Mexico's Agricultural Dilemma* (Tucson: University of Arizona Press, 1981), p. 162.

16. Ibid., p. 134.

17. Reyes Osorio and others, *Estructura agraria*, p. 214.

18. World Bank, "The Economy of Mexico," table 7.4 and 7.5.

19. Yates, *Mexico's Agricultural Dilemma*, pp. 156–59; Teresa Rendón, "Utilización de mano de obra en la agricultura Mexicana, 1940–1973," *Demografía y economía*, vol. 10, no. 3 (1976), p. 366.

20. Kaja Finkler, "From Sharecroppers to Entrepreneurs: Peasant Household Production Strategies under the Ejido System of Mexico," *Economic Development and Cultural Change*, vol. 27 (October 1978), pp. 103–20.

21. Yates, *Mexico's Agricultural Dilemma*, p. 159.

22. Enrique Contreras S., *Estratificación y movilidad social en la ciudad de México* (Mexico, D.F.: Universidad Nacional Autonoma de México, 1978), p. 375.

23. Rendón, "Utilización de mano de obra," pp. 367–68.

24. Gabriel Maldonado Lee, *La mujer asalariada en el sector agricola* (Mexico, D.F.: Centro Nacional de Información y Estadísticas del Trabajo, 1977), pp. 69, 74.

25. Alemán, *Investigación socioeconomica directa*, p. 112.

26. Yates, *Mexico's Agricultural Dilemma*, p. 163; Roger D. Norton and Leopoldo Solís M., eds., *The Book of CHAC: Programming Studies for Mexican Agriculture* (Baltimore,

Md.: Johns Hopkins Universtiy Press, 1983), pp. 346–47; Centro de Investigaciones para el Desarrollo Rural (CIDER), *Mercado de trabajo del algodón* (Mexico, D.F., n.d.).

27. Jorge Balan, Harley L. Browning, and Elizabeth Jelin, *Men in a Developing Society* (Austin: University of Texas Press, 1973), p. 79.

28. George M. Foster, *Tzintzuntzan: Mexican Peasants in a Changing World*, rev. ed. (New York: Elsevier, 1979), pp. 275–76.

29. Douglas S. Butterworth, *Tilitongo: Comunidad mixteca en transición* (Mexico, D.F.: Instituto Nacional Indigenista, 1975), pp. 173–93.

30. Billie R. DeWalt, *Modernization in a Mexican Ejido* (London: Cambridge University Press, 1978), p. 221.

31. Lourdes Arizpe, *Migración, etnicismo y cambio económico* (Mexico, D.F.: El Colegio de México, 1978), pp. 230–31. Workers from rural communities often migrate together, taking with them one or two women to keep house for them. Sometimes villages specialize in a certain occupation: one village might be a source of masons, another of welders, and so on.

32. A. René Barbosa-Ramírez, *Empleo, desempleo y subempleo en el sector agropecuario*, vol. 1 (Mexico, D.F.: Centro de Investigaciónes Agrarias, 1976), p. 159.

33. Alemán, *Investigación socioeconomica directa*, pp. 69–71.

34. The existence of a substantial differential between wages reportedly paid day laborers by smallholders and large farm units is puzzling. One would expect the local rural labor market to be highly competitive and for wage differentials among various employing units to be narrow. It is possible, of course, to hypothesize about factors that could give rise to a differential within such a market. These would include quality differences among workers, longer commuting distances to large farms, a difference in the timing of peak periods of hiring by small and large farmers, and so on. It may be that the larger farms pay wages equal to the legal minimum even though the effective supply price of labor lies below that level. However, since rural employers in most parts of Mexico at that time were reputed to ignore the legal requirements of employment, why should they not have been doing so here? Unfortunately, Alemán offers us no clue.

35. Reyes Osorio and others, *Estructura agraria*, p. 353.

36. Ibid., p. 401.

37. Ibid., pp. 399, 1084–85.

38. A. René Barbosa-Ramírez, *El Bajío* (Mexico, D.F.: Centro de Investigaciones Agrarias, 1973), chap. 3.

39. A. René Barbosa-Ramírez, *Empleo, desempleo y subempleo en el sector agropecuario*, 3 vols. (Mexico, D.F.: Centro de Investigaciones Agrarias, 1976, 1977, and 1979).

40. Ibid., vol. 2, p. 135.

41. Ibid., vol. 1, p. 229.

42. Ibid., pp. 132–33.

43. Gobierno Constitucional de los Estados Unidos Mexicanos and Gobierno Constitucional del Estado de Oaxaca, *Programa de desarrollo rural integral de las Mixtecas Oaxaqueñas Alta y Baja 1984–1988* (Mexico, D.F.: Secretaría de Programación y Presupuesto, 1984), pp. 45–59.

44. Secretaría de Agricultura y Recursos Hidraulicos, Centro de Estudios en Planeación Agropecuaria (CESPA), *El desarrollo agropecuario de México*, vol. 6, *El empleo de mano de obra en las actividades productivas agropecuarias* (Mexico, D.F., 1982), pp. 53, 61, 84–85, 186.

45. Rendón, "Utilización de mano de obra," pp. 368, 372–73.

46. Cynthia Hewitt de Alcantara, *Modernizing Mexican Agriculture: Socio-economic Implications of Technological Change 1940–70*, Report no. 76.5 (Geneva: United Nations Institute for Social Development, 1976), pp. 64–72.

47. Barbosa-Ramírez, *Empleo, desempleo y subempleo*, vol. 1, p. 138.
48. CESPA, *El empleo de mano de obra*, p. 49.
49. CESPA, *El desarrollo agropecuario de México*, vol. 9, *Inversión predial y formación de capital* (México, D.F., 1982), p. 28.
50. Rendón, "Utilización de mano de obra," pp. 371–72.
51. CESPA, *El empleo de mano de obra*, p. 62.
52. Ministry of the Presidency, Government of Mexico, "A Program for Mexican Agriculture," in *The Book of CHAC*, ed. Norton and Solís, p. 191.
53. Rendón, "Utilización de mano de obra," pp. 372–73.
54. CESPA, *El empleo de mano de obra*, p. 52.
55. Rendón, "Utilización de mano de obra," pp. 369–71.
56. CESPA, El empleo de mano de obra, p. 78.
57. Rendón, "Utilización de mano de obra," p. 374.
58. CESPA, *El empleo de mano de obra*, pp. 103–06.
59. Ibid., p. 113.
60. Ibid., p. 135.
61. Barbosa-Ramírez, *Empleo, desempleo y subempleo*, vol. 1, pp. 173, 239; vol. 2, p. 136; vol. 3, pp. 120, 261.
62. CESPA, *El empleo de mano de obra*, p. 83. CESPA advances different estimates for the size of the labor force without venturing an explanation for the differences. In deriving the estimate of days worked in 1977, the authors computed a labor force size of 5.754 million. Earlier in the same study (p. 52), a figure of 6.557 million was used. Both numbers would appear to represent substantial overestimates of the actual agricultural labor force. For example, the latter number would imply an annual rate of growth of 3.6 percent since 1970, far above the approximately 0.1 percent rate of the preceding decade. In table 2-5 I estimated its growth at an annual rate of 0.5 percent. The unadjusted census data for 1970 and 1980 indicate an annual growth rate of 1 percent.
63. Reyes Osorio and others, *La estructura agraria*, pp. 343–44.
64. Teresa Rendón cites a study undertaken by the Colegio de México in thirteen rural localities in 1975. It found that in eleven of these communities the median agricultural wage was below the legal minimum. In six, the median was at least 40 percent below the legal. Rendón, "Utilización de mano de obra," p. 365*n*.
65. The reader is referred to Chapter 7 for a discussion of the course of minimum wages since 1940.
66. Centro de Investigaciones Agrarias, *Estructura agraria y desarrollo agricola de México*, vol. 1 (Mexico, D.F., 1970), p. 593.
67. CESPA, *El empleo de mano de obra*, p. 183.
68. Ministry of the Presidency, "A Program for Mexican Agriculture," pp. 162–63, 171–72.
69. CESPA, *El empleo de mano de obra*, pp. 157–62.
70. Barbosa-Ramírez, *Empleo, desempleo y subempleo*, vol. 1, p. 168.
71. Ibid., p. 222.
72. Ibid., vol. 2, pp. 127–28.
73. Ibid., vol. 3, p. 114.
74. Ibid., p. 208.
75. Ibid., vol. 2, p. 128.
76. Ibid., vol. 3, p. 252.
77. Ibid., p. 249.
78. Ibid., p. 254.
79. Ibid., pp. 259–61.

80. Banco Nacional de Crédito Rural (BANRURAL), Fideicomiso para Estudios y Planes de Desarrollo Agropecuario (FEDA), *Empleo, subempleo y desempleo en el sector rural, por subregiones economicas*, 31 vols. (Mexico, D.F., 1981–83). Although a research report was published for each state studied, only eighteen were available to me. The data cited, therefore, refer only to these states.

81. Barbosa-Ramírez, *Empleo, desempleo y subempleo*, vol. 2, p. 123.

82. Ibid., vol. 1, pp. 222–39.

83. Ibid., pp. 130–33.

84. Ibid., pp. 226–27. Another example of the change in the traditional allocation of labor services in rural communities can be found in the passing of the practice of *tequio*. This was the provision of free labor by local residents for various social or public works, such as maintenance and construction of local roads, schools, public buildings, and churches. Volunteer labor has been largely replaced by wage labor. Ibid., pp. 230–31.

85. Reyes Osorio, *La estructura agraria*, p. 426.

86. Barbosa-Ramírez, *Empleo, desempleo y subempleo*, vol. 3, p. 317.

87. Ibid., p. 112. See also, Arturo Warman, . . . *Y venimos a contradecir* (Mexico, D.F.: Ediciones de la Casa Chata, 1976), as cited in ibid., p. 112.

88. Michael Belshaw, *A Village Economy* (New York: Columbia University Press, 1967), pp. 135–54; Rendón, "Utilización de mano de obra," p. 353*n*.

89. Rodolfo Stavenhagen, "Los jornaleros agricolas," *Revista de México agrario*, vol. 1, no. 1 (1967), p. 165.

90. Luz María Bassoco and Roger D. Norton, "A Quantitative Framework for Agricultural Policies," in Norton and Solís, *The Book of CHAC*, chap. 5; Ministry of the Presidency, "A Program for Mexican Agriculture," p. 191.

91. Hewitt de Alcantara, *Modernizing Mexican Agriculture*, pp. 64–72; Yates, *Mexico's Agricultural Dilemma*, p. 129.

92. Banco Nacional de Crédito Rural, S.A., Fideicomiso para Estudios y Planes de Desarrollo Agropecuario, "Principales indicadores del estudio del empleo, subempleo y desempleo rural" (1983), table 9-A.

93. Ibid., table 9-A.

94. As is the case with several of the tables reporting labor force–related data, the 1980 census reports a considerable number of individuals (about 16 percent of the total) for whom no earnings data were available or who could not be classified according to a sector of employment even though earnings were reported. In calculating the sectoral median earnings, I have limited myself to only those for whom earnings and sector of employment are reported. Earnings recipients are divided into two categories: those assigned to agricultural employments and all other. The totals for each state, however, include the earnings of those who were not assigned a sector of employment.

5. Internal Migration and Regional Development

THE PROCESS OF economic development involves both an increase in the quantity of productive factors and a reorganization in the manner in which existing resources are employed. Expansion of these factors is usually dominated by growth in capital, both physical and human. The reorganization of production involves concomitant change in the structure of demand for labor that will have several dimensions: sectoral, occupational, and geographic. Successful development will therefore require a labor force that is willing and able to adapt to these changes.

In a free labor market, the changing structure of demand for labor will be reflected in changing wage relationships that are designed to encourage flows of workers to expanding areas and occupations. The responsiveness of the labor force (as well as of potential members of the labor force) to these inducements to move or adapt will be governed by a number of economic, cultural, and institutional factors. The greater the responsiveness of workers to the shifting structure of demand, the smoother will be the process of growth and the more favorable the prospects for increasing the degree of equality in the distribution of income over time.

Mexican workers would seem to be very willing to migrate when the incentives are present. Seasonal migration of labor within the agricultural sector, as well as between the rural and urban sectors, has long been a feature of the Mexican labor market. Short-term migration across the northern border to the United States has a history extending back into the nineteenth century when the building of the transcontinental railroads through the Southwest attracted large numbers of Mexican laborers. That migration has continued into the present century, in the form of both formal recruitment programs, for example, the *bracero* program of the 1940s and 1950s, and informal, illegal border crossings.

Within Mexico, the rapid economic development that has characterized the country since 1940 has seen large numbers of people willing to make permanent moves in response to new and improved opportunities of employment. The accelerated development of an improved transportation system and the expansion of the means of communication facilitated the mobility of labor and provided for the dissemination of information that was vital to its efficient redeployment.[1] The institutional changes flowing from the revolution also removed any barriers to mobility that might have been posed by the traditional organization of agriculture. Unlike those in other poor lands, agricultural workers were not tied to the land or to a particular landowner by caste or bonds of servitude. Thus, they were free to exercise choice with respect to their location and, to a lesser extent, to a sector of employment.

In this chapter, the size and direction of internal migratory flows in the years since 1940 will be examined. The correlates of these flows will be reviewed, as these data have been defined by econometric studies of migration. In addition, the characteristics of migrants will be described, along with their economic status prior to and following their moves. Attention will be given to the process by which the migrant becomes integrated into the labor market at the destination point. Migration would be expected to represent a factor shaping regional differences in productivity and incomes. Therefore, in the final section of this chapter, there will be a discussion of changes in regional measures of income that have emerged over four decades of economic expansion and migration.

The literature is dominated by two broad views of the underlying motivation for and consequences of migration in Latin America. One, which is descriptive and is based on more or less casual empiricism, holds that migration is motivated by rural poverty, which "pushes" the population out of an economically hopeless environment into an urban environment that is as bad or worse. In this scenario, employment opportunities adequate to the absorption of the migrant flow are held to be lacking. Survival becomes dependent on the meager returns from casual self-employment or very low-wage jobs in an urban "informal" sector, particularly in the service sector. The literature speaks of migration as leading to the "marginalization" of populations or to the "tertiarization" of the urban economy. Migration is said to contribute neither to increased efficiency in the use of resources nor to an improvement in the lot of the migrants. Essentially, this represents a rather negative evaluation of migration and is a view that is frequently expressed in references to the migration phenomenon in Mexico.

The alternative approach treats migration as a product of the economically rational decisions of individuals who are responding to the perceived costs and benefits of their moves. The analytical framework for the study of migration derives from modern human capital theory. Individuals seek to maximize the present value of their net income streams by evaluating their employment prospects in alternative settings. In this view, migration represents a response to differences in wage levels and employment opportunities, and it contributes both to increased economic efficiency and to improvement in the economic well-being of the migrants. In the case of Mexico, this evaluation is supported by the findings of anthropologists who have studied peasant communities or followed migrant populations in urban areas over time. It is also given credence by analyses of aggregated data drawn from population censuses or special sample surveys. Once the available evidence has been reviewed, validity of these two clashing views can be determined.

The Size and Direction of Migration Flows

The primary source of information regarding migration is the various population censuses. Unfortunately, the information that is contained in the censuses before 1970 provides no more than a partial indicator of population movement. Prior to that year, the only pertinent data were a count of persons residing in a state other than that of their birth. As such, this measure represented a stock of persons who at some time in their lives had changed their state of residence at least once and were currently residing in a state other than that in which they had been born. Not included, therefore, were those who, at the time of the census, were living in the state of their birth but who had resided elsewhere and had returned. This measure is to be distinguished from an accounting of migration that is a flow of population per unit of time. Furthermore, the procedure takes no account of intrastate migration.

As a measure of migration, changes over time in the number of persons residing in a state other than that of their birth are far from ideal. First, they do not reflect the gross flows of populations, only the net flows. Thus, the movement of one non-native person in each direction between Jalisco and Querétaro would not be detectable as two cases of migration since they would leave unaffected the number of non-natives in each state. In addition, this measure does not provide a way to detail the multiple moves of any individual. At best, it may provide only a rough indication of the relative importance of population movements for the course of population change in the states over time. Yet, the data probably do serve to identify faithfully those states that have been significant losers and gainers of population through migration.

The 1970 census marked a significant improvement in the way information relating to migration was presented. The traditional measure of non-native residents in each state appeared. Moreover, all those who reported ever having made an interstate move were classified according to the length of residence in the state of current residence. Not only did this measure include migrants returning to the state of their birth but it also permitted the isolation of the migrants who changed their state of residence within certain time intervals prior to the census. Before a discussion of the 1970 census, however, a review of the data based on non-native residents of the states is in order.[2]

For each census year between 1940 and 1970, table 5-1 shows the non-native population as a percentage of the total population of each state and the relative importance of the non-native population in the intercensal growth. For the country as a whole, the data suggest an increase in the frequency of migration coinciding with the onset of rapid growth in the 1940s. The 1940 census recorded 10.6 percent of the population as residing in a state other than that of their birth. The proportion rose over the next two censuses and leveled off at just under 15 percent of the population. As might be expected, there was considerable variation among the states in the proportion of the population consisting of non-natives as well as in the rates of change in that subgroup over time. States with low income levels per capita tended to report small proportions of non-natives. Among these would be the southern states of Chiapas, Oaxaca, Guerrero, Tabasco, and Yucatán, as well as the depressed states in the Central and North Central region: San Luis Potosí, Michoacán, Hidalgo, Puebla, Querétaro, Tlaxcala, and Zacatecas.

At the other extreme are the high-income states, which have constituted the development poles of the Mexican economy. In absolute terms, the entity with the largest concentration of non-natives is the Federal District. The three censuses from 1940 through 1960 recorded over 40 percent of the population as being non-native. Between 1960 and 1970, however, the natural rate of increase in the District became a more important contributor to population growth, and the proportion of non-natives fell to one-third of the total.[3] However, the continued growth in the concentration of economic activity in the Mexico City metropolitan area resulted in spillover effects. When the limits of the absorptive capacity of the District were reached, further activity and population growth engulfed the state of México, which surrounds the District on three sides. This also occurred to a lesser extent in the state of Morelos, which abuts the District on the south. In 1940, only 3.5 percent of the state of México's population was non-native. By 1970, this proportion had risen to over one-fourth. During the 1960s, this state was the principal destination of people emigrating from the District, accounting for one-third of these migrants. The increase in non-natives in the state of México accounted for 37 and 40 percent of the total increase in population during 1950–60 and 1960–70, respectively.

Table 5-1. *Non-Native Population as a Proportion of Total Population and as a Source of Population Growth, by State, 1940–70*

	Percentage of non-native residents to total population				Percentage of intercensal growth[a] accounted for by change in non-native population		
State	*1940*	*1950*	*1960*	*1970*	*1940–50*	*1950–60*	*1960–70*
Aguascalientes	18.3	19.7	17.8	17.1	28.4	11.4	15.1
Baja California N.	48.2	59.9	59.3	39.6	66.1	58.8	10.5
Baja California S.	4.5	4.4	14.2	16.9	4.3	43.0	21.6
Campeche	6.9	9.3	12.7	16.8	15.5	21.9	25.1
Coahuila	21.6	19.7	17.2	12.3	13.9	6.9	−51.8
Colima	22.8	24.2	27.2	27.7	27.5	33.5	28.7
Chiapas	2.0	2.3	4.1	2.3	3.4	9.4	−97.6
Chihuahua	11.3	12.1	16.8	10.2	14.2	27.3	−63.7
Durango	11.1	10.9	10.3	6.6	10.4	7.3	−86.8
Federal District	46.7	45.4	40.2	33.0	43.6	31.4	15.6
Guanajuato	3.7	4.2	6.2	5.6	5.9	12.7	3.5
Guerrero	2.0	3.1	3.6	3.3	7.4	5.3	2.4
Hidalgo	4.4	4.2	6.4	4.2	1.5	19.7	−110.5
Jalisco	4.5	5.3	7.9	10.2	8.5	14.4	16.8
México	3.5	5.0	13.4	26.9	12.4	36.6	40.2
Michoacán	3.7	3.9	4.2	3.7	4.5	5.2	2.0
Morelos	20.7	23.8	26.3	26.6	29.9	32.5	27.1
Nayarit	15.4	15.8	16.1	15.1	17.4	16.6	12.5
Nuevo León	14.7	18.4	23.6	23.6	28.4	35.0	23.6
Oaxaca	1.6	3.1	3.2	2.7	10.9	3.6	−4.2
Puebla	4.4	5.7	5.9	5.9	10.5	7.0	5.9
Querétaro	5.4	5.5	5.8	8.3	6.3	7.0	14.9
Quintana Roo	26.1	24.8	39.2	43.3	22.0	56.0	48.7
San Luis Potosí	7.1	7.5	7.0	6.5	8.9	4.9	4.2
Sinaloa	6.4	6.6	9.1	11.7	7.6	16.8	16.9
Sonora	10.1	12.3	18.2	14.8	17.7	29.2	6.4
Tabasco	3.3	3.0	4.0	6.3	1.9	6.9	10.6
Tamaulipas	23.9	30.9	28.5	21.8	43.3	22.7	6.2
Tlaxcala	5.2	6.0	6.2	6.1	8.8	7.2	5.4
Veracruz	8.4	8.1	10.2	8.6	6.9	16.4	4.7
Yucatán	1.8	1.5	2.1	2.0	0.4	5.1	1.6
Zacatecas	6.6	5.7	4.8	4.6	0.3	0.9	3.4
Mexico	10.6	12.8	14.9	14.5	n.a.	n.a.	n.a.

n.a. Not available.

a. A negative sign indicates a decline in the non-native population. A negative percentage greater than − 100 indicates a decline in non-natives greater than the growth in population.

Source: Secretaría de Industria y Comercio, Dirección General de Estadística, *Censo de Población*, 1940, 1950, 1960, and 1970.

The other focal points of growing concentrations of non-native residents are to be found in the northern border states, which are also relatively high-income states. Most notable among these has been the state of Baja California. Between 1940 and 1970, the population of the state expanded elevenfold, an increase attainable only with a large infusion of migrants. As can be seen from table 5-1, the expansion of the non-native population accounted for approximately 60 percent of the increase in total population during the first two intercensal periods. Over those same years, Tamaulipas, Sonora, and Nuevo León likewise recorded significant growth associated with large increases in the non-native population.

A clearer picture of the distribution of the migrant population both by state of origin and state of residence is provided by table 5-2, which is based on the 1970 census. The information presented is of two kinds. One is that based on the state of residence in 1970 and state of birth. The ratio of the number of non-natives residing in a given state to the number of persons originating in that state but residing in others provides a rough notion of relative gains and losses of population from migration. For example, the ratio of 7.5 for Baja California Norte implies a gain of 7.5 non-native residents for every person born in that state who was found residing in other states. Conversely, the ratio of 0.12 for Zacatecas implies that for every increase of one non-native in its population, the state recorded a loss to other states of more than eight persons. The second basis of recording gains and losses is a broader one; it refers to the destination and state of immediate previous residence of all those reporting any change in the state of residence. This measure therefore includes those who have moved back to the state of their birth from another state. Although the size of the ratio changes for some states, the general orders of magnitude are very similar. The states in table 5-2 are ranked in accordance with their per capita income in 1970. The direct relationship between the migrant ratios and income is readily apparent. The correlation between income and the broader measure of migration yields a coefficient of 0.41, significant at the 2 percent level.

As mentioned above, the use of the changing proportions of non-native residents as an indicator of geographic mobility has severe limitations. Some clues to the limitations of this measure can be gleaned from the 1970 census inclusion of movers by length of residence in their current state. In the country as a whole, some 7,190 thousand persons, or 14.9 percent of the total population, were reported to have changed their state of residence at any time in the past. Over half of these, or 55 percent, had made at least one interstate move during the preceding ten years. As a proportion of the total population, this group represented about 8.1 percent. More revealing, however, is the extent of movement in the single year preceding

Table 5-2. *States as Sources and Destination of Interstate Migrants, 1970*

State in rank order by per capita GDP *in 1970*	*Ratio of in-migrants to native out-migrants*	*Ratio of in-migrants to all out-migrants*
Federal District	3.96	2.95
Nuevo León	3.13	2.92
Baja California N.	7.50	5.15
Sonora	1.94	1.72
Coahuila	0.60	0.60
Tamaulipas	2.11	1.83
Baja California S.	1.53	1.32
Sinaloa	1.02	1.01
Chihuahua	1.44	1.39
Campeche	1.50	1.45
México	2.32	2.23
Colima	1.96	1.69
Veracruz	0.98	0.98
Jalisco	0.64	0.71
Tabasco	0.70	0.69
Yucatán	0.16	0.18
Morelos	2.53	2.01
Aguascalientes	0.69	0.69
Quintana Roo	5.97	5.36
Durango	0.26	0.28
Nayarit	1.03	1.01
Querétaro	0.32	0.35
Guanajuato	0.23	0.26
San Luis Potosí	0.25	0.27
Puebla	0.37	0.39
Guerrero	0.23	0.24
Chiapas	0.39	0.41
Michoacán	0.14	0.16
Hidalgo	0.15	0.17
Zacatecas	0.12	0.13
Tlaxcala	0.23	0.26
Oaxaca	0.16	0.18

Source: Secretaría de Industria y Comercio, Dirección General de Estadística, *IX Censo de población, 1970.* Per capita GDP from Luis Unikel, *El desarrollo urbano de México*, 2d ed. (México, D.F.: El Colegio de México, 1976), appendix table VI-A3.

the census. Fully 723,000, or 10 percent of all movers, reported a change in their state of residence within the past year; they represented 1.5 percent of the total population. If 1969 was a typical year with respect to the frequency of mobility, this would imply a much higher rate of mobility than is suggested by any of the other measures reviewed thus far. What may also be implied is that, once an initial move from the home state is made, an individual is more prone to make a further interstate move. This act would not normally be detected as a move by the data as it is currently garnered by the census.

Another indication of the size of net population flows may be gleaned from the census-based measures of growth of the urban and rural populations. Such flows would, of course, include intra- as well as interstate movements. In common with most other developing countries, Mexico has experienced a significant shift of population from the countryside to towns and cities. If one adopts the census definition of urban centers as those with populations of 2,500 or more, then the proportion of the population that is urban increased from 35 percent in 1940 to almost 59 percent in 1970. The annual rate of growth of the urban population over the thirty-year period was 4.8 percent. In contrast, that for the rural population was only 1.5 percent. Estimates of the net migration flow from the rural to urban areas amounted to some 3.755 million for the decade 1960–70.[4] This was equivalent to 35.4 percent of the intercensal growth of the urban population. Although the rural-urban flow was a rather general phenomenon, not all urban areas were recipients of the flow. Urban areas in several states have grown at a rate below the natural rate, indicating a net out-migration. As might be expected, these tend to be located in the lower-income states. For the decade 1960–70, they included Aguascalientes, Coahuila, Durango, Hidalgo, San Luis Potosí, Yucatán, and Zacatecas.[5] Several of these states had suffered net out-migration of their urban populations during the preceding decade as well.

Unfortunately, the final 1980 census results did not become available for the country as a whole in time for me to report the contribution that migration during the 1970s may have made to the distribution of population in 1980.

Research Findings on Migration

There is an extensive literature on internal migration based on empirical research. This literature is divisible into two broad categories that are based on the character of the methodology employed and the data sources. One of these groupings uses data drawn from the population censuses.

The treatment of the data ranges from pure description to the analysis of the correlates of migration by the application of econometric techniques. The other class of research is based on sample surveys of migrants in two metropolitan areas (Mexico City and Monterrey) and on anthropological studies of rural communities and urban migrants. These studies are rich in detail and permit one to gain considerable insight into the motivations underlying migration. They also shed light on the process of migration and the integration of workers into the labor market at their destination point. Most of the other empirical studies adopt an approach that is based explicitly on a human capital framework or have collected information that can be analyzed and interpreted within that structure.

The econometric studies typically use multiple regression analysis. This method relates variations in the rates of migration among states to a number of independent variables that might be expected to influence the costs and prospective gains of migration. Among the variables are distance between origin and destination points, income or wage levels at each point, unemployment rates, size of total or urban population, and a variety of other ecological or social variables.[6] By and large, the results conform to expectations generated by human capital theory.[7]

Distance proves to be highly significant and is inversely related to migration rates. Longer distances may have a deterrent effect, not only because of the higher costs associated with a move, but also because information may be less readily available. Destinations characterized by high wages or average incomes have a more powerful drawing effect than do poorer regions. Clearly, the probability of improving one's economic position is greater if the destination is a high-wage rather than a low-wage area. Unemployment rates tend to be lower in the destination and higher in the points of origin; this finding suggests that there is movement from areas with more restricted employment opportunities to areas with less.

The only unexpected result is the positive sign of the income or wage variable at the point of origin. Human capital theory would lead one to expect a negative sign, that is, that lower incomes would be associated with higher rates of emigration. However, several other empirical studies have reported a similar direct relationship. The rationalization that has been offered for it holds that, in developing countries, the poorest groups are too poor to migrate—they are unable to muster the resources to defray the costs of migration. In addition, the poorest areas are likely to be the most deficient in human capital, especially education, so that prospects of improvement in employment and income may be perceived as being very dim. In short, these three variables emerge as the most significant factors in explaining the variance in migration rates among alternative pairs of points.[8]

As indicated above, the sample surveys studied the migrant populations of Mexico City and Monterrey. These cites would appear to be natural choices for students of migration since both have been among the principal foci of migrants. Mexico City has long held a dominant position in the country, not only because it serves as the seat of the national government, but also because of its role as the major financial and service center for the rest of the country. In addition, the rapid industrial development of the metropolitan area over the past four decades has provided expanded employment opportunities, not only in the industrial sector, but also in the others that serve it. An appreciation of the impact that migration has had on the population of the metropolitan area can be gained from the 1970 census datum of the proportion of non-natives in the total: 33.4 percent, equivalent to 2.8 million people.

Monterrey has emerged as a prominent metropolitan center only in more recent times. In 1930, the census reported a population of only 134,202. Within twenty years, the population of Monterrey had virtually tripled, and by 1970 had reached 1.1 million. Its growth has been characterized by the rise of a modern heavy industrial sector that currently represents the largest source of employment; it provides jobs for 37 percent of the employed labor force.[9] The fact that the rapid population growth of Monterrey is more recent explains the large relative importance of migrants in the population. In 1965, only 29 percent of the population was native born. An additional 14 percent had been born there, but had emigrated at some time in the past and subsequently returned. If the latter are not counted among the migrants, the non-native population still accounted for 57 percent of the total.

Because men are believed to have a greater independent voice than women in the decision to migrate, most studies of migration limit their samples to male migrants. The Mexican studies are no exception. All of them concern themselves primarily with male migrants. The characterization of the migration that follows should be understood to apply only to men unless otherwise explicitly noted.[10] This preoccupation with males would be understandable if they dominated the migrant flow. In the case of Mexico City, however, female migration has exceeded male by a large, though secularly declining, margin. During the 1930s, female migrants outnumbered male by 40 percent and by 20 percent in the 1950s.[11] During the 1960s, the margin declined further to 17.2 percent.[12]

Characteristics of Migrants

The sample surveys and other empirical studies confirm the importance of distance as a factor that channels migration flows. Two-thirds to three-fourths of the migrant flow originated in neighboring states. In the case of migration to Monterrey, this proportion includes migrants originating within the state of Nuevo León itself.[13] Between 80 and 90 percent of the migrants originated within a radius of 600 kilometers of the metropolitan areas.[14]

Rural areas have long been a source of population that has contributed to urban growth. It is only more recently, however, that migrants with rural origins have constituted the majority in the flow to Mexico City. For example, of those arriving prior to 1955, only 40 percent had originated in communities with populations under 5,000 whereas the cohort arriving between 1965 and 1970 was 53 percent rural.[15] The rural component of the flow to Monterrey has been marginally greater than that to Mexico City, and it, too, has shown a slight increase over time.[16] Most of the migrants to Monterrey with rural origins, almost 60 percent, moved to the city in a single step with no intermediate moves; the balance was almost evenly divided between those who had left their place of birth less than and more than ten years prior to arriving in Monterrey.[17]

One interesting observation made by Contreras is the inverse relationship between the distance traveled to Mexico City and the relative importance of rural residents in the flow.[18] Migrants from neighboring areas within 400 kilometers were 70 percent rural, and the percentage rural declines to 43 and 28 as the distance increases to between 400 and 600 kilometers and to more than 600 kilometers, respectively. (In this case, rural communities are defined as those with populations of less than 10,000.) One may hypothesize that the greater prevalence of urbanites among the long-distance migrants reflects their higher levels of education and the greater access they had to information that would have reduced the risks of migration. Given the large income differences between urban and rural families that exist in Mexico, it is also likely that the interurban migrants were better able than rural residents to finance the longer moves.

Only Anson reports that a significant proportion—41 percent—of the migrants had considered alternative urban destinations (to Monterrey), while Balan, Browning, and Jelin found that only 11 percent did so.[19] Yet it cannot be said that moves are made blindly, without considerable information. Migrants to Monterrey were found to have been influenced by a prior acquaintance with the city. Nearly two-thirds had visited the city for some purpose prior to moving there, and this proportion shows a steady increase among the more recent cohorts of migrants. Furthermore, 84 percent of the migrants had friends or relatives already living in Monterrey before their move. Adult migrants to Mexico City reported the presence of friends and relatives almost as frequently as did their Monterrey counterparts, and over half had made prior visits to the city.[20] As might be expected, the significance of relatives and friends already at the destination point was not limited to their value as a source of information. They also served as an important source of assistance upon arrival. Over half of the adult migrants received free room and board. This form of assistance probably far outweighed any help received from families at the point of origin. Most migrants received no aid at all from the latter. What aid was received was limited to some cash or a one-way bus ticket.[21]

It has generally been held that migration is a selective process; migrants are not chosen at random from the population at the point of origin. Indeed, one would expect that the migrants would be drawn from among those who are best equipped to succeed and who have the greatest probability of recouping their investment in migrating. Thus, migrants would be expected to be young and to be drawn from among those with higher levels of education. Mexican migrants conform to this characterization. Actually, a very substantial number of urban non-natives, about one-third, leave their place of origin prior to reaching age 16, presumably as part of a family move in most cases. The bulk of the remainder, who are more likely to move independently of their families, also fall into the ranks of the young. Only 14 percent of the migrants to Mexico City were over 30 years of age at the time of arrival. In Monterrey, fully two-thirds of the migrants were no older than 21.[22] Rural migrants tend to be older than the interurban, a factor that may pose an obstacle to prospects for upward occupational mobility.

It is more difficult to generalize with complete confidence about the educational levels of migrants because of differences in the way in which data are presented. The data for Mexico City suggest that, among those whose education can be presumed to have been completed prior to their move, the number of years of schooling completed has been rising over time.[23] While the educational attainments of the migrants would appear to compare favorably with those of the general population of Mexico (3.5 years of primary schooling on average in 1975), they remain well below the average level of the native population of Mexico City. For example, male migrants aged 21 to 40 who arrived in the Mexico City metropolitan area between 1965 and 1970 reported an average level of schooling of five completed years. Since, in 1970, only 16.8 percent of the population over 15 years old had completed six years of primary education, the migrants were, on the average, clearly better educated than the population at large.

In comparison with the average educational levels of native males, however, the migrants' achievements were more modest. Native males aged 21–30 had completed eight years while those 31–40 had completed 7.6 years. Furthermore, it would appear that the difference between the educational levels of migrants and natives has been increasing over time.

The oldest group of migrants, who arrived prior to 1935, reported only 1.3 years of schooling less than the natives. This increased to a two-year difference for young adult males arriving between 1935 and 1955 and further to three years for the most recent young arrivals included in the study. Of course, men over 40 among the recent arrivals to the area reported much lower levels of education than did the young arrivals. The gap between their level of schooling and that of their native peer groups was even greater than that noted for the younger migrants. But the older recent migrants were relatively few in number, and it may be presumed that at least some of them did not migrate for economic reasons.

A more adequate notion of the selectivity of migrants requires a comparison of the educational levels of migrants with those of the population at the point of origin rather than at the destination. The available evidence seems to confirm the expectation that the migrants are those with characteristics most likely to achieve success. The anthropological studies of the village of Tzintzuntzan in Michoacán found that the migrants to urban centers came from the minority of households with above-average standards of living, education, and occupational skills. Half of the men who had achieved a sixth grade education in the interval 1942–79 had migrated.[24]

A more formal comparison of educational attainments of migrants and nonmigrants is provided by Balan, Browning, and Jelin for migrants to Monterrey.[25] The basis of comparison is the proportion of men among the migrants with six or more years of schooling and the proportion in the zones in which they originated. The zones are classified into five categories according to the level of socioeconomic development. The proportion of migrants who completed primary school is significantly greater than that in the population in their zones of origin. However, the difference has narrowed over time. For example, among those migrants who arrived before 1941, the proportion with completed primary education was ten times greater than that in the zone they had left for the two lowest of the five socioeconomic categories. The proportion was six times greater in another category and a little more than twice as great in a fourth. Among those arriving in the decade of the 1950s, the ratios had narrowed significantly from a high of three for one zone and to two or less for the remaining four zones. This suggests that the degree of selectivity has been declining even as the average level of schooling of migrants has been increasing.

Two reasons may be offered for this apparent decline in selectivity. First, there has been a significant narrowing of differences in average educational attainment among regions. The progressive extension of primary educational opportunities to the less urbanized areas of the country has had a larger relative impact on educational achievement there than it has had in the largest urban centers. These centers have enjoyed greater access to education, particularly through the primary level, for a longer period of time. The increasingly mass nature of migration has tended to dilute the distinctiveness of the migrant. In particular, the increase in the number of migrants with rural origins, whose educational attainments are more modest than those of urban natives, would tend to lower the average educational level of migrants relative to the region of origin.[26]

It should not be surprising to find an increasing flow of rural migrants to the larger urban areas. Findings by Kemper and others suggest that this increase was a consequence, in part at least, of the termination of the bracero program. Many of the migrants from Tzintzuntzan and the Mazahuan region, for example, were men who, as surplus labor in the village, had been siphoned off as temporary migrants to the United States. Following the end of the program in 1964, the rate of migration to Mexico City increased sharply. These moves, however, proved to be different—neither temporary nor seasonal. Only 6.6 percent of these emigrants returned to the village.[27]

Other fundamental changes have contributed to this increase. Of the greatest importance has been the extension of educational opportunities to rural areas; this has enhanced the competitiveness of the rural population in urban labor markets. Furthermore, education, once acquired, appears to make little difference in the income levels attainable in rural areas. The economic returns to education are significantly greater in urban employments. In 1968, an additional year of schooling was associated with an increase in monthly earnings among male nonagricultural workers that was 3.2 times greater than that accruing to workers in agriculture, Mex$283 to Mex$89. By 1977, the relative difference in the returns from an additional year of schooling had increased to 4.5, the absolute returns being Mex$854 and Mex$189 in nonagriculture and agriculture, respectively.[28] Given these very substantial differences in returns from education, the incentives to migrate from rural to urban areas must appear very powerful to those with some schooling. Indeed, the most important reasons given for migrating to the metropolitan areas were economic; 60 to 65 percent of the respondents offered employment or income-related reasons for moving.

Of course, these reasons for moving could also be interpreted in a somewhat different light. Moves could be made, not so much in response to the attractiveness of opportunities at the destination point ("pull" factors), as to the absolutely desperate economic conditions prevailing in the place of origin ("push" factors). However, the push factors would not seem to be present in an extreme form among the sampled migrants. Most workers were employed before migrating and expressed a high degree of job satisfaction in their last job. In the Mexico City sample, only 4.2 percent of the migrants had been unemployed and actively searching for work before migrating. Another 0.5 percent were classed as discouraged unemployed; about 13 percent reported that their jobs had recently terminated.[29] The proportion of men in the Monterrey studies whose work had ended apparently was higher, but the significance of this is not clear. The period between the end of employment at the point of origin and the departure for Monterrey was reported by Anson to be very short, 10.3 days on average. Migrants to Mexico City also reported only a short interruption between the end of employment and departure. Fully 43 percent left the very next day, another 31 percent left within a month; 5 percent were being transferred by their employers and did not experience any interruption in their work.

Nevertheless, one should not discount completely the significance of poverty and restricted employment opportunities in the rural areas of origin as a compelling force for migration. The decline in mortality rates resulted in an increasing rate of population growth in areas with limited land resources. Although many of the plots assigned to landless laborers during the land reform movements of the 1930s and 1940s had been adequate to support the rural population at an improved standard of living, pressures on the land began to become apparent during the 1950s. By 1960, the ratio of cultivated land to labor in some of the more congested and poorer regions of Mexico, including the central and southern zones, appears to have fallen to below two hectares per member of the agricultural labor force. With shrinking land resources available for redistribution, the diminishing prospects of acquiring one's own holding might be expected to induce the more adventuresome among the rural population to seek their fortunes elsewhere.

The rural origins and modest educational attainment of most migrants is reflected in their occupational experience before migration. Agricultural employment was reported as the last premigration job for from 40 to 55 percent of the migrants; this proportion shows a secular increase among successive cohorts. Approximately one-fourth of the migrants had held low-skilled jobs in construction or artisan or factory production. In short, from two-thirds to three-fourths of the migrants were unskilled manual workers prior to migrating. The balance were employed in commerce and services; some of these may also have been in low-skilled jobs. Those with prior experience in skilled, technical, or professional employment appear to have numbered no more than 15 percent of the migrants.[30]

Only limited information is available about the employment status of migrants prior to migrating, and that refers largely to the status of those whose jobs had been in agriculture. By and large, it is the wage laborer and the unpaid family worker who migrate, which, in view of the youth of the migrants, is not surprising. *Ejidatarios* or *aparceros* (share croppers) appear as a small minority in the flow, on the order of 11 percent in the Mexico City sample.[31] The degree of stability in employment was reported to be low for Anson's Monterrey sample; only 31 percent held an *empleo de planta* (permanent job).[32] In contrast, the survey of migrants to Mexico City found that three-fifths of the respondents held permanent remunerated jobs before migration.[33]

Integration in Urban Labor Market

The process of integration into the metropolitan labor market appears to have been a relatively painless one. Although only a small proportion, approximately one-quarter, either were certain of a job or had the promise of a job prior to migration, the delay in finding employment was short. Over 60 percent found a job within two weeks of arrival in Mexico City.[34] Anson's migrants averaged 11.5 days to find their first job in Monterrey.[35] The importance of friends and relatives in the destination point becomes apparent again, for between one-half and three-quarters of the new arrivals found their first jobs with their help. Most migrants arrive with few definite job preferences. In view of the prevalence of agricultural workers with nontransferable skills, this should not be surprising. Seventeen percent of the migrants to Mexico City expressed a preference for employment in manufacturing, construction, or unskilled service occupations; another 15 percent wished to continue exercising their artisan skills. Only 8 percent aspired to nonprofessional white-collar occupations.[36]

Migrants' first jobs are heavily concentrated in the unskilled manual categories in manufacturing and construction and, to a lesser extent, in services. However, an important distinction can be drawn between those who had and had not held jobs before migrating. Those who took their first job ever in Mexico City reported an occupational structure that was more favorable than that of natives in their first job. Particularly notable were the larger proportion entering nonmanual jobs, including the highly skilled occupations, and the lower proportion entering unskilled manual work. Conversely, those who reported prior work experience fared significantly worse than natives in their first employment in the city.[37]

The work histories of the migrants offer little support for the commonly expressed view that migration is the cause of the "tertiarization" of cities. The proportion of the migrants entering the service sector in low-skilled jobs shows a progressive decline among the cohorts arriving in each decade since 1930. Of the migrants arriving during 1930–39, almost half found their first employment in the service sector. By the decade of the 1960s, this proportion had fallen to 27 percent.[38] In fact, nonmigrant unskilled entrants to the labor force were to be found in services in greater proportions than were migrants during that decade, and a growing proportion of migrants flowed into the industrial sector. During the 1960s, 56 percent of the unskilled entrants found jobs there, a larger proportion than that among nonmigrants. Nor should it be assumed that the manufacturing activity in which the migrants became employed was of an artisan or "informal" nature; fully 70 percent of those entering manufacturing did so in the capital goods sector. Construction activity has also shown a gradual decline in importance as a port of entry. Whereas about one-fourth of the unskilled male migrants entered that sector during the 1930–49 interval, only 17 percent did so in the more recent decade. The fact that none of the migrants to Mexico City reported employment as itinerant vendors or in a self-employed status for their first jobs is significant.[39] Butterworth also found it "noteworthy that none of the migrants [to Mexico City of Mixtec origins from Oaxaca] is an ambulatory salesman, 'peddler' or vendor of any kind."[40]

Migration to the metropolitan areas resulted in an increase in employment stability. Anson found that, on the one hand, 36 percent held a permanent job, or empleo de planta, in their first year, but, by the end of the interval of his study, 52 percent enjoyed that status. On the other hand, he found that in each year between 29 and 51 percent of his sample had suffered at least four weeks of unemployment. Whether that represents an improvement or deterioration as compared with the premigration employment cannot be determined in the absence of data about the latter.[41] To the extent that premigration jobs were in agriculture, some seasonal unemployment might have been expected. The authors of the Mexican City study define employment instability in terms of the frequency of job changes rather than unemployment. In that case, rather than representing a negative quality of employment, changes of jobs proved to be a medium of occupational mobility and improvement in job status.[42]

Migrants to Mexico City were more heavily concentrated at the lower end of the earnings distribution than were native male members of the labor force. The proportion of male migrants aged 21 to 60 earning less than the legal minimum wage was 28.1 percent, as compared with 15.8 percent for the natives. However, the average performance of the migrants was heavily weighted by the number of rural migrants with agricultural work histories, who tended to fare less well; 32.6 percent of these workers earned less than the minimum, in part because they are less educated and older as a group upon arrival in Mexico City. Migrants whose first employment was in a nonagricultural sector fared no worse than natives with respect to earnings below the legal minimums.

Earnings were also a function of the length of residence in Mexico City. The most recent arrivals, workers with fewer than ten years of residence, were most likely to be earning less than the minimum; 38.6 percent did so. Among those with ten to nineteen years of residence, 28.2 percent earned below minimum wages; 26.4 percent of those with more than 20 years in the city did so.[43] Since Mexico City had among the highest legal minimum wages in the country, exceeded only by some of the zones bordering the United States, this finding does not preclude the possibility that unskilled migrant workers in the metropolitan area realized earnings greater than those of the vast majority of unskilled workers in the rest of the country.

The anthropologists' studies of migrants also concur that migration enhanced their economic welfare. Kemper found most Tzintzuntzeños earning the minimum in Mexico City in 1969–1970, or the equivalent of US$2.54 per day. By contrast, few Tzintzuntzan villagers earned more than a dollar a day in the traditional occupations in farming, pottery making, and shopkeeping.[44] Butterworth's Mixtecan community in Mexico City reported earnings ranging from Mex$400 to Mex$1,000 a month in 1960, which averaged Mex$550, or about 33 percent more than the minimum.[45] Nine years later, in 1969, only 7 percent of the workers employed in agriculture in the state of Oaxaca earned as much as Mex$500 a month. In manufacturing jobs, 30 percent did so, as did minorities of employees in construction, commerce, and services.[46] Arizpe reported a growing differential rate of earnings between those migrants from the Mazahua region in the western part of the state of México who had become established in Mexico City and agricultural laborers in the Mazahuan villages. The weekly wage of an *albañil* in construction in the capital averaged Mex$90 in 1955, had doubled by 1965, and had reached Mex$224 by 1971. By contrast, the daily agriculture wage rose from Mex$42 a week in 1955 to Mex$60 in 1965, and to Mex$90 in 1971. The inflation of the mid-1970s apparently reduced the relative advantages of urban employment, however, and Arizpe reports a trickle of return migrants in the face of disillusionment with the high cost of living in Mexico City.[47]

In spite of this reservation, all of the studies conclude that, in most cases, migration to the metropolitan areas resulted in an immediate improvement in the employment status of migrants.[48] However, the full implication of migration for the employment position of workers depends not only on the immediate gains but also on the opportunities for subsequent improvement. In this respect, the evidence is again encouraging. Balan,

Browning, and Jelin analyzed the experience of men entering the Monterrey labor market in an unskilled category and found that, within a ten-year interval, 54 percent had moved out of the unskilled category. Even the remaining 46 percent showed a high frequency of occupational change within the unskilled ranks. Furthermore, the younger groups showed a higher incidence of upward mobility than did the older, 59 to 48 percent, respectively.[49]

In Mexico City, migrants entering the city's labor force in an unskilled manual job reported a high frequency of upward movement, 25 percent a one-step move and 44 percent a two-step move within a seven-step occupational structure. This experience compared favorably with that of natives whose first employment was in an unskilled job. Their proportions of one- and two-step movements were 25 and 50 percent, respectively. Furthermore, migrants entering skilled manual or nonmanual occupations reported higher frequencies of upward mobility than did the natives.[50]

Among manual workers, industrial employment offered a higher probability of advancement than did any other. This was probably attributable to the practice in modern industry of advancing workers through an occupational hierarchy according to seniority. Workers with premigration jobs in agriculture tended to experience somewhat lower rates of upward mobility than did others. This may reflect the fact the the former tended to migrate at a later age and to have less education than those with nonagricultural backgrounds. Although workers with agricultural backgrounds may thus appear to be at a disadvantage relative to those with other work experience, compared with those who remain in agriculture, where the opportunities for upward mobility are extremely limited, they have done well.

All of the surveyed populations view themselves as having made significant improvements in their status and living standards as a result of migration. Overwhelmingly, they pronounced themselves satisfied with the economic results of their move. Anson is the only researcher to have gathered detailed information about earnings before and after migration, and these show very substantial improvements.[51] Whereas 43 percent of the migrants earned less than Mex$10,400 in the year prior to migration, only 5 percent did so in the first year following the move. (The income figures are all in terms of constant 1975 Mexican pesos.) At the other end of the earnings structure, 31 percent earned more than Mex$20,800 before migrating, while 51 percent exceeded that amount in their first year in Monterrey. By the end of the five-year interval under study, fully 80 percent reported earnings in excess of Mex$20,800. On the average, family incomes for the first and last postmigration years exceeded the last premigration income by 30 and 64 percent, respectively.

Anson then proceeds further to calculate the returns to migration after adjusting for differences in the cost of living between Monterrey and the migrants' places of origin and for changes in their opportunity cost.[52] In the first year, a median internal rate of return of 13.5 percent was realized. On the assumption that income increased at a constant rate over the interval studied, the rate of return increases to 37.8 percent by the year prior to the study.[53] To be sure, some respondents, about 10 percent of the sample, reported either small positive or negative returns in their first year in Monterrey. In virtually all cases, however, these were migrants who had previously enjoyed "high" incomes, so that they were not denied the essentials of living by their move. Compensating for this lack of immediate improvement was the more stable or permanent character of their employment. Furthermore, by the end of the period, half of those who initially had experienced negative returns had begun to realize positive net returns.

A final point of interest is the very low cost of migration reported by Anson's sample. The total cost for rural migrants amounted to Mex$471 (US$38), and Mex$899 (US$72) for interurban migrants. This difference in cost can largely be ascribed to the difference in forgone earnings during the move—the cash outlays differed by only Mex$76. The low cost of migration reflects the low price of bus transportation in Mexico and the important subsidy in the form of free room and board which most migrants receive upon arrival in the city.[54]

The limited information available about female migration indicates many similarities to that of males.[55] The age structure is very similar as is the proportion originating in rural areas. As among men, there is an inverse relationship between distance and the number of migrants who come from states outside the Federal District. The greater the distance moved, however, the greater is the incidence of urban antecedents among the migrants. Women are much less likely than men, 24 versus 57 percent, according to one sample, to have had any work experience prior to migration; they also have had fewer years of schooling than men. Among those with prior work experience, the incidence of nonmanual employment appears to be higher than among male migrants or among the female labor force as a whole. But this group does not offset the lack of work experience and low levels of formal education of the bulk of the migrants. Female migrants in the labor force are heavily concentrated in low-skilled jobs, particularly in services. One of the most common ports of entry to the urban labor market is domestic service. Given the ready availability of work and the assurance of room and board, it reduces the risks and costs of migration considerably.

The researchers of El Colegio de México provide some earnings data for female migrants that are differentiated by length of time since migration to

Mexico City. By and large, women's earnings were lower than those of men at all points in time, but especially in the first employment in Mexico City. Whereas 64 percent of recent female migrants earned less than the legal minimum wage in their first employment, only 27 percent of males did so. Earnings of both sexes improved with longer residence, however. Indeed, females exhibited a relatively higher incidence of improvement if earnings above the minimum wage were taken as the criterion. Among long-established migrants, the proportion still earning less than the minimum wage fell by 46 percent to 34.7 percent of the women, and by 38.4 percent to 16.7 percent among men.

Migrant females did relatively worse than men when compared with natives of their own sex. Whereas the proportion of long-time resident male migrants receiving less than the legal minimum wage was only slightly greater than that among natives, the proportion among migrant women was almost twice that of natives. Thus, in spite of the considerable absolute improvement in the economic status of migrant women, they appear to be more disadvantaged than native women. Because these data do not control for differences in age or educational levels, however, they may reflect very different demographic characteristics of the two populations, rather than simply their status as migrants or natives.[56]

Migration and Regional Income Differentials

To the extent that migration flows respond to differences in income among regions, it is to be expected that regional disparities in incomes would tend to decline over time. As the population moves to regions with high average incomes, the rate of growth in earnings might be expected to decline, while the exodus from low-income regions might be expected to raise the rate of increase there. Typically, however, the process of narrowing may be expected to be spread over several decades. Indeed, early in periods of accelerating growth, regional income differentials are more likely to increase; sustained narrowing occurs only after the development process has begun to approach maturity.

From 1900 to 1940, the metropolitan region comprising Mexico City and the surrounding area of the state of México led all others in the rate of increase in both population and per capita income. Two other high-income areas, the Northwest and Gulf regions, experienced higher rates of growth in both per capita income and population than did the remaining regions. Conversely, the poorer regions suffered slower rates of growth in both income and population.[57] Income disparities among the regions thus increased during the early part of the century. Between 1940 and 1970, the income position of the capital and the state of México declined relative to all but one region, but the high-income border regions in the North and Northwest gained relative to all the others.

The course of income dispersion can best be summarized by reference to the coefficient of variation (V), taking Unikel's measures of per capita gross domestic product of the individual states as observations. In 1900, V had a value of 52.5 percent. A sharp increase in dispersion occurred in the interval to 1940; V in that year was 80.5 percent. Over the next decade, V declined to 66.6 percent and remained at that approximate level through 1970. Thus. while some decline in dispersion seems to have occurred between 1940 and 1950, resource mobility was not sufficient to bring about a continued narrowing of regional income differentials. Indeed, the poorer states in the southern and central regions continued to lose ground relative to the average for the country as a whole through 1970. During the ensuing decade, however, returns from the 1980 census suggest that a reversal in this widening tendency may have set in. (See table 4-7 and the accompanying discussion for evidence of such a reversal.) Whereas Unikel's data are derived from the national accounts, the population census reports monthly incomes earned by labor force members. These income data yield measures of dispersion that are considerably smaller than those derived from the national accounts. In 1970, V stood at 49.4 percent. By 1980, it had declined to 27.1 percent. In view of the reservations I have expressed regarding the reliability of the 1980 census, it would seem prudent to await the emergence of additional evidence before accepting the finding of narrowing income differentials at face value.

Summary

The evidence reviewed here offers little support for the view that migration has been "excessive" or immiserizing. In terms of private costs and benefits, it would seem that migration has proceeded in directions predicted by theory and has resulted in substantial net gains to the migrants. Migration is a self-selective process whereby individuals who already have the best chances of succeeding move to a more challenging environment. In the Mexican context of steady and rapid economic growth, urban employment opportunities have emerged at wage levels that are comfortably above rural alternatives and have survived in spite of the large migratory flow. The expansive nature of urban labor markets is illustrated by the promptness with which most migrants were absorbed on advantageous terms. I attach considerable significance to the persistence of large urban-rural differentials and to the favorable character of the employment conditions of migrants prior to migration. They suggest strongly that migration represented a response to perceived opportunities for economic improvement, rather than simply an act of desperation to escape impossible economic conditions at home. Nor are economic gains limited to the short run following migration. Apparently, upward mobility was commonly realized among migrants. Within a few years, their socioeconomic position (at least, for males) was indistinguishable from that of urban natives with similar demographic characteristics. Regional differentials in income may be expected to narrow as a result of migration, but only after a lag. In Mexico, prior to 1970, there was little such change, but preliminary indications suggest that a significant narrowing may have finally occurred during the past decade.

Notes

1. For example, during the decade of the 1940s there was an almost fourfold increase in the number of kilometers of paved road from 768 in 1939 to 2,623 in 1950. The number of radios increased tenfold between 1940 and 1960, from 325,000 to 3,200,000. Rising literacy levels also contributed to improved information flows.

2. Throughout this book, references to Mexico's states should be understood to include the Federal District, which is not a state, and Baja California Sur, which until recently had the status of a territory.

3. The proportion of non-natives in the population of the metropolitan Mexico City area in 1970 was approximately the same, 32 percent.

4. Gustavo Cabrera Acevedo, "Población, migración y fuerza de trabajo," in *Mercados regionales de trabajo* (México, D.F.: Instituto Nacional de Estudios del Trabajo, 1976), pp. 283–84. Unikel estimates the flow to have included 4.5 million people between 1950 and 1970, but he defines urban centers as those with 15,000 or more population (Luis Unikel, *El desarrollo urbano de México*, 2d ed. [Mexico, D.F.: El Colegio de México, 1978], p. 213).

5. Unikel, *El desarrollo urbano*, appendix table VI-A19.

6. Michael J. Greenwood and Jerry R. Ladman, "An Economic Analysis of Migration in Mexico," *Annals of Regional Science*, vol. 12, no. 2 (1978), pp. 16–31; Jonathan King, "Interstate Migration in Mexico," *Economic Development and Cultural Change*, vol. 27, no. 1 (1978), pp. 83–102; Joseph P. Stoltman and John M. Ball, "Migration and the Local Economic Factor in Rural Mexico," *Human Organization*, vol. 30, no. 1 (1971); Luis Unikel, C. Ruiz Chiapetto, and O. Lazcano, "Factores de rechazo en la migración rural en México, 1950–1960," *Demografía y economía*, vol. 7, no. 1 (1973), pp. 24–57; Unikel, *El desarrollo urbano*.

7. Of the studies cited, that of Greenwood and Ladman offers the clearest results, and their regressions have the greatest explanatory power of all. The others suffer weaknesses that impair their effectiveness. King includes a large number of variables, many of which are closely interrelated; as a result, his regressions are plagued with problems of multicollinearity, which pose serious problems for the interpretation of his findings. Unikel's approach appears to have several shortcomings. Some of his equations are misspecified; for example, he includes measures of both inputs and outputs of a production function as independent variables in the same equation. In addition, some of his variables might be expected to be

interrelated; there is thus the possibility of multicollinearity. He groups states of origin by reference to a particular characteristic and runs separate regressions for each group, a method that reduces the variance within the sample of the independent variables presumably associated with migration rates. Finally, in his analysis of destinations, his groupings result in a small number of observations relative to the number of independent variables, thus reducing the degrees of freedom.

8. In the Greenwood and Ladman study ("An Economic Analysis of Migration, p. 21), these three variables, plus population size, accounted for 70 percent of the variance.

9. Secretaría de Programación y Presupuesto, *Encuesta continua sobre ocupación* (ECSO), vol. 7, 1st quarter (1979), p. 238.

10. An exception is represented by Enrique Contreras S., *Estratificación y movilidad social en la ciudad de México* (Mexico, D.F.: Universidad Nacional Autonoma de México, 1978), p. 89. His sample of migrants consisted of heads of families; as a result it included only a small number of female migrants, which can hardly be considered representative.

11. Gustavo Cabrera A., "Población, migración y fuerza de trabajo."

12. Secretaría de Industria y Comercio, Dirección General de Estadística, *IX Censo general de población, 1970, Resumen general* (Mexico, D.F., 1972), table 14.

13. Ricardo Anson, "La relación entre la politica de migración interna y la realidad de las consecuencias personales de la migración interna: el caso de Monterrey" (Monterrey, Nuevo Leon: Instituto Tecnologico y de Estudios Superiores de Monterrey, n.d.; processed), p. 14; Jorge Balan, Harley L. Browning, and Elizabeth Jelin, *Men in a Developing Society* (Austin: University of Texas Press, 1973), p. 64; Mercedes Pedrero N., "Corrientes migratorias internas de México (1950–60)," in *Conferencia regional latinoamericana de población, Actas 1* (México, D.F.: El Colegio de México, 1972), pp. 547–52; Contreras, *Estratificación y movilidad*, p. 68.

14. Pedrero reports ("Corrientes migratorias internas," pp. 547–52) that 81 percent of the migrants to the Northwest region, another area of dynamic growth in recent years, originated in neighboring zones.

15. Humberto Muñoz, Orlandina de Oliveira, and Claudio Stern, *Migraciones internas a la ciudad de México y su impacto*, Temas de la Ciudad no. 8 (Mexico, D.F.: Delegación del D.D.F. en Venustiano Carranza, 1978), p. 35.

16. Balan, Browning, and Jelin, *Men in a Developing Society*, p. 64.

17. One-step migration to Mexico City was found to be typical of more recent migrants by other studies as well. Whereas some of the earlier migrants would first move to regional urban centers, later migrants overwhelmingly left for Mexico City directly. George M. Foster, *Tzintzuntzan: Mexican Peasants in a Changing World*, rev. ed. (New York: Elsevier, 1979), p. 273; Douglas S. Butterworth, "A Study of the Urbanization Process among Mixtec Migrants from Tilatongo in Mexico City," in *Peasants in Cities*, ed. William Manglin (Boston, Mass.: Houghton-Mifflin, 1970), p. 101.

18. Contreras, *Estratificación y movilidad*, pp. 70–72.

19. Anson, "La relación entre la politica de migración," p. 14; Balan, Browning, and Jelin, *Men in a Developing Society*, p. 154.

20. This information about the migrants to Mexico City was extracted from unpublished tables (hereafter referred to as Tabs.), to which I was kindly given access by Orlandina de Oliveira at the Colegio de México. The presence of relatives and friends in Mexico City is cited as a significant factor guiding migration by Larissa A. Lomitz, *Networks and Marginality: Life in a Mexican Shantytown* (New York: Academic Press, 1977).

21. Balan, Browning, and Jelin, *Men in a Developing Society*, p. 160; Tabs.

22. Ibid., p. 150; Contreras, *Estratificación y movilidad*, pp. 82–83. Cabrera reports ("Población, migración y fuerza de trabajo") that migrants in Mexico generally are young. In

each of three intercensal decades since 1930, about half of the male migrants were between the ages of 10 and 24 years and an additional 14 percent between 25 and 29. The proportion of women in the 10–24 age bracket consistently exceeded that of men although by a narrow margin. Among both sexes, the proportion arriving in the youngest age groups showed a small upward trend.

23. Muñoz, de Oliveira, and Stern, *Migraciones internas*, p. 47.

24. Foster, *Tzintzuntzan*, p. 273; Robert V. Kemper, "Tzintzuntzeños in Mexico City: The Anthropologist Among Recent Migrants," in *Anthropologists in Cities*, ed. George M. Foster and Robert V. Kemper (Boston, Mass.: Little, Brown, 1974), p. 83.

25. Balan, Browning, and Jelin, *Men in a Developing Society*, pp. 144–47.

26. The difference in educational attainments between urban and rural migrants is suggested by Anson's finding ("La relación entre la politica de migracion," p. 14) that, among his sample of adult male migrants arriving in Monterrey between 1969 and 1974, the former had completed seven and the latter three years of school.

27. Kemper, "Tzintzuntzeños in Mexico City," p. 83; Lourdes Arizpe, *Migración, etnicismo y cambio económico* (Mexico, D.F.: El Colegio de México, 1978), pp. 78–79.

28. These returns were estimated from a multiple regression equation of monthly earnings on education, age, occupational status (that is, employer, employee, self-employed, and so on), and size of community of residence. The data were drawn from the 1968 and 1977 household surveys of incomes and expenditures and were processed for this project by the Banco de México, S.A. The absence of large differences in income associated with differences in educational levels among men employed in agriculture was also demonstrated by unpublished data drawn from the 1970 population census by the Grupo de Estudio del Problema del Empleo.

29. Tabs.

30. Balan, Browning, and Jelin, *Men in a Developing Society*, pp. 154–55; Muñoz, de Oliveira, and Stern, *Migraciones internas*, pp. 43–45; Anson, "La relación entre la politica de migración interna," p. 14.

31. Tabs.

32. Anson, "La relación entre la politica de migración interna," p. 21.

33. Tabs.

34. Ibid.

35. Anson, "La relación entre la politica de migración interna," p. 12.

36. Tabs.

37. Humberto Muñoz and Orlandina de Oliveira, "Migración y movilidad ocupacional," in *Migración y desigualdad social en la ciudad de México*, ed. Humberto Muñoz, Orlandina de Oliveira, and Claudio Stern (Mexico, D.F.: El Colegio de México, 1977), p. 94.

38. Muñoz, de Oliviera, and Stern, *Migraciones internas*, p. 43. Migrants with prior employment in agriculture have consistently evinced a higher incidence of service sector employment as a port of entry than those with nonagricultural or no previous work experience. See also Humberto Muñoz and Orlandina de Oliveiros, "Migración, oportunidades de empleo y diferencias de ingreso en la ciudad de México," *Revista mexicana de sociología*, vol. 38, no. 1 (1976), pp. 55–56.

39. Brigida García, Humberto Muñoz, and Orlandina de Oliveira, "Migraciones internas y grupos populares urbanos: Ciudad de México (1950–70)," in *Población y desarrollo en América Latina*, ed. Víctor L. Urquidi and José B. Morelos (Mexico, D.F.: El Colegio de México, 1979), p. 122. The group of migrants described here is limited to those who had been employed prior to their arrival in Mexico City. It thus excludes migrants who arrived as children and later entered the labor market.

40. Butterworth, "A Study of the Urbanization Process," p. 106.

41. Anson, "La relación entre la politica de migración," pp. 21–22.

42. García, Muñoz, and de Oliveira, "Migraciones internas y grupos populares urbanos," p. 123.

43. Humberto Muñoz, Orlandina de Oliveira, and Claudio Stern, "Migración y marginalidad ocupacional," in *Migración y desigualdad*, pp. 80–83.

44. Kemper, "Tzintzuntzeños in Mexico City," p. 87.

45. Butterworth, "A Study of the Urbanization Process," pp. 106–107.

46. *Censo general de población, 1970*, table 48.

47. Arizpe, *Migración, etnicismo y cambio económico*, pp. 85–86.

48. A caveat must be entered regarding the interpretation of this finding. Migrants who fail to improve their economic status in the city may simply return to their places of origin and thus escape detection.

49. Balan, Browning, and Jelin, *Men in a Developing Society*, pp. 132–33. Another dimension of socioeconomic mobility associated with migration is the intergenerational one. Migrants improve not only their premigration position but also their socioeconomic status relative to their fathers. See, for example, Instituto Nacional de Estudios del Trabajo, *La incorporación al trabajo obrero en un medio de industrialización reciente*, Folleto Tecnico no. 1 (Mexico, D.F., 1977), p. 24.

50. Muñoz and de Oliveira, "Migración y movilidad ocupacional," pp. 95–97.

51. Anson, "La relación entre la politica de migración," pp. 19–26.

52. The opportunity cost in each year is calculated by adjusting the migrant's last premigration rate of earnings by the average rate of change in earnings in his zone of origin.

53. The nominal rate of return was calculated to be 288 percent in the first year. The way in which this was adjusted to account for differences in the cost of living in the premigration residence is not spelled out in Anson's paper. The maximum possible number of years of residence of his sample in Monterrey was less than six.

54. Anson, "La relación entre la politica de migración," pp. 16–17. In his summary table 1, Anson refers to the costs of migration as the *family* costs, implying that they refer to the costs of moving the migrant *and* his family. Furthermore, in the text he notes that 65 percent of the migrants made the move together with the complete family. Since the average size of the family unit was 4.4 persons, this total cost of moving strikes me as surprisingly low.

55. Contreras, *Estratificación y movilidad*, pp. 89–91.

56. Muñoz and de Oliveira, "Migración y movilidad ocupacional," p. 84.

57. Unikel, *El desarrollo urbano*, pp. 179–84.

6. Migration to the United States

THE RIO GRANDE and the northern border of the states of Chihuahua, Sonora, and Baja California define the political boundary between Mexico and the United States. Historically, however, they have not posed an effective barrier to the movement of population. Until the mid-nineteenth century, of course, the U.S. area that now abuts Mexico was an extension of that country, having been part and parcel of the Spanish domain before Mexican independence. Much of southwestern United States and California had been settled by Spaniards, and after independence Mexicans continued to be free to move to the northern territories. But migration to these territories was in fact relatively small. Only New Mexico had received a substantial flow of settlers.

In 1849, when the Treaty of Guadalupe Hidalgo ceded to the United States Mexico's northern territories, the Hispanic population was estimated to be on the order of 73,000–100,000. Of these, approximately 60,000 were in New Mexico, 7,500 in California, and 5,000 in Texas.[1] Mexicans continued to move northward throughout the nineteenth century in response to a demand for labor in mining, agriculture, and railway construction, but in little more than a trickle. Only in the decade of the 1870s did as many as 5,000 Mexicans migrate across the border.[2] At the turn of the century, the total Mexican population in the United States amounted to only 103,393. As Barton Clark has observed, the significance of that number lies, not in its absolute size, but in its geographical distribution. Heavily concentrated in the Southwest and California, it defined the region toward which most of the twentieth-century migration would be directed.[3] Indeed, the great bulk, 85 percent, of the population of Mexican origin is still concentrated in the Southwest.

The turn of the century marked a watershed in the course of Mexican migration to the United States, for the flow suddenly assumed major proportions. In the first decade alone, more Mexicans migrated to the United States than had done so during the entire preceding eighty years since independence. With the exception of the depression decade of the 1930s, this flow has continued unabated (see table 6-1). Mexico did not become subject to numerical immigration quotas until the amendment of the Immigration and Naturalization Act in 1965. The number of legal immigrants averaged around 44,000 annually during the remainder of that decade and has increased to between 60,000 and 70,000 during the 1970s.

These documented immigrants, however, constitute only part of the flow across Mexico's northern border. Indeed, that legal movement has been overshadowed by a much greater flow of illegal migrants who cross the border seeking temporary employment or an extended residence in the United States. Although the impact this phenomenon has had on conditions in the U.S. labor market has been of considerable concern, if not controversy, this is not the primary focus here. Rather, this chapter views the flow as an extension of the process of internal migration that was discussed in Chapter 5. What will be examined are the size of the flow, characteristics of migrants, the motivation underlying the decision to migrate, the nature of their migratory experience, and some of the possible consequences for employment conditions in Mexican labor markets.

Measures of Stocks and Flows of Migrants

Clearly, the total number of temporary and permanent migrants across the frontier has been influenced by conditions in both countries. For example, the sharp increase in migration recorded in table 6-1 during 1911–30 is traceable to the political and economic turmoil that characterized the revolutionary period in Mexico. At the same time in the United States, the labor shortages experienced during World War I and the general prosperity that extended for a decade beyond that war provided attractive employment opportunities for Mexicans. Particularly with the

Table 6-1. *Immigration to the United States from Mexico, 1821–1977*

Years	*Immigrants*	*Years*	*Immigrants*
1821–1900[a]	28,002	1951–60	299,811
1901–10	49,642	1961–70	443,301
1911–20	219,004	1971–75	318,075
1921–30	459,287	1975	62,205
1931–40	22,319	1976	57,863
1941–50	60,589	1977	62,205

a. No record of Mexican immigration is available for 1886–93. As a result, the number given understates somewhat the actual size of the nineteenth-century flow.

Source: U.S. Immigration Service, *Annual Report*, 1974 and 1977.

termination of free immigration from Europe in 1921, Mexican workers were ideally positioned to respond to any rightward shift in the U.S. demand for unskilled labor.

The reestablishment of order and stability in Mexico in the 1930s and the concurrent severe economic depression in the United States brought an abrupt end to the growing stream of registered immigrants. That decade also saw the first concentrated effort to expel illegal immigrants already resident in the United States; the goal was to alleviate some of the economic distress resulting from the widespread unemployment. Between 1929 and 1937, some 400,000 Mexicans were repatriated. In addition, the Border Patrol was more intensively employed to reduce the illegal entry of Mexicans.[4]

The economic expansion and labor shortages spawned by World War II again created an environment favorable to renewed Mexican migration. Immigration regulations were relaxed to permit a larger flow of legal migrants. In addition, the bracero program was adopted as a vehicle for the recruitment of temporary migrants for employment in agriculture. Although the program was intended to expire at the end of the war, pressures from agrarian interests caused the U.S. Congress to extend it to 1951 and then until 1964. During its lifetime, some 4.8 million workers were contracted to work in the United States.[5]

Illegal Migration

However, these recorded flows of immigrants and braceros did not constitute the total count of migrants to the United States. The flow of illegal migrants began to exceed that of the legal in the 1940s. Returning braceros spoke glowingly of high earnings and of their desire to return to the United States. Others were undoubtedly influenced by such reports and experienced similar desires. Since the number of Mexican workers seeking bracero contracts exceeded the certificates of need issued by the secretary of labor, all those wishing temporary employment in the United States could not be accommodated by the bracero program. Furthermore, a bribe was frequently required to ensure selection. Thus, to many and particularly those who had acquired a familiarity with the United States through previous entries as braceros, it must have seemed easier simply to cross the border on their own.[6] The other side of the coin was the ready demand for illegal migrants among agricultural employers who preferred to avoid being bound by the conditions of employment and government supervision that were imposed by the formal bracero program.[7]

The apprehension and expulsion of illegal migrants mounted substantially after the end of World War II. From 26,689 in 1944 they reached a peak of 1,075,165 in 1954 when a concentrated effort, Operation Wetback, was mounted to sweep from the interiors of Texas, Arizona, and California to the border. In the process, some of the accumulated backlog of migrants undoubtedly fell into the net. Perhaps because of the success of this effort, the number of apprehensions declined over the following decade to fewer than 100,000 a year. Still, over the whole lifetime of the bracero program, 1942–64, more than 5 million illegal migrants were apprehended.[8] Since no account can be taken of multiple crossings and apprehensions, however, this figure undoubtedly overstates the number apprehended.

A large proportion of deportable Mexican aliens—62 percent in 1974—are apprehended within seventy-two hours of their crossing into the United States.[9] Since they failed to realize the objective of their entry, the temptation to try again is likely to prove irresistible. Indeed, interviews with apprehended Mexicans have recorded multiple apprehensions for many. Furthermore, the efforts of the Border Patrol to control the flow of aliens have varied in intensity over time. During periods of economic expansion and tight labor markets in the southwestern United States the patrol seems to have relaxed its vigilance, only to return to more restrictive postures when unemployment mounted. Thus, after the intensive sweep of 1954 apprehensions may have declined at least in part because a return to routine control procedures permitted a large flow of migrants to enter undetected and to remain undisturbed.

Finally, the accuracy and significance of the reported numbers of apprehensions have been called into question. As part of its study of migration to and across the northern frontier, the Centro Nacional de Información y Estadísticas del Trabajo (CENIET) manned all of the sites on the Mexican side of the border to which the Immigration and Naturalization Service (INS) delivered the illegal aliens apprehended. CENIET researchers counted the returnees and administered a brief interview to almost all of them. It is disturbing to find a very large discrepancy between the number of apprehensions of deportable aliens reported by the INS and the count of expulsions made by CENIET during August 1978. Whereas the CENIET enumerators registered fewer than 33,000 expulsions, the figure estimated from INS sources amounted to almost 89,000, a discrepancy of approximately 56,000.[10] No reasonable methodological basis for this large discrepancy could be advanced, which suggests the possibility that a systematic inflation of the actual number of detentions and deportations has occurred in the INS.[11] An unlikely alternative explanation is that more than half the apprehensions of deportable aliens do not result in expulsions.

In the absence of any effective method of enumerating the undocumented Mexican aliens in the United States the estimating procedures employed have given rise to widely disparate conclusions. Some of the more extreme estimates of the number of illegal aliens issued by the INS during the 1970s placed the number of illegal aliens between 1 million and 12 million, though the empirical basis for most estimates were weak at best. In 1976 the INS contracted Lesko and Associates to determine the number of undocumented workers. The report, which has been widely criticized on methodological grounds, estimated between 4.2 million and 11 million, with a probable number of 8.2 million of which 5.2 million were Mexicans.[12] With the accession of a new director of the INS, Leonel Castillo, another estimate was released in 1978 that placed the number between 3 million and 6 million.

The controversy over the number of illegal aliens stimulated several more serious efforts to resolve the issue.[13] One such study, by Lancaster and Scheuren, placed the number of all illegals, including non-Mexicans aged 18 to 44, at between 2.9 million and 5.7 million in 1973 with a suggested specific figure of 3.9 million.[14] Members of the white race, which presumably include Mexicans, were placed at between 2.0 million and 3.7 million. The estimates were derived by application of "capture and recapture" techniques that are appropriate for estimating populations not subject to census counts. The authors relied on a matching by the Bureau of the Census of households enumerated in the Current Population Survey (CPS) that also appeared in any one of the following three registers: Internal Revenue lists of taxpayers, contributors to Social Security, and recipients of Social Security benefits. An estimate of the population, including illegal aliens, was calculated from this matching. It was then compared with an estimate derived from an adjustment of the 1970 census figures forward to 1973; this accounted for births, deaths, and net legal migration but excluded illegal migration. The difference between these two population estimates was attributed to the presence of illegal aliens. The authors recognized the fragility of some of the assumptions underlying the procedure and tried to compensate by allowing for a generous margin of error. Although the estimates may be subject to some question, they at least have the virtue of being based on data and procedures that are explicitly described; readers are thus allowed to make adjustments as they see fit.[15]

Mexicans are presumed to form a preponderant though unknown proportion of illegal aliens in the United States. Although Mexicans constitute about 85–90 percent of all deportable aliens apprehended, this proportion cannot be taken to represent the true incidence of Mexicans within the total alien population. Multiple entries and apprehensions within any given period are realistically possible only for Mexicans and Canadians (the latter, however, do not avail themselves of the opportunity in significant numbers). Furthermore, since the apprehensions of Mexicans are concentrated in the border region, they are easier to effect than are those of persons originating in other countries who are dispersed over a wider area. North and Houstoun have estimated that Mexicans make up between 60 and 65 percent of the illegal alien population.[16]

The Flow of Migrants

The measures offered thus far are concerned with the size of the stock of illegal migrants. To appraise the impact of migration on the Mexican labor market, however, one needs the rate of change in the stock of Mexican permanent residents in the United States and the size of the flow of temporary migrants. As in the case of the stock, the flows have been subject to widely divergent estimates. For example, Secretary of Labor Marshall was cited as stating in 1977 that probably 2 to 3 million illegal aliens enter the United States each year. The INS has offered estimates of a similar order of magnitude. During the 1970s, the INS apprehended about 700,000 deportable aliens annually. Based on its presumption that, for every apprehension, two aliens escape detention, the number of illegal entries would be estimated to exceed 2 million.[17] However, these appear to be rather arbitrary measures that do not distinguish between gross and net flows or between permanent and temporary residence in the United States.

Several attempts have been made to estimate the net flow of illegal immigrants from demographic statistics. Using U.S. population statistics from the 1970 census and subsequent counts from the CPS, David Heer estimated the growth of the population of Mexican origin between 1970 and 1975. After allowing for undercounting of this subgroup in the census and for net documented immigration, he obtained a residual increase that could not be accounted for by the national growth rate and was therefore attributed to net illegal immigration. He actually derived seven estimates by employing cross-classifications of various assumptions about the ratio of net to gross documented migration and the proportions by which the population of Mexican origin was undercounted in the 1970 census. His preferred estimate of the annual rate of growth of the illegal immigrant population was 116,000 between 1970 and 1975.[18]

An alternative method was employed by J. Gregory Robinson.[19] He departed from an assumption that neither the population census nor the CPS capture the alien population, but that reported deaths do include most aliens. If so, age-specific death rates, especially those from violent causes, should be higher in those regions in which aliens are presumed to be concentrated. In fact, he did find a persistent deviation in the death rate trend for ten states since 1960 for white males aged 20–44, but for no other group. By applying different death rates and varying assumptions regarding the proportion of illegal alien deaths that go unrecorded and the proportion of the illegal population captured by the population census, he derived a range of estimates of the illegal alien population at various points in time. Thus an estimate of the annual rate of change was provided. The two estimates of the growth considered most plausible by the author for the five southwestern states that are presumed to host most Mexican migrants are given in table 6-2. The annual rate of increase for the decade of the 1960s would thus lie in the range of 36,000–46,000 a year and 230,000–267,000 a year during the 1970–75 interval. Robinson considered these to be of the same general order of magnitude as the estimates made by Heer or those derivable from the estimates of Lancaster and Scheuren.

Apparently only one demographic study based on Mexican census data has estimated the growth in the stock of undocumented migrants in the United States.[20] Howard Goldberg compared the 1970 and 1960 Mexican population census and, using the residual method, concluded that 1.6 million Mexicans who were living in Mexico in 1960 could not be accounted for in 1970 by either death or legal emigration to the United States. He attributed this loss to illegal emigration. The Goldberg estimate implies an annual net flow four times greater than Robinson's. It is my belief that Goldberg's estimate is likely to be biased upward. Had the legal emigrants and the presumed number of illegal emigrants remained in Mexico, the population would have been greater by some 2,045,000 in 1970, plus any offspring they would have had. Not including the latter, this would have implied a rate of population growth of 3.84 percent a year rather than the 3.45 percent actually recorded. A natural rate of increase of that magnitude is extraordinarily high even in the developing world. Only the Ivory Coast, Kuwait, and Libya reported growth rates equal to or higher than 3.8 percent per year during the 1960–76 interval, and the first two were recipients of large flows of immigrants.[21]

Table 6-2. *Estimates of the Growth in Illegal Alien Population for Five Southwestern U.S. States, 1960–75*
(thousands)

Estimate	*1960–70*	*1970–75*	*1960–75*
1	363	1,136	1,499
2	464	1,335	1,799

Note: The five states are Arizona, California, Colorado, New Mexico, and Texas.

Manuel García y Griego adopted an extensive estimating procedure and applied it to the flow of illegal migrants over a five-year period, 1972–77.[22] This approach used as its empirical input the INS statistics on apprehensions and the migration histories of Mexicans who were expelled to Mexico and interviewed by staff researchers of CENIET. The latter information was culled from the first of three border surveys that were undertaken by CENIET and extended over a three-week period during October and November 1977. Since the INS reports a distribution of persons expelled by the duration of their stay in the United States, it is possible to classify the migrants into cohorts according to the year of entry to the United States.

Of course, the aliens apprehended are only part of the flow across the border. In addition, there are those who escape detection and return to Mexico of their own volition. The size of this flow is estimated from information derived from the migration histories of a sample of those people apprehended and delivered to the Mexican reception centers during the first survey of 1977. For every expulsion recorded, there were between 0.7 and 1.2 voluntary returns over the 1970–77 period. Slightly more than half of the sample of 3,686 persons interviewed, or 1,857, reported that they had crossed into the United States on previous occasions for a total of 4,687 entries.[23] These individuals were likewise distributed into cohorts defined by the year of each entry. For each cohort, the ratio of voluntary to involuntary departures was computed and applied to the INS data on apprehensions for an estimate of the number of undetected illegal entries. A final component of the flow of migrants was derived from the data on documented, or legal, entries to the United States. If documented entrants reported previous periods of residence, they were assumed to have been illegal aliens and thus were assigned to a cohort by year of entry.

Obviously, one component of the flow of undocumented aliens cannot be accounted for by the available data: those who entered and were not detected. It is axiomatic, however, that all who entered at some point in the past and have not been recorded as exiting, must exit from the stock of aliens in the United States at some point in the future either by expulsion, voluntary departure, legalization of status, or by death. An estimate of the distribution of these future exits from each entering cohort thus provides a basis for adjusting the numbers of known and estimated entries, as described above. It can serve further to estimate the net change in the stock of illegal migrants in the United States. The basis for this estimate is found in the distribution of aliens by duration of their stay. From the data of the INS and the employment histories of the expelled interviewees, it is evident that the bulk of the migrants remain in the United States for less than a year; the proportion ranges from 83 to 87 percent of those exiting between 1972 and 1976. The balance reported durations of more than a year, and the number reporting each additional year of residence declined in a fairly steady sequence. A projection of the rate of change in the number of migrants with from two to seven years' residence yields a number of undetected individuals with longer stays in the United States. The figure so estimated can then be assigned to cohorts defined by year of entry. (It is assumed that the number of aliens in the United States of any entering cohort goes to zero in forty years.) This calculation is required if a full consideration of stocks and flows is to be derived.

Two estimates of entries, departures, and net flow are then presented. The high approximation is based on the apprehensions reported by the INS. However, since the CENIET researchers found such a large discrepancy between the apprehensions reported and the expulsions recorded at the Mexican reception centers, a low estimate is offered that reflects the size of the discrepancy recorded by CENIET. The method so devised thus permits an estimate of a net change in the stock of undocumented Mexican aliens in the United States.

The approximate flow for the years 1972–76 can be seen in table 6-3. The estimated number of entries increased substantially over the period and averaged between 629,000 and 2,043,000 a year. Estimated exits did not increase as rapidly and gave rise to an increasing net addition to the stock of Mexicans who were in the United States permanently or for

Table 6-3. *Flow of Undocumented Workers to the United States, 1972–76*
(thousands)

	Low estimate			*High estimate*		
Year	*Entries*[a]	*Exits*[b]	*Net flow*	*Entries*[a]	*Exits*[b]	*Net flow*
1972	465	453	12	1,497	1,458	39
1973	545	517	28	1,770	1,638	131
1974	651	632	20	2,139	2,062	77
1975	680	606	75	2,239	1,983	256
1976	799	687	113	2,571	2,286	284
Average	629	579	50	2,043	1,885	158

a. Entries refer to border crossings into the United States or to changes in the legal status of migrants that lead to their classification as deportable.

b. Exits refer to returns to Mexico, voluntary or by expulsion, and to legalization of one's presence in the United States. Exits through death are not considered here.

Source: Manuel García y Griego, *El volumen de la migración de mexicanos no documentados a los Estados Unidos*, Estudios no. 4 (Mexico, D.F.: CENIET, 1980).

extended durations. The last two years suggested an annual expansion of the stock of Mexican aliens in the United States of between almost 100,000 and 125,000. The stock of deportable aliens in the United States on January 1 of each year, from 1972 to 1977, was also calculated. The low and high approximations were 234,000 and 436,000 for 1972, and 482,000 and 1,224,000 for 1977. As of those moments in time, the stock was estimated to contain, as its largest component, individuals with less than one year's residence in the United States, or approximately 45 percent of the total.

A totally different approach to calculating the number of undocumented Mexicans is based on the volume of remittances from individuals in the United States to individuals in Mexico. Although there have been other studies adopting such an approach, only the work of Juan Díez-Canedo will be reported here.[24] There exists persuasive evidence that most individual remittances originate with workers temporarily in the United States. Permanent Mexican residents there have their families with them and only infrequently send money to Mexico. When they do, they are likely to do so by personal check. In contrast, remittances by temporary residents is by certified check and postal money orders. These instruments are recorded in Mexico so that it is possible to identify the names of the sender and recipient; the source and destination, by state, of the check; and the amount remitted.

Díez-Canedo employs the findings of North and Houstoun to define the proportion of Mexican aliens in the United States that does send money home and the average size of remittances made. Low, high, and medium estimates are reached by varying the values of the parameters of the estimating equation. The results are as follows: in any month of 1975, the number of undocumented workers in the United States ranged from 235,000 to 2,900,000. Applying the "most reasonable" values of these parameters as revealed by North and Houstoun, one would reach a "more realistic" figure of 815,000. This estimate can be compared with those of García y Griego. For example, if one takes the average of the latter's estimated undocumented stock for January 1 of 1975 and 1976 as indicative of the average stock during 1975, one gets an upper limit of 812,000 and a lower limit of 332,000. The upper limit proves virtually identical to Díez-Canedo's most reasonable estimate.

The most comprehensive effort to explore the migration phenomenon has been undertaken by CENIET. Their studies include three border surveys in which undocumented workers who were returned to Mexico by the INS have been enumerated and interviewed. Also included is a national household survey designed to yield the number of Mexicans, aged 15 or older, who were currently working or looking for work in the United States and those currently in Mexico who had been to the United States with similar intentions at any time during the previous five years (1974–78).[25] Some 60,000 households were polled during December 1978 and January 1979. The results of this survey provide a measure of the number of temporary migrants: 405,467 Mexicans who habitually reside in Mexico were reported to be either working or looking for work in the United States.[26] This measure differs from other estimates in that it does not distinguish between legal and illegal aliens.

Except for border communities from which a Mexican labor force commutes daily to work legally in the United States (the so-called green-card holders), no region is a significant source of legal temporary workers.[27] The daily commuters are excluded from this survey measure, however, because they were not "absent from their habitual residence." It should also be noted that the survey was conducted at a time when the number of undocumented workers temporarily in the United States was likely to have been at its minimum. Because of the importance of agriculture as an employer of undocumented workers, there is a pronounced seasonal pattern in the migration flow that corresponds to the peaks of agricultural activity. Furthermore, the survey coincided with the Christmas season, which may be presumed to have further minimized the number away from home.

Permanent Leakage

That there is a significant permanent leakage out of the migrant stream into the United States is suggested by one additional bit of information yielded by the CENIET household survey. This is the number of persons 15 years or older and residing in Mexico at the time of the interview who had been to the United States to work or to look for work at least once at any time during the previous five years (1974–78). The preliminary number of these Mexicans is given as approximately half a million.[28] If, as appears to be the case, most migration is temporary, one would expect the stock of Mexicans in Mexico with migration experience to be considerably larger than the number in the United States at any time.

Consider the following. If migration were purely temporary, and the average duration of stays were six months, the maintenance of a stable group of 500,000 workers in the United States at all times over a year would require a stock of approximately 1 million Mexicans in Mexico and the United States who would rotate between the two countries. A stock of this size would require that all those in it spend six months in the United States each year and that there be no infusion of new migrants. If not all those with migration experience wished to rotate at six-month intervals, and if there were a constant infusion of new migrants, then the total stock of Mexicans with migration experience could be expected to expand rapidly and to be captured by the CENIET survey.

That there has been a significant infusion of new migrants is suggested by the data on apprehensions. Although first-time migrants were probably disproportionately represented among those detained by the Border Patrol, they probably made up a substantial proportion of each cohort of successful entrants to the United States. For example, of the expelled Mexicans interviewed by CENIET in its first border survey, 58 percent were first-time migrants. If the probability of apprehension were only twice as great for a first timer as for others, this ratio of apprehensions would imply that first timers constituted approximately 40 percent of the flow of successful crossers. If the probability of getting caught were three times as great, the proportion of first timers to successful crossers would decline to about 30 percent. If migration were purely a seasonal or temporary phenomenon, this infusion of 160,000 to 200,000 new migrants into every cohort would very quickly build up the stock of workers in Mexico with migration experience to levels greater than those recorded by CENIET's migration study.[29] An average stay of six months further implies that two cohorts of migrants would enter the United States a year.

If the stock of returned migrants in Mexico remained relatively constant at around 500,000, this would imply an annual leakage into the U.S. labor force that approximately equalled the number of new entrants into the migration stream. An estimate can be made of the absolute size of that leakage based on the available information regarding the average number of workers in the United States over the year and the past rate of apprehension, as revealed by the North and Houstoun study. This can be done, however, only by assuming an appropriate differential rate of apprehension for first timers and experienced border crossers. Adopting 500,000 as the size of each cohort, an average probability of 0.81, and a probability of apprehension for first-timers that is from two to four times the probability for experienced crossers would yield a permanent or long-term leakage into the U.S. labor force of between roughly 100,000 and 200,000 from each cohort. Given two cohorts a year, the annual range of leakage would be twice as great. The high estimate of the net leakages offered for 1975 and 1976 by García y Griego, about 250,000–280,000, lies near the bottom of this range. If the increasing trend of leakages noted by him were projected further to 1978–79, the time of the national household survey, the leakage could more nearly approximate the upper limit of the range, 400,000, suggested by my tentative calculation.

The conclusion about the nature of the migrant flow that I have drawn from this large infusion of first timers departs sharply from that drawn by

CENIET. After the study observed that 58 percent of the apprehended migrants interviewed in the first border survey were first timers, it concluded: "The large proportion of 'first-timers,' in principle, tends to demonstrate a large renewal in the composition of those who migrate to the U.S. If these data reflect the general character of the undocumented migration phenomenon, it would lend support to the hypothesis that the career of the undocumented emigrant is shorter than is usually thought."[30] In view of the unexpectedly small size of the returned migrant stock enumerated by the household survey, the opposite conclusion would appear to be more tenable. It is, of course, possible that the CENIET household survey underenumerated the Mexicans with migration experience. If this is the case, this estimate of the permanent leakage will prove to have been exaggerated.

Net Outflow

The CENIET survey thus offers grounds for concluding that temporary and permanent migration to the United States adds up to a significant withdrawal of labor from the market in Mexico. At the end of the decade of the 1970s, this implied the withdrawal of 500,000 man-years in the category of temporary migrants and a net leakage of up to 400,000 a year into the U.S. labor market on a longer term basis. The latter would represent the highest annual rate of all those offered here, and, in the light of the data reviewed immediately below, it would also seem to be the least plausible.

Ordinarily, one would expect to derive more precise estimates of migration flows for the 1970–80 decade once the 1980 census data became available. A procedure could then be adopted that would apply expected survival rates to each age cohort of the 1970 census to estimate the number of individuals that would be expected to be in the same cohort in 1980 in the absence of any migration. The comparison of this expected number with the actual enumeration of the 1980 census would then provide a measure of net migration for each age cohort. Unfortunately, the data currently available do not permit conclusions that can be advanced with much confidence. None of the available sources agree on the age distribution of the population in 1970 or 1980 and, therefore, yield very different estimates of emigration.

For example, the age distribution of the population as published in the official censuses of 1970 and 1980 yields the numbers recorded in table 6-4. Although the 10–14 age group is included in the table, I consider these numbers less reliable than the others because of the greater margins of error in the 1970 enumeration of infants and young children. As can be

Table 6-4. *Estimated Net Migration by Sex and Age Group, 1970–80*
(thousands)

Age group	*Males*[a] *Census*	*Males*[a] CONAPO	*Females*[a] *Census*	*Females*[a] CONAPO
10–14	−(80.3)	(49.0)	(21.0)	(98.5)
15–19	−133.7	−128.0	64.3	107.1
20–24	−306.6	−265.0	34.0	41.7
25–29	−178.4	−278.5	−89.8	−101.2
30–34	−32.6	−198.0	−141.0	−95.3
35–39	122.0	−49.8	71.3	35.5
40–44	124.9	23.0	91.4	47.4
45–49	−1.3	−9.7	−34.6	−3.8
50–54	14.5	−10.1	11.8	−8.8
55–59	−9.0	58.5	−18.8	−3.3
60–64	27.1	48.7	26.9	16.8
Total[b]	−373.1	−808.9	15.5	43.7

a. A negative number represents net emigration, a positive number net immigration.
b. Totals do not include the 10–14 age group.
Sources: Secretaría de Industria y Comercio, Dirección General de Estadística, *IX Censo general de población, 1970: Resumen general* (Mexico, D.F., 1972); Secretaría de Programación y Presupuesto, *X Censo general de población y virienda, 1980: Resumen general abreviado* (Mexico, D.F., 1984); Consejo Nacional de Población, *México demografico* (Mexico, D.F., 1982).

seen, the count of the male population between the ages of 15 and 34 was 651,000 smaller than "expected"; for the age group 35 to 64, it was about 278,000 greater than expected. The result was a net outflow of 371,000 men. For women, this method yielded a number 15,500 greater than the expected number in the 15–64 age groups and implied a small net immigration of women. In view of the size of the legal outflow of adult women during the 1970s, this result would seem to be implausible. Thus, this set of data yields a net outflow of 357,600 people 15–64 years of age, a number smaller than the outflow of almost 400,000 legal migrants of that age.[31] This would imply a net return to Mexico of illegal migrants over the decade.

An alternative estimate of the net outflow is derived from population distributions estimated for 1970 and 1980 from census and other data by the National Population Council (CONAPO), which appeared in a 1982 publication, *México demografico*. The age distributions in this publication for both years have been adjusted for a presumed undercounting of infants and young children as well as for other presumed shortcomings of the published censuses. These data yield estimates of net migration considerably greater than those derived immediately above. As can be seen in table 6-4, male net emigration amounted to about 809,000, females record a net return migration to Mexico of some 43,000, and the aggregate net emigration was 766,000. Since legal migration in the age group 15–64 was estimated to have amounted to approximately 390,000, this would place illegal migration at about 375,000 for the entire decade, well below most other estimates.

A third source of population estimates is another, later publication that officials of CONAPO consider to contain the most authoritative estimates of Mexico's population by age group for 1970 and 1980. These calculations were the product of a joint effort by CONAPO, the Ministry of Programming and the Budget (SPP), and the Latin American Center for Demography (CELADE).[33] The age distributions offered by this publication reflect adjustments for undercounting as well as a level of migration that is assumed to have taken place. Migration is assumed to be constant in each year of the 1970s at a level of 70,000, a number that is only 12,000 greater than the annual average number of legal migrants to the United States. This would imply a net illegal outmigration of only 120,000 Mexicans of all ages over the decade.

Thus, it would seem that the attempt to employ census data for estimation purposes does not contribute much to resolve the controversy surrounding the volume of illegal migration to the United States. This effort only serves to increase the reservations regarding the accuracy of the census enumerations that were expressed in Chapter 2 and its appendix. Not only do the Mexican sources based on the most recent censuses show significant differences among themselves, but they provide little support for any of the estimates reviewed earlier in this section. The CONAPO data (37,500) would appear to come closest to the low estimate of average annual emigration (50,000) offered by García y Griego for the years 1972–76 but still fall far short of the latter. But it seems inconceivable to me that the census sources, even though deemed deficient, could fail to capture the volume of population loss if the actual annual loss approached the high estimate of 158,000 offered by García y Griego or even half of the 400,000 figure that I suggested might be derived from the procedure applied to the CENIET household survey. After all, these rates of net outmigration would imply a net population loss over the whole decade of between 1.5 and 2 million in addition to the almost 600,000 legal migrants. The failure of the census to record losses of such magnitude would suggest that perhaps the annual volume of net undocumented migration over the decade did not exceed the 50,000 lower estimate of García y Griego. This would, of course, place the annual level of illegal migration below the other estimates reviewed in this section.

Summary

In summary, the various studies reviewed here exhibit a fairly wide range of estimates of both the stock of undocumented Mexican aliens in the United States and their annual rate of flow to this country. With respect to the flow, the CENIET survey results reporting over 400,000 workers temporarily in the United States at the seasonal trough would seem to be a reasonable number. The seasonal peak number of migrants is therefore likely to exceed half a million; on average over the year, the flow may represent a withdrawal from the internal Mexican labor market of something on the order of a half a million work years. The possible implications of this withdrawal for employment conditions in the domestic labor market will be explored at a later point in this chapter.

With respect to the annual leakage into the United States on a prolonged or permanent basis or the stock of undocumented residents, less can be said with great certainty. One conclusion that can be drawn from the various studies that measure the stock of illegal aliens in the United States, however, is that none lend much support to some of the INS "official" estimates issued during the middle of the 1970s regarding their total number. The order of magnitude appears not to have been between 8 million and 12 million, but rather fewer than 6 million and perhaps as few as 4 million. Within this total, Mexicans were a significant number, perhaps 2 million to 3 million. The annual net additions to this stock, however, are believed by some to have been increasing toward the end of the decade. It would not be surprising if this in fact were so. As the stock of resident Mexicans in the United States increases, the information costs of migration are significantly reduced as are the out-of-pocket costs. With a decline in the ratio of costs to benefits associated with migration, one would expect the size of the flow, as well as the leakages out of that flow, to increase.[34] Having said this, however, I find it difficult to offer with much conviction an estimate of the actual size of the net annual leakage into prolonged residence in the United States. If pressed hard, I would offer only a qualified opinion that the rate of leakage during the decade of the 1970s is unlikely to have exceeded an average of 100,000 individuals a year.

Characteristics of the Migrant Flow

Apparently, there have been at least some constants in the character of the migrant flow to the United States over time. One of the most striking is the stability in the relative importance of various states as a source of migrants and the disproportionate share of migrants contributed by a small number of states. The CENIET household survey found that 61 percent of the migrants originated in six states of central Mexico and another 18 percent from two of the border states. These same areas contained less than a third of Mexico's population but provided 80 percent of the migrants. Of special importance are the states of Guanajuato, Jalisco, Zacatecas, Michoacán, San Luis Potosí, Durango, Chihuahua, and Baja California. Only the last two border on the United States. The relative importance of these states as sources of migrants has changed little over time except for the emergence of Baja California as a major point of origin. Studies dating back to the 1920s by Gamio and Foerster confirm the preponderance of the central plateau as the source of migrants.[35]

Similarly, there has been little change over time in the relative importance of the areas in the United States to which the migrants flow. Over three-fourths of the migrants flow to the four southwestern states bordering on Mexico, although California alone is the destination of fully half the migrants and Texas of another fifth. Arizona and New Mexico, however, are no more important than other states farther removed from the border. In Gamio's study, these same four southwestern states were the recipients of over half of the migrants; outside the Southwest, only Illinois was a primary destination.[36]

Díez-Canedo's study of remittances provides an alternative source of information on the destination of migrants. Based on the number of remittances recorded from the various states north of the border, California is first by a wide margin. In second place is Illinois, followed by Texas, New York, and Minnesota. That northern states do not appear as a major destination for migrants, as recorded by the CENIET surveys, suggests that the remittances may originate with the longer-term migrants or permanent legal residents, contrary to the temporary status attributed to them by Díez-Canedo.[37]

It would seem to be consistent with rational behavior for temporary Mexican migrants to the United States to minimize travel cost, particularly if they qualify only for low-skill employment. However, those remaining in the United States may begin to consider regional differences in earnings and may be prepared to undertake the larger investment associated with a long move. A further positive factor favoring such moves may be a reduced probability of detection, apprehension, and expulsion. But this line of reasoning does not seem to derive much support from the distribution of legal Mexican aliens in the United States. INS data show that, of the 882,606 Mexican aliens who reported under the alien address program in 1974, 52 percent resided in California, 29 percent in Texas, and 7 percent in Illinois. New York was insignificant as a place of residence.[38]

A similar distribution is yielded by INS data on the chosen states of residence for Mexican immigrants admitted in 1974. Of the 71,586 so admitted, 47 percent settled in California, 32 percent in Texas, 9 percent in Illinois, 4 percent in Arizona, and 1.3 percent in New Mexico. No other state was chosen by as many as 1 percent of the immigrants. New York and Minnesota were chosen by only 422 and 57, respectively.[39] Thus, it would appear that migration currents, both legal and undocumented, during the 1970s retained their traditional destinations.

The flow of migrants from different points in Mexico shows different patterns of distribution over the principal destinations. The states of western Mexico—Baja California, Sonora, Jalisco, and Michoacán—are more closely linked to California; those in the central and northeastern part direct a larger proportion to Texas. These movements cannot be explained solely by considerations of distance. For example, Texas is much closer to Jalisco and Michoacán than is California, yet the flows from these favor California by a better than 7:3 ratio.[40] Custom and the higher wage levels prevailing in the latter apparently are sufficient to overcome the obstacles of distance.

The recorded personal characteristics of the legal and illegal migrants exhibit considerable differences. The legal immigrant flow is characterized by roughly equal numbers of men and women and by complete family units with young children. It is a youthful stream; 40 to 45 percent of the immigrants are under 20 years of age and most of the rest between 20 and 39.[41] The sex and age distribution of undocumented Mexicans differs sharply from the legal flow.

The first CENIET border survey of apprehended aliens returned to Mexico in 1977 was dominated by males of labor force age; 88 percent were males. Very few small children were recorded; only 1.4 percent of the total returnees were younger than 15. The age distributions of apprehended men and women were very similar, with the bulk, 81.9 and 77.5 percent, respectively, falling in the 15–34 age bracket. The men with rural residences in Mexico outnumbered those from urban areas by only a slight margin.[42] Yet women were predominantly urban; 76 percent reported urban residences, mainly from the border communities.[43] The sex and age distribution of the apprehended aliens matched closely that of workers in the United States as enumerated by the household survey.[44] One exception, however, was the proportion of migrants with rural origins which, at 78.3 percent, was significantly larger than the 48.5 percent recorded by the border interviews. Carlos Zazueta also reported the marital status of the absentee workers; they were evenly divided between single and married individuals.

The educational level of workers absent from home revealed the mean years of schooling as 4, somewhat above the mean of the population 15 years and older in 1970 (3.1 years). Women however, recorded a higher level of schooling (4.7 years) than did men (3.9); this probably reflected the predominance of urban residents among the former.[45] Although the migrants would appear to boast an average educational level higher than that of the Mexican adult population in 1970, the difference could be expected to have narrowed substantially by 1977–78, when the migration survey was undertaken, as educational opportunities continued to expand. In fact, in view of the significant negative association of educational level and age within the general adult population, it may very well be the case that a comparison of age-specific educational attainments of the migrants would reveal them to have no more schooling than their nonmigrant counterparts. If a comparison were to be made with only the rural population, however, the migrants are likely to report more than the average years of schooling.

The occupational experience of the undocumented migrant group reflects the low average levels of schooling and the rural origins of most migrants. A majority of those who had been employed in Mexico during the month before their departure for the United States worked in agriculture. The border interviewers recorded the primary sector as the sector of employment of 52 percent of the expelled migrants; the national household survey recorded approximately 65 percent. This difference is obviously a reflection of the difference in the incidence of rural origin recorded by the two surveys, which was noted above. The household survey recorded 16 percent with secondary sector jobs, roughly half of which were in manufacturing, and 19 percent with tertiary, of which one-third were in commerce.[46] The sector of employment in the United States of a plurality of the temporary migrant workers is still agriculture; 34 percent of the sample of returnees had worked there. Following close behind agriculture is the service sector with 32.3 percent. These are mainly unskilled jobs in restaurants or domestic work. Manufacturing and construction also emerged as significant sectors of employment for 17.8 and 9.2 percent, respectively, of the returnees. However, the employment status referred to November 1978, a month of relatively low agricultural activity in the United States; had a month during the principal growing season been chosen as a reference, Zazueta and Mercado believe a larger proportion would have been found in agriculture.[47]

The literature on undocumented migration to the United States places great emphasis on its seasonal and temporary nature. There exists a considerable body of evidence that supports this view, such as some of the microcosmic studies of rural communities undertaken by social scientists. Certainly, the years of the bracero program were so characterized. Foster, in his study of Tzintzuntzan, noted that in 1960 half of the village's men had been to the United States, many of them ten or more times—a testimony to the temporary nature of migration as it was structured under the terms of the program.[48] A more recent study of the ejido Las Tortugas, in the municipio of Puruandiro, Michoacán, found no fewer than 70 men away, illegally in the United States, from this community of 165 families. While such migration had become an established practice over the preceding thirty years, only one person had succeeded in legalizing his presence in the United States and remaining there permanently.[49] In his study of nine communities in northeastern Jalisco that have a long traditon of migration, Cornelius found temporary migrants outnumbering permanent settlers in the United States by a margin of 8:1 during 1930–76. Furthermore, fewer than 19 percent of the returned illegal migrants expressed any interest in permanent migration to the United States.[50]

The impression of short stays in the United States is also reinforced by some of the CENIET findings. For example, the first border survey of undocumented workers expelled from the United States yielded a median stay of only 1.5 days. This short duration is a consequence of the large proportion of individuals apprehended within a day or two of crossing the border. Since 5.6 percent had been in the United States for more than a year, 588 days on average, however, the average length of stay for the apprehended group as a whole was 87 days. With the exclusion of those detained almost immediately after crossing the border, the modal group reported a stay of two to six months. However, this sample is dominated by individuals—58 percent—making their first attempt to enter the United States and is surely not representative of the Mexican population illegally present at one time.[51] Repeated attempts at crossing are likely to improve the evasive skills of the undocumented workers. Thus, the average stay of successful crossers is lengthened in excess of an average that includes the unsuccessful crossers.[52] Furthermore, if the probability of detection and apprehension declines with the length of a successful stay, as seems reasonable to expect, longer-term residents will be underrepresented in the sample of expelled workers.

The national household survey offered two measures of the length of stays of migrants in the United States. For those who had migrated during the previous five years but were in Mexico at the time of the survey, the average length of stay was 160 days, or slightly more than five months. Fully 68 percent remained six months or less; 13 percent remained more than a year. Among those who were currently in the United States but whose usual residence was still considered to be in Mexico, only 36 percent had been away for fewer than six months, while 32 percent had been absent for over a year.[53] Omitted from consideration, however, have been those who are in the United States and who no longer consider Mexico to be their usual place of residence. This imparts a downward bias to the average length of stay of illegal migrants. Unfortunately, the CENIET survey was not structured to yield information regarding the number of Mexicans who have remained in the United States for an indefinite or permanent duration.

The view that most Mexican migration is only temporary and of short duration receives further support from the findings of the North and Houstoun study of illegal aliens in the United States. Their subjects are hardly a random sample of illegal aliens in the United States at any one time. The sample included few Mexicans who had been picked up in the U.S.-Mexican border states and was further limited to those who had worked at least two weeks in the United States at some time (although not necessarily during the last trip that ended in apprehension). By recording the migration histories of the sample, North and Houstoun were able to determine the accumulated time spent in the United States and the number of trips back and forth from Mexico. The accumulated average was 2.4 years. Since the Mexicans averaged 4.5 trips, this suggests an average duration of about six months per trip.[54] A projection of such a figure to the entire population of Mexican undocumented workers in the United States, however, would require the assumption that the probability of apprehension was the same for all individuals, regardless of the duration of their stay. If, as would seem more reasonable to expect, the relationship were an inverse one, then the duration of stays yielded by a sample of those apprehended would yield an average duration that is downward biased.

The migration experiences of some communities stand in sharp contrast to those reported above for Las Tortugas or to the general impression that migration is largely temporary. Robert Shadow's study, in 1975–76, was of a community with a well-established tradition of migration to the United States, Villa Guerrero in northern Jalisco. He found a substantial number of permanent migrants among those with migration experience. Of 564 persons with such experience, 133 had withdrawn from the migrant stream because of age. The rest were almost evenly divided between temporary and permanent migrants—40 and 37 percent of the total with migration experience, respectively. The great majority of the permanent migrants of both sexes were married and living in the United States with their spouses.[55]

Shadow's reported findings in Villa Guerrero, however, would seem to stand as an exception rather than as a rule. Most microstudies emphasize the temporary nature of migration and report a lack of enthusiasm among potential and returned migrants for permanent residence in the United States. In so doing, they would seem to reinforce the conclusion tendered in the preceding section that the past net leakages into prolonged residence in the United States are better characterized as modest flows rather than as torrents.

Causal Factors in Migration

Much of the professional and popular literature on migration has focused on the relative strength of "push" and "pull" factors in motivating the movements of populations. The literature on Mexican migration to the United States is no exception. Articles in the U.S. press that treat the subject rarely fail to stress the "high" levels of unemployment and underemployment as the primary forces impelling Mexican workers northward. Commenting on the causes of the increasing flow of illegal migrants to the United States over time, Wayne Cornelius states, "Since the late 1960s, however, 'push' factors on the Mexican side seem to have been more important [than demand fluctuations in the U.S.]. Indeed, there is no other way to explain the large increases in illegal migration from Mexico to the U.S."[56] The dominant long-term factor is held to be the growth of unemployment and underemployment, which follows from the failure of the economy to create enough jobs to keep up with the increase in the labor force. Thus, Cornelius characterizes the migration as "crisis-induced, income-maintenance migration." Since migrants' households operate at the margin of subsistence, any disaster, such as a crop failure or major illness in the family, creates a situation of short-term, acute economic necessity that can be met most easily by temporary migration to the United States.[57]

"Push" Factors: Conditions in Mexico

In a similar vein, John Evans and Dilmus James write, "In our examination of the factors contributing to the immigrant flow we focus upon three closely interrelated 'push' factors: the inadequate growth of productive employment opportunities, income inequality, and rapid population growth. We recognize that other variables are determinants of migration, but we are confronted by the evidence that the factors stressed are of outstanding importance".[58] As evidence of the dominance of push factors, the authors also cite numerous other studies that reported that the primary motives for migration were work- or income-related. Although most writers on the subject have chosen to interpret such responses of migrants as indicative of the strength of push factors, there is nothing in the responses that would preclude their interpretation as pull factors. In other words, migration to the United States for reasons of employment and wages may also reflect the relative attractiveness of job opportunities there.[59]

A work by Blejer, Johnson, and Porzecanski purports to provide an empirical foundation for the conclusion that unemployment in Mexico is the principal determinant of migration to the United States.[60] Their econometric study concluded that a significant statistical relationship existed between unemployment in Mexico and migration to the United States over the period 1960–75. Separate regressions were estimated for legal, illegal, and total migration. The Mexican rate of unemployment was the single most powerful "explanatory" variable. The inclusion of the ratio of Mexican-to-U.S. unemployment or of relative wages in the two countries did little to the explanatory power of Mexican unemployment alone. Although the proportion of the explained variance in the three measures of migration was impressively high, one cannot help but view the results with some degree of skepticism because of the dubious quality of the information used for estimating the size of migration flows and for deriving a measure of Mexican unemployment. The data on legal migration, of course, represent actual counts, but they would not seem to be an appropriate measure of the response to Mexican labor market conditions in the year of migration. In the face of the new constraints on legal migration to the United States introduced by the 1965 amendments to the Immigration and Naturalization Act that became effective in 1968, the backlog of immigration applications quickly mounted. Thus, immigration in any given year represents the termination of an application process begun several years earlier.

As a measure of illegal immigration, the authors used the INS figures on the number of deportable Mexicans apprehended. Implicit in the use of these figures is the existence of a constant relationship between the number of detentions and the number of illegal migrants, something for which no empirical verification exists. This procedure makes no allowance for the vagaries of the apprehension process. It is widely acknowledged that the INS reacted to the migration flows with different degrees of vigor and effectiveness during the studied period, perhaps responding more to unemployment rates and political pressures in the United States than to conditions in Mexico.

Finally, the unemployment data used for Mexico are not measured unemployment but represent a residual derived from aggregate output and estimated labor force measures. Employment growth is estimated from sectoral growth of output under an assumption of a constant ratio of output to labor inputs. Intercensal projections provide the estimates of the size of the labor force, and unemployment is the difference between this and the employment estimate.

In the absence of direct measures of the labor force and its components, one can sympathize with the need to improvise. However, the questions that surround the correspondence of the derived measures to the actual values make it difficult to give heavy weight to the findings of this imaginative work. In any case, the events of the decade of the 1970s would appear to have provided a counterexample. As has been shown in an earlier chapter, open unemployment rates appear to have been in a declining trend; at the same time, the rate of illegal migration is held to have been on the increase.

Two more recent attempts to identify the determinants of undocumented migration to the United States have also concluded that conditions in Mexico, or push factors, seem to dominate. Walter Fogel employs multiple regression analysis, with the number of apprehensions (in the role of a proxy for the flow of migrants) as the dependent variable.[61] Several regressions are run on the size of the labor force in Mexico, the average annual unemployment rate in the United States, the annual average manufacturing wage in the United States, the annual average manufacturing wage in Mexico, and time as independent variables. The data were drawn from the years 1965 to 1977. Fogel interprets the results as showing that the U.S. economic variables have had relatively little influence on the migrant flow. The most important variable proves to be the growth of the Mexican labor force; this variable accounted for 98 percent of the changes in annual migration.

Unfortunately, serious reservations remain regarding the significance of Fogel's findings. One arises from the adequacy of the use of apprehensions as a proxy for successful migration. Another stems from the labor force measure that is employed. Since there are no actual counts of the labor force for the period studied, its size is simply a projected figure based on 1960 and 1970 census figures and thus is largely determined by estimated changes in the size of the population of working age. Therefore, a larger Mexican population is associated with a larger flow of migrants, a finding that does not seem to be particularly illuminating. The use of the Mexican average wage in manufacturing also may not be fully appropriate. That datum is drawn from a nonrepresentative sample of important manufacturing firms and may or may not represent a suitable proxy for the wage opportunities faced by the migrants in Mexico.

The second study citing push factors, by Alberto Davila, is intended to identify the determinants of changes in migration flows over time, not the magnitude of such flows.[62] Davila's study covers the period 1973–82. His model includes proxies for both pull and push forces. The former include the demand for labor in the United States as represented by U.S. employment in agriculture, manufacturing, and construction in the four states bordering on Mexico. The push factor purports to measure the demand for labor in Mexico. For this purpose, he adopts the ratio of employed individuals in the 20–34 age group to the population of this group in the three major metropolitan areas of Mexico City, Guadalajara, and Monterrey. Changing conditions in these areas are held to be indicative of employment conditions generally.

Finally, Davila examines the impact of the Mexican currency devaluation of 1976 as an explanatory variable. Multiple regression techniques are applied to twenty-four quarterly observations, and the estimates reported are in double-log functional form. Most of the elasticity coefficients associated with the pull variables are positive, as expected, although only those for U.S. agricultural employment are statistically significant. The sign of the push variable, the proportion of the population aged 20–34 employed in Mexico, is negative and the coefficient is statistically significant. The magnitude of the coefficients leads Davila to conclude that migration is much more sensitive to this proportion than it is to the pull factors. The 1976 devaluation, which had the effect of increasing the U.S. wage defined in terms of Mexican pesos relative to wages in Mexico, is found to have the expected positive and significant immediate influence on the flow, although its influence declined over time.

Again, the robustness of Davila's conclusions depend on the appropriateness of the data employed. The use of apprehensions data as measures of the flow is subject to the usual reservations. Of the independent variables used, the one most likely to be open to question is the push factor, the ratio of employed to total population in the 20–34 age group. It would appear that, as a proxy for general employment conditions, this ratio is inappropriate since it contains an inherent bias in the direction of "deterioration." This is the case because of the very substantial increase in the proportion of the population of both sexes in the 20–24 year age group enrolled in school. The proportion increased by about 50 percent over this interval. Its effect is to build in a declining ratio of the employed to the population. Unless one assumes that enrollment in school is merely a form of disguised unemployment, this ratio may prove misleading. If Davila had used the proportion of the nonschool population that was employed, he might have emerged with strikingly different results; this ratio either increased or remained unchanged in the three regions considered. In view of these considerations, one cannot place much confidence in the validity of his conclusions.

Although no one familiar with labor market conditions faced by many Mexicans (especially those in rural areas) would deny that employment and income opportunities there leave much to be desired, there is ample ground for questioning whether migration to the United States is motivated primarily by poverty and unemployment. Indeed, an interpretation that attributes migration solely to either push or pull forces is likely to provide an oversimplified characterization of the process.

The CENIET household survey, for example, inquired into the employment status of the apprehended and returned migrants prior to their departure for the United States. Only 3.1 percent of the migrants did not work in the month preceding their departure and were actively seeking employment. The interpretation of this datum must be undertaken with care, however, since it could obscure the employment prospects in Mexico for some of those who reported themselves as employed during the month preceding their migration. If recent agricultural jobs had just ended because of seasonal factors, and if the workers who chose to migrate had not done so, some may have been faced with a prospect of open unemployment. A significant portion of the migrants, one out of five, were reported not to have been employed. Part of this group, of course, was made up of the openly unemployed, but the bulk did not actively seek employment.[63]

Whether or not this failure to look for work is indicative of discouraged unemployment cannot be determined from this survey's reported findings. It is instructive to observe that the border survey of 1977 reported that 26 percent of the apprehended migrants, exclusive of those who had spent all of 1977 in the United States, had not held any job in Mexico during 1977. In other words, they chose to seek their first job for 1977 in the United States.[64] Again, the interpretation of this datum is made difficult by the absence of additional information. Traditionally, however, there is a very small amount of long-term unemployment reported in Mexico, and the migrant population is relatively young. Rather than being discouraged unemployed, migrants who did not work in Mexico during 1977 may either have departed from Mexico early in the year or be new entrants to the labor force. One factor contributing to the nonemployed status of this group is the very low labor force participation rate in Mexico of female migrants; female labor force members apparently are underrepresented among the female migrant workers.[65]

If push factors were the dominant determinants of migration to the United States, one might expect to see that the least advantaged members of the labor force would be heavily represented in the migrant flow. This might be evidenced in a larger migration from the poorest states of the country or in higher rates of migration among the poor within communities. However, the available information about the origins or migrants does not support these expectations. Some of the poorest states in the republic, such as Chiapas or Oaxaca, are very minor sources of migrants. The relatively unchanging importance of the various Mexican states over time as sources of migrants suggests that factors other than a precarious position in the labor market may be playing a significant determining role.

Even within states, migrants do not necessarily originate in those communities with the poorest employment prospects. El Bajio, in the state of Guanajuato, is a relatively rich agricultural region of commercial farm production that is fairly heavily capitalized. There is generous use of purchased and labor inputs per hectare, and it is widely irrigated. Several industrialized urban areas are nearby and offer possibilities for temporary off-farm employment. Yet the rural population of the region is heavily engaged in off-farm employment away from home, with the United States dominating all other migration destinations.[66] Other rural areas with income levels half those of El Bajio send no one to the United States.

Similarly, within the sending communities, the characteristics of migrants do not suggest a selective process heavily weighted by negative considerations. Various community studies that have observed the migration phenomenon have noted that it is not the poorest households that provide the migrants to the United States.[67] Nor is it the landless who dominate the flow. Ejidatarios, small landholders, and sharecroppers represented half of the CENIET border sample of migrants with agricultural antecedents in Mexico.[68] In his study of Villa Guerrero, Shadow found that the incidence of migrants from the various landholding statuses was almost identical.[69] Raymond Wiest, on the other hand, found landless laborers greatly underrepresented in the migrant flow from Acuitzio, Michoacán.[70] Whereas they made up 43 percent of the total male labor force, they accounted for only 22 percent of the migrants. The incidence of migration was highest among the minifundistas, the small private farmers. A similar finding is attributed to Cornelius's study of Los Altos de Jalisco by Roberts.[71] United States-bound migrants were not the landless but the small private farmers and ejidatarios.

That the poorest elements of rural Mexico are not a significant part of the northbound flow should not be surprising. After all, there are out-of-pocket costs associated with migration and the risk of failing to breach the frontier. Especially for first timers, the risks are likely to appear higher. One way of minimizing the risk of being caught is to engage the services of a "coyote," one who will smuggle the illegal alien across the border in return for a fee. According to the first CENIET border survey, about 20 precent of the apprehended migrants had employed the services of a coyote. Although these migrants were not classified by the number of crossings attempted, they were more heavily represented in those Mexican regions from which the largest proportions of first timers were to be found.[72] The price of the service varied widely from less than US$50 to over US$300, for an average of US$175. The destination of the illegal migrant also figured into the amount. The price for being smuggled into California exceeded that for Texas, US$180 to US$150, respectively. The differential may reflect a greater difficulty of evading the Border Patrol along the California border, the higher prospective earnings obtainable in that state, or both. Nevertheless, this sum represents a very significant outlay, which would be beyond the resources of the poorest rural people.

Almost one-third of the apprehended migrants reported having borrowed to finance their trip. On average, the debt incurred amounted to US$97.[73] Migrants originating in the border areas borrowed the least, as one might reasonably expect. The largest sums borrowed were reported, not from the region most distant from the U.S. border, but from the central plateau. It has had a long-established tradition of migration and apparently also shows the highest level of earnings realized in the United States. In this region, CENIET's household survey found a significantly higher than average proportion (42 percent) of borrowers in its sample; an average of $130 was borrowed.[74] Since an individual's borrowing capacity is usually at least partly determined by the income or assets (or both) of his family, the poorest elements were likely to be the highest-risk candidates for loans and therefore the most likely to be excluded. Thus, one might expect to find a dichotomy between those who opt for migration to the United States and those who limit their migration to internal destinations. Since the latter may involve smaller cash outlays and also a smaller risk of total loss, one might expect to find the poorer residents more heavily represented in the domestic migration stream or in local off-farm employment, while the less poor choose to go to the United States.

Clearly, the financial returns to a successful stay in the United States exceed those available from the existing alternatives in Mexico. For example, in CENIET's border survey, the apprehended migrants who had been employed in Mexico during 1977 reported average daily earnings in agriculture of Mex$65.7, and Mex$95 in construction and other activities, for an average of Mex$79.2.[75] In contrast, the legal minimum wage in the United States in 1977 was US$2.60 an hour, or US$20.80 for an eight-hour day. At the exchange rate then current (Mex$23 to US$1), this translates into Mex$480. Put another way, a migrant employed at the U.S. legal minimum wage could earn in one day the equivalent of a six-day week's earnings in Mexico. For agricultural workers it would be the equivalent of 7.3 days of Mexican wages. Net earnings after deductions for social security and income taxes would reduce the size of the premium somewhat but would still leave it at a substantial level of five to six times the Mexican rate of earnings.

Actual earnings of migrants are available only in a preliminary form, but even these are instructive. The CENIET household survey collected earnings information as given by the returned migrants—at hourly, daily, or weekly rates—without attempting to reduce them to a single consistent basis. Of those reporting hourly earnings, three-fourths earned less than US$4 and only 2 percent earned more than US$8. Nearly 60 percent of those reporting daily earnings earned less than US$20; most of the rest earned between US$20 and US$50.[76] Finally, half of the respondents earned less than US$100 a week, while another 40 percent earned between US$100 and US$200.[77] However, these rates of earning refer to trips completed in the past and are not time-specific. Nevertheless, although most earnings did not depart much from the 1977 legal minimum wage, they clearly represented large premiums over the rates of earnings current in Mexico in 1978. It is understandable that prospective wages in the United States would have a strong attraction for young mobile workers.

Perhaps the most persuasive evidence that migration to the United States is not undertaken by the neediest is to be found in the way in which the accumulated earnings are spent. While some proportion may surely go to finance current consumption, substantial sums are destined for other purposes.[78] Virtually all who have observed the impact of these earnings at the community level imply that they are used more as discretionary rather than subsistence incomes. The most common expenditures seems to be on home improvements, ranging from the addition of rooms or installation of plumbing and flooring materials to the acquisition of furnishings and appliances. Returning migrants frequently arrive home laden with clothing or appliances purchased in the United States. Other common uses to which savings are put are the purchase of land, the financing of an independent business venture, or the purchase of trucks, automobiles, or tools relating to a trade. Visible differences in material levels of well-being can thus be observed in the villages between U.S. migrant and other households.[79]

Household Decisionmaking

As has been indicated, the motivations underlying migration can be discussed in terms of push and pull factors. While this approach may have the virtue of simplicity, it also is likely to do violence to reality. The decision to migrate to the United States is undoubtedly not based on only one or the other of these two forces. Indeed, both push and pull forces are frequently at work simultaneously. A more fruitful line of analysis is likely to result from a model that considers migration to the United States as only one of several options faced by Mexican workers. The choice among those options would be governed by the perceived costs and benefits and the degree of risk aversion characterizing the individuals and their households.

Kenneth Roberts follows this approach. He develops a model of migration in which the rural household is the decisionmaking unit, pursuing the objective, not necessarily of income maximization, but rather of a stable minimum level of income designed to ensure the survival of the household.[80] In this view, the household takes stock of its manpower resources and the labor requirements of cultivating its own land and decides how much labor time can be spared for off-farm wage employment. By allocating family labor over different employments, the household can reduce the risk posed to its survival by unexpected variations in income from any one source. An added incentive for realizing cash earnings from off-farm employment is that it allows for household participation in a network of reciprocal relationships, a system designed to provide for unforeseen contingencies through loans.[81] While migration to the United States provides one way of earning the cash required to participate in this network, it is by no means the only one.

The variety of responses of households to the range of choices available to them has been well documented. Oaxaca is one of the poorest states of Mexico, and one in which great reliance is placed on off-farm earnings. It ranks third as a state of origin for Mexican internal migration; over half of the flow is destined for Mexico City alone. Yet very few undocumented workers in the United States are from Oaxaca. Nor can distance be the sole determining factor in the decision of Oaxaceños to shun the U.S. labor market. Other poor communities much closer to the northern border are equally averse to choosing the United States as a destination for temporary migration.[82] The existence of an element of choice is illustrated by the experience of at least one sample of temporary migrants to the United States. Cornelius reports that 45 percent of the individuals who had illegally crossed into the United States had worked in Mexican communities other than their own and thus were familiar with local alternative destinations.[83]

On the basis of his comparison of four contrasting zones, Roberts concludes that the key factor determining the incidence of off-farm employment is the degree of penetration of capitalist agricultural production in the zone.[84] By capitalist penetration, he means the degree to which the local agricultural sector is integrated into markets for agricultural inputs and outputs and for consumer goods. Penetration appears to imply a degree of technological "modernization" that proves to be labor-displacing. The resulting labor surplus can be funneled into off-farm employment. Furthermore, the increased dependence on markets for purchased agricultural inputs and consumer goods is offered as a source of pressure that necessitates the search for off-farm employment.[85]

Although the changing mode of production that releases labor may provide sufficient ground for explaining the incidence of off-farm employment, it is not adequate for predicting the choice among work alternatives. Only one of Roberts's four zones was characterized by a significant flow of workers to the United States. This was El Bajío in the state of Guanajuato, a region that has long been a source of migrants to the United States. Within that region, Roberts detected only one factor that clearly distinguished households with U.S. migrant members from those with none: the size of the household, or, more precisely, the number of adult males in the household. The relation between size and the incidence of international migration was direct. This is interpreted by Roberts as indicating that a large household is better able to assume the risk of sending one of its members to the United States. Given the fact that El Bajío is a relatively prosperous agricultural zone, Roberts finds support for his contention that "higher levels of family income encourage extended family relationships which permit the riskier alternative of U.S. migration."[86]

While Roberts's conclusions seem plausible enough, it would appear premature to raise them to the status of generalizations. If the size and income of a household were the determining factors in U.S. migration, then it should be possible to observe them at work in other rural states. Most states have farm units that are run by households ranging in size, and in corresponding income, from small to large. Yet, if one observes the heavy concentration of U.S. migrants in only a handful of states, one is compelled to look further for variables that may affect a household's calculation of the expected income derivable from migration to the United States.

The "Pull" of the United States

Cornelius disposes of the question of why the United States is chosen as a destination in a simple and direct manner. His sample of migrants chose the United States because jobs were deemed easier to find there than in Mexico and because of the higher earnings that were obtainable there.[87] In rephrasing this response, one could state that the migrants' expected income from employment in the United States exceeded that from alternatives present in Mexico. Again, however, this fails as a satisfactory general explanation of why the United States was chosen. If jobs were more easily obtainable and expected incomes higher in the United States for those that had successfully migrated there, why would this same perception not be shared and acted upon by Mexicans throughout the country?

In fact, both Cornelius and Roberts mention what may be a key factor, even though they do not exploit fully its significance for their migration models. All of the literature points out the "long tradition" of migration to the United States from certain areas in Mexico.[88] Cornelius and Roberts, in addition, emphasize the importance of networks and extended family relationships that can be built and relied upon to insure survival in the face of some unexpected disaster or interruption to income. In addition, however, tradition and networks can be interpreted as significantly affecting the perceived costs and benefits of migration to the United States. That migration continues to originate in certain highly concentrated localities is at least partially explainable in terms of the reduction in information costs and, therefore, in the degree of risk incurred by a prospective migrant. "Tradition" implies the accumulation of a fund of information available locally and at no cost through household and community networks. The information can include such vital intelligence as how best to elude the *migra*, the Mexican expression for the Border Patrol; the relative prospects of employment at different destinations in the United States; the mechanics of job search; and a whole catalogue of do's and don'ts that are critical to the successful realization of a migrant's goals.

In other ways, too, the longstanding tradition of migration to the United States from certain regions stands to reduce costs of migration. As leakages have occurred from the migration stream into permanent residence in the United States, the network of household relationships extending from communities in Mexico to communities in the United States has expanded. Thus, information flows about employment possibilities are facilitated, and the degree of uncertainty is reduced. Relatives or fellow-villagers in the United States may provide a temporary free refuge until a job is secured and thus reduce the investment the migrant himself must make in his employment quest. They may also represent a source of credit for the financing of other migration costs. Thus, the existence of an established Mexican community in the Chicago area would explain its continuing importance as a destination of temporary migrants in spite of its considerable removal from the border. Similar communities in the U.S. border states offer these same advantages in addition to that of proximity. The greater and more prolonged the past flow of Mexicans from a particular area to the United States, the lower become the risks associated with migration of subsequent generations.

The combination of greater information and reduced risk serves to increase the expected returns to U.S.-bound migration relative to those from internal migration. The converse applies for those regions in Mexico that did not serve as important sources of migrants to the United States in times past, when such migration was either legal or easier. The relative scarcity of information and lack of a stateside family or village network increase the risk of failure considerably and, consequently, reduce the expected returns to migration relative to returns from internal migration.

Areas from which internal migration has become traditional have also built networks of information and assistance in both the source and destination communities. These network relationships raise the expected returns to internal migration relative to those from moves to the United States. Perpetuation of past patterns of behavior is thus strengthened. A change can probably occur only gradually, as individuals willing to accept high risks in order to migrate to a destination outside the established network do so successfully and establish a beachhead. As this foothold expands, the relative attractiveness of that destination increases, and the flow of migrants could be expected to increase. Viewed in these terms, the persistence of migration from a rather small area of Mexico can be explained as the workers' rational response to perceived returns from either international or internal migration. It also suggests that the past pattern will extend into the future with only gradual modifications.

The fact that the traditional pattern of migration is likely to persist tells us nothing about the level at which that migration will be sustained. The number of workers who will attempt migration to the United States will obviously be a function of developments on both sides of the border. To the extent that the process of economic growth is more rapid in Mexico and is reflected in rising wage levels, the relative attractiveness of the United States will tend to decline. Given the very large absolute differentials that currently exist, however, U.S. wages are likely to be perceived as relatively attractive for some time to come.

One study has developed an estimate of real wage differences between the various minimum wage zones of Mexico and the southwestern United States. The real wage estimates take into account differences in purchasing power among areas. Between 1969 and 1975, the differential declined from 5.56:1 to 4.12:1 on average. The Mexican devaluation of 1976 led to an increase in the differential to 7.43:1 and 7:1 in 1977 and 1978, respectively, a change that might be expected to increase the attractiveness of temporary migration.[89]

This same study also undertook a broader comparison of certain attractions in both countries that could be expected to influence permanent migration. The authors developed a socioeconomic opportunity index that included the availability of social services such as education, health, housing, and so on, for both U.S. and Mexican districts. Within this index, all sixteen of the U.S. regions included were at least 1.75 standard deviations above the composite mean for both Mexican and U.S. districts. Only three Mexican districts were comparably rated and thus competitive with those in the United States. They were the three largest metropolitan regions of the country: Mexico City, Guadalajara, and Monterrey—the chief destinations of internal migrants. Incidentally, these large urban conglomerations have been only minor sources of U.S. migrants, which confirms that they compete with the United States as destinations.

Conditions on the U.S. side of the border also help determine the volume of migration. Over the past few years, the United States has become increasingly concerned about the implications of recent levels of migration for the U.S. labor force. This concern also extends to the social consequences of greater "permanent" migration. With the rate of unemployment in the United States approaching 10 percent at the height of the 1981–82 recession, the clamor that "something be done to stem the tide" became more strident. Both the Carter and Reagan administrations have advanced a series of proposals to reduce the flow of illegal migration; the U.S. Congress currently has before it a bill intended to deal with the issue. The ultimate form and effectiveness of any measures that may be adopted cannot be foreseen nor can they be taken into consideration for purposes of this discussion. Nevertheless, it may be presumed that an effective demand for Mexican workers will continue to exist in the United States. On the basis of past experience, it is not unreasonable to expect that more legal strictures against migration might not be stringently enforced if the unemployment level declined or "labor shortages" developed.

Indeed, given the demographic profile of the U.S. population and recent birth rates, it is quite possible that the next two decades may see a decline in the growth rate of the domestic labor force. The current impressions of a labor "surplus" may then convert to one of "shortage." Clark Reynolds has estimated the supply of, and demand for, labor in the United States for 1990 and 2000. Given an annual rate of growth in the GNP of 3 percent, he adopts different assumptions concerning the rate of growth in productivity and labor force participation rates.[90] Assuming a 1.38 percent annual increase in productivity (the average rate for the period 1960–77) and stable labor force participation rates, a sizable labor deficit of 5 million is forecast for the year 2000. (These estimates allow for an annual immigration of 400,000.) Reynolds holds that the shortfall of supply will occur in those jobs at the bottom of the occupational hierarchy. As minority and other disadvantaged groups improve their educational and skill levels, fewer such workers will be available to fill these positions. Thus, a large and growing demand for unskilled Mexican labor will be evidenced in the United States in years to come.

Reynolds's projection of a shortage of unskilled labor echoes the findings of a study undertaken by the National Planning Association in the middle 1970s. That study concluded that by the latter part of the 1980s, the supply of people available to fill low-skill occupations will have grown more slowly than the demand. The absolute decline in the available supply foreseen for the 1980s is predicated on the declining size of the teenage population—a primary supplier of such labor—and on the upgrading of skills of disadvantaged groups, the other principal labor source.[91] To be sure, adjustments to this perceived shortage can take many forms, including substitution and changes in relative wages. The authors of the study also foresaw a surplus of labor for the more highly skilled jobs. Therefore, a realignment of wages across occupational groups may bring the various subsectors into a state of equilibrium without an allowance for immigration. It would not be surprising, however, to find the low-wage employers resisting market pressures on wages and opting for the employment of Mexican migrant labor.

The Impact of Migration on the Mexican Labor Market

The option of migrating to the United States in search of employment has frequently been likened to a safety valve. Implied is a belief that, in the absence of migration, conditions in the Mexican labor market would deteriorate significantly, with greater open unemployment and underemployment, lower wage levels, or both. Conversely, the persistence of the migration phenomenon would be expected to raise wages above the levels that would otherwise have held.[92] As far as I can determine, however, there has been no attempt to quantify the changes that would be associated with different levels of migration—and with good reason. In order to estimate the impact on the wage level, one would need to delineate the spatial and occupational boundaries of the relevant labor market and would require measures of the price elasticities of supply and demand for labor. In addition, it would be necessary to know the proportion of the migrants who would have been in the labor force in Mexico had they not migrated. Unfortunately, all of these bits of essential information remain in the realm of the unknown. Therefore, any estimate of the wage effects of migration must be largely speculative in nature, dependent on the assignment of rather arbitrary values to the parameters of the market equation. Although little confidence can be placed in such estimates, they may at least establish the general order of magnitude of the wage effect of migration.

The question examined in this section is, by how much are wages in the Mexican labor market likely to be affected by illegal migration to the United States? The first issue to be addressed is the impact that migration has on the domestic supply of labor. The CENIET household survey estimated that something on the order of 500,000 Mexicans were temporarily in the United States at any one time. If my estimate of the Mexican labor force in 1980, amounting to about 20 million were reasonably correct, these temporary migrants amounted to only 2.5 percent of the total. Migrants are not potential competitors of all other members of the labor force, however, since they lack the skills appropriate to many occupations. Furthermore, since migrants tend to originate in relatively few areas of the country, the effects on the Mexican labor force in these originating areas might prove to be greater than in those regions providing few migrants.

For example, CENIET's survey indicated that migrants represented 6.5 percent of the labor force of the eight major source states.[93] Thus, if the migration option were suddenly to be removed, and if all the suspended migrants were to remain in their own local labor markets, the wage effects in those markets could be quite substantial. In such an event, it would seem reasonable to assume that these migration-prone individuals would substitute internal for international migration; thus, the wage effects would be spread more evenly over the national labor market as a whole.[94] (For the sake of convenience, I will assume that the migrants would, in fact, be greatly dispersed internally.)

It has been noted that migrants are competitive in only some occupations. The occupational distribution of the national labor force, as estimated by the national household labor force survey in 1979, is presented in table 6-5. It also offers a crude estimate of the proportion of each occupational category with which the migrants might be competitive. Given the low educational levels of most migrants, it is safe to assume that they would be negligible participants in the markets for professional, managerial, and administrative personnel. I arbitrarily assume that they

Table 6-5. *Percentage Distribution of the Labor Force by Occupational Group, and the Percentage of Each Group Subject to Competition from Migrants, 1979*

Occupational group	*Percentage distribution of labor force*	*Percentage subject to competition from migrants*	*Percentage of total employment subject to competition from migrants*
Professional and technical workers	7.6	0	0
Managers	2.7	0	0
Administrative personnel	8.6	0	0
Salespeople	11.0	33.3	3.7
Workers in services and operators of motor vehicles	16.0	50.0	8.0
Agricultural laborers	28.6		28.6
Nonagricultural laborers	25.4	66.6	16.9
	99.9		57.2

Source: Secretaría de Programación y Presupuesto, *Encuesta continua sobre ocupación*, vol. 7, 1st quarter 1979 (Mexico, D.F., February 1980).

would be competitive in one-third of the sales and one-half of the service employments. Finally, migrants are assumed to be competitive in all agricultural and two-thirds of the nonagricultural laborer jobs. The areas of effective competition thus add up to approximately 57.2 percent of all occupations. According to the 1980 census, the labor market from which migrants are withdrawn would have measured some 11.4 million participants, and migration would result in a reduction of 4.4 percent in that force. For purposes of this estimating procedure, a 5 percent reduction will be adopted as a rough approximation of the likely actual change.

Assigning values to the price elasticities of demand for, and supply of, labor is not as easily done. Therefore, an expedient method of calculating the wage effect is to use different values for these elasticities drawn from a range within which the true values are likely to occur. For the elasticity of demand, three values are adopted, ranging between -0.5 and -1.5, and three for supply between 0.2 and 0.7. Each of the three demand elasticities is combined with each of the three supply elasticities to yield a total of nine estimates of the change in wages associated with a 5 percent reduction in the supply of labor. The percentage change in the wage is calculated using the formula

$$w = \frac{-h}{\epsilon - \eta}$$

where w is the percentage change in the wage, h the percentage change in the supply of labor (representative of a horizontal shift in the supply schedule), ϵ is the price elasticity of the supply labor, and η is the price elasticity of the demand for labor.[95]

Table 6-6 presents the results of the various computations. The estimated changes in the wage range from a low of 2.27 percent, when the highest absolute values are assigned the two elasticities, to 7.14 percent at the other extreme, when both elasticities are assumed to be at their lowest values. Most of the combinations of the elasticities yield estimated changes on the order of 3 to 4 percent. This interval would appear to be based on elasticities most likely to approximate the actual ones. The recent estimated flow of migrants would thus imply a wage level in low-skill occupations 3 to 4 percent higher than would otherwise prevail.

Conversely, a sudden suspension of migration would have a once-and-for-all negative impact of the same magnitude. A decline of this order is clearly much smaller than that which most students of the migration phenomenon seem to assume when they contemplate the possibility that migration might be impeded or halted. To place a decline in the domestic wage level of this magnitude in perspective, it should be pointed out that it is approximately equal to the average annual rate of increase in real wages

Table 6-6. *Percentage Change in the Wage Level in Labor Markets Subject to Competition from Migrants, Given Different Price Elasticities of the Supply of, and Demand for, Labor*

Elasticity of supply	*Elasticity of demand*		
	−0.5	*−1.0*	*−1.5*
0.2	7.14	4.17	2.94
0.5	5.00	3.33	2.50
0.7	4.17	2.94	2.27

of workers in the smallest enterprises in the industrial, service, and commercial sectors between 1960 and 1975.[96] In other words, the reintegration of the migrants into the domestic labor market during the 1970s would have implied a fall in wages about equal to a single year's rate of advance; real wages would thus have been left unchanged for about a year.

This estimate of the size of the change in wages that might follow a suspension of opportunities for migration to the United States was predicated on a wide dispersal of the would-be migrants over the entire country. To the extent that the labor force in some of the traditional source areas is not dispersed widely but remains concentrated in local or regional labor markets, the wage effect in those markets might be expected to be greater. Such a decline in real wages could be expected to spur out-migration to areas boasting more favorable employment conditions, however, and the local depression of wages would thus be moderated over time.

The estimated wage effect was predicated on the assumption that all of the U.S.-bound migrants would enter the labor market in competition with other workers, but in fact this might not be so. For example, if migrants to the United States were to have land of their own that was left uncultivated during their absence, loss of the migration opportunity could lead some simply to self-employment rather than to entry into the wage labor market. Indeed, a substantial number of migrants apparently do leave their plots uncultivated. Cornelius's sample found that 19 percent of the migrants who were ejidatarios or small landholders left their plots uncultivated, a surprising revelation in view of the household and community labor surplus conditions that are presumed to characterize rural areas.[97] He also cites work by Richard Mines that suggests that productive resources are not fully exploited in areas given to heavy migration to the United States as the area under cultivation declined.

The estimates of the wage effect of migration offered above were based on the assumption held by CENIET that migration is largely a circular phenomenon with insignificant permanent leakage out of the Mexican labor force. If a permanent leakage does occur, as the discussion earlier in this chapter suggests, then the above estimates understate the positive impact that migration has had on wage levels in Mexico. A major difference between temporary (or circular) and permanent migration is that the former has only a once-and-for-all impact while the latter impact is exponential.

For illustrative purposes, let us assume that the elasticities of supply of, and demand for, labor are 0.5 and − 1.0, respectively, values that may be regarded as plausible. Furthermore, out of each cohort of 500,000 migrants, 100,000 leak out permanently into the U.S. labor market. Since two cohorts are assumed to migrate to the United States each year, this implies a permanent leakage of 200,000 workers and a constant circulating group of 400,000 in the United States. Under the formula introduced above, the once-and-for-all effect of the withdrawal of the circulating 400,000 workers would then raise wages in the relevant Mexican labor market by 2.57 percent. The first-year impact of the permanent withdrawal of 200,000 workers would be an additional 1.28 percent, for a total increase of 3.85 percent. In each subsequent year, however, the leakage of an additional 200,000 will have a further impact on the wage level that is cumulative. At the end of five years, for example, the annual leakage of 200,000 will have resulted in a wage level 7.3 percent higher than that associated with a constant circulating stock of 400,000.

If, instead of a leakage of 100,000, there were one of 200,000 from each cohort of 500,000 going to the United States, the longer-term impact on the Mexican wage level would, of course, be greater. With the same elasticities, the once-and-for-all increase associated with a constant 300,000 stock of circulating workers in the United States would be 1.9 percent, while the first-year impact of the permanent withdrawal of 400,000 workers would be on the order of 2.56 percent. After five years, the Mexican wage level in the relevant market would be 14.5 percent higher than it would have been had there been a constant circulating stock of 300,000 in the United States.

As a general rule, the larger the proportion of each cohort of migrants to the United States that remains there, the greater the long-run impact migration will have on the wage level in Mexico. Obviously, a suspension of migration to the United States, including that of permanent illegal migrants, would also have a cumulative impact on the Mexican wage level since the domestic supply of labor would expand more rapidly. If an annual leakage of 400,000 workers were halted, the rate of real wage increase in the relevant part of the Mexican labor market would probably fall below 1 percent, given rates of economic growth of the same order of magnitude as those that held over the 1960–75 interval. If the actual leakage were closer to the 200,000 level, absorption of this number in the Mexican labor market might imply a reduction in the annual rate of increase in real wages to perhaps 2 percent.

Clearly, these estimates of changes in wages associated with different levels of circulating and permanent illegal migration should not be taken to represent anything more than illustrative and crude measures. At best, they may offer measures of a general order of magnitude under plausible assumptions regarding the elasticities of supply and demand and the size of migration flows. Implicit in these estimates was the maintenance of sustained and high rates of economic growth such as those characterizing the Mexican economy over the past four decades. Naturally, a significant decline in the rate of growth might be expected to produce less favorable conditions in labor markets generally, although the marginal effect of migration on wage levels might not prove to be much different.

In addition to the favorable consequences of migration for wage and employment conditions in Mexican labor markets, there are the consequences for the Mexican balance of payments. Two recent estimates of the approximate total contribution of migrant remittances to the flow of U.S. dollars to Mexico in the second half of the past decade are surprisingly similar: approximately US$315 million. One of these is derived from Díez-Canedo's study of checks cleared through Mexican banks; the other was a product of CENIET's household survey.

More visible, of course, is the impact of migration on the income level of households with migrating members. Given the wide disparity between wage levels in the United States and Mexico, even temporary employment in the United States makes possible a substantial improvement in living standards over those that would otherwise be achievable. Of lesser importance are likely to be the additions to human capital associated with migration. By and large, migrants are employed in occupations requiring little skill or training. Since most migrants do not remain in their U.S. jobs for more than a few months, they are unlikely to become candidates for training for more highly skilled jobs. Whether migrants return to Mexico with attitudes that may render them more productive is open to question. Cornelius observes that psychological profiles of migrants reveal they have a greater need for achievement than nonmigrants, and some evidence exists that this trait is enhanced by experiences in the United States.[99] Such individuals might also be more likely to perceive greater long-run opportunities for advancement in the U.S. labor market and, as a result, form a disproportionate share of the permanent leakage from the migration flow. If that were the case, Mexico would suffer a loss of highly motivated producers that it could ill afford.[100]

Summary

This chapter has reviewed the present status of our knowledge and understanding of the migration phenomenon of Mexicans to the United States. While considerable gaps exist in quantitative data, at least it can be said that the several attempts to estimate empirically the flow of workers to the United States have narrowed the range within which the estimated measures lie. In contrast to off-the-cuff estimates of government officials and others that the United States was being inundated by a flood of Mexican workers, the more serious efforts of researchers suggest flows of much more modest proportions. The available estimates of gross flows across the northern border would seem to be more reliable than those of net flows.

A proper assessment of the long-run impact of migration on the Mexican labor market depends heavily on the extent of permanent leakage of labor out of the circular migratory flow and into the United States. The cumulative effects of such a leakage can be considerable. My attempt to assess the impact of circular migration on wage levels in the relevant parts of the Mexican labor market suggests that, while positive, it is likely to have been quite modest, raising the wage level by no more than 3 to 4 percent. Even this conclusion must be treated with considerable care, for it is based on a rather arbitrary, although plausible, definition of the "relevant labor market" and on arbitrary elasticity coefficients.

It is likely that the U.S. labor market will continue to appear attractive to Mexican workers for some time to come. The large wage disparities that currently exist will probably survive well into the next century. Indeed, if the U.S. domestic supply of labor to low-skill occupations declines during the rest of this century, a faster increase in wages for these jobs relative to the general wage level may well occur; thus, the differential between unskilled wage rates in the United States and Mexico may be maintained or even enhanced.

It is difficult to foresee the steps that may be taken in the United States to stem the illegal migration flow from abroad and especially from Mexico. Although the measures ultimately adopted may serve to reduce the flow, it is hard to believe that they will stop it. As long as the gains to prospective migrants loom large and the advantages to U.S. employers of employing Mexican workers remain, there will be workers and employers willing to bear the increased risk of detection. Indeed, one may hypothesize that an attempt to close the border will give rise to more "permanent" illegal migration relative to circular since successful border crossers may be reluctant to test their luck again.

Some part of the clamor in the United States that the authorities do something to reduce the flow is surely related to the high levels of unemployment that were characteristic of the U.S. labor market during the early 1980s. Should the U.S. economy revert to a state of moderately full employment, the pressures to act on the migration issue or to enforce any new legislation might also subside. Further down the road, if actual shortages of unskilled labor were to materialize in the United States, we might see a de facto relaxation of barriers to migration or even an outright encouragement of migration through an organized program similar to the bracero program of the mid-century decades. It would thus appear that the United States would be unlikely to sever completely, or for long, the links that bind the two countries' labor markets.

Notes

1. Carey McWilliams, *North from Mexico: The Spanish-Speaking People of the U.S.* (New York: Greenwood Press, 1968), p. 52.
2. U.S. Immigration and Naturalization Service (INS), *Annual Report 1974* (Washington, D.C.: Government Printing Office, 1975), pp. 56–58.
3. Barton M. Clark, "Mexican Migration to the United States," in *Mexican Migration*, ed. T. Weaver and T. E. Downing (Tucson: University of Arizona, Bureau of Ethnic Research, 1976), p. 52.
4. Ibid., p. 54.
5. Julian Samora, *Los Mojados: The Wetback Story* (South Bend, Ind.: University of Notre Dame Press, 1971), p. 19.
6. Ibid., pp. 44–45.
7. Paul R. Ehrlich, Loy Bilderback, and Anne H. Ehrlich, *The Golden Door* (New York: Ballantine Books, 1979), pp. 211–14.
8. Samora, *Los Mojados*, pp. 44–45.
9. INS, *Annual Report 1974*, p. 10.
10. Carlos H. Zazueta, "Consideraciones acerca de los trabajadores mexicanos indocumentados en los Estados Unidos: Mitos y realidades" (Mexico, D.F.: Secretaría de Trabajo y Previsión Social, Centro Nacional de Información y Estadísticas del Trabajo [CENIET], March 27, 1979; processed), pp. 18–24. Monthly data on expulsions were not available for 1978 from the INS, but the total for the year was. For 1972–77, however, the proportion of the annual total attributable to August of each year varied within a narrow range of 8.2 to 10.2 percent. Zazueta applied the extreme percentage values to the 1978 annual total of apprehensions to obtain a high and low estimate for August of that year, 97,219 and 77,604 respectively. The value cited in the text is simply the mean of these extreme values.
11. Ibid., pp. 25–31. A similar large discrepancy was reported between the number of expulsions reported by the INS and by CENIET over a three-week interval, October 24–November 13, 1977. Although some conceptual or juridical differences could give rise to a discrepancy between "illegal aliens apprehended" and expulsions, these are not likely to suffice as explanations. An extended and careful discussion of this issue appears in Manuel García y Griego, *El volumen de la migración de mexicanos no documentados a los Estados*

Unidos (nuevas hipótesis), Estudios no. 4 (Mexico, D.F.: CENIET, 1980), pp. 215–44. A discussion of the conceptual differences of measures employed by the INS and their significance is contained in Charles B. Keely, "Counting the Uncountable: Estimates of Undocumented Aliens in the United States," *Population and Development Review*, vol. 3, no. 4 (1977), pp. 473–81.

12. Lesko and Associates, "Final Report: Basic Data and Guidance Required to Implement a Major Illegal Alien Study during Fiscal Year 1976," Contract no. CO-16-75 (Washington, D.C.: Office of Planning and Evaluation, U.S. Immigration and Naturalization Service, 1975; processed). The estimate of the total number of illegal aliens was based on the personal opinions of seven "experts" canvassed by Lesko. The estimate of Mexican aliens was derived from an assumed and constant ratio of apprehensions to entries. Furthermore, it was assumed that only 2 percent of the successful entrants returned to Mexico of their own free will. No empirical foundations for these proportions were offered.

13. Ideally, the number of illegal aliens in the United States could be derived by an enumeration based on census or other sampling procedures. One such attempt was made under contract from the INS in 1976 by Joseph Reyes and Associates. The practical difficulties confronting this effort apparently proved overwhelming, however, and the project was abandoned after two years. (García y Griego, *El volumen de la migración*, pp. 31–34.)

14. Clarise Lancaster and Frederick J. Scheuren, "Counting the Uncountable Illegals: Some Initial Statistical Speculations Employing Capture-Recapture Techniques," *1977 Proceedings of the Social Statistical Section of the American Statistical Association* (Washington, D.C., 1978), pp. 31–34.

15. For a fuller critique of this study, see Ehrlich, Bilderback, and Ehrlich, *The Golden Door*, pp. 182–90; and García y Griego, *El volumen de la migración*, pp. 45–47.

16. David S. North and Marion F. Houstoun, *The Characteristics and Role of Illegal Aliens in the U.S. Labor Market* (Washington, D.C.: Linton, 1976), pp. 40–45.

17. David M. Heer, "What is the Annual Net Flow of Undocumented Mexican Immigrants to the United States?" *Demography*, vol. 16, no. 3 (1979), pp. 417–23.

18. Ibid. This estimate assumes a 10 percent undercount in the 1970 census and a 70 percent net migration rate among documented immigrants. The seven estimates ranged from a low of 426,000 to a high of 1,201,000 over the entire five-year period.

19. J. Gregory Robinson, "Estimating the Approximate Size of the Illegal Alien Population by the Comparative Trend Analysis of Age-Specific Death Rates," *Demography*, vol. 17, no. 2 (1980), pp. 159–76.

20. Howard Goldberg, "Estimates of Emigration from Mexico and Illegal Entry into the United States, 1960–70 by the Residual Method" (Washington, D.C.: Center for Population Research, Georgetown University, n.d.), cited in North and Houstoun, *Characteristics and Role of Illegal Aliens*, p. 72.

21. World Bank, *1978 World Bank Atlas* (Washington, D.C., 1978), p. 8.

22. García y Griego, *El volumen de la migración*.

23. An additional 162 crossings were reported but proved unusable because certain information was lacking. Only the latest fifteen entries previous to the most recent one were recorded.

24. Juan Díez-Canedo, "La migración indocumentada a Estados Unidos; un enfoque," Documento de investigación no. 24 (Mexico, D.F.: Banco de México, July 1980).

25. CENIET, "Análisis de algunos resultados de la primera encuesta a trabajadores mexicanos no documentados devueltos de los Estados Unidos, octubre 23–noviembre 13 de 1977" (Mexico D.F., n.d.); Carlos H. Zazueta, "Consideraciones acerca de los trabajadores mexicanos indocumentados en los Estados Unidos; mitos y realidades" (Mexico, D.F.: CENIET, 1979; processed); Carlos H. Zazueta, "Mexican Workers in the United States: Some

Initial Results and Methodological Considerations of the National Household Survey of Emigration (ENEFNEU)," paper prepared for the Working Group on Mexican Migrants and U.S. Responsibility, Center for Philosophy and Public Policy, University of Maryland, March 1980; César Zazueta, "Investigación reciente sobre migración mexicana indocumentada a los Estados Unidos," (Mexico, D.F.: CENIET, February 19, 1980; processed).

26. César Zazueta, "Investigación reciente sobre migración," p. 79.

27. The daily commuters hold immigrant status that is renewable every six months as long as they continue to be employed in the United States. At the end of fiscal 1978, these numbered 49,290 (U.S. Senate, Committee on the Judiciary, 96th Congress, *Temporary Worker Programs: Background and Issues* [Washington, D.C.: Government Printing Office, 1980], p. 82). In addition, seasonal commuters with a legal (H-2) status are admitted, primarily during the peak agricultural season. These workers were estimated to number approximately 8,000 in 1974 (Anna-Stina Ericson, "The Impact of Commuters on the Mexican-American Border," in *Mexican Workers in the United States*, ed. George C. Kiser and Martha W. Kiser [Albuquerque: University of New Mexico Press, 1979], p. 215).

28. César Zazueta, "Investigación reciente sobre migración," p. 79.

29. This number is derived as follows. If the average size of each cohort of successful crossers into the United States were approximately 500,000 workers, the number of first timers might range from 30 to 40 percent of that number, or 160,000–200,000. Of course, if the probability of apprehension for first timers were actually more than three times that of experienced migrants, then the absolute number of first timers would be smaller. There is no way of knowing what these probabilities are. An average probability over repeated successful entries can be derived from North and Houstoun's data on Mexican migrants (*Characteristics and Role of Illegal Aliens*, pp. 86–87). Their respondents reported an average of 4.5 successful trips to the United States and 0.8 apprehensions, for a 0.18 average probability of apprehension. If the probability of detention were three times greater for first timers than for repeaters, this would imply a probability of 0.374 for the former and 0.124 for the latter.

30. CENIET, "Análisis de algunos resultados," p. 41.

31. INS, *Annual Report*, various years.

32. Consejo Nacional de población, *México demografico, breviario 1980–81* (Mexico, D.F., 1982), pp. 38–39.

33. Consejo Nacional de Población (CONAPO), Secretaría de Programación y Presupuesto (SPP), and Centro Latinoamericano de Demografía (CELADE), *México: estimaciones y proyecciones de población, 1950–2000* (Mexico, D.F., 1982), p. 18.

34. However, the benefits derived from temporary migration, measured in Mexican pesos, should have been declining from 1978 through the beginning of 1982 as a consequence of increasing overvaluation of the peso. Conversely, the sharp devaluations of 1982 and the deep recession that followed in Mexico should have had the opposite effect.

35. Manuel Gamio, *Mexican Immigration to the United States* (Chicago: University of Chicago Press, 1930); Robert F. Foerster, *The Racial Problem Involved in Immigration* (Washington, D.C.: Government Printing Office, 1925).

36. Carlos Zazueta, "Mexican Workers in the United States," p. 50.

37. Díez-Canedo, "La migración indocumentada." Díez-Canedo speculated that remitters are more likely to be temporary or undocumented migrants. Long-term or permanent migrants were held to be more likely to have their immediate families with them and their financial responsibilities to family members in Mexico correspondingly weakened. The CENIET household survey limited its inquiry to the work force in the United States that nonetheless maintained its customary residence in Mexico. Thus, longer-term residents in the United States would be less likely to be recorded.

38. INS, *Annual Report, 1974*, p. 104.

39. Ibid., pp. 51–55.

40. CENIET, "Análisis de algunos resultados," p. 25.

41. INS, *Annual Report, 1974*, pp. 51–52.

42. Rural localities are defined by these studies as those with fewer than 20,000 inhabitants.

43. CENIET, "Análisis de algunos resultados," pp. 26–34.

44. Carlos Zazueta, "Mexican Workers in the United States," pp. 34–44.

45. Ibid., pp. 41–43.

46. Ibid., pp. 58–59; CENIET, "Análisis de algunos resultados," pp. 35–36; Cesar Zazueta and Fernando Mercado N., "El mercado de trabajo norteamericano y los trabajadores mexicanos: algunos elementos teoricos y empiricos para su discusion," paper read at the Mexico-United States Seminar on Undocumented Migration, September 4–6, 1980, University of New Mexico, Albuquerque, New Mexico, pp. 20–22.

47. Zazueta and Mercado, "El mercado de trabajo norteamericano," pp. 20–22.

48. George M. Foster, *Tzintzuntzan: Mexican Peasants in a Changing World*, rev. ed. (New York: Elsevier, 1979), p. 297.

49. Luis M. Fernandez O. and Maria T. de Fernandez, "Capitalismo y cooperación: el caso de un ejido en Michoacán," in *Capitalismo y campesinado en México* (Mexico, D.F.: Instituto Nacional de Antropología e Historia, 1976), p. 216.

50. Wayne A. Cornelius, "Mexican Migration to the United States: Cause, Conseqences, and U.S. Responses" (Cambridge, Mass.: Center for International Studies, Massachusetts Institute of Technology, July 1978; processed), pp. 25–26.

51. CENIET, "Análisis de algunos resultados," pp. 40–46.

52. Cornelius reported that first timers had a much higher rate of apprehension than repeaters ("Mexican Migration to the United States," p. 24).

53. Zazueta and Mercado, "El mercado de trabajo norteamericano," p. 24.

54. North and Houstoun, *Characteristics and Role of Illegal Aliens*, pp. 84–86.

55. Robert D. Shadow, "Differential Out-Migration: A Comparison of Internal and International Migration from Villa Guerrero, Jalisco (Mexico)," in *Migration Across Frontiers: Mexico and the United States*, ed. Fernando Camara and Robert V. Kemper (Albany: State University of New York at Albany, 1979), pp. 71–72.

56. Cornelius, "Mexican Migration to the United States," p. 36.

57. Ibid., pp. 38, 29.

58. John S. Evans and Dilmus D. James, "Conditions of Employment and Income Distribution in Mexico as Incentives for Mexican Migration to the United States: Prospects to the End of the Century," *International Migration Review*, vol. 13, no. 1 (1979), p. 5.

59. Indeed, even Cornelius, perhaps unwittingly, illustrates the role of pull forces in his discussion of short-term economic push factors: "But the recent economic development which has undoubtedly had the greatest impact on migration to the United States was the devaluation of the Mexican peso in September, 1976—the first such devaluation in 22 years. Before September 1, 1976, if a migrant working in the U.S. sent one U.S. dollar to his family in Mexico, it brought 12.50 pesos. With U.S. dollars now yielding nearly twice as much as before, rapid inflation, and a high unemployment rate in Mexico, a large increase in illegal migration during 1977 was inevitable." ("Mexican Migration to the United States," pp. 36–38.) One would have thought that a sudden increase in the attractiveness of U.S. employment would constitute a pull rather than push factor.

60. Mario I. Blejer, Harry G. Johnson, and Arturo C. Porzecanski, "Un análisis de los determinantes economicos de la migración mexicana legal e ilegal hacia los Estados Unidos," *Demografía y economía*, vol. 11, no. 3 (1977), pp. 326–40.

61. Walter Fogel, "Twentieth-Century Mexican Migration to the United States," in *The*

Gateway: U.S. Immigration Issues and Policies, ed. Barry R. Chiswick (Washington, D.C.: American Enterprise Institute, 1982), pp. 193–221.

62. Alberto E. Davila, "Economic Determinants of Illegal Mexican Immigration to the U.S.," *Economic Review*, Federal Reserve Bank of Dallas, May 1983, pp. 13–23.

63 Carlos Zazueta, "Mexican Workers in the United States," pp. 56–59.

64. CENIET, "Análisis de algunos resultados," pp. 35–36.

65. César Zazueta, "Investigación reciente sobre migración mexicana," pp. 91–92.

66. Kenneth Roberts, *Agrarian Structure and Labor Migration in Rural Mexico: The Case of Circular Migration of Undocumented Workers to the United States* (Austin: Institute of Latin American Studies, University of Texas at Austin, 1980), pp. 266, 248–49.

67. Ibid., p. 266; Shadow, "Differential Outmigration," pp. 72–75; Raymond E. Wiest, "Implications of International Labor Migration for Mexican Rural Development," in *Migration Across Frontiers: Mexico and the United States*, ed. Fernando Camara and Robert V. Kemper (Albany: State University of New York at Albany, 1979), p. 87.

68. CENIET, "Análisis de algunos resultados," p. 36.

69. Shadow, "Differential Outmigration," p. 72.

70. Wiest, "Implications of International Labor Migration," pp. 88–90.

71. Roberts, *Agrarian Structure and Labor Migration*, p. 75.

72. CENIET, "Análisis de algunos resultados," pp. 56–61. Cornelius reports that 30 percent of the migrants in his sample employed coyotes on their first attempt to cross the border; 41 percent of his sample had used them on their most recent trip ("Mexican Migration to the United States," p. 23).

73. CENIET, "Análisis de algunos resultados," p. 63.

74. César Zazueta, "Investigación reciente sobre migración mexicana," pp. 88–90. Male migrants were reported to be much more likely to finance their trip by borrowing than were women, the respective ratios of borrowers to total migrants being 45 to 20 percent. In part, this may reflect the relatively greater female migration from the border cities rather than from the interior and, subsequently, a lesser need for a cash reserve.

75. CENIET, "Análisis de algunos resultados," pp. 37–39.

76. There appears to have been no attempt to distinguish between the gross rate of earnings and the net rate after payroll deductions. Both were probably reported by the respondents.

77. Zazueta and Mercado, "El mercado de trabajo norteamericano," p. 23.

78. Apparently, there are some households for which migrant earnings constitute the "only source of income" (Fernandez and Fernandez, "Capitalismo y coperación," p. 216).

79. Shadow, "Differential Outmigration," p. 75; Wiest, "Implications of International Labor Migration," p. 88; Michael Belshaw, *A Village Economy* (New York: Columbia University Press, 1967), p. 31; P. Lamartine Yates, *Mexico's Agricultural Dilemma* (Tucson: University of Arizona press, 1981), p. 245.

80. Roberts, *Agrarian Structure and Labor Migration*, pp. 68–73.

81. In his discussion of household networks, Roberts relies on the findings of Ina R. Dinerman in her study of rural households in Huecorio, Michoacán, "Patterns of Adaptation among Households of U.S.-Bound Migrants from Michoacán, Mexico," *International Migration Review*, vol. 12, no. 4 (1979), p. 496.

82. Shadow, "Differential Outmigration," p. 70; Roberts, *Agrarian Structure and Labor Migration*, pp. 129–34.

83. Cornelius, "Mexican Migration to the United States," p. 22.

84. Roberts, *Agrarian Structure and Labor Migration*. The four zones studied were Las Huastecas, San Luis Potosí; Mixteca Baja, Oaxaca; Valsequillo, Puebla; and El Bajío, Guanajuato.

85. Why the increased reliance on purchased farm inputs should lead to a greater need to earn off-farm cash income in order to finance those purchases is not clear. If a move away from peasant and toward commercial agriculture increases total output and the cash income from farming, as it apparently does, then the earnings from farming should suffice to cover the costs associated with that mode and still leave the household better off. Otherwise, there would be no incentive to shift from subsistence to commercial agriculture.

86. Roberts, *Agrarian Structure and Labor Migration*, pp. 263–67.

87. Cornelius, "Mexican Migration to the United States," p. 22.

88. Cornelius makes much of the persistence of tradition within families as an intergenerational phenomenon. In 62 percent of the families having some history of migration to the United States, members of two generations have gone there. An additional 8 percent reported participation in the migratory flow through three generations. Eighty-seven percent of the migrants also reported having brothers or sisters working in the United States. He also cites other studies confirming this intergenerational pattern. ("Mexican Migration to the United States.," p. 21.)

89. Michael E. Conroy, Mario Coria S., and Felipe Villa G., "Socio-economic Incentive for Migration to the United States: Cross-Regional Profiles, 1969–1978," paper presented at the 1980 Annual Meeting of the Population Association of America, April 11, 1980, Denver, Colorado, pp. 15–30.

90. Clark W. Reynolds, "Labor Market Projections for the United States and Mexico and their Relevance to Current Migration Controversies," Food Research Institute Studies no. 17 (Stanford, Calif.: Stanford University, 1979; processed).

91. Harold Wool, "Future Labor Supply for Lower Level Occupations," *Monthly Labor Review*, vol. 99, no. 3 (1976), pp. 22–31.

92. In localities where a large proportion of the labor force migrated to the United States, the wage and employment effects have been found to be quite visible. Wiest observed in Michoacán that the large wage differential in earnings between the United States and the local community raised the reservation price of local workers and created labor "shortages" in agriculture. Local labor requirements for the sector were satisfied by recruiting workers from outlying hamlets. ("Implications of International Labor Migration," p. 91.)

93. César Zazueta, "Investigaciones recientes sobre migración mexicana," p. 80.

94. There is some empirical foundation for the assumption that internal and international migration are substitutes for each other. A finding of the CENIET household survey was a lower frequency of internal migration involving a change in residence among those who had experienced migration to the United States.

95. This formula is derived from the reduced form equations of supply and demand as discussed in Micha Gisser, *Introduction to Price Theory*, 2d ed. (Scranton, Penn.: International Textbook, 1969), pp. 378–80.

96. See Chapter 7. The three sectoral annual rates of increase were 4.5, 3.6, and 3.2 percent, respectively.

97. Cornelius, "Mexican Migration to the United States," p. 48.

98. Díez-Canedo, "La migración indocumentada;" Carlos Zazueta, "Mexican Workers in the United States," pp. 51–54.

99. Cornelius, "Mexican Migration to the United States," p. 20.

100. For a discussion of the presumed benefits and costs to Mexico of illegal migration to the United States, see Allen R. Newman, "Some Theoretical Considerations for Mexican Illegal Migration to the United States," paper presented at the annual meeting of the Rocky Mountain Council for Latin American Studies, February 14, 1981, Las Cruces, New Mexico.

7. Wages in Mexico, 1935 to the Present

ANYONE WISHING to chronicle the course of wages over the past fifty years in Mexico is faced with a formidable challenge. Systematic collection of wage data has still to be undertaken in Mexico. Thus, the data that have been available originate from different sources, are not comparable, and certainly not representative. Compounding the problem of wage data scarcity is that of converting nominal wages into real wages. The course of real wages varies significantly depending on the choice of a deflator, particularly for the years prior to 1960. An evaluation of the evidence on the course of wages will be attempted in this chapter.

Much of the discussion on the course of wages in Mexico takes as its point of departure changes that have occurred in the level of legal minimum wages. Since these do represent an observable datum, it is understandable that they should be cited often. It is almost universally recognized, however, that legal minimums have had only a very limited effective coverage and that departures of actual wages from the minimums have been significant and of different magnitudes and signs over time. Nevertheless, since the legal minimums have served as a sort of benchmark for the course of wages, they do deserve attention.

History of Minimum Wages

Minimum wages have a relatively long history in Mexico. The Constitution of 1917 provided for their establishment, but it was not until 1934, during the administration of Lázaro Cárdenas, that this provision was implemented. The law provided for a very complex structure of minimums. The country was divided into 111 zones for which regional boards were to define two separate minimums, one for the agricultural sector and another for all other wage-earning employment. In addition, the regional boards were empowered to establish occupational wage minimums for unorganized workers; eighty-six were in effect in 1983. The number of covered occupations has been increasing over time. As recently as 1974–75, only sixty-five occupational rates were in force.[1] The original statute provided for a revision of rates every other year. With the acceleration of inflation, however, an interim adjustment was made near the end of the 1971–73 biennium, and thereafter minimums have been revised at least once a year.

The decentralization of the minimum wage setting process was intended to allow each zone to determine rates that, to some extent, reflected local labor market conditions. As a result, a structure of minimum wage rates emerged that was marked by large disparities. For example, in the early 1940s, the highest rural minimum wage was 4.3 times the lowest. That differential almost doubled over the rest of the decade. Since then, it has steadily narrowed and by the end of the 1970s stood at a ratio of approximately 2:1. The nonagricultural structure of minimums has undergone similar changes over time. During the early 1940s, the highest rate stood in a ratio of 4.8:1 to the lowest. After widening to 7.7:1 at the end of that decade, this ratio had shrunk to 2.3:1 by 1979. The highest minimums have generally obtained in the regions bordering the United States and the large metropolitan areas, while the lowest were assigned the depressed zones of the southern peninsular and Pacific regions and parts of the central plateau. The ratio of urban-to-rural rates has also varied sharply over time. The initial urban minimum measured only 6 percent above the rural, a differential that increased to 26 percent by 1950–51, only to narrow gradually thereafter to under 10 percent in 1979.

A significant change in the policy orientation for wages emerged during the administration of President López Portillo. Over the preceding twenty-five years, adjustments in the minimum wage had been designed to prevent a decline in its purchasing power and to advance its real value gradually over time. Toward the end of the decade of the 1970s, minimum wage administration was invested with an expanded purpose. One of these was redistributive in nature. A narrowing of minimum wage differentials among zones was advocated as a means of raising the lowest wage incomes of the covered population in order to achieve greater degree of equality in the distribution of income. Therefore, the national commission on minimum wages began adjusting the lowest urban and rural minimums at an accelerated rate, narrowing the differentials between urban and rural minimums within, as well as across, zones. A second rationale offered for the narrowing of differentials was the expectation that it would reduce the incentives for "improper," that is, excessive, rural–urban migration.[2]

Beginning with the determinations for 1978, the number of different minimum wage rates has been reduced rapidly—first from 144 to 59, by 1980 to 18, and to only 4 in 1983. This sharp reduction was facilitated in

1981 by the consolidation of the rural and urban rates within each zone; thus, one of the differentials that had characterized the system ever since its inception was eliminated. The wide relative differential that had existed between the highest and the lowest minimum rate was also sharply narrowed, from a ratio of 3.28:1 as recently as 1977, to only 1.4:1 in 1983.

The course of the legal minimums over time from their inception to the present is set forth in table 7-1. For most years, the nominal and real minimums are presented and indexed in two ways. The first is a simple arithmetic average of minimums across all zones; the second presents the minimums as weighted averages, with the size of each zone's labor force serving as the weight. As can be seen, the weighted average minimum is consistently larger than the simple average, a reflection of higher wage levels in more densely populated zones. The nominal rates are deflated by the consumer price index for Mexico City since a national price index does not become available until 1968.

No sooner had the initial legal minimums been declared for the biennium 1934–35 than they began an uninterrupted decline in real terms as increases in the general price level outpaced adjustments in the minimums. The urban minimum bottomed out during the 1946–47 biennium at a level 48 percent below the initial 1934–35 level; the rural minimum reached its lowest point in 1950–51, 56 percent below its initial level. Both rates then began to recover, but the minimums did not exceed their initial real values until the 1964–65 biennium.[3] Over the next twelve years to 1977, the weighted minimums increased by about 60 percent, peaking in 1977 on a full-year basis. Thereafter, in the face of accelerating inflation, the urban real minimum wage lost ground. During 1983, it averaged between two-thirds and three-fourths of the peak 1977 level. In contrast, the rural minimum, which underwent a more rapid rate of increase until it was finally merged with the urban, continued to increase in real terms through 1981, after which it moved together with the urban minimum.

The Course of Real Wages, 1940–55

The question that has troubled students of Mexican economic development is the extent to which the course of the minimums accurately reflects that of actual wages paid. Particularly troublesome has been the sharp decline, noted above, in the real minimums between 1934 and the end of the 1940s. In general, the consensus seems to be that actual real wages paid also fell, though by a narrower margin than the minimums. Little agreement exists on the extent to which real wages fell and the proportion of the labor force affected by the decline.

Unfortunately, the wage statistics that are available for those years have

Table 7-1. *Average Nominal and Real Legal Minimum Wages, 1934–35 to 1983*
(Mexican pesos)

	Nominal unweighted average minimum wage		*Real unweighted average minimum wage index (1978 = 100)*[a]		*Nominal weighted average minimum wage*		*Real weighted average wage index (1978 = 100)*[a]	
Years	*Urban*	*Rural*	*Urban*	*Rural*	*Urban*	*Rural*	*Urban*	*Rural*
1934–35	1.15	1.09	53.2	57.8	n.a.	n.a.	n.a.	n.a.
1936–37	1.31	1.21	52.3	55.4	n.a.	n.a.	n.a.	n.a.
1938–39	1.46	1.31	47.0	48.3	n.a.	n.a.	n.a.	n.a.
1940–41	1.52	1.30	46.8	45.9	n.a.	n.a.	n.a.	n.a.
1942–43	1.52	1.35	34.7	35.3	n.a.	n.a.	n.a.	n.a.
1944–45	1.90	1.65	29.4	29.3	n.a.	n.a.	n.a.	n.a.
1946–47	2.48	2.05	27.9	26.4	n.a.	n.a.	n.a.	n.a.
1948–49	3.01	2.40	29.3	26.8	n.a.	n.a.	n.a.	n.a.
1950–51	3.35	2.66	28.2	25.7	n.a.	n.a.	n.a.	n.a.
1952–53	5.35	4.55	37.4	36.5	n.a.	n.a.	n.a.	n.a.
1954–55	6.34	5.26	39.5	37.8	n.a.	n.a.	n.a.	n.a.
1956–57	7.25	5.99	39.0	37.0	n.a.	n.a.	n.a.	n.a.
1958–59	8.13	6.86	37.7	36.4	n.a.	n.a.	n.a.	n.a.
1960–61	9.89	8.83	42.8	43.8	n.a.	n.a.	n.a.	n.a.
1962–63	12.44	10.92	52.6	52.9	n.a.	n.a.	n.a.	n.a.
1964–65	16.00	13.47	54.9	62.6	17.33	14.78	64.0	61.3
1966–67	18.69	15.72	70.3	67.7	20.01	17.42	68.6	67.0
1968–69	21.58	18.32	77.5	75.4	23.12	20.12	76.0	74.0
1970–71	24.91	21.20	81.1	79.1	26.99	23.48	80.1	78.2
1972–73	29.29	24.94	83.6	81.6	31.93	27.73	83.1	81.0
1973[b]	34.56	29.43	88.3	86.2	37.68	32.73	93.1	90.8
1974[c]	39.38	33.52	89.4	87.3	43.42	37.79	87.6	85.6
1974–75[d]	48.04	40.90	92.5	90.2	52.97	46.10	91.4	89.3
1976[e]	58.68	49.87	98.9	95.1	64.74	56.66	96.2	94.4
1976[f]	72.18	61.34	107.3	104.5	79.63	69.55	107.8	105.8
1977	79.37	67.45	102.5	99.8	87.56	76.48	103.1	101.1
1978	90.55	78.99	100.0	100.0	99.37	88.50	100.0	100.0
1979	105.80	96.26	99.2	103.5	116.02	106.81	99.1	102.5
1980	124.53	121.33	92.3	103.1	136.62	134.16	92.3	101.7
1981	167.00	167.00	95.1	101.7	178.87	178.87	93.8	105.3
1982[g]	224.00	224.00	87.3	100.1	240.00	240.00	85.2	95.7
1982[h]	291.20	291.20	80.9	92.8	312.00	312.00	79.0	88.7
1983[i]	364.00	364.00	78.2	89.7	390.00	390.00	76.4	85.8
1983[j]	400.40	400.40	67.2	77.0	429.00	429.00	65.6	73.6

n.a. Not available.
a. Deflated by the consumer price index for Mexico City.

(Notes continue on the following page.)

serious deficiencies. The only official data derive from the annual October wage surveys of selected manufacturing firms. These companies are not necessarily representative of the whole sector nor even of the industries of which they form a part.[4] The surveyed firms are described simply as being among the "most important" in Mexico. Prior to 1964, establishments in only six cities were surveyed; since then, twelve cities have been surveyed. Usually the included firms are among the largest in their respective industries. In 1939, probably no more than 43,000 workers were employed in the surveyed establishments. By 1950, the number of workers covered had increased to 54,000, or by 25 percent, distributed over approximately 600 establishments. Since employment in the modern industrial sector had virtually doubled in the intervening decade, the full impact this expansion may have had on wage levels is not captured by the survey.[5] Furthermore, since no employment weights are available, the average wage can be computed only as a simple average of the wage paid in the included industries. Since only the average daily wage appears, no account can be taken of the impact on earnings of variations in hours or days worked. Utilizing these data, López Rosado and Noyola Vázquez estimated that real wages in the covered industries had fallen by approximately 27

Table 7-1 (*notes continued*)

b. Effective September 17 to December 31, 1973.

c. Effective January 1 to October 7, 1974.

d. Effective October 8, 1974, to December 31, 1975.

e. Effective January 1 to September 30, 1976.

f. Effective October 1 to December 31, 1976.

g. Effective January 1 to October 30, 1982. In addition to the adjustment recorded here, a further graduated general wage increase was decreed by the secretary of labor on March 19. All wages under Mex$20,000 per month were increased by 30 percent, those between Mex$20,000 and Mex$30,000 by 20 percent, and all higher wages by 10 percent. The increases were made retroactive to February 18. Since the highest minimum wage in effect yielded a monthly wage of less than Mex$10,000, the decree effectively raised all workers at the minimum wage by 30 percent in February. The legal minimums were not officially increased by 30 percent until November 1. If account is taken of the decreed increase, the weighted index of urban minimums would have averaged 107.0 over the January–October interval; the rural, 120.1. The weighted minimums for the year are approximate only.

h. Effective November 1 to December 31, 1978. The weighted minimums are approximate only.

i. Effective January 1 to May 31, 1983. The weighted minimums are approximate only.

j. Effective June 1 to December 31, 1983. The weighted minimums are approximate only.

Sources: Comisión de los Salarios Minimos, *Salarios minimos*, various issues; prices 1934–35, James W. Wilkie, *Statistics and National Policy* (Los Angeles: University of California, L.A., Latin American Center, 1974), p. 229; prices 1936–60, Nacional Financiera, S.A., *50 años de revolución mexicana en cifras* (Mexico, D.F., 1963); prices 1961–83, Banco de México, *Informe anual*, various issues.

percent between 1939 and 1947, although these were believed to have recovered slightly over the following two years.[6]

A rather different estimate of the drop in real wages is obtained from another official source cited by these same authors that surveyed twenty-four industrial groups with roughly one-sixth of the total industrial labor force in 1949. According to this source, real wages fell by a lesser amount, 18 percent between 1939 and 1948. Two additional groups for which data were presented also revealed substantial declines: railway workers by 14 percent and public (federal) employees by 31 percent over the decade 1939–49.[7] While substantial, these declines appear to have been less severe than those for the urban minimum wage.

Two other analyses of the course of wages deserve mention since they attempted a less aggregative approach. John Isbister concludes that annual earnings of blue-collar workers in the manufacturing sector fell by 11 percent between 1940 and 1945 and then remained relatively stable until 1955.[8] During that same interval, the real value of the legal minimum wage for urban workers had fallen by 40 percent. Stylianos Perrakis examined the course of earnings of unskilled workers in Mexico City manufacturing industries.[9] Between 1940 and 1944, the legal minimum applicable to the Federal District and actual earnings fell together by about 27 percent. Thereafter, unskilled earnings leveled off even as the legal minimum continued its decline to 1951.

As discussed in Chapter 2, the decade of the 1940s was one of substantial economic growth. Gross national product grew at an average annual rate of 6 percent, while per capita income rose at a 3.7 percent rate. Output per worker also increased at an average annual rate of 3.2 percent, although the intersectoral disparities were large: from 3.6 percent in agriculture to 0.5 percent or less in the secondary and tertiary sectors. A decline in real wages in such an expansionary context is something of an anomaly and has led to numerous attempts to analyze and interpret these findings.[10] The anomaly is heightened by Adolph Sturmthal, who traced changes in the functional distribution of national income and concluded that the weighted real average wage must have risen by at least 10 to 12 percent over the decade of the 1940s.[11]

One possible explanation offered by both López Rosado and Sturmthal is the changing weight in the structure of employment. Although wages in the canvassed sectors may have been falling in real terms, a shift of labor from even lower absolute wage sectors could have resulted in a rising average wage. The unweighted wage data do not fully reflect the impact of probable changes in the occupational structure within the industrial sector, which may have been moving toward more skill-intensive employments. And to the extent that individual workers experienced upward occupational mobility within the expanding industrial sector, the decline in average earnings might provide a misleading guide to the course of earnings of individuals employed in the sector over a period of years. Both of these sources also hold out the possibility that daily wage rates may underestimate earnings if hours or days worked increased over the decade. While this possibility was not empirically tested, Sturmthal believes such increases would seem plausible in view of the substantial industrial expansion of the decade.

Alternatively, the decline in real wages is viewed as a consequence of a lag in the adjustment of nominal wages to changes in the general price level. While it is not unusual for wages to lag prices at the beginning of an inflationary period, one would expect that, if the real wage prior to the onset of inflation were equal to the market price of labor, the nominal wage would soon adjust so as to restore the market clearing real wage. The revised expectations of workers would lead to an increase in the reservation price of labor expressed in nominal terms that would be sufficient to restore the real wage.

In the Mexican case, the accelerated rate of price increases dated from the mid-1930s and continued through the 1940s. On the one hand, it might have been expected that, if the base year wage level had been truly indicative of the market price of labor, the initial decline in the real wage would have led to an earlier recovery than could be observed from the available data. On the other hand, it has been observed that the decline in real wage rates was accompanied by increases in fringe benefits, social services, and probably in hours worked that would have offset at least part of the welfare loss occasioned by declining wage rates.[12]

Finally, all the students of this issue concur in the view that the wage data that are available are drawn from a very narrow sample of firms and therefore cannot be taken to be representative of the industrial sector as a whole or of the urban labor market. Some question of the reliability of the data themselves may also be raised, although the trend they establish is so pronounced and pervasive that it is hard to dismiss them as completely misleading for the sampled firms.

There may be an alternative explanation for the observed decline in the wage rates of the sampled firms. First, this sample is drawn from among the largest firms in each of the industries sampled. These firms in the "modern" sector are those most likely to observe the legal minimum requirements of employment. Furthermore, since they are also the best candidates for organization, the trade unions would serve an enforcement function to ensure the payment of wages at least equal to the minimum wage.

Next, it can be inferred that the minimum wages established in the initial 1934–35 years were well in excess of the market price of labor. For example, the output per worker in 1934 in the economy as a whole can be estimated to have been equal to approximately Mex$567 in current pesos. The average urban minimum wage defined in annual terms (365 × Mex$1.52) was equal to Mex$420, or 74 percent of GDP per worker. The annualized average rural minimum was only slightly smaller: Mex$398, or 70 percent of the average output per worker in the economy as a whole. Since agricultural output per worker in that period was less than half of the national average, the annualized rural minimum exceeded the value of output per worker. The share of wages and salaries in GDP for a proximate year, 1940, has been estimated at 29.7 percent, and it can therefore reasonably be inferred that the minimums had been set well above the market price of labor.[13] Given the strong pro-labor sympathies of the Cárdenas government, it would not be surprising to find the establishment of minimum wages reflecting such sympathies, with little reference to actual market wage conditions. Thus, it may be surmised that the adoption of wages at least equal to the legal minimums in the large, modern sector firms yielded substantial economic rents to the workers employed there.

Subsequently, as the real value of the minimum wage rates began their decline in 1936 and as the nominal minimums were adjusted at rates below the rate of inflation, these firms were under no market compulsion to adjust the actual wages paid by more than the adjustment in the nominal legal minimum. Real wages could therefore fall at an equal rate with the legal minimum until the latter was a more accurate reflection of the market supply price of unskilled labor. As Perrakis pointed out, this occurred in Mexico City in 1944, when the real wage paid for unskilled labor stabilized even though the real minimum continued to decline for several additional years.[14]

Thus, it is entirely possible that the course of neither the legal minimum wage nor the wages in these surveyed firms provides a true reflection of what was happening to wages generally in either the urban or rural labor markets. In the case of the legal minimum, it has always been widely accepted that it serves as an effective wage only in the larger establishments of the modern urban sector or in the modern large-scale commercial agricultural sector. Such employers probably accounted for no more than 20 percent of total employment in the late 1930s or early 1940s. Since the surveyed firms were not representative of jobs outside the effective range of the minimum wage, there is no way to conclude from these wage data what the general course of wages may have been. Wages for urban unskilled labor beyond the scope of legal minimum wage coverage could have been rising in real terms at the same time that wages in the surveyed sector were declining.

Indeed, there are several bits of information that, taken together, would lead one to treat with caution, if not skepticism, the conclusion that urban wages suffered a general decline during the decade of the 1940s. It is an axiom of economic theory that the price of a factor of production to any particular use is determined by its opportunity cost. In the case of urban unskilled labor in a developing economy, its opportunity cost is generally taken to be defined by forgone earnings in the rural or agricultural sector. Thus, a clue to the course of unskilled urban wages might be provided by the course of incomes or earnings in the rural sector.

Urban-Rural Wage Differences

The first development that would influence the reservation price of labor is the changing land tenure relationships in agriculture. One might expect that the conversion from landless laborer to landowner would have resulted in an increase in the income of the land recipient, particularly since there is no evidence available that would suggest a decline in output on the plots transferred to their new owners. In the late 1930s, the distribution of almost 18 million hectares of land might have been expected to induce workers to remain in the sector in hopes of becoming the beneficiaries of further distributions. Indeed, there are references in the literature to urban residents returning to their rural communities of origin in order to establish and pursue their claim to land. The decade of the 1940s saw a continuing process of distribution. While not acquiring the scope of the process during the Cárdenas regime (1934–40), the land reform did distribute an additional 8 million hectares during 1941–49.[15] The transfer of land might therefore be viewed as resulting in a once-and-for-all increase in the returns to rural labor or as creating an anticipation of such an increase. In either case, the reservation price of labor to the urban sector would not be expected to decline under such conditions.

Although land redistribution effected an immediate change in the level of income of many rural laborers, the trend of income over time would also be relevant to the wage trend for unskilled work in the urban sector. Data reviewed in Chapter 2 indicate that output per worker in the agricultural sector was increasing at a faster rate than the rest of the economy during the 1940s and by a very considerable margin, 3.6 percent a year to less than 0.5 percent. To be sure, this is not sufficient evidence of an increase in incomes among those strata of the rural population most likely to view urban unskilled employment as an alternative source of work.

One may come closer to approximating the income trend of these groups, however, from the output data of the agricultural sector classified by size or form of land tenure. Presumably, the relevant group is the small landholder and his family. Although there are no income data for farm families, the value of output per plot is available for 1940 and 1960. Measured in constant Mexican pesos, output on plots of less than five hectares increased at a rate of 4 percent per year, while on ejido plots it increased at a rate of 3.9 percent. A very significant part of this growth, and perhaps most of it, was realized during the decade of the 1940s; Sergio Reyes Osorio and his coauthors hold that output on the smallest farm units remained virtually unchanged between 1950 and 1960.[16] Most of the increase in output per plot is traceable to an increase in productivity of approximately 2.7 percent a year; the balance is attributable to a growth in the average size of plots.

Furthermore, the increases in the value of output during the 1940s were accompanied by an improvement in the rural-urban terms of trade. Agricultural prices rose during the decade by 279 percent. The wholesale price index of Mexico City increased by 191 percent and the consumer price index by 228 to 254 percent, depending on which source is cited.[17] In the face of such increases in rural income, one would not expect to find the reservation price of rural labor to the urban sector falling.

The contribution that rural-urban migration has made to the evolution of intersectoral wage differentials is also at issue here. For example, Perrakis attributes the decline in the real minimum wage to "a delayed effect of the land redistribution program of the late thirties and the subsequent massive immigration into the cities."[18] Implied is the dominance of push factors in the rural zones, which propelled people into the urban areas and resulted in a depression of wages for unskilled labor. It is certainly true that the decade of the 1940s saw a sharp increase in the rate of growth of the urban population, defined here as people residing in communities with at least 15,000 inhabitants. Although this segment of the population had grown at a rate of only 3.1 percent a year during the 1930s, it accelerated to 6.2 percent in the succeeding decade.[19] An alternative hypothesis could be that the accelerated flow to urban areas was a response to an increase in the relative attractiveness of urban employments.

Had the flow been simply the product of push factors, one could reasonably have expected that the "excess" supply would have encountered difficulties in finding acceptable employment, that open unemployment would have become more prevalent, and that the wage level would have been lowered. The evidence on unemployment, however, offers little support for such a scenario. According to data reviewed in Chapter 3, unemployment in 1940 was estimated at about 3.1 percent of the labor force, while the 1950 census reported a decline to 1.3 percent.

Most of the literature on Mexican internal migration supports the view that it has been strongly motivated by differential income opportunities, as has been documented in Chapter 5. If unskilled wages had been declining in the urban centers during the 1940s, this would have implied that migration accelerated as the relative attractiveness of urban employment declined. Of course, urban wages apparently still remained above those in the rural sector. It may therefore be argued that the existence of an absolute differential was the critical condition giving rise to migration and that the narrowing of the urban unskilled–rural wage differential need not have served as a disincentive to a high rate of migration.

In my opinion, however, the data that elicit skepticism about the alleged general decline in urban earnings are those that trace the trend in consumption and vital statistics during the years between 1940 and 1960. The prevailing view is that average real wages for industry declined during the 1940s and into the early 1950s, reaching their lowest level in 1952. They recovered to the 1940 level and fluctuated within 10 percent above that level until 1958 when the beginning of a sustained rise in average earnings began. In the case of the legal minimum wage and the earnings of unskilled workers in the large-plant sector in Mexico City, the 1940 real wage level was not achieved until 1964 and 1962, respectively. Yet the data on consumption levels seem to indicate increases of substantial proportions during this period.

Consumption and Income

Table 7-2 provides per capita measures of apparent consumption for three agricultural commodities that might be expected to vary with changes in income. As can be seen, consumption of these commodities, regarded as staples in the diet of lower-income groups, increased in a continuous fashion in each five-year interval since 1935–39. Some might interpret the increase in corn and bean consumption as support for the conclusion that wages declined during the 1940s and early 1950s. Estimates of the income elasticity of demand, calculated from cross-section studies of households at different income levels, suggest that it is negative, in other words, that consumption would increase in the face of a decline in income. While cross-section studies apparently do invariably yield negative values for the income elasticity of demand for corn and beans, time series data suggest positive values. Furthermore, a negative value over all income groups is not necessarily inconsistent with positive values within the lower income groups.

In any case, the continued rise in per capita consumption, even after real wages surpassed their 1940 levels, casts doubt on the presumed negative values of the income elasticity of demand. In the case of sugar, the income elasticity of demand is consistently considered to be positive. As can be

Table 7-2. *Apparent Annual Per Capita Consumption of Selected Agricultural Commodities, 1935–39 to 1960–64*

	Consumption in kilograms, five-year averages		
Years	*Corn*	*Beans*	*Sugar*
1935–39	91.4	6.2	15.7
1940–44	100.8	7.2	18.8
1945–49	108.4	8.0	22.3
1950–54	134.3	11.4	24.6
1955–59	158.9	15.1	28.1
1960–64	199.2	18.0	28.2
1965–69	171.3	18.5	35.4

Note: Apparent internal consumption is estimated from production plus imports minus exports.

Source: Secretaría de Agricultura y Recursos Hidraulicos, Dirección General de Economía Agricola, *Consumos Aparentes de Productos Agricolas, 1925–1978* (Mexico, D.F., 1979).

seen in table 7-2, large increases in consumption were recorded in each successive subperiod. Estimates of the caloric intake of the population suggest a very significant increase between 1934–38 and 1960. Data provided by Reyes Osorio indicate an average increase of 47 percent in per capita caloric intake over the period, from 1,800 to 2,654.[20]

There are other products whose use was suggestive of rising incomes. A large increase was recorded in the production of beer. From 83 million liters in 1935, production, and apparent consumption, expanded to 180 million in 1940, 353 million in 1945, 572 million in 1953, and 745 million in 1957.[21] The proportion of the population without shoes also fell steadily in the intercensal period 1940–60, from 27.6 percent in 1940 to 19.1 and 14.3 percent in subsequent census years. The ratio of radios to population increased sharply from 1:52 in 1940 to 1:16 in 1960.[22] These data suggest a growth in the discretionary income available to households that is not consistent with a decline in real wages. Of course, if the number of employed household members had increased during this period, then an upswing in consumption in the face of a decline in real wages would still have been attainable. However, the data on labor force participation offer little support for such a possibility: the male rate proved constant between 1940 and 1950. While the female participation rate doubled over the same interval, from 4 to 8 percent, the absolute increase that this implies is far too small to account for the substantial expansion in consumption we have observed.

Vital statistics for the period are suggestive of improved living standards. For example, infant mortality, which is very sensitive to consumption levels among the lower-income groups, declined during the twenty-year period 1940–60. In 1940, there were 123 infant deaths per thousand births; the two subsequent census years recorded declines to 106 and 74. Over the same period, the proportion of deaths attributable to parasitic and intestinal diseases dropped from 43 percent to 36 and 27 percent.[23]

Thus, a plausible alternative can be offered to the view that wages fell generally during the 1940s and into the 1950s. Those wages in the traditional large-scale manufacturing sector that had been raised well above the market price of labor through institutional intervention in the wage determination process may, indeed, have declined during that period. But it would be reasonable to posit that, in the face of a rising opportunity cost of urban labor, wages in that part of the labor market unaffected by institutional intervention rose, and the differential rate of earnings within the urban manual labor force was thus narrowed. The narrowing that is documented below for the years after 1960 would then appear to be a continuation of a process that had begun earlier. Although wages in large, long-established firms may have been falling in real terms, we have no data indicating the course of wages in the new or growing firms of the industrial sector that were responsible for the impressive growth of industrial output during those years.

Narrowing of Wage Differentials

Although it may be thought that unskilled labor abounded at a constant wage, it is not at all clear that the supply of workers with the minimal educational requisites for industrial employment was perfectly elastic. After all, even as late as 1950, 42.5 percent of the population over 15 years of age was classified as illiterate, a proportion somewhat smaller than that of the population with no formal schooling.[24] The 1960 census recorded the median level of education of this same population at only 2.4 years. Since the educational attainment of the adult population in 1940 was even more modest, it is quite possible that the shift in the demand for urban labor resulted in increases in real wages. At the very least, unskilled wages may have shown little change, but it is not likely that they could have declined as sharply as the limited available data would suggest. As one scholar has observed, "One cannot believe that political stability could have so easily endured if real wages had halved at a time of such rapid overall growth."[25]

There are fragmentary data reinforcing the belief that the legal minimum wages declined to levels below the market wage for unskilled labor during the 1940s and remained there until the 1960s. These data originate in community studies, usually by anthropologists, that record the nature of economic activity by the various classes of residents. The most common source of information is interviews with individuals during which work histories are compiled.

Although such information may not be completely representative or may be distorted by faulty memories, it may be indicative of the closeness of actual wages paid to the prevailing minimums. For example, Lourdes Arizpe reports that young men from the rural districts of the northwestern part of the state of México would migrate to participate in harvesting and other peak season activities in the fields around Xochimilco, in the Federal District. In 1945, the going wage for such work was on the order of Mex$25 a week, or Mex$4.16 a day. At the time, the legal minimum for rural workers was only Mex$2.45 a day.[26] The same source reports that men from the same rural district seeking casual employment in Mexico City in the early 1950s could work nights as stevedores in La Merced market and earn on the order of Mex$30–40 a week.[27] During 1950–51, the daily legal minimum for the Federal District was on the order of Mex$4.50, although it was increased sharply during the following biennium to approximately Mex$6.70. In 1955, masons (*albaniles*) in construction were earning Mex$15 per day, roughly 60 percent more than the minimum wage; this differential was to narrow over the subsequent decade to 40 percent in 1965.

Rural wages in some areas also seemed to exceed the legal minimums. For example, López Rosado cites data for 1948–49 that permit a comparison of regional daily wages with legal minimums.[28] Wages paid in the northern border states in 1949 were approximately 50 percent above the legal minimum; in the central and coastal regions, they were about 40 and 100 percent higher, respectively. In 1955, Arizpe reported daily wages in agriculture in the Mazahua region in the northwestern part of the state of México as Mex$7 while the rural daily minimum wage for the zone was Mex$3.31. Even in Chiapas, one of the poorest states of the republic, wages above the minimum have been reported for 1957. In the center of the state, not far from Santiago de las Casas, wages during the corn harvest season were Mex$30 plus maintenance for a six-day week, while the legal minimum was Mex$3.48 a day. Furthermore, it was noted that the larger farmers of the region typically faced an upward-sloping supply schedule for labor and generally had to offer more than the wage prevailing among small landholders in order to recruit a sufficient number of workers.[30]

Beginning in 1960, the pace of adjustment in legal minimums quickened. The first three bienniums produce rates of increase in the unweighted national urban average minimum wage of 21.6, 25.8, and 28.6 percent; the rural minimums were adjusted upward by similar proportions. In view of the impressive stability in consumer prices, which rose only 10 percent between 1960 and 1965, these raises in the minimums represented large increases in their real values. Clearly, had the minimums been effective at the beginning of the decade, such rates of increase would have propelled the whole wage structure in the covered sectors upward at a rate inconsistent with the observed stability of prices. Instead, these increases first served to narrow the gap between the minimums and the higher market wage. In the Chiapas region mentioned above, the minimum and the market wage reached a virtual equality by 1963. Thereafter, the going wage lagged behind adjustments in the minimum.

By 1966, the nominal cash wage had reached Mex$7.50 a day, only 3.5 percent above the 1957 level in real terms. However, the legal minimum had increased to Mex$13. Not even the addition of the cost of maintenance—estimated to range from Mex$2.30 to Mex$3.85 a day—sufficed to close the gap. Payment of wages in kind (namely, corn) was also common. Indeed, 90 percent of the employing farmers paid wages, at least in part, if not entirely, in kind. According to Frank Cancian, payment in kind had increased over the same interval by a larger proportion than the cash wage, by about 13 percent.[31] In the Mazahua area, the rural wage by 1965 had increased to Mex$10 a day but now was below the legal minimum of Mex$11.50. During peak seasons, however, the daily wage would rise to equal the legal minimum. Indeed, by 1968, local shortages of agricultural labor began to appear in the region and the daily wage rose to Mex$15, slightly above the legal minimum.[32]

A similar changing relationship between the legal minimum wage and actual daily wages of urban unskilled workers in the modern manufacturing sector has been documented by Isbister.[33] In 1950, actual wages stood in a ratio of 1.45:1 to the legal minimum in the six industrial cities surveyed. By 1960, the ratio had shrunk to 1.16:1 and reached parity in 1964. An additional six cities surveyed in the latter year yielded a similar ratio. Since these actual wage data were drawn from larger establishments, which normally tend to pay wages above the minimum, the achievement of parity suggests that, in other urban employments (the so-called informal sector), actual wages may have been surpassed by the legal minimum. Perrakis's observation of earnings in small establishments during the middle of the decade led him to conclude that the legal minimum had once again become an effective minimum.[34]

Wage Data from Economic Censuses, 1960–75

The course of wages since 1960 can be charted by data appearing in the economic censuses that are taken every five years. For table 7-3, wage data

Table 7-3. *Average Real Annual Total Remunerations in Services, Industry, and Commerce by Establishment Size, 1960–75*
(1960 pesos)

Sector and size of establishment	Average total remunerations[a]				Percent change
	1960	1965	1970	1975	1960–75
Establishments with no paid employees					
Services	6,315	5,625	6,918	8,245	30.6
Industry	2,710	5,173	5,102	7,058	160.4
Commerce	4,059	4,089	7,501	7,768	91.4
Establishments with paid employees					
Small					
Services, 1–2 workers[b]	5,397	n.a.	9,799	8,655	60.4
Industry, 1–5 workers	4,973	6,005	6,855	9,610	93.2
Commerce, 1–2 workers	6,279	7,197	7,973	10,613	69.0
Medium					
Services, 3–8 workers[c]	7,869	n.a.	10,437	11,096	41.0
Industry, 6–25 workers	8,119	8,940	10,534	12,977	59.8
Industry, 1–25 workers	6,644	7,945	9,308	12,003	80.7
Commerce, 3–8 workers	9,465	9,941	10,957	14,505	53.2
Large					
Services, 9 or more workers[d]	16,470	n.a.	18,637	18,044	9.6
Industry, 26–100 workers	10,272	11,969	14,419	17,185	67.3
Industry, 101–500 workers	11,854	15,058	18,148	22,116	86.6
Industry, over 500 workers	12,877	18,241	23,225	28,236	119.3
Commerce, 9 or more workers	14,259	16,611	16,595	20,135	41.2
National average urban minimum wage[e]	3,610	5,328	6,978	7,617	110.0

n.a. Reliable data for 1965 are not available.

a. Nominal remunerations are deflated by the consumer price index for Mexico City.

b. 1–3 workers in 1960.

c. 4–10 workers in 1960.

d. 11 or more workers in 1960.

e. Since a weighted average minimum wage was not available for 1960, the unweighted average is used throughout to maintain comparability.

Sources: Secretaría de Industria y Comercio, Dirección General de Estadística, *Censo de servicios*, 1961, 1966, and 1971; *Censo industrial*, 1961, 1966, and 1971; *Censo comercial*, 1961, 1966, and 1971. Secretaría de Programación y Presupuesto, *Censo de servicios, 1976*; *Censo industrial, 1976*; *Censo comercial, 1976*. Comisión Nacional de los Salarios Minimos, *Salarios minimos*, various issues.

from the censuses for the industrial, commercial, and service sectors have been extracted; the industrial census includes manufacturing, construction, and electric power generation and distribution. The data are available in most cases by size of establishment; therefore, this basis for analysis has been chosen to avoid the bias inherent in the wage data drawn from only the large-firm manufacturing sector. It is generally accepted that, to the extent that they lie above the market price of labor, the legal minimum wages are observed only in larger establishments. Small employers are more likely to respond to supply conditions in the labor market in setting the wages they pay. Thus, the observation of the course of wages in the small establishments of the three sectors ought to provide a better guide to the market-determined wage for low-skill labor than the data originating in large manufacturing firms. Annual total remunerations per worker are expressed in real terms.

Before a discussion of the trends revealed by the data, a few remarks are in order about the data themselves. First, although data for very small establishments are included in the table, it should be kept in mind that these are likely to be subject to wide margins of error. As is generally recognized, such establishments keep poor records, and caution is advisable in accepting their data at face value.

Second, there is little consistency in the manner in which employment is reported. In some of the earlier censuses, the only employment figure given was one as of a given date, for example, June 30. In others, it appeared as an average of two points in time. In the 1975 census of manufactures, the employment figure is an average of three observations. But the remunerations datum refers to total wage payments made during the year. Thus, some unknown proportion of the changes in measured annual remunerations per worker may be attributable to these differences in the way "annual" employment is measured.

A third difficulty encountered in estimating remunerations of workers in small establishments was the absence of sufficient detail in the industrial censuses since 1960 to permit the separation of unpaid workers from paid employees. According to the 1960 census, over 98 percent of the unremunerated workers (including proprietors, the self-employed, and unpaid family workers) were to be found in establishments with twenty-five or fewer workers. In subsequent censuses, there was the problem of allocating the unremunerated workers over the various size strata in order to compute the remunerations of paid personnel. The solution was to follow rather closely the distribution of unremunerated workers among establishments of different sizes that appeared in the 1960 census, with an added constraint that the bulk of this class of worker had to fall within the two smallest establishment categories.

As a result of this allocation, it is quite possible that the average remuneration in the size categories of 1–5 and 6–25 workers may be somewhat distorted. The overallocation of unpaid workers to one of these two categories would have the effect of raising the average remuneration of the remaining paid workers in that category and lowering that in the other small establishment category. For this reason, the average remuneration for the composite category of establishments with 1–25 workers has also been included, which should provide a very close approximation of the average remuneration of paid employees for the entire group of small establishments.

Fourth, the concept of remunerations used includes all wage and salary payments plus fringe benefits. The latter tend to be proportionately larger in the larger establishments.

Since so many small establishments employed very few or no paid workers, it seemed desirable to try to estimate the returns to unremunerated labor, particularly in light of the common belief that a self-employed or unpaid family labor status represents a last refuge in a jobs-scarce labor market and, therefore, one that is characterized by extremely low income. It is possible to arrive at such an estimate for those establishments with no paid employees. This was done by deducting from net value added an imputed return to capital.[35] The latter, in turn, was calculated by applying a rate of interest to the capital employed equal to the return on a highly liquid asset that would have been easily accessible to individuals with modest means. (For this purpose, I adopted the interest rate payable on hipotecarios ordinarios, a form of mortgage bond that is available in units as small as Mex$100; in 1970 the interest payable on these bonds was 8 percent.)[36] The residual of net value added, less the imputed returns to capital, was then divided by the number of unremunerated persons reported as working in the establishments with no paid employees.

To the extent that unremunerated workers are likely to include a larger proportion of part-time workers than is true of the remunerated labor force, the estimated return to the former may be understated. In any case, while the absolute value of the returns to the former may contain a significant margin of error, it may not be unreasonable to hope that the trend in these returns does reflect their actual course. With these caveats in mind, let us now examine the course of remunerations over time.

Increases in Wages by Size of Establishment

The data in table 7-3 reveal substantial increases in the real average remunerations of employees in all size strata of the establishments and in all three sectors.[37] The total increases in the last column of the table translate into annual rates of growth in real wages in excess of 3 percent for most strata. Furthermore, a notable narrowing can be observed in the differential rate of earnings between the smallest and the larger establishments within sectors. Only in the industrial sector does a widening occur between the smallest and the largest establishment strata, but narrowing is again evident between the smallest and all the other large establishment strata. Among the small and medium-size firms, intersectoral differentials appear to have narrowed as well.

The one observation that stands out as a significant departure from the general observable tendencies is that for the industrial establishments with 500 or more employees. Whereas in 1960 such firms paid wages that were lower than those in "large" establishments in either commerce or services, by 1975 earnings there had surpassed wages in the other two sectors by a large margin. Indeed, they recorded the largest rate of increase of any observation within the set of data originating in firms with paid employees.

This rapid growth in reported earnings may be attributable to several possible factors. First, it could represent an increasing weight of technologically more complex industries that employ a larger proportion of skilled manual workers; thus the large increase in average earnings would reflect a change in the occupational structure in large firms. Second, it may be a reflection of a growing structure of managerial and administrative personnel in modern industrial firms. Since the reported remunerations include all personnel and not only wage earners, changing weights between manual and nonmanual employees could be a contributing cause of the high rate of change in average earnings. A third possibility is that wages in large firms have been increased as a result of collective bargaining. Trade unions are heavily concentrated in the large-firm sector. (The effectiveness of this kind of intervention in the wage determination process will be discussed later in this chapter.) Fourth, the faster rate of increase in large firms may reflect movement along an upward-sloping supply curve of labor. Depending on how "high" the hiring requirements of this sector are relative to the average characteristics of the manual and nonmanual labor force, the notable expansion of employment there may have required a faster rate of increase in offered wages than in the rest of the large-firm sectors. (In commerce or services a "large" firm is one with only nine or more workers, rather than 500 or more.)

Although notable gains in real earnings can be observed among the small establishment strata, these may, in fact, understate the actual gains realized by workers over time. One would not expect that the establishments in the stratum with the smallest number of employees in 1975 would necessarily be the same ones that were recorded in 1960. To the extent that firms were "successful," they may have grown and moved into larger size strata in subsequent censuses. Since earnings per worker and establishment size are so highly correlated, one might expect that the rate of salary increase in a panel of small firms followed in a longitudinal manner would exceed that recorded within any of the smaller size classes.

It is reassuring to note that the course of the imputed earnings of unremunerated labor (including those of the self-employed and unpaid family labor) resembles that observed for paid labor. The increases reported for this class of labor in the industrial and commerce sectors ranked among the largest recorded for any of the strata; thus, the differential in earnings between wage and nonwage labor was narrowed. Furthermore, the same narrowing of intersectoral earnings differentials that was observed for wage labor is present within the category of firms with no paid employees.

It was observed above that the legal minimum wage had ceased to be an effective wage from the latter half of the 1940s until sometime in the 1960s. The earnings data from the small establishment strata (table 7-3), which are most likely to reflect labor market conditions, seem to confirm this. In 1960, the average total remunerations were well in excess of the legal minimums, which in annual terms amounted to Mex$3,610.[38] The lowest rate of earnings is that for the smallest industrial establishments at Mex$4,973. Even if one allows for the various labor charges that render total remunerations greater than wage payments to employees, it is clear that the going wage comfortably exceeded the legal minimum in1960.

By 1965, however, the margin had narrowed significantly. The annualized legal minimum expressed in 1960 pesos is Mex$5,328. Earnings in the two sectors for which data are available for 1965, industry and commerce, were well in excess of the legal minimum. By 1970, annual remunerations in the smallest industrial establishments, at Mex$6,855, had slipped below the legal minimum of Mex$6,978. It may be surmised that a substantial proportion of workers so employed were receiving wages below the legal minimum. Average earnings in small establishments in the other two sectors continued to exceed the minimum. Between 1970 and 1975, however, earnings surged and again surpassed the legal minimum in the smallest establishments of all three sectors. Throughout these years, wages in the larger establishments lay above the minimum in all sectors.

Productivity of Labor

The advances in real wages that occurred during the 1960–75 interval had their foundations in increases in the productivity of labor. Tables 7-4 and 7-5 present several relevant measures per worker for the industrial sector. The preferred measure of productivity, net value added per worker, increased significantly in all strata. Only in one intercensal interval, 1960–65, were there widely disparate rates of increase among the various size strata; the rate of increase during that interval proves to be directly related to establishment size. Thereafter, however, the rates of change tended to converge, and in the 1970–75 interval these are slightly inversely related to size.

Underlying this growth in productivity are increases in the amount of capital per worker employed. These were particularly large, in real terms, between 1960 and 1970. For the 1970–75 interval, the increase in invested capital per worker progressed at a rate slower than the consumer price index; this implies that, in real terms, investment was negative. In fact, it is difficult to believe that this happened, especially in light of the increase in net value added per worker that exceeded the surge in prices by a substantial margin. It may be that the 1975 census valuation of capital reflects an original cost rather than a current replacement value. Thus, the amount of capital per worker in 1975, as well as its rate of increase, may be greatly understated.

Of interest is the relationship between the rate of growth in productivity and remunerations in the three intercensal intervals. Expansion in productivity outran wage increases by a considerable margin between 1960 and 1965. The difference narrowed significantly during the next five-year period. Finally, during 1970–75, remunerations increased more rapidly than productivity. This changing relationship is consistent with a growing relative scarcity of labor in the market.

A rather mixed pattern of change can be observed within the service sector (see table 7-6). Unfortunately, data for net value added are not available for the census periods before 1970. A substitute measure of productivity that can be employed is the volume of sales per worker. During the 1960–70 interval, remunerations outran by a considerable margin the increases in sales receipts per worker in the two larger establishment strata; they did so again over the 1970–75 interval, but by a smaller margin. In the case of the smallest establishments, remunerations increased faster than receipts per worker in both periods as well, but the margin of increase was greater in the latter period. For the 1970–75 interval, it is possible to compare changes in net value added and remunerations per worker. As in the case of sales per worker, increases in remunerations far outdistanced those in value added.

In table 7-6, the observation of rates of increase in remunerations in excess of those in productivity in both the service and industrial sector would seem to imply a redistribution of income in favor of wage and salary recipients, particularly during the 1970–75 interval. Indeed, the national income accounts for the decade do indicate a growth in the share of wages

Table 7-4. *Output, Net Value Added, Capital Employed, and Remunerations Per Worker in the Industrial Sector by Size of Establishment, 1960–75*
(current pesos)

Year and establishment size (number of workers)	*Value of production per employed person*	*Net value added per employed person*[a]	*Capital per employed person*	*Total remuneration per paid employee*[b]
1960				
No paid employees	9,351	3,243	6,663	2,710
1–5	22,681	9,223	11,037	4,973
6–25	46,478	12,521	37,046	8,119
1–25	32,913	10,643	22,232	6,644
26–50	60,867	13,642	52,221	10,272
51–100, 101–250, 251–500	66,065	15,641	62,726	11,854
501 and over	76,540	16,535	74,959	12,877
Annual minimum wage[c]				3,610
1965				
No paid employees	12,168	6,027	4,346	5,680
1–5	28,154	12,227	10,489	6,593
6–15	49,833	19,826	31,488	8,824
6–25	57,716	22,167	38,327	9,816
1–25	44,919	17,864	26,276	8,724
26–100	82,897	29,797	61,247	13,142
101–500	104,500	39,852	87,406	16,534
501 and over	124,620	48,744	104,776	20,029
Annual minimum wage[c]				6,325

a. For 1960 and 1965, net value added figures represent an estimate derived by subtracting from the total value of production and receipts the cost of all purchased inputs and contracted services.

b. For establishments with no paid employees, the returns to labor were estimated by subtracting from net value added the imputed returns to capital. For all other establishments, total remunerations include all wage and salary payments plus fringe benefits and payroll taxes.

and salaries in the national product. From 35.7 percent of GDP in 1970, their share increased to 38.1 percent in 1975. A further rise to 40.3 percent was recorded for 1976. The interpretation of this increase is clouded by cyclical considerations, however, since it coincides with a sharp slowdown in the rate of expansion of the economy. In any event, this last proportion was not maintained, for by 1978 the share had declined back to the approximate level of 1975, to 37.7 percent.[39]

Year and establishment size (number of workers)	*Value of production per employed person*	*Net value added per employed person*[a]	*Capital per employed person*	*Total remuneration per paid employee*[b]
1970				
No paid employees	17,739	7,329	8,074	6,683
1–5	46,672	19,336	20,383	8,980
6–15	71,745	28,937	46,233	12,499
6–25	84,822	33,149	54,279	13,799
1–25	69,823	27,718	40,952	12,193
26–100	120,256	44,382	86,756	18,889
101–500	155,953	60,027	118,893	23,774
501 and over	187,674	74,546	142,637	30,425
Annual minimum wage[c]				9,851
1975				
No paid employees	46,112	17,639	13,982	16,311
1–5	98,576	39,468	29,110	22,208
6–15	152,006	58,324	61,743	27,449
6–25	169,026	63,621	71,873	29,990
1–25	143,613	54,908	56,447	27,739
26–100	243,579	88,505	110,861	39,715
101–500	319,061	121,630	175,446	51,110
501 and over	360,420	144,440	227,803	65,252
Annual minimum wage[c]				19,334

c. The annual minimum wage for 1965–75 is a weighted average of all urban zone rates. Each zone rate is weighted by the zone's labor force. Weighted averages were not available for 1960. The 1960 wage is a simple arithmetic average of all the urban minimums. As a rule, the weighted average tends to exceed the simple average by approximately 8–10 percent.

Sources: Same as for table 7-3.

Wages since 1975

An alternative source of wage data for the years since 1968 is the Banco de México. These data, however, are limited to a sample of large firms primarily in the manufacturing sector. Table 7-7 presents an index of nominal and real earnings, including fringe benefits, from 1968 through 1982. An index of the weighted average, real urban minimum wage is also included for comparison purposes. As can be seen, the course of the two wage series is quite similar. That for earnings is somewhat smoother than

Table 7-5. *Rates of Change in the Value of Production, Net Value Added, Invested Capital, and Total Remunerations Per Worker in the Industrial Sector by Establishment Size, 1960–75*
(percent)

Factor and establishment size (number of workers)	*1960–65*	*1965–70*	*1970–75*	*1960–75*
Value of production per worker				
No paid employees	30.1	45.8	159.9	393.1
1–5	24.1	65.8	112.1	334.6
6–15	n.a.	44.0	118.7	n.a.
6–25	24.2	47.0	99.3	263.7
26–100	36.2	45.1	102.6	300.2
101–500	58.2	49.2	104.6	382.9
501 and over	62.8	50.6	92.0	370.9
Net value added per worker				
No paid employees	85.8	21.6	140.7	443.9
1–5	32.6	58.1	104.1	328.0
6–15	n.a.	46.0	101.6	n.a.
6–25	77.0	49.5	91.9	408.1
26–100	118.4	48.9	99.4	548.8
101–500	154.8	50.6	102.6	676.6
501 and over	194.8	52.9	93.8	773.5
Invested capital per worker				
No paid employees	−34.8	85.8	73.2	109.8
1–5	−5.0	94.3	42.8	163.7
6–15	n.a.	46.8	33.5	n.a.
6–25	3.5	41.6	32.4	94.0
26–100	17.3	41.6	27.8	112.3
101–500	39.3	36.0	47.6	179.7
501 and over	39.8	36.1	59.7	202.9
Total remunerations per worker				
No paid employees	109.6	17.7	144.1	501.9
1–5	32.6	36.2	127.3	346.6
6–15	n.a.	41.6	119.6	n.a.
6–25	20.9	40.6	117.3	269.4
1–25	31.3	39.8	127.5	317.5
26–100	27.9	43.7	110.3	286.6
101–500	39.5	43.8	115.0	331.2
501 and over	55.5	51.9	114.5	406.8
Average legal minimum wage	62.0	55.7	96.3	395.7
Consumer price index	9.8	19.3	76.4	131.1

n.a. Not available.

Sources: Secretaría de Industria y Comercio, Dirección General de Estadística, *Censo industrial*, 1961, 1966, and 1971; Secretaría de Programación y Presupuesto, *Censo industrial, 1976.*

Table 7-6. *Service Sector Receipts, Value Added, and Remunerations Per Worker, 1960–75*

Year and establishment size (number of workers)	*Receipts per worker*	*Value added per worker*	*Annual wages and salaries per worker*	*Total remuneration per worker*[a]
	Current pesos			
1960				
No paid employees	14,540	n.a.	—	6,315
1–3 workers	20,796	n.a.	5,259	5,397
4–10	35,485	n.a.	7,260	7,869
11 and over	69,368	n.a.	14,911	16,470
1970				
No paid employees	21,144	13,249	—	9,062
1–2 workers	48,412	33,816	11,484	12,837
3–8	45,389	29,689	12,043	13,673
9 and over	89,058	58,509	20,817	24,415
1975				
No paid employees	37,781	21,390	—	19,055
1–2 workers	68,797	43,402	18,197	20,002
3–8	82,399	49,127	22,427	25,643
9 and over	128,955	73,304	34,656	41,678
	Percentage change			
1960–70				
No paid employees	45.4	n.a.	—	43.5
1–3 or 1–2	132.8	n.a.	118.4	137.9
4–10 or 3–8	27.9	n.a.	65.9	73.8
11 or 9 and over	28.4	n.a.	39.6	48.2
Consumer price index, 31.0				
1970–75				
No paid employees	78.7	61.4	—	110.3
1–2	42.1	28.3	58.5	55.8
3–8	81.5	65.4	86.2	87.5
9 and over	44.8	25.3	66.5	70.7
Consumer price index, 76.4				
1960–75				
No paid employees	159.8	n.a.	—	201.7
1–3 or 1–2	230.8	n.a.	246.0	270.6
4–10 or 3–8	132.2	n.a.	208.9	225.9
11 or 9 and over	85.9	n.a.	132.4	153.1
Consumer price index, 131.1				

n.a. Not available.

— Not applicable.

a. See table 7-4, note b.

Sources: Secretaría de Industria y Comercio, Dirección General de Estadística, *Censo de servicios*, 1961, 1966, 1971; Secretaría de Programación y Presupuesto, *Censo de servicios,* 1976.

Table 7-7. *Index of Nominal and Real Average Remunerations of Production Workers in Manufacturing, 1968–82*
(1978 = 100)

Year	Index of nominal earnings	National consumer price index	Index of real earnings	Index of real weighted average urban minimum wage
1968	24.2	29.7	81.5	78.6
1969[a]	25.6	30.7	83.4	76.1
1970	26.8	32.2	83.2	84.4
1971[a]	29.4	34.0	86.5	79.9
1972	31.3	35.7	87.7	90.0
1973	35.2	40.0	88.0	85.1
1974	44.2	49.5	89.3	93.1
1975	53.5	57.0	93.9	93.5
1976	66.7	66.0	101.1	104.4
1977	86.5	85.1	101.6	103.5
1978	100.0	100.0	100.0	100.0
1979	117.2	118.2	99.2	98.8
1980	144.7	149.3	96.9	92.1
1981	194.0	191.1	101.5	94.2
1982	303.6	303.6	100.0	100.7[b]

Note: Remunerations include wages plus fringe benefits of production workers.
a. Years in which no adjustment in minimum wages was made.
b. Takes into account the increase decreed in March (see note g of table 7-1).
Sources: Remunerations in manufacturing: Dirección General de Estadística, *Estadística industrial mensual* (Mexico, D.F., various issues); minimum wages: Comisión Nacional de los Salarios Minimos, *Salarios minimos* (Mexico, D.F., various issues).

that for the minimum wage and reflects the discontinuous adjustment of the latter in the face of a changing price level. Real earnings continued to increase throughout the early and middle years of the 1970s despite an acceleration in the rate of inflation.[40]

Beginning in 1978, however, the rate of increase in earnings lagged behind that in prices, so that by 1980 real earnings had fallen 4.6 percent below their 1977 level. The real minimum wage declined 10.5 percent over the same interval. These declines in real wages coincided with an acceleration of the rate of inflation from 17.5 percent in 1978 to 26.3 percent in 1980. Not all forms of wage payment nor all groups of workers were equally affected. For example, during 1978, the real wages of salaried white-collar workers suffered a greater decline in average earnings than did those of manual workers in industry. During this interval, a somewhat steeper decline in wage rates was partially offset by an increase in fringe benefits.[41] As will be seen below, fringe benefit payments increased relative to wage rates in 1979 and 1980 as well.

The course of real earnings was reversed in 1981 as earnings climbed back to their 1977 level. They continued to rise during the first five months of 1982 even though the pace of inflation was quickening. During the rest of the year, however, real wages again declined as the Mexican economy slid into a serious economic crisis with output falling and inflation accelerating. On average, earnings were only slightly below the 1981 level but were clearly deteriorating from midyear on, a course that was to extend into 1983.

The declines in real earnings reported for 1979 and 1980 are surprising in view of the strong expansionary forces that were in evidence in those years. Industrial output expanded at a 9 percent rate in each year, and industrial employment increased by an estimated 7.3 and 6.7 percent. Labor shortages were reported, not only of skilled workers, but even of unskilled in several sectors and urban centers of the country.[42] Increases in total employment were held to have outrun the growth of the labor force. Under these conditions, one would not ordinarily expect to observe real wages falling. These divergent trends in economic activity and employment, on the one hand, and in real wages, on the other, would seem to raise important questions about the determinants of wages in this part of the manufacturing sector. Attention might also be directed to the relationship between these wages and those in the broader labor market. These issues will be addressed later in the chapter.

Wages of Domestic Servants

In an earlier section, which traced the evolution of wage payments in three major sectors by size of establishment, we observed that real earnings appeared to have risen substantially in all size strata, even in those in which the impact of institutional forces might be expected to be weak or absent. Those findings suggested that labor market forces of supply and demand were effectively pushing wage levels upward in such firms. This observation may be checked against the behavior of wages in another market which is widely acknowledged to lie beyond the influence of institutional factors—the market for domestic servants. Within this market wage changes over time might be expected to reflect changes in supply and demand conditions in the broader market for low-skilled female labor. Wage data for female domestics in Mexico City for the years 1963 through 1975 are available in a study appearing in a publication of the labor ministry.[43] A wage series was constructed from the monthly wages offered in advertisements in two of the leading newspapers of the city,

Excelsior and *El Universal*. Between 1963 and the early 1970s, the real cash wage of domestic servants in Mexico City was estimated to have risen on the order of 25–35 percent (see table 7-8). While this rate of increase lagged behind the rise in the real legal minimum wage for Mexico City of about 50 percent by 1970, it did not compare unfavorably with the rate of increase in earnings in consumer goods manufacturing of about 36 percent. Nor is it much different from the advance recorded between 1960 and 1970 for the small-establishment strata of the commerce and industry sectors in table 7-3.

The course of real cash wages, however, took an abrupt turn following 1972 as inflation began to accelerate. By 1975, real cash wages had fallen by about 19–27 percent.[44] Most of the decline occurred in 1974 and coincided with the more than quadrupling of the rate of inflation in that year compared with the rates characteristic of the first three years of the decade. The decline in real cash wages may simply reflect the lack of experience with inflation in a society that had enjoyed two decades of relative price stability. Lacking sophistication or any organizational support, domestic servants may not have adjusted their reservation price sufficiently rapidly to prevent a decline. The fact that they usually receive a very substantial proportion of their remuneration in kind (that is, room and board) may also have tended to blunt their awareness of the full extent of the decline in the purchasing power of their cash wage.

The pattern of domestic servant remunerations since 1975 is not recorded in any statistical source in Mexico. As a first approximation to the measure of the change that has occured since 1975, samples of cash wages offered for live-in household help had to be culled from the same two newspapers employed in the survey cited above. The samples were drawn from various issues in the months of July and August 1979, July 1980, and May 1981. They provided evidence that the loss suffered earlier in the decade had not only been recouped but that substantial further gains in real earnings had been made. The offers observed for 1979 averaged 70 percent above those for 1975 and almost one-third higher than the previous peak of 1970. A year later, the average real wage offered had increased again. It was double that of 1975 and 55 percent greater than 1970.

Lest the sample not be representative of the actual average offered wage but rather biased upward, the lowest frequently quoted wage offer was also compared with the past recorded averages. A cash wage of $2,500 was adopted as the minimum for 1980. It was at the bottom of the Mex$2,500–3,000 interval within which just 50 percent of the observations fell. (Only six of the seventy-eight offers were for less than Mex$2,500 per month.) Even this wage, in real terms, proved to be 50 and 19 percent greater than the 1975 and 1970 averages, respectively.

The sharp upward trend in real wages continued into 1981. The average of sixty-nine wage offers was Mex$4,862 per month, or 89 percent greater in real terms than the previous high of 1970. The most frequently cited minimum of Mex$3,500 was 40 percent above the preceding year's minimum and 14 percent higher in real terms. A notable feature of the 1981 advertisements was that there was a much wider range of offers than in earlier years. The coefficient of variation measured 29.1 percent as compared with 22.1 and 23.2 percent in 1979 and 1980, respectively. If one were to judge by the incidence in 1981 of extremely high salary offers, those between $6,500 and $8,000, market pressures on wages must have continued to be strong.

Table 7-8. *Average Monthly Cash Wages Offered to Domestic Servants, Mexico City, 1963–81*
(current pesos)

Year	*Method I monthly wage*[a]	*Index of real wages (1963 = 100)*	*Method II estimated monthly wage*[b]	*Index of real wages (1963 = 100)*
1963	277	100.0	258	100.0
1964	288	101.8	283	107.3
1965	320	109.0	308	112.6
1966	349	114.1	333	117.0
1967	360	114.5	358	122.3
1968	363	113.9	383	128.9
1969	356	107.4	408	132.2
1970	447	128.2	433	133.5
1971	427	116.1	458	133.7
1972	478	123.6	483	134.1
1973	511	118.7	508	126.8
1974	532	101.1	533	108.7
1975	615	99.8	558	97.3
1979, July	2,164	152.8	n.a.	n.a.
1980, July	3,260	198.8	n.a.	n.a.
1980, July[c]	2,500	152.4	n.a.	n.a.
1981, May	4,862	242.4	n.a.	n.a.
1981, May[c]	3,500	174.5	n.a.	n.a.

n.a. Not available.

a. Method I is a simple average of the sample offers in each year.

b. Method II estimated an annual wage from a regression line fitted by least squares to the sample averages. Both methods are reported as published.

c. Minimum wage offered.

Sources: "Análisis del mercado de los servicios domésticos en México," *Cuadernos de empleo*, no. 1 (Mexico, D.F.: Secretaría de Trabajo y Previsión Social, 1976), pp. 55–114. The data for 1979–81 were culled from issues of *Excelsior* and *El Universal*.

That this was the case should not be surprising. Domestic service is not considered a preferred form of employment, and the widespread labor shortages, even of unskilled labor, should have meant a wider range of alternative employments open to women at higher wages. For example, even the most casual empiricist could not have failed to notice the sharp increase in the number of women employed in construction projects between 1979 and 1981 in Mexico City. Not only did their number increase, but also the variety of tasks to which they were assigned.

What is notable about this wage series is that it stands in such sharp contrast to that recorded in recent years for the large-firm segment of the industrial sector in table 7-7. Real wages for domestic servants evidenced a strong upward movement at the same time that those in the large-firm stratum of the industrial sector appear to have been falling. In the absence of additional information about wages in other parts of the labor market, these cross-currents are difficult to interpret. However, past wage trends in the market for domestic help do not suggest that that market was isolated from the broader market for low-skilled labor. If, indeed, these two markets are closely integrated, then it is reasonable to expect that other unskilled wage rates that are largely market determined may also have been rising generally.

The possibility cannot be ruled out that the sharp advance in the real wages of domestics was a unique occurrence and hardly representative of the course of other wages for low-skill jobs. After all, it is not ususual to observe money wages lagging price increases in the context of accelerating inflation. What sets off these years in Mexico from other inflationary episodes in Latin America is the very strong expansionary process that was unfolding at the same time. With open unemployment at very low levels, the large increases in the demand for labor may very well have overwhelmed the common tendency for money wages to lag prices.

Industrial Wages

Conversely, if real wages were rising throughout most of the labor market, then the lackluster performance of industrial earnings, as represented by the Banco de México wage index, would appear to be the anomaly, somewhat reminiscent of their behavior during the decade of the 1940s. At least two possible explanations of their relatively poorer performance during 1978–80 can be offered. The first to be considered here is the institutional setting within which wages in the large-firm industrial sector are determined; the second is a possible change in the composition of the work force.

The large-firm sector is also one in which workers are most likely to be organized and in which wage levels are subject to determination by collective bargaining. All collective bargaining agreements in industries falling under federal jurisdiction must be registered with the Dirección General de Conciliación. In cases in which the parties are unable to agree to terms, the conciliation service intervenes in an attempt to facilitate an agreement. It is at this juncture that the government is in a position to exert its influence on the course of wages in the organized sector.[45]

At the end of each year, the administration formulates guidelines defining the desired rate of wage adjustment for the coming year. The adjustment of the legal minimum wage, which becomes effective at the beginning of each year, signals the target rate of adjustment that the government considers appropriate for the private and public sector wage contracts. In the past, these guidelines seem to have been arrived at by a process of discussion and negotiation within the leadership of the government party, the Partido Revolucionario Institucional (PRI). Since the labor movement and the private sector are represented at the highest levels of the party, the definition of guidelines acceptable to the principal political and economic interest groups could be achieved before their promulgation.[46]

In recent years, however, the guidelines appear to have taken on an increased significance. In view of the high rates of inflation experienced since the middle of the 1970s, the guidelines have been formulated with two objectives in mind. One is the defense (preservation) of the real wage to protect the standard of living of the wage-earning class, the other to restrain the inflationary impact of wage adjustments on costs. Thus, the annual wage adjustments have been greatly influenced by the expected rate of inflation during the ensuing year. In 1979, when inflation was expected to approximate a rate of 15 percent, a guideline was adopted allowing for a 13.5 percent adjustment. In fact, the price level rose at a faster rate than predicted, and wages that did conform to the guidelines tended to suffer declines in real terms, as did the minimum wage.

In 1980, the guidelines at the beginning of the year defined a 19 percent rate of adjustment. For the first time since the declaration of the interim emergency wage adjustment of 22 percent, following the devaluation of 1976, the government revised its guidelines as the year progressed. For contracts negotiated from March through June, a 20 percent rate was set, 22 percent for July and August, 25 percent for September through November, and 27 percent for December.[47] Since the price level rose by over 26 percent during 1980, those bargains concluded earlier in the year were subject to attrition in real terms to the extent that their terms adhered closely to the guidelines. Since the guidelines adopted were based on the expected rate of inflation for the coming year and did not attempt to recoup any loss in real wages that might have occurred during the preceding year, an underestimation of the rate of inflation would tend to lead to a progressive decline in the real wage. This was observed in the wage index of the Banco de México.

In view of the shortfall of the guidelines relative to the rate of inflation, actual wages would decline in real terms only to the extent that they actually conformed to the guidelines. In fact, of course, the guidelines do not constitute a rigid ceiling on the size of wage increases. Rather, they defined the floor on the size of adjustments acceptable to the trade unions. Indeed, some large-firm managers expressed the view that their wage bargains were expected to exceed by 1–1.5 percentage points the adjustment in the minimum wage which also served to define the guideline.

An extensive study of the terms of settlement of a sample of agreements concluded in 1977 and 1979 has been undertaken by César Zazueta and his associates at CENIET.[48] These provide a basis for comparing the actual rates of adjustment with those of the guidelines for those years. The 1977 guideline was set at a modest 10 percent increase, coming as it did on the heels of the major emergency readjustment of 22 percent in October 1976. In addition, a new administration had just entered office with the declared objective of reducing the rate of inflation. Given the economy's decline into recession and the general air of crisis that prevailed following the devaluation, the government was able to gain a widespread commitment to wage adjustments conforming to the guidelines. Zazueta's data reveal that departures from the guidelines did occur in 1977, but that these were relatively infrequent and were held within narrow bounds. Before a review of his findings, a few comments are appropriate on the way in which his data are organized.

The organization corresponds to the two fundamental kinds of contract negotiation that occur under the Mexican industrial relations system. Basic contracts are negotiated for a two-year term, and negotiations may treat not only basic salaries and fringe benefits but other nonwage terms of employment as well. A reopening clause permits renegotiation only on basic wages during the term of the contract, but it is possible to seek adjustments in particular occupational rates as well as general wage changes. Zazueta's data are drawn from thirty industrial groups that have been designated as lying within the jurisdiction of the federal authorities. These include the largest manufacturing industries as well as electric power generation, construction, transportation, and communications industries. Public as well as private sector firms are included. The covered sectors account for the bulk of the trade union members of the country.[49] For each of the covered industries, the average rate of change in basic wages is provided separately according to the nature of the settlement, contract renegotiation, or wage reopening.

Thus, in 1977, there were fifty-one observations of rates of wage change distributed over the twenty-seven industrial groups that were involved in negotiations and conciliation during the year. Each of these observations represents an average of all bargains reached within the industry with the participation of the conciliation service. In all, 396 separate agreements were so concluded. Of the fifty-one average change rates, fully forty-two provided for adjustments in basic wages that averaged within plus or minus one percentage point of the 10 percent guideline established for the year. An additional six fell between 11.1 and 12 percent; only three rates exceeded 12 percent.

No trend in the size of settlements is discernible over the year. Given the air of economic crisis that characterized much of the year and the honeymoon period that any new administration ordinarily enjoys, it may have been easier to persuade the parties to the collective bargaining process to practice the restraint the government was urging. In addition, the recent grant of the emergency adjustment may have removed some of the urgency of larger adjustments during 1977. That adjustment proved to have effectively assured workers of no loss of real earnings, on average, over the year.

In the case of those parties negotiating a new contract, restraint on basic wages could be offset, at least in part, by more generous concessions on fringe benefits. Indeed, this seems to have occurred in 1977. Whereas the average increase in basic wages of 10.05 percent, agreed upon in the renegotiation of contracts, was virtually identical to the official guideline, the increase in total remunerations averaged 11.16 percent. When adjustments in remunerations accorded both in contract reopenings and in renegotiations are considered, the overall average increase amounted to 10.94 percent. This proves to be smaller than the actual increase in remunerations recorded in the large-establishment sector by the wage index of the Banco de México. According to that index, the November 1977 level of remunerations stood 13.2 percent above that of the previous November.[50] Whether the latter figure is the product of wage drift within the covered sector, higher rates of increase in firms that reached accords without benefit of conciliation or that are nonunion, or a general prevalence of large overtime payments cannot be determined on the basis of the information at hand.

The close adherence of contract settlements to the guidelines observed during 1977 was not duplicated in 1979. The guideline for the latter year was set at 13.5 percent. Zazueta's data, disaggregated on a monthly basis, reveal a very close adherence in those settlements concluded in January. Basic salaries were adjusted by 13.76 and 13.95 percent in the renegotiated and the reopened contracts, respectively. As the year progressed, however, deviations from guidelines become increasingly evident. During the last three months of the year, wage adjustments were averaging between 15 and 16.5 percent. Much less restraint was shown in the adjustment of fringe benefits, perhaps as the price of closer adherence to the guidelines of adjustments in the more visible basic wages. This can be observed in the settlements achieved in contract renegotiations. Whereas basic wages were adjusted upward by 14.36 percent on average over the year, total remunerations increased by 18.75 percent. The average of the contracted changes in total remunerations over both contract reopenings and renegotiations amounted to 17 percent, well in excess of the guidelines. But even this change failed to equal the rate of inflation of over 18 percent. This negotiated increase in remunerations virtually matched the increase of 16.3 percent recorded by the Banco de México's wage index (table 7-7).

The experience of 1979 revealed the impracticability of promulgating a single guideline for the year in the face of accelerating inflation. It had already become evident that the rank and file of organized labor was becoming increasingly impatient with the lag of wages behind prices and increasingly unwilling to accept the limitations on wage increases posed by the guidelines. Furthermore, 1980 saw a continuation of the strong expansionary trends in output and employment of the previous year. This continued buoyancy of the economy might reasonably be expected to reduce employers' resistance to the wage demands made by organized labor. A recognition of these conditions led to successive increases in the guidelines as 1980 progressed and it became obvious that the actual rate of inflation would surpass the 19 to 20 percent rate that had been expected to prevail at the beginning of the year.

A review of the contractual changes agreed upon with the intervention of the conciliation service during 1980 reveal a close adherence of basic wage changes to the guidelines of each subperiod during the year. Departures from the guidelines in most months averaged no more than 1 percentage point above the guideline. Only in July and August did actual wage adjustments exceed the guideline by more, 1.6 and 4 percentage points, respectively. The average rate of adjustment for all contract settlements over the year proved to be 22.5 percent, as compared with the 26.3 percent rate of increase in the consumer price index. Only the settlements effected in December provided for a wage adjustment greater than the rise in the price index.[51] As in 1979, however, concessions made in the form of fringe benefits increased the rate of adjustment in total remunerations to 25.6 percent, less than 1 percentage point short of the change in prices.[52] Thus, on average over the year, contractual arrangements provided for wage adjustments that maintained real remunerations at a level virtually constant with respect to 1979.

In view of these contractual adjustments, the decline of 3.1 percent in average real remunerations reported by the Banco de México wage index comes as a surprise. Of course, the contractual adjustments reported above refer only to those that were achieved under the aegis of the conciliation service. An unknown number of additional wage bargains were concluded without the intervention of the service. It is highly unlikely, however, that any of those bargains settled for less than the guidelines—the union could be assured of getting at least the guidelines by taking the dispute to the conciliation service. More likely, those bargains concluded independently of the service granted wage concessions equal to or greater than those obtainable through conciliation.

The second possible explanation of the reported decline in average remunerations may lie in a change in the composition of the work force. In both 1979 and 1980 employment in the industrial sector increased by about 7 percent. Employers faced with expanding labor requirements have two options available. They can hire workers at the entry level wage and, after the probationary period of three months, change their status to permanent employees, whereupon they become tenured and dischargeable only at heavy cost to the employer. Alternatively, if employers are uncertain about the permanence of the higher staffing levels occasioned by the economic boom, they are more likely to opt for the hiring of *eventuales*, or temporary workers, on short-term renewable contracts of up to three months' duration. Such workers are generally employed at wages below those of the permanent work force and enjoy none of the fringes accorded the latter. Thus, a sizable expansion of the industrial labor force based on temporary workers would tend to bias downward the level of average earnings of the work force as a whole. The decline in the average level of real remunerations in the large-firm sector reported by the Banco de México wage index is therefore not necessarily inconsistent with the maintenance of stable real wages for each of the various components of the industrial labor force.

The relative stability, or possibly the small decline, in real earnings in this large-firm industrial sector in the face of rapidly expanding employment suggests that wage levels there may have been above the market price of the classes of labor employed. Thus, some attrition in the real wage, relative to wages elsewhere, could occur without increased turnover rates or difficulties in hiring. Also mitigating an immediate turnover response to a deteriorating relative wage position is the value of vested property rights associated with permanent employment status.

It does not follow that the stability or small decline in real wages observed in the organized large-firm sector extended to other segments of the labor market. Indeed, in an environment of vigorous economic expansion, one might expect to find wage differentials narrowing as lower-wage firms are the first to feel the impact of a tightening labor market. If the increases recorded in the wages offered to domestics are indicative of market conditions for low-skilled labor generally, then such a narrowing may well have occurred as real wages rose in those parts of the market in which institutional constraints on wages were not operative. Unfortunately, the paucity of timely and representative wage data make it impossible to determine the course of wages for various subsectors during these boom years.

The trends in wages in the large-enterprise sector could be interpreted as indicating that the trade union movement in Mexico has had relatively little independent power to affect the monetary terms of employment. Whatever influence it has is derived from its institutional role within the structure of the dominant political party, the PRI. Alternatively, it might be argued that the organized sector has had bargaining power independent of government support but has chosen not to exercise it in deference to the economic policy objectives of the government. The organized sector would have had an opportunity to influence these objectives through bargaining within the inner councils of the party. Thus, once a policy has been adopted, the labor movement, as represented by the dominant labor federation, the Confederación de Trabajadores de México (CTM), falls into line. However, some of its affiliates with a greater than average degree of independence and power may hold out for settlements that exceed the agreed-upon guidelines. In either event, the government would emerge as a formidable influence on the course of wages in many large industrial firms.

Effects of the Minimum Wage

Since the government's discretion in defining the money terms of employment, through the minimum wage mechanism and its intervention in collective bargaining, is so broad, one might appropriately pose a question regarding the result of its decisions. Has government intervention tended to produce substantial distortions in actual wages compared with the market price of labor? By and large, if the wage policies of Mexican government administrations were viewed over the long run, it would not seem that these have had serious distortive effects even though wages have occasionally been pegged well above the market price of the relevant class of labor. For example, the Cárdenas administration, which expressed strong sympathies for the objectives of organized labor, encouraged and supported trade unions in their pursuit of high wages. These same concerns for the status of wage earners were reflected in the establishment in the middle 1930s of legal minimum wages that were well in excess of the opportunity cost of labor. Nevertheless, even the Cárdenas administration was unable, or proved unwilling, to protect the gains made in the early years of the administration. Real wages in large firms and the real minimum wage had already begun to decline during the last half of Cárdenas's administration. As was observed earlier, the fall in both wage measures was to continue through the 1940s and into the early 1950s before they stabilized. Apparently, organized labor lacked the independent power to resist the decline.

By the late 1960s, the legal minimum wage had once again been raised to a level at which it became an effective minimum. However, the distortive effects of a minimum that lies above the market price of unskilled labor would appear to be fairly minimal in Mexico since evasion is so widespread throughout the small-enterprise sector. The limited effectiveness of the legal minimum has been demonstrated by a survey of 2,500 households in Mexico City that reported that 26.9 percent of the employed and remunerated labor force between the ages of 21 and 60 in 1969 earned less than the legal minimum wage then in force.[53] (The respondents included self-employed as well as salaried workers, however, and the survey did not distinguish part-time from full-time earnings.) Particularly among low-skilled occupational groups characterized by low levels of formal education there were large proportions that earned less than the minimum wage. For example, 36 percent of the unskilled and 27 percent of the semiskilled production workers, 65 percent of the unskilled and 24 percent of the semiskilled construction workers, and 35 percent of the retail clerks reported earnings less than the minimum wage (see table 7-9). Virtually no occupational group, including technical, semiprofessional, and managerial classes, was without individuals reporting subminimum earnings. To be sure, some of these low earnings were undoubtedly associated with part-time employment, but a majority probably reflected earnings for a full work week.

What is noteworthy about the data is that the average earnings of occupational groups with substantial numbers of subminimum earners lie well above the minimum wage. This suggests a large variance in the earnings distribution within each group. Only the unskilled construction workers and unskilled service workers reported average earnings below the minimum. The latter, however, include domestic workers who receive substantial income in kind for which no accounting is made. Also worthy of note is the close direct relationship between earnings and years of schooling.

Whether the legal minimums have had substantial distortive effects on wages in the modern industrial sector is more difficult to determine with any degree of confidence. In practice, most large firms treat the legal

Table 7-9. *Earnings and Educational Levels of Selected Occupational Groups in Mexico City, 1970*

Occupation	*Average monthly earnings (pesos)*	*Proportion earning less than the minimum wage (percent)*	*Average years of schooling completed*
Professionals	5,679	0.0	15.4
Technicians	3,293	9.0	11.6
Semiprofessionals	2,542	8.8	11.5
Upper- and middle-level public employees	2,643	6.6	10.7
Owner-managers			
Construction	2,538	55.2	5.5
Manufacturing	3,225	13.0	7.1
Commerce	3,187	22.4	6.2
Services	3,056	20.8	8.0
Office employees	1,890	8.6	9.1
Mozos and office boys	1,134	22.2	6.1
Retail clerks	1,376	34.9	5.9
Peddlers	1,113	62.4	3.2
Service workers			
Skilled	1,374	27.3	5.2
Unskilled	605	77.9	3.4
Drivers	1,608	9.8	5.0
Production workers			
Skilled	1,631	18.1	6.0
Semiskilled	1,215	26.7	4.7
Unskilled	1,016	35.5	4.1
Construction workers			
Skilled	1,198	20.7	4.8
Semiskilled	1,122	24.3	2.8
Unskilled	810	64.9	2.2
Legal minimum wage	847		

Note: In 1970 the exchange rate was 12.5 pesos to the U.S. dollar.

Source: Humberto Muñoz García, Orlandina de Oliveira, and Claudio Stern, "Migración y marginalidad en la ciudad de México," *El perfil de México en 1980*, vol. 3, 6th ed. (Mexico, D.F.: Siglo Veintiuno Editores, 1979), pp. 354–57.

minimum as an entry-level wage for unskilled workers, but most low skill occupations are reimbursed at rates above the minimum. Although the wage paid for unskilled labor may thus exceed that paid in the informal labor market, the quality of labor demanded by the larger establishments may also be quite different. To the extent that the relevant labor market for more skilled occupations is "internal," that is, skilled positions are filled by the progressive advancement of workers from less skilled jobs rather than from outside the firm, newly hired workers entering unskilled job positions may be expected to have the qualifications required for advancement. Clearly, the reservation price of such workers must be higher than that of workers unlikely ever to qualify for advancement beyond the ranks of unskilled labor. Had the legal minimum been substantially higher than the market wage for the quality of workers recruited by the large-firm sector, one might have expected a continuing slide in wages in this sector as the real minimum declined. As can be seen in tables 7-1 and 7-7, however, wage declines match those in the legal minimum from 1976 through 1980. Thereafter, earnings stabilized while the minimum continued its downward course.

To test whether the minimum wage has substantially distorted the price of unskilled labor to the modern sector relative to its market price, one might observe the course of occupational differentials within the modern sector after the legal minimum had begun to increase in real terms and had once again assumed its role as an effective wage. One might hypothesize that, if the minimum were increasing over time relative to the market-determined price of unskilled labor, this would tend to produce a narrowing in skill differentials as unskilled rates were pressed upward. Unfortunately, reliable data on occupational earnings are scarce, and studies of occupational wages are understandably also scarce.

One effort by Jesús Reyes Heroles traced the course of differentials in manufacturing in Mexico City for a very reduced number of occupational titles from 1940 to 1976.[54] His findings suggest a fairly small degree of compression from the early 1950s, when the legal minimum was below the market wage, to 1976. The ratio of a mechanic's wage to that of entry-level occupational titles, such as *mozo* or *peón*, fell from 2.1:1 to 1.8:1.[55] All of the narrowing occurred between 1960 and 1968, an interval during which the real urban minimum wage was increased by about 80 percent. It is not clear that even this contraction can be attributed to a legal minimum wage pegged at above the market level. Reyes Heroles's tables imply that the mozos' wages and, by exension, other unskilled wage rates were consistently above the legal minimum.[56] This can be inferred from data showing the ratio of the mechanic's wage to the legal minimum to be substantially greater than that of the mechanic's wage to the mozo's; during the 1970s, the former ratio fluctuated between 2.3:1 and 2.7:1 in contrast to the 1.8:1 ratio of the latter.[57]

Apparently, skill differentials of all kinds were markedly narrowing during the decades of the 1960s and 1970s. Reyes Heroles followed the ratio of the highest paid manual occupational title to the mozo's wage over time and found the ratio declining continuously from about 3.3:1 in the early 1950s to about 2.4:1 in the middle 1970s.[58] White-collar occupational earnings are also shown to have declined relative to blue-collar wages. Reyes Heroles charts the ratio of various office salaries to those of mechanics over the period 1962–75. Earnings for a bilingual secretary declined from about 1.8:1 to 1.4:1; those for a cashier fell from 1.7:1 to 1.2:1.[59] Since the wage of a mechanic had declined relative to unskilled rates, this implies that the white-collar earnings had also declined relative to the low-skill manual occupational groups. It is quite possible that part of the narrowing that occurred during the decade of the 1960s was traceable to the rapid increase in the real value of the minimum wage. However, that this contraction can be observed at most points within and between the manual and office worker wage structures suggests contributing factors other than the legal minimum. One such factor could be the large expansion of the supply of individuals with greater formal educational and vocational training.

In any event, over the decade of the 1970s, it would appear that any gap that might have existed between the legal minimum and the market price of urban unskilled labor must have diminished substantially. It was noted earlier in the chapter, for example, that, in contrast to the decade of the 1960s when wage-level changes in the small-enterprise sectors lagged behind changes in minimum wage, during the first half of the 1970s remunerations in those sectors advanced at a faster rate than did the minimum wage. In real terms, the former increased almost three times more rapidly, 29 to 11 percent. If the rapid rise of domestics' earnings at the end of the decade is indicative of conditions in the unskilled labor market generally, market-determined wages must have been outstripping the advances in the minimum, especially since the latter were falling in real terms after 1976.

Although minimum wage policy may appear to have had only limited distortive effects on the price of industrial labor, can the same be said for rural labor? As was mentioned in an earlier section, a sharp change in policy occurred during the late 1970s with respect to the rural minimums. The minimum wage was invested with new purposes: to effect a redistribution of income in favor of the lowest-wage workers and to reduce the income incentives for migration from rural to urban areas. As a result, the differential between rural and urban minimum wages was rapidly reduced as rural and urban minimums were merged within zones and the number of different minimums was sharply reduced.

On the surface, the results of this procedure would not appear to have had a serious distortive effect. After all, the real rural minimum wage was increased between 1976 and 1981 by only about 9 percent on average. However, the increases in the lowest wage zones in Chiapas, Oaxaca, and Querétaro were more on the order of 89 percent. Were these to represent the effective increases in wages paid in such traditionally poor and low-wage areas, one might expect some substantial labor-saving adjustments to follow. This might obtain especially in commercial agriculture, which is a major employer of rural labor and in which it may be more difficult to evade the legal minimum. In the small landholder sector, the new higher legal minimums are unlikely to have any more impact than they have had in the past. Nor is commercial agriculture in the northern regions likely to have been greatly affected by the accelerated change. There, since rural minimums and actual wages paid have always been relatively high, the impact of the policy change is likely to have been minimal.

The efficacy of the legal minimum wage for achieving these expanded policy objectives was neither tested nor questioned by the authorities responsible for their promulgation. In order to realize the objective of income redistribution, employment of the poorest wage earners must first be assured. Higher minimum wages will do little to increase the incomes of those who may find fewer days of employment available to them in rural areas.

Agriculture is a sector in which substitutions in production are relatively easy to make.[60] As was pointed out in Chapter 4, this substitution may take the form of machinery for labor, or less labor-intensive cropping patterns, or both. The result of such substitutions could be a redistribution of income within the low-income rural population that could leave some displaced workers and their families even worse off than they were.

Furthermore, higher rural minimum wages are not likely to be effective deterrents to rural-urban migration. To the extent that they result in a reduction in wage-earning opportunities in agriculture, the differential between expected annual earnings in the country and the city may very well increase and serve to stimulate a greater flow of migrants than would otherwise have occurred. Indeed, the very rationale of the migration objective may be open to question. The authors of the policy assume that migration has been "excessive" and, therefore, undesirable. Yet the weight of the evidence examined in Chapter 5 seems to indicate that, from the point of view of the welfare of the migrants, migration has had favorable consequences. Whether the social costs of migration have exceeded the benefits is a question that has not yet been addressed in Mexico.[61]

If legal minimum wages have had only a limited impact on actual wages in most of the labor market, what then is the significance of the government's wage policy as effected through its intervention in collective bargaining? The studies of the CENIET group seem to suggest that the government's guidelines, which tend to parallel its minimum wage policies, may be effective in gaining compliance of that part of the organized sector that is subject to the conciliation procedures of the government. The relevant question that remains, then, is, how far does the impact of the guidelines extend? We have observed that the rate of change in wages in the large-firm stratum of the industrial sector seemed to parallel the changes in the legal minimum more closely than did wages in the small-enterprise strata. Is this to be interpreted as evidence of the effectiveness of the government's guidelines over a substantial part of the modern sector?

If the guidelines, in fact, exercised a wide influence over firm wage adjustments, one would expect, not only that the average wage would move in tandem with the legal minimum, but also that the individual rates of change would be clustered within narrow bands around the mean rate of change. Whether or not the wage structure shows signs of stability over time can be empirically tested by reference to the available data.

The annual October surveys of the industrial sector provide average straight-time hourly earnings of the manual labor force in a number of industries in twelve urban centers.[62] Following the extension of the areas surveyed in 1964, the sample encompassed some 800 firms; the number has grown gradually to 867 firms in 1975, which employ some 255,000 workers. I have calculated the rate of change in earnings over the 1965–75 period for twenty-five industrial groups that appear to be identical in the first and last years.[63] The simple arithmetic rate of change over the decade would be 204 percent, virtually identical to the change in the legal minimum wage of 205 percent. However, underlying that average is a considerable dispersion in the rates of change among industries. The changes ranged from 122 percent in electric generation to 385 percent in tire manufacturing. The standard deviation was 63.2, which indicates that fully a third of the rates of change lay beyond plus or minus 63.2 percentage points of the mean. This dispersion hardly bespeaks a close adherence to guidelines.

Unfortunately, the survey does not provide other information that might serve as a basis for explaining differential rates of increase. One can only observe that the rate of change was inversely related to the wage of the base year. The simple coefficient of correlation between the base year wage and the rate of change in the wage was − 0.42, significant at the 5 percent level. It can also be observed that, as expected, the degree of dispersion in hourly earnings in the terminal year 1975 was somewhat smaller than in 1965. The coefficients of variation were 37.6 and 34.4 percent for the first and last years, respectively.

Given the nonrepresentativeness of the data provided by this survey, one can only speculate about the significance of these observed trends. A narrowing of the interindustry wage structure could be a consequence of a progressive tightening of labor markets. An increasing scarcity of labor may be expected to be felt first and foremost by firms and industries at the lower end of the wage structure. Thus, the faster rate of increase in wages there may reflect an attempt to remain competitive in the recruitment of labor.

The behavior of wages in this rather select sample of firms would thus appear to mirror that which was observed in table 7-3; there, wage data drawn from the industrial censuses found wage differentials narrowing between the lower-wage small enterprises and the higher-wage large firms. One possible inference could be that, although government constraints have had some effect on the higher-wage industries and firms, market forces have been more important determinants of wages in the lower-wage sectors. The faster rate of increase in the low-wage industries may have been achieved within the framework of collective bargaining as well. As long as employers consider it desirable or necessary to surpass the increases defined by the guidelines, agreements could be reached without an impasse in negotiations and without submission to the official mediation procedures. Since the guidelines are enforceable largely in the context of the mediation process, agreements reached outside that process are at least partially insulated from their influence.[64]

It would seem to follow that resort to the conciliation process would tend to be more common during periods of economic recession or reduced profitability. If employers offer a wage adjustment smaller than that implied by the guidelines, the union would have every incentive to create an impasse and carry the negotiations to the conciliation board in hopes of securing support for a settlement more closely approximating the guidelines. Conversely, an employer confronted by a demand in excess of these would follow a similar strategy. During such periods, the guidelines may therefore represent tentative minimum and maximum sizes of adjustments viewed from the perspective of unions and employers, respectively.

Of course, the guidelines serve to define these limits in times of expanding economic activity as well. In such times, however, it may be in the interests of both parties to reach an accord independently of the conciliation process, particularly if employers consider the guidelines too restrictive in view of their staffing requirements.

One might also expect the bargaining power of the unions to be enhanced during prosperous times as the credibility of a strike threat may appear greater. In fact, it is not clear that posing such a threat has gained for unions substantially better terms than those assured by the guidelines. The study of negotiated settlements by Zazueta and his associates distinguished between those achieved without the threat of a strike and those concluded after an actual strike or the threat of one. In 1980, settlements concluded without a strike threat yielded increases in remunerations almost 5 percentage points greater than those in which a strike was threatened but not effected, and 2.6 percentage points greater than those in which a strike preceded the settlement.[65] If these findings are representative, they would tend to reinforce the judgment offered above that Mexican trade unions generally have only limited independent power to affect the monetary terms of employment.

Summary

Sustained growth of the Mexican economy from 1940 to 1982 appears to have carried with it widespread improvements in the wage conditions of employment. Some controversy surrounds the course of real wages during the period 1940–55, which saw a steep decline and gradual recovery in the real wages earned in the modern industrial sector. However, reasons and limited evidence have been offered in support of the view that even that period was one of steadily advancing real wages in those parts of the urban labor market that lay beyond the purview of the legal minimum wage and collective bargaining.

For the period since 1960, improved data contribute to the conclusion that increases in real wages were widely distributed over the urban economy. Between 1960 and 1975, earnings data drawn from the economic censuses indicate an annual rate of increase in real earnings approximating 3 percent. Furthermore, a narrowing of earnings differentials was observed between the low- and high-wage classes of establishments, not only within sectors but across them as well. The course of wages, at least through 1975, would not seem to be consistent with the existence of a large volume of surplus labor overhanging the labor market. On the contrary it would appear that the demand for labor in the nonagricultural sectors shifted to the right more rapidly than did supply and thus accounted for the persistent increase in real wages.

While institutional intervention in the labor market in the form of legal minimum wages and collective bargaining enjoys high visibility, it would not appear to have played a decisive role in determining the course of wages in most of the labor market. As was observed, the relationship of legal minimum wages to market-determined wages has evinced frequent and substantial changes at different times during the past, and increases in the former were not a necessary precondition for raising real wage levels of those employed toward the lower end of the urban wage structure.

With respect to the period since 1975, the limited availability of data makes it difficult to offer conclusions invested with a high degree of certainty. Earnings data for the large, modern industrial enterprises indicate a peaking of real earnings in 1977 and a subsequent decline, in spite of an unprecedented rate of economic expansion from 1978 through 1981. In this sector, institutional intervention would appear to have exercised a restraining influence on the course of wages. With respect to the rest of the economy, there are no official wage statistics available. A sharp increase in the offering price for domestic services was noted, and it was suggested that this might be indicative of similar changes in other market-determined wages for low-skilled labor. Certainly, the widespread reports of labor shortages in1980 and 1981 would lead one to expect equally widespread rising real wages. But the acceleration of inflation in recent years may have overwhelmed increases in money wages. To the extent that inflation is not fully anticipated or that workers, in the face of rising nominal earnings, do not readily perceive their declining purchasing power, it is quite possible that a rapid expansion of employment could take place in an environment of generally falling real wages.

I am skeptical, however, about the lasting influence of such misapprehensions. While money wages might lag price increases in the early stages of an inflationary episode, I would not expect them to continue to do so indefinitely, especially in the context of a rapid expansion in real output and employment. Only when the economic censuses for 1980 are published will it become possible to determine the net change in earnings of various groups over the 1975–80 interval. Even those figures, however, will not shed light on the year-to-year variations that might have occurred within that period.

Of course, the entire panorama and the outlook for real wages has changed drastically since 1981. High rates of inflation combined with a widespread deterioration in general economic conditions do not create an environment favorable to a continued increase in real wages. Indeed, it is certain that part of the impressive gains made by workers generally over the past decades has been lost. The concluding chapter will include a brief discussion of recent changes in the Mexican labor market conditions and their possible implications.

Notes

1. Comisión Nacional de los Salarios Minimos, *Salarios Minimos*, various issues.
2. Ibid., 1979 and 1980.
3. Clark W. Reynolds deflated the nominal minimum wages by the wholesale price index for Mexico City and reported a much faster recovery of real minimums. According to his method, real minimums had recovered most of their loss by the middle of the 1950s. *The Mexican Economy* (New Haven, Conn.: Yale University Press, 1970), pp. 84–85.
4. Secretaría de Industria y Comercio, Dirección General de Estadísticas, *Trabajo y salarios industriales* (Mexico, D.F.), various issues. Since 1975, the survey has been published by the Secretaría de Programación y Presupuesto (SPP), Coordinación General del Sistema de Información.
5. Diego G. López Rosado and Juan F. Noyola Vázquez, "Los salarios reales en México, 1939–50," *Trimestre económico*, vol. 18, no. 2 (1951), p. 204; John Isbister, "Urban Employment and Wages in a Developing Economy: The Case of Mexico," *Economic Development and Cultural Change*, vol. 20, no. 1 (1971), p. 44.
6. López Rosado and Noyola Vázquez, "Los salarios reales," p. 206.
7. Ibid., pp. 204–206.
8. Isbister, "Urban Employment and Wages," p. 36. How Isbister derived annual earnings is not explained in his article. For several years beginning with 1950, he cites the annual October wage survey, *Trabajo y salarios industriales*. However, that publication provides only hourly and weekly earnings data. The source cited for the observations of the 1940s, *Revista de estadistica*, is not available to me, and I know neither the form in which the data appeared nor their origin.
9. Stylianos Perrakis, "The Surplus Labor Model and Wage Behavior in Mexico," *Industrial Relations*, vol. 11, no. 1 (1972), pp. 80–95.
10. Ibid.; Isbister, "Urban Employment and Wages;" López Rosado and Noyola Vásquez, "Los salarios reales"; Horacio Flores de la Peña and Aldo Ferrer, "Salarios reales y desarrollo económico," *Trimestre económico*, vol. 18, no. 4 (1950), pp. 617–28; Adolf Sturmthal, "Economic Development, Income Distribution, and Capital Formation," *Journal of Political Economy*, vol. 63, no. 3 (1955). pp. 183–201.
11. Sturmthal, "Economic Development, Income Distribution," pp. 187–88.
12. Ibid., pp. 189–90.
13. Reynolds, *Mexican Economy*, p. 84.
14. Perrakis, "The Surplus Labor Model," p. 88.
15. Sergio Reyes Osorio, Rodolfo Stavenhagen, Salomon Eckstein, and Juan Ballesteros, *Estructura agraria y desarrollo agricola en México* (Mexico, D.F.: Fondo de Cultura Económica, 1974), p. 50.
16. Ibid., p. 213.
17. Ibid., table 11-22; Nacional Financiera, S.A., *50 años de revolución en México* (México, D.F., 1963), p. 109; and World Bank data.
18. Perrakis, "The Surplus Labor Model," p. 91.
19. Luis Unikel, *El desarrollo urbano de México*, 2d ed. (México, D.F.: El Colegio de México, 1978), table 11-A3.
20. Reyes Osorio and others, *Estructura agraria*, pp. 90 and 101–102.
21. Nacional Financiera, *50 años de revolución en México*, p. 83.
22. World Bank data.
23. World Bank data.

24. Organization of American States, *América en cifras 1977*, vol. 3 (Washington, D.C., 1979), p. 102.

25. Timothy King, *Mexico: Industrialization and Trade Policies since 1940* (London: Oxford University Press, 1971), pp. 26–27.

26. Lourdes Arizpe, *Migración, etnicismo y cambio económico* (Mexico, D.F.: El Colegio de México, 1978), p. 75.

27. Ibid., p. 80.

28. López Rosado and Noyola Vásquez, "Los salarios reales," pp. 201–02.

29. Arizpe, *Migración, etnicismo y cambio económico*, p. 86.

30. Frank Cancian, *Change and Uncertainty in a Peasant Economy: The Maya Corn Farmer* (Stanford, Calif.: Stanford University Press, 1972), pp. 50–130.

31. Ibid., pp. 129–30.

32. Arizpe, *Migración, etnicismo y cambio económico*, pp. 118–19.

33. Isbister, "Urban Employment and Wages," p. 38.

34. Perrakis, "The Surplus Labor Model," p. 85.

35. The census before 1970 did not include a measure of net value added. I therefore estimated it by subtracting from total receipts the value of all purchased inputs.

36. Banco de México, *Indicadores Económicos*, vol. 4, no. 8 (1976).

37. Between 1970 and 1975, the real earnings of workers in the smallest size of service establishments recorded a significant decline in contrast to all other categories and sectors. The significance of this decline is difficult to gauge. It may flow from data deficiencies that assigned to 1970 an unexpectedly high value to earnings in this stratum. Note that the 1970 earnings figures for services depart from their previous relation to those in commerce, only to return to the earlier relation in 1975.

38. The annualization of the minimum wage is computed according to the provisions of the labor code, which states that workers are entitled to a normal day's pay for Sundays. Thus, the annualized minimum wage is computed as the daily rate times 365. Whether this provision is normally observed by small employers, however, is open to question. As indicated in the notes to table 7-3, the unweighted average minimum wage is recorded there in order to retain comparability with 1960, for which a weighted minimum was not available. Had the weighted average been used, the averages for 1965 and subsequent years would have been between 8.3 and 10 percent higher, or Mex$5,771, Mex$6,978, and Mex$8,391. However, the rate of change in the legal minimum is virtually the same, regardless of which measure, the weighted or unweighted, is used.

39. SPP, *Sistema de cuentas nacionales de México*, vol. 1 (Mexico, D.F., 1981).

40. The increases in real earnings yielded by this index between 1970 and 1975 approximates that derived from the largest-firm stratum of the industrial census, 17.7 and 21.7 percent, respectively.

41. Banco de México, *Informe anual 1978* (Mexico, D.F., 1979), pp. 62–64

42. Banco de México, *Informe anual 1980* (Mexico, D.F., 1981), pp. 32–35.

43. "Análisis del mercado de los servicios domésticos en México," *Cuadernos de empleo*, no. 1 (Mexico, D.F.: Secretaría del Trabajo y Previsión Social, 1976), pp. 51–114.

44. The range of increases and decreases in remunerations reflects the use of two different methods to estimate the rate of change. The lower values are derived from the data as recorded in each year of the survey. Since the annual values showed rather sharp and irregular year-to-year variations, however, a trend line was fitted to the nominal wage data by least-squares method, and a series of estimated annual remunerations was derived. The larger values appearing in the text are attributable to the wage series so derived.

45. Richard U. Miller, "Labor Legislation and Mexican Industrial Relations," *Industrial Relations*, vol. 7, no. 2 (1968), pp. 171–82.

46. It was impossible to obtain from government officials a definitive view of how the guidelines are formulated. The process described here was considered to be the most plausible one in the opinion of several well-informed individuals both in government and in the private sector.

47. César Zazueta, José L. Vega, and Jaime Rozenel, *Comportamiento de la negociación de salarios contractuales, México 1977 y 1979* (Mexico, D.F.: Secretaría del Trabajo y Previsión Social, CENIET, 1981), p. 13.

48. Ibid.

49. César Zazueta and Simon Geluda, *Población, planta industrial y sindicatos*, Serie Estudios 7 (Mexico, D.F.: Secretaría del Trabajo y Previsión Social, CENIET, 1981).

50. November was chosen as the month of year-to-year comparison because of the prevalence during December of irregular year-end bonuses and other payments that might distort the change in regular wage payments. The December-to-December change was 12.8 percent.

51. César Zazueta, Jaime Rozenel, and José Luis Vega, *Reporte sobre la negociación de salarios en México, 1980* (México, D.F.: Secretaría del Trabajo y Previsión Social, CENIET, 1981), p. 61.

52. Ibid., p. 68.

53. Humberto Muñoz García, Orlandina de Oliveira, and Claudio Stern, "Migración y marginalidad en la ciudad de México," *El perfil de México en 1980*, vol. 3, 6th ed. (Mexico, D.F.: Siglo Veintiuno Editores, 1979), pp. 354–57. There are no data for a later year with which to compare this ratio of people earning less than the legal minimum.

54. Jesús F. Reyes Heroles, "Welfare Effects of Short-run Macroeconomic Policies in a Dual Economy: The Case of Mexico," Ph.D. dissertation, Massachusetts Institute of Technology, 1980.

55. Ibid., p. 111. The occupational title *mozo* refers to an entry-level position similar to that of an office boy who runs errands, carries internal communications from office to office, serves coffee or other beverages, and performs similar functions. The wage rate assigned mozos was virtually identical to that reported for *peón*, or laborer. Reyes Heroles used the former only because it was more frequently reported than peón.

56. Table 7-9 shows that, in 1969 as well, earnings of mozos were about 34 percent above the legal minimum wage. In fact, just half of the individuals in this job category earned an amount at least 20 percent greater than the minimum wage.

57. Reyes Heroles, "Welfare Effects of Short-run Macroeconomic Policies," p. 116.

58. Ibid., p. 114.

59. Ibid., p. 122.

60. The empirical measures of the elasticity of substitution of capital for labor that are available refer only to the short run, that is, to a single crop year, or to two at most. These have been estimated to be on the order of 0.25 to 0.4 on average. Given a longer period of adjustment, however, one would expect substantially higher coefficients to hold. Hunt Howell, "Machinery-Labor Substitution in Mexico's Central Plateau," in *The Book of CHAC: Programming Studies for Mexican Agriculture*, ed. Roger D. Norton and Leopoldo Solís M. (Baltimore, Md.: Johns Hopkins University Press, 1983), pp. 375–411; Luz María Bassoco and Roger D. Norton, "A Quantitative Framework for Agricultural Policies," in *The Book of CHAC*, ed. Norton and Solís, pp. 127–35.

61. While the sharp increases in rural minimums thus had the potential for introducing great distortions in the price of rural labor to some employers, subsequent developments have reduced their probable impact, at least for the time being. The lag in the adjustment of the legal minimums to recent high rates of inflation has, in effect, reduced their real value substantially (see table 7-1). A tour of rural areas in four states in central Mexico taken by me

in May 1985 revealed that, in many areas, the legal minimum was not an effective minimum. Small farmers in some zones were paying wages 40 percent above the legal minimum. In others, wages more closely approximating the legal minimum were being paid. Only infrequently was a farmer found offering less than the legal minimum.

62. *Trabajo y salarios industriales*, 1965 and 1975.

63. The industries selected for this comparison include meat packing and canning, milling, baking, edible oils and shortenings, beer, nonalcoholic beverages, synthetic fabrics, footwear (except plastic and fabric), plywood, wood furniture, paper, boxes and containers, printing and publishing, leather tanning, tires, soaps and detergents, matches, insecticides, glass containers, cement, foundries, automobile assembly, automobile parts, construction, and electric generation.

64. Unions confronted with an offer in excess of the guidelines would have a strong incentive to settle without a dispute since disagreement would then require submission to the mediation process. Given the guidelines, the union could not count on improving on the employer's offer by such a submission.

65. Zazueta, Rozenel, and Vega, *Reporte sobre la negociación*, p. 72.

8. Conclusion

In Chapter 1, it was argued that an appreciation of Mexico's employment "problem" could be gained only by identifying the variables critical to evaluating the performance of the labor market and then charting their course over time. The key or critical variables can be determined by reference to various models of labor markets that have been advanced in the economic literature. Furthermore, these models provide an analytical framework for guiding empirical inquiries into labor market performance since they offer a statement of the relationship among variables and the outcomes that can be expected to follow from their interaction. By comparing the Mexican experience with the outcomes predicted by the various models, I hoped to identify the model most closely corresponding to the conditions prevailing in the Mexican labor market. This can now be done.

The most widely held perception of the Mexican labor market was one that conformed most closely to the Todaro variant of the surplus-labor, or dual-market, model. The distinguishing features of that model included a compartmentalized, or dual, urban labor market. Institutionally determined wage levels in the "modern" or "formal" market were greatly in excess of those in the "informal." An "excessive" flow of labor to urban areas was to be found, as was the formation of queues of unemployed or "marginally" employed awaiting access to preferred employments in the formal, high-wage sector. Consequently, extremely depressed wage levels would prevail in the informal labor market—wages equal to or even below those available from rural employment. Implicit here is a perfectly elastic supply of labor to the urban sector at the wage prevailing in the formal sector. Indeed, given the existence of "surplus labor" in the agricultural sector, the supply of labor to the urban sector would be perfectly elastic at any wage above the average product of rural labor.[1]

Does such a model provide a "close fit" to the Mexican experience? If the observations of the performance of the labor market over a forty-year period, as recorded here, are even approximately valid, one would have to answer an unqualified "no."

Review of Labor Market Conditions

Consider the characteristics of Mexican internal migration. The empirical evidence that was brought to bear on this issue represents the antithesis of the conditions of the Todaro model. Rather than flowing into a queue to await the opening of improved employment opportunities, migrants moved quickly and easily into employments in both the formal and informal sectors at wages above those earned prior to migration. As Anson's study of migrants to Monterrey showed, positive rates of return were forthcoming during the first year rather than in some more distant future. Over time, improved earnings were not contingent on intersectoral mobility within the urban economy, that is, from informal to formal; earnings levels rose continuously in all of the principal sectors of the nonagricultural economy. Of course, it is this recorded behavior of real wages that renders any of the surplus labor models inapplicable to the Mexican case.

In the face of a perfectly elastic supply schedule of labor to the urban economy, one would expect wages to remain stable in that part of the urban economy in which wages were market determined until the labor surplus has been absorbed. Yet, there has been in Mexico a steady upward trend in wages in enterprises that are likely to be representative of the informal sector as well as in the domestic service market. Since institutional intervention is absent or ineffective in these markets, the upward trend in real wages is explainable only in terms of the forces of supply and demand. Consistent with this behavior of wages is the inference that the growth of employment in the tertiary and informal sectors has not been simply supply determined, but rather has represented a market response to increases in effective demand for the output of those labor services.

I could find no convincing evidence of a large labor surplus overhanging the urban labor market. Recorded open unemployment rates in Mexico have been low by developing-country standards, and although the quality of these measures for the most part is less than ideal, it is hard to detect a significant increasing trend. Much of the qualitative evidence suggests that a large part of the urban unemployment may be frictional in character. Both the frequency of voluntary separation from employments and the short period of job search recorded bespeak a labor market in which job scarcity is not perceived to be a problem. Underemployment in the form of less than full-time employment is largely a voluntary phenomenon rather than evidence of market failure.

Even the agricultural sector, which is frequently held to be a repository of large quantities of surplus labor, seems not to live up to this characterization. While the rural labor force may be surplus to the agricultural sector, it need not be surplus to the economy as a whole. This follows from the close integration of rural and urban labor markets (discussed in Chapter 4) and the easy movement of labor from one to the other. Other indications that labor has been a scarce commodity in rural areas are the prevalence of hired labor on even small farm units, the reported resistance of small peasants to technological changes that require larger inputs of labor, and the widespread trend toward mechanization and less labor-intensive cropping patterns. At least one rural household study established that a far smaller quantity of rural family labor was effectively available for employment than was estimated by the rather simple and crude methods customarily used.

Thus, virtually all of the elements that have conventionally added up to a pessimistic appraisal of labor market performance seem to have been laid open to question by the available empirical evidence. Rather than an economy that has failed to provide a "sufficient" volume of employment, Mexico emerges from this account as one that has coped remarkably well. Not only has a rapidly growing labor force been absorbed in productive employment, but the terms of employment have shown a steady improvement throughout the course of forty years. The labor market has proved to be an efficient mechanism for reallocating labor resources in response to changes in sectoral and regional demands for labor. By avoiding institutional interventions that seriously distorted the price of labor, Mexico has also avoided the misallocation of labor characteristic of the Todaro model, a misallocation that would be evidenced by high rates of open urban unemployment and the queuing of labor at the entry points to the formal sector. Because the labor market was allowed to price labor at its opportunity cost, labor-intensive productive activities have been able to thrive alongside a more capital-intensive productive sector that requires a substantially different class of labor. The flexibility of the labor market thus facilitated a high level of employment and utilization of the labor force. In turn, the relatively full employment has implied that the steady growth of the economy since 1940 has exerted an equally steady upward pressure on the general wage level as new or expanding sectors had to attract labor from other employments. As the price of labor has risen, a gradual adjustment of producers in labor-intensive activities was also observed. Capital-labor ratios and labor productivity also rose gradually to support the higher wage levels. In short, the period 1940–80 witnessed a steady transformation of the Mexican economy along a relatively smooth path with the benefits of growth widely distributed over a growing labor force.

No claim is made here that the allocation of investment responded solely to market forces or that it was not influenced by distortions introduced by institutional intervention. For example, government trade, credit, and investment policies obviously played an important role in influencing the allocation of capital resources. Since such intervention was not necessarily guided by market criteria, it is quite possible that the growth path followed by the economy was not the most efficient one potentially available. However, once the parameters that guided the allocation of capital were defined, the labor market responded to the resulting pattern of demand for labor with a high degree of efficiency.

If this account of the development process is a reasonably accurate portrayal of what has actually unfolded, how can one explain such a great preoccupation with an "employment problem?" This question was addressed in Chapter 3, in which concepts of labor underutilization were discussed. It was noted there that what is commonly labeled an employment problem can more appropriately be called a concern with the existence of low incomes and poverty. Specifying the object of concern accurately is important; the conditions associated with or "causing" it can then be identified and policy measures appropriate to the amelioration of that condition can be formulated. For example, recognition that the concern is with low incomes rather than with employment opens up a much wider range of alternative policy responses. Measures can be framed that can address the problem directly and with a greater degree of efficiency than would more generalized responses, such as accelerated employment creation. There is no reason to presume that the principal beneficiaries of the latter would be those who form the intended target population, the poorest strata of society. The importance of the proper specification of the problem to be attacked will become apparent in the discussion that follows of recent developments in Mexico.

The Economic Crisis

Recent employment conditions in Mexico would appear to belie the rosy scenario of the past that has been spelled out in the preceding chapters. In mid-1982 Mexico began a slide into a severe recession that left rising open unemployment and declining real wages in its wake, a clear and sharp interruption of the trends that extend back to 1940. While the crisis is very real, it should be emphasized that it in no way represents an inevitable consequence of the growth pattern that held sway in Mexico in the years before the latter part of the 1970s. Nor can it be ascribed to a failure of the labor market. The origins of the crisis and the changes that it has spawned are examined below. More important for the future, however, are the lessons to be drawn for policy initiatives from an understanding of the labor market and the manner in which it has functioned in the past.

The crisis of the Mexican economy was the result of several factors, including a misreading of the employment problem of the country, faulty management of the economy, and serious miscalculations regarding the future price of petroleum and the prospective foreign exchange earnings that would be forthcoming from petroleum exports. The government of López Portillo appears to have been persuaded that Mexico faced both a short-term and a longer-term employment problem. The short-term problem stemmed from the reduced rate of growth in the first year of the administration, a consequence of the program of austerity initiated by the new government in an effort to stem inflation and to reduce the fiscal deficit and its reliance on external financing. As noted in Chapter 3, open unemployment in the large urban areas did rise in 1977 as economic activity continued at the rather depressed levels of 1976, although the increase can hardly be viewed as alarming. Unemployment rates in 1977 in the three major metropolitan areas of Mexico City, Guadalajara, and Monterrey averaged only 0.7, 1.2, and 1.5 percentage points, respectively, above their 1973–75 average.[2] Nevertheless, according to Leopoldo Solís, the government decided to accelerate growth in 1978 to close the breach that was presumed to have appeared between the growth in the labor force and the level of employment. It was estimated that a 7.5 percent growth rate would be required to absorb the increase in the labor force and to reverse the deterioration in employment conditions associated with the recession of the two preceding years.[3]

All of the studies of the employment situation also pointed to the existence of a long-term employment problem in the form of serious underemployment. Thus, the government apparently opted to go beyond a limited response to the cyclical problem and to force a more prolonged accelerated rate of growth. Expanded investment in import-substituting activities in both the industrial and agricultural sectors were advanced to further the twin goals of employment creation and an increased degree of self-sufficiency.

The administration also sought to address the social issue of income distribution by introducing or increasing the subsidization of basic foods and services. Since these decisions coincided with a rapidly increasing flow of petroleum from the new southeastern fields and with an expanding availability of credit from abroad, the resources required for the ambitious program of the government appeared to be clearly in hand. Furthermore, the government chose to ignore the past volatility in the price of petroleum and to assume that oil prices would continue to rise at a rate high enough to sustain the higher level of government expenditures and to service its foreign debt. (In fairness to the Mexican government, it was not alone in forecasting a monotonic upward trend in petroleum prices.)

Unfortunately, the requirements of expanded investment and consumption quickly outran the resources available to government. Unable to divert additional resources to itself by increased taxation, the government resorted to massive deficit financing. In each of the final four years of the administration, the deficit increased as a proportion of GDP until, in 1982, it amounted to 18 percent of aggregate output. The deficit was financed by an accelerated rate of monetary creation and by foreign credits. The private sector, as well, was encouraged by an increasingly overvalued exchange rate to turn to foreign sources of funding. The economy responded to these stimuli with four years of rapid growth.

The boom collapsed following the worldwide glut of petroleum and the subsequent fall in its price. A severe balance of payments disequilibrium ensued as export revenues faltered, the cost of servicing the burgeoning external debt mounted, and capital flight intensified as the inevitability of devaluation of the peso became increasingly apparent. A further extension of foreign credits and the renegotiation of existing debt was made conditional on the adoption of policies designed to restrain domestic inflation, reduce the fiscal deficit, and address the disequilibrium in the balance of payments. The impact on economic activity was quickly felt. After peaking early in 1982, national output declined during the second half of the year, canceling out the entire growth of the first half. Over the entire year, GDP declined by 0.5 percent from the level of 1981, and there was further contraction in 1983 as GDP fell by 4.7 percent.

Construction activity was an early casualty of the restrictive measures and was sharply curtailed during the second half of 1982. Manufacturing output also fell, with the production of capital and consumer durable goods leading the way. On balance, industrial output fell by 2.7 percent in 1982 and by a further 8.3 percent in 1983.[4] By the end of 1983, the contractionary forces had run their course and the economy appeared to have stabilized.

As would be expected, the recession had a visible impact on open unemployment. By the end of 1982, unemployment in the three major metropolitan areas had risen to an average of over 8 percent, more than double the rate during the first quarter of the year.[5] The unemployment rate appears to have stabilized at about that level during 1983 and early 1984.

Real wages in the large-enterprise portion of the industrial sector began to slip during 1982 as the pace of inflation accelerated. Reflecting the leftward shift in the demand for labor and government restraints on advances in nominal wages, real earnings declined sharply during 1983. By midyear they were some 25 percent below their average level of 1981.[6] The adjustments made in legal minimum wages were a further manifestation of the government's policy of wage restraint. As can be seen in table 7-1, through the first half of 1983 the real value of the minimum wage had declined by almost 20 percent from its average value in 1981. In spite of a midyear adjustment, it continued to slide during the latter half of the year, averaging 70 percent of its 1981 value. If the trends in modern industrial sector earnings and in legal minimum wages are representative of the course of remunerations in the labor market at large, these declines have completely wiped out the gains realized over the decade of the 1970s and have carried real wages to levels prevailing during the latter half of the 1960s.

While the recession appears to have had a severe impact on real wages, its impact on the level of unemployment has been less drastic than one might have expected, in view of the severity of the decline in output. An estimate of the expected level of unemployment can be derived by applying a rather simple procedure. This would take into account the normal growth in the labor force and the employment elasticity of output over the two-year interval 1982–83 and would yield a prediction for urban unemployment of over 13 percent by the end of 1983.[7] If the actual rate were closer to the 8 percent level reported, this would appear to have been a major achievement.

Confirmation of the limited impact that the recession had on employment is provided by data from another source—the social security system, which extends over most of the modern sectors of the economy. After adjustments for changes in coverage, the number of registrants in 1983 was only 0.36 percent below that of 1982.[8] Also consistent with this observation is the precedent recorded during the 1976–77 recession. Although that recession was not as deep as the current one, it will be recalled that the response of the open unemployment rate must still appear to have been mild. These experiences suggest that the economy and labor market are quite flexible and adaptive to cyclical disturbances, just as they have been to secular changes. In the current environment, the absence of wage rigidity is likely to have been a major factor in maintaining employment at a higher than expected level.[9] Had real wages remained at their prerecession levels, the employment effects of the economic decline might have been considerably more severe.

It is not possible to chart empirically with precision how markets have accommodated the labor force in productive employment over the past two years. I can only suggest, in a general way, some of the adjustments that appear to be taking place.

The immediate implication of a decline in real wages is that some productive activities that were not worth undertaking in an environment of expanding employment at higher wages will now be viewed as viable. For example, rural workers, who had abandoned cultivation of their plots in response to higher returns to wage labor in urban construction and manufacturing activities, would now be expected to return to agricultural production as urban employment opportunities shrink. The surprisingly large increase in agricultural output in 1983 over 1982 of 8 percent would be consistent with this expectation.[10] The decline in real wages could also induce producers who enjoy considerable short-run scope for substituting labor for machinery to opt to employ labor more intensively. For example, small farmers may substitute lower priced labor for the rental of farm machinery. Small contractors in the construction industry may enjoy similar options.

Furthermore, one might expect a change in the output mix between labor- and capital-intensive goods. The price of the former should decline relative to the latter, thus encouraging substitution in consumption in favor of labor-intensive goods. While empirical data do show much sharper declines in production levels of consumer durable and producer goods relative to nondurables, it is not possible to distinguish the contribution to this shift of the decline in incomes from the pure substitution effect. Within agriculture, one might expect to see a reversal of trends in cropping patterns as recorded in Chapter 4. Forage crops might give way to the cultivation of more labor-intensive subsistence or commercial crops. In fact, this does appear to have occurred. The production of corn, the principal subsistence crop, exceeded the predicted output for 1983 by 35 percent; at 13.5 million tons, it was almost double that of 1982.[11] Data on exports of agricultural commodities also show large increases in labor-intensive fruits and vegetables as well as of cotton.

In view of the large devaluation of the peso in 1982 and the subsequent continual adjustment in the exchange rate, one would also expect to see an increase in exports of other nonpetroleum products, although with a lag. Again, labor-intensive goods would appear to enjoy the greatest comparative advantage and to be prominently represented in the export basket. In 1983 there was in fact a notable increase in such exports, especially to the United States: exports of manufactured goods increased more than 21 percent over 1982, and there were large increases in processed foods, textile products, machinery, and automotive products.[12] This expansion extended into early 1984 as well. During the first two months of the year, manufactured exports were running 74 percent ahead of the previous year, while agricultural exports were up by 37 percent.[13]

Significant increases of less labor-intensive goods have also been reported, as an expanded national capacity in the production of petroleum derivatives and automobiles has emerged. The labor-intensive tourist industry has also enjoyed a resurgence; incoming tourism advanced by a record 24 percent in 1983 over 1982.[14]

The devaluation of the peso also had the effect of promoting a substitution of domestic goods for those imported. Of course, the sharp reduction in imports was attributable in considerable part to administrative restrictions, but the unprecedented change in relative prices made itself felt not only in the consumption of imported goods but also of services, like tourism abroad. Numerous examples of substitution have been recorded, beer bottles for imported aluminum cans, wood for imported plastics in furniture, services for repairing machinery or replacing parts previously imported, and so on.[15] For the first time in many years, the consumption of domestic goods exceeded that of imported goods in the states bordering the United States.[16]

Finally, the devaluation increased very sharply the peso value of wages earned in the United States relative to those earned domestically. An expected consequence would be an increase in the flow of undocumented workers to the United States, a phenomenon that might be a factor accounting for the reported increase in apprehensions by the Border Patrol in 1983 and the early months of 1984.

Thus it is possible to observe a reallocation of resources taking place that will raise Mexico's average labor-output ratio. As long as conditions favorable to this reallocation are not affected by policy interventions that would distort real wages and exchange rates, there is no reason to believe that it will not continue. In short, past experience in Mexico suggests that the cyclical increase in unemployment may prove to be just that, a relatively short-term phenomenon.

Of course, the longer the economy remains in a depressed state, the less likely it becomes that the process of absorption of people displaced from employment by the recession and those new entrants to the labor force can be achieved without depressing wages still further. Nor will a return to full employment imply an early return to the levels of labor productivity and real wages that held before the onset of the crisis. Although even a restoration of reasonably full employment might be considered a major achievement, the conventional measures for determining the degree of underutilization will yield an uncomfortably large proportion of the labor force in the "underemployed" category; the open unemployment equivalent of this proportion will also appear "unacceptably high." A recent economic review of the Mexican economy reported that 50 percent of the labor force is underemployed, a proportion little changed from what has been advanced periodically over the past decade.[17]

Recent Developments

Before these numbers become a basis for public policy measures designed to accelerate the absorption of the "underemployed," it would be well to pause and recall the lessons that recent experience offer. The large measure of underemployment will not represent an accurate measure of the idle labor resources available for immediate employment in newly created vacancies. Indeed, even under the present conditions of economic recession, there are regions that report "shortages" of particular classes of labor. For example, the annual report of the Banco de México for the year 1983 is cited as pointing to labor shortages in the northwestern and northcentral provinces.[18] The World Bank in January 1984 likewise reported that "the 1983/84 cotton production estimate for Mexico was lowered by 10,000 tons in November on evidence that an acute shortage of harvesting labor in Mexicali has reduced the prospective yield."[19]

Interviews with small private farmers and ejidatarios during a tour of rural areas of central Mexico in the spring of 1985 also revealed a preoccupation with labor shortages. In several regions, farmers complained of such shortages in spite of wages offered that were well in excess of the legal minimum. Furthermore, they held that they and other members of their communities were able to obtain as much employment as they desired. In these areas, at least, it did not appear that the recession had resulted in a surplus of available workers in the labor market according to potential employers.[20] Whether this perception was fully shared by landless workers who were dependent on wage employment for all their earnings could not be established.

Although a process of adjustment to the sharp changes in the parameters of the Mexican economy is clearly under way, it is not characterized by an instantaneous movement to a new equilibrium position. Once resources are engaged in a particular pattern, they adapt to a new set of changed conditions only with a lag. When the economy resumes a pattern of growth it will again require reallocation of labor resources.

Historically, the supply of labor responded to shifting patterns of demand with a lag sufficient to exert a continuous upward pressure on the general wage level. Although labor may be disposed to respond somewhat more quickly to changes now than in the past, it would not seem reasonable to expect it to abandon completely its traditional caution. Certainly the experience of 1978–82 would counsel against an attempt to "resolve the employment problem" rapidly by vigorously accelerating the rate of expansion "to make up for the employment growth forgone during the recession." Such accelerated growth could very quickly exhaust the ranks of the employables among the ranks of the open unemployed, and labor shortages could again become the order of the day.

Even if full employment is restored, a question remains concerning the real wage level at which the labor force will be employed and the prospects for the future course of wages. In the context of a declining national product in both 1982 and 1983, the absorption of a labor force growing on the order of 3.8 percent a year could be achieved only at declining real wages. The expected growth in 1984, on the order of 1 percent, will not suffice to reverse the course of real wages. Given the expected growth in the labor force, real wage constancy is likely to require a rate of growth in GDP approximating 4 percent.[21] A faster rate of growth could be expected not only to absorb a growing labor force but also to do so at rising average real wages as labor shifts from low- to higher-productivity employments. Past experience had demonstrated that an annual rate of growth averaging about 6 percent sufficed to raise average real wages at a 3 percent rate during the 1960–75 interval.[22] In view of the faster current rate of growth of the labor force, by approximately 1 percentage point, a return to a 6 percent rate of growth in GDP would be expected to yield a smaller rate of increase in real wages unless substantial changes were to occur in the structure of production toward a greater intensivity in the employment of labor.

Short-Term Prospects

It is not within the scope of this study to predict how soon the Mexican economy will regain its past momentum; this will depend, in part, on an external environment that lies beyond the control of the Mexican government and that is difficult to foresee. The future price of petroleum, Mexico's ability to tap foreign savings, and the degree of openness of foreign markets will all influence the country's command over foreign exchange—a critical variable in the determination of the rate of investment.

Although external factors will play a contributory role in determining the course of Mexican economy, one should not minimize the role of domestic policies in shaping the manner in which productive resources, including labor, will be employed. Since the state, directly (and indirectly through parastatal institutions) accounts for a large share of the domestic product, its investment and other expenditures will play a critical role in the evolution of economic activity in general and in determining the quantity and quality of the new employment opportunities. By structuring the incentives to which private investment decisions respond, the government can influence these same employment outcomes in the private sector. By intervening in the determination of minimum conditions of employment, it can influence the pattern of investment among alternative productive activities, as well as the choice of factor proportions within any particular activity. Thus, the responsibility of government decisionmakers is very great. Particularly since resources available for investment are likely to be relatively scarce during the next few years, the country can ill afford to squander resources on activities that do not maximize yields in output and employment.

It is easier to outline the actions that government should avoid than to suggest what they should do in the furtherance of efficient economic growth and favorable employment conditions. Measures that subsidize the price of capital will tend to favor investment in capital-intensive productive activities and the substitution of capital for labor. Unless the price of capital is allowed to reflect its true opportunity cost, it is unlikely to flow to its most efficient applications. The policies that influence the price of labor to the modern or formal sector of the economy should avoid distorting that price. A price in excess of its opportunity cost will tend to encourage responses similar to those flowing from the subsidization of capital.

Although a rising real wage level is a laudable social objective, it has been demonstrated here that acting on the price of labor through, for example, the legal minimum wage, is not likely to be an effective mechanism for improving the wage conditions of most of the lowest-wage earners. More important for raising the wages of those at the lower end of the wage structure is the achievement and maintenance of a high and sustained rate of economic growth and a pattern of growth that minimizes the variance in the productivity of labor of any given quality. Avoidance of a dualistic pattern of development argues heavily in favor of pricing both capital and labor resources in accordance with their opportunity costs.

The exchange rate is another critical price that will affect the internal allocation of resources. Maintenance of an overvalued exchange rate favors consumption of foreign over domestic goods, lowers the price of imported capital goods relative to the price of domestic labor, and limits the growth of output and employment in the production of goods and services in which Mexico is likely to enjoy a comparative advantage in international trade—goods and services that tend to be labor-intensive in production. In short, these prescriptive measures reduce to an application of efficiency criteria for guiding resource allocation.

Although these criteria are acknowledged to be important, governments ordinarily pursue multiple policy objectives, some of which conflict with others. For example, a great emphasis is being placed in Mexico on increasing the self-sufficiency of the country in agricultural as well as in intermediate and capital goods. The rationale that is offered for the pursuit of this goal is that Mexico will then be freed from the vagaries of foreign supplies and the country will economize on the foreign exchange needed to service the large external debt. To some extent, pursuit of this objective may involve a cost in the form of forgone employment. For instance, self-sufficiency in agricultural goods refers primarily to basic grains. Yet their production requires fewer labor inputs than do the principal export commodities of the sector.[23] To the extent that agricultural resources are diverted from export to production for domestic consumption, employment of labor and real income will be sacrificed.

The promotion of intermediate and capital goods production is also likely to conflict with the goal of maximizing the employment effects of new investment since these sectors are frequently relatively capital-intensive in nature. And, to the extent that such production is promoted by protective barriers against imports, efficiency and employment are further compromised by the creation of secure domestic monopolies. To judge from the experience of most countries that have pursued vigorous import-substitution policies, the irony of these measures is that they proved ineffective in achieving one of their principal stated goals, the conservation of foreign exchange. Furthermore, the resource cost of saving a dollar of foreign exchange has all too frequently exceeded that of earning a dollar, with a consequent loss of economic welfare. However, since the economic costs associated with such measures are rarely clearly discernible and the measures themselves appear politically attractive, it is too much to expect Mexico or any other government to abstain completely from such intervention. At best, one may hope that an awareness of the existence of costs associated with them will serve as a restraint on their proliferation.

The next few years will continue to be difficult ones for Mexico. Policymakers will be faced with enormous pressures to respond to various individual and collective hardships associated with the economic crisis and its aftermath. In particular, the deteriorating employment conditions during 1982 and 1983 have intensified public and official concern over the "employment problem." The familiar characterizations of the past have carried over to the present. As noted above, underemployment now (as in the past) affects half of the labor force. While the language describing the employment problem is unchanged, one can only hope that the interpretation or significance assigned by policymakers to such a statistical artifact will reflect learning gained from the labor market experience of the recent period of accelerated growth. An appreciation of that experience, as well as of the secular developments documented here, would provide a persuasive basis for altering past perceptions about the way in which the labor market has functioned in Mexico. It would also place in perspective the significance to be attached to conventional measures of labor force underutilization. A modification of those perceptions would give Mexicans a greater sense of pride in the success of their past development efforts, as well as provide a sounder basis for charting responses to the cyclical and secular challenges that currently confront the country.

Notes

1. Surplus labor, as used here, refers to the theoretical concept of labor employed at a zero or near-zero marginal product.

2. See table 3-2.

3. Leopoldo Solís M., "Reflexiones sobre el panorama general de la economía mexicana," in *El sistema económico mexicano* (Mexico, D.F.: Premia Editora, 1982), p. 348.

4. Banco Nacional de México (Banamex), *Review of the Economic Situation of Mexico*, vol. 60, no. 700 (March 1984), p. 85.

5. The Mexico City and Guadalajara metropolitan areas reported 8 percent; Monterrey, with its concentration of heavy industry hard hit by the recession, suffered 12 percent. Its experience is likely to be less typical of urban areas generally than that of Mexico City and Guadalajara with their more diversified production bases.

6. Monthly earnings statistics for 1983 were obtained from the Banco de México.

7. This would result from an initial level of unemployment of 4 percent at the beginning of 1982, an annual rate of growth of 3.8 percent in the labor force, and declines in GDP of 0.5 and 4.7 percent times 0.6, the output elasticity of employment that held during the 1970s. Since manufacturing and construction activity were much harder hit than agriculture and the other major sectors, applying the average output elasticity of employment for the economy as a whole to changes in GDP probably underestimates the expected impact on urban unemployment.

8. "La economía mexicana en 1983," *Comercio exterior*, vol. 34, no. 4 (April 1984), p. 360. This article presents a summary review of the annual report issued by the Banco de México.

9. Some firms in the modern sector may have been inhibited from reducing their permanent work forces by the large severance payments that are mandated by the labor code. These legal provisions do not apply to temporary employees, however, and are not observed in the informal sector of the economy.

10. Economic Intelligence Unit, Ltd., *Quarterly Economic Review of Mexico*, no. 1 (London, 1984), p. 15.

11. Ibid., p. 13.

12. Ibid., p. 10.

13. *Comercio exterior*, vol. 34, no. 5 (May 1984), pp. 462–66.

14. *Review of the Economic Situation of Mexico*, vol. 60, no. 698 (January 1984), p. 39.

15. *Quarterly Economic Review of Mexico*, no. 2 (1984), p. 8.

16. *Comercio exterior*, vol. 34, no. 4 (April 1984), p. 360.

17. *Quarterly Economic Review of Mexico*, p. 12. Whether the proportion of the labor force defined as underemployed has increased or decreased during the recession cannot be predicted a priori. For example, if the minimum wage is adopted as the benchmark separating the underemployed from the fully employed, it is possible for the proportion to have declined.

This would follow if actual earnings of low-wage workers have fallen by less than the decline in the legal minimum.

18. *Comercio exterior*, p. 360.

19. World Bank, "Quarterly Review of Commodity Markets" (Washington, D.C., January 1984).

20. It would be difficult to offer with confidence a full interpretation of such reports alleging regional shortages of labor in the agricultural sector. They may reflect a declining willingness of the youthful rural population to enter and remain in the agricultural labor force; as my informants observed, higher levels of education have led to a decreased willingness of rural youth to perform the heavy manual work demanded by current agricultural practice on smallholdings. The alleged shortages may also stem from an increased demand for agricultural labor in response to higher real guaranteed prices recently promulgated by the government for many basic agricultural commodities. In the face of a relatively fully employed rural labor force, such a shift in demand for labor could give rise to perceptions of shortages. None of the regions visited had a tradition of relying on migrant labor for manual work. Most of them, however, happened to be traditional exporters of labor to the United States on both a temporary and permanent basis. The decline in nonagricultural real wages in Mexico should have had the effect of increasing the relative attractiveness of work in the United States and may have induced a larger than usual migration.

21. If the aggregate production process is approximated by a Cobb-Douglas production function, the average wage level is defined as

$$W = \alpha X/L$$

where W is the average wage level, X is total output, and α is the coefficient of the labor term in the production function. Converting to log form and differentiating, the rate of change in wages will be approximated by

$$\Delta W/W \doteq \Delta\alpha/\alpha + \Delta X/X - \Delta L/L.$$

If α is constant in the short run, then the increase in output required to yield no change in average wages is equal to the rate of change in the size of the work force. Over time, α may change in response to structural changes in production, for example, toward more labor-intensive processes of production. In that case, W might be expected to increase.

22. See Chapter 7.

23. Secretaría de Agricultura y Recursos Hidraulicos, Centro de Estudios en Planeación Agropecuaria, *El desarrollo agropecuario de México*, vol. 6, *El empleo de mano de obra en las actividades agropecuarias* (Mexico, D.F., 1982), pp. 124–25.

Bibliography

Books and Articles

Alemán, Eloisa. *Investigación socioeconómica directa de los ejidos de San Luis Potosí.* Mexico, D.F.: Instituto Mexicano de Investigaciones Económicas, 1966.

Altimir, Oscar. "La distribución del ingreso en México, 1950–1977." In *Distribución del ingreso en México: Ensayos.* Vol. 1. Mexico, D.F.: Banco de México, November 1982.

———. "La medición de la población economicamente activa de México." *Demografía y economía,* vol. 8, no. 1 (1974), pp. 50–83.

"Análisis del mercado de los servicios domesticos en México." *Cuadernos de empleo,* no. 1 (Mexico, D.F.: Secretaría del Trabajo y Previsión Social, 1976), pp. 51–114.

Anson, Ricardo. "La relación entre la politica de migración interna y la realidad de las consequencias personales de la migración interna: El caso de Monterrey." Monterrey: Nuevo Leon: Instituto Tecnologico de Estudios Superiores de Monterrey, n.d. Processed.

Arizpe, Lourdes. *Migración, etnicismo y cambio económico.* Mexico, D.F.: El Colegio de México, 1978.

Balan, Jorge, Harley L. Browning, and Elizabeth Jelin. *Men in a Developing Society.* Austin: University of Texas Press, 1973.

Barbosa-Ramírez, A. René. *El Bajío.* Mexico, D.F.: Centro de Investigaciones Agrarias, 1973.

———. *Empleo, desempleo y subempleo en el sector agropecuario.* 3 vols. Mexico, D.F.: Centro de Investigaciones Agrarias, 1976, 1977, 1979.

Belshaw, Michael. *A Village Economy.* New York: Columbia University Press, 1967.

Bergsman, Joel. *Income Distribution and Poverty in Mexico.* World Bank Staff Working Paper no. 395. Washington, D.C., June 1980.

Blejer, Mario I., Harry G. Johnson, and Arturo C. Porzecanski. "Un análisis de los determinantes económicos de la migración mexicana legal e ilegal hacia los Estados Unidos." *Demografía y economía,* vol. 11, no. 3 (1977), pp. 326–40.

Butterworth, Douglas S. "A Study of the Urbanization Process among Mixtec Migrants from Tilantongo in Mexico City." In *Peasants in Cities,* ed. William Manglin. Boston, Mass.: Houghton Mifflin, 1970.

———. *Tilantongo: Comunidad mixteca en transición*. Mexico, D.F.: Instituto Nacional Indigenista, 1975.

Cabrera A., Gustavo. "Población, migración y fuerza de trabajo." In *Mercados regionales de trabajo*. Mexico, D.F.: Instituto Nacional de Estudios del Trabajo, 1976.

———. "Selectividad por edad y por sexo de los migrantes en México." In *Conferencia regional latinoamericana de población (Actas I)*. Mexico, D.F.: El Colegio de México, 1972.

Camara, Fernando, and Robert V. Kemper, eds. *Migration Across Frontiers: Mexico and the United States*. Albany: State University of New York, 1979.

Cancian, Frank. *Change and Uncertainty in a Peasant Economy: The Maya Corn Farmer*. Stanford, Calif.: Stanford University Press, 1972.

Cervantes G., Jesús A. "México: Análisis de la distribución de ingreso—Aspectos metodologicos." *Comercio exterior*, vol. 32, no. 1 (1982), pp. 43–50.

Clark, Colin. *The Conditions of Economic Progress*. 3rd ed. London: Macmillan, 1957.

Conroy, Michael E., Mario Coria Salas, and Felipe Vilá Gonzalez. "Socio-economic Incentives for Migration from Mexico to the United States: Cross-Regional Profiles, 1969–1978." Paper presented at the 1980 Annual Meeting of the Population Association of America, April 11, 1980, Denver, Colorado.

Contreras S., Enrique. *Estratificación y movilidad social en la ciudad de México*. Mexico, D.F.: Universidad Nacional Autonoma de México, 1978.

Cornelius, Wayne A. "Mexican Migration to the United States: Causes, Consequences, and U.S. Responses." Cambridge: Massachusetts Institute of Technology, Center for International Studies, July 1978.

Corona V., Rodolfo, and Crescencio Ruiz C. "Migración interna e internacional." Paper presented at the Simposio Nacional sobre Migración y Distribución Espacial de la Población, December 5–9, 1979, Guadalajara, Jalisco.

DeWalt, Billie R. *Modernization in a Mexican Ejido*. London: Cambridge University Press, 1978.

Díez-Canedo, Juan. "La migración indocumentada a Estados Unidos: Un enfoque." Documento de investigación no. 24. Mexico, D.F.: Banco de México, July 1980.

Díez-Canedo, Juan, and Gabriel Vera. "La importancia de la escolaridad en la determinación del nivel de ingreso." In *Distribución del ingreso en México: Ensayos*. Vol. 2. Mexico, D.F.: Banco de México, 1982.

Dinerman, Ina D. "Patterns of Adaptation among Households of U.S.-Bound Migrants from Michoacán, Mexico." *International Migration Review*, vol. 12, no. 4 (1970), pp. 485–501.

Economic Intelligence, Ltd. *Quarterly Economic Review of Mexico*. London, 1984.

Ehrlich, Paul R., Loy Bilderback, and Anne H. Ehrlich. *The Golden Door*. New York: Ballantine Books, 1979.

Ericson, Anna-Stina. "The Impact of Commuters on the Mexican-American Border." In *Mexican Workers in the United States*, ed. George C. Kiser and Martha W. Kiser. Albuquerque: University of New Mexico Press, 1979.

Eriksson, John R. "Wage Change and Employment Growth in Latin American Industry." Research Memorandum no. 36. Williamstown, Mass.: Williams College, Center for Development Studies, June 1970. Processed.

Evans, John S., and Dilmus D. James. "Conditions of Employment and Income Distribution in Mexico as Incentives for Mexican Migration to the United States: Prospects to the End of the Century." *International Migration Review*, vol. 13, no. 1 (1979), pp. 4–24.

Fei, John C. H., and Gustav Ranis. *Development of the Labor Surplus Economy: Theory and Policy*. Homewood, Ill.: Irwin, 1964.

Felix, David. "Trickling Down in Mexico and the Debate over Long Term Growth-Equity Relationships in the LDCs." St. Louis, Mo.: Washington University, n.d. Processed.

Fernandez O., Luis M., and María T. de Fernandez. "Capitalismo y cooperación: El caso de un ejido en Michoacán." In *Capitalismo y campesinado en México*. Mexico, D.F.: Instituto Nacional de Antropología e Historia, 1976.

Finkler, Kaja. "From Sharecroppers to Entrepreneurs: Peasant Household Production Strategies under the Ejido System of Mexico." *Economic Development and Cultural Change*, vol. 27, no. 1 (1978), pp. 103–20.

Flores de la Peña, Horacio, and Aldo Ferrer. "Salarios reales y desarrollo económico." *El trimestre económico*, vol. 18, no. 4 (1950), pp. 617–28.

Fogel, Walter. "Twentieth Century Migration to the United States." In *The Gateway: U.S. Immigration Issues and Policies*, ed. Barry R. Chiswick. Washington, D.C.: American Enterprise Institute, 1982.

Foerster, Robert F. *The Racial Problem Involved in Immigration*. Washington, D.C.: Government Printing Office, 1925.

Foster, George M. *Tzintzuntzan: Mexican Peasants in a Changing World*. Rev. ed. New York: Elsevier, 1979.

Foster, George M., and Robert V. Kemper, eds. *Anthropologists in Cities*. Boston, Mass.: Little, Brown, 1974.

Fuentes M., Olac. "Enseñanza media basica en México, 1970–76." *Cuadernos Politicos*, no. 15 (1978), pp. 91–104.

Gamio, Manuel. *Mexican Immigration to the United States*. Chicago: University of Chicago Press, 1930.

García, Brigida. "La participación de la población en la actividad económica." *Demografía y economía*, vol. 9, no. 1 (1975), pp. 1–31.

García y Griego, Manuel. *El volumen de la migración de mexicanos no documentados a los Estados Unidos (nuevas hipotesis)*. Estudios no. 4. Mexico, D.F.: Centro de Información y Estadísticas del Trabajo (CENIET), 1980.

Gisser, Micha. *Introduction to Price Theory*, 2d ed. Scranton, Penn.: International Textbook Co., 1969.

Goldberg, Howard, "Estimates of Emigration from Mexico and Illegal Entry into the United States, 1960–70 by the Residual Method." Washington, D.C.: Center for Population Research, Georgetown University, n.d.

Gomez O., Luis. "Crisis agricola, crisis de los campesinos." *Comercio exterior*, vol. 28, no. 6 (1978), pp. 714–27.

Greenwood, Michael J., and Jerry R. Ladman. "An Economic Analysis of Migration in Mexico." *The Annals of Regional Science*, vol. 12, no. 2 (1978), pp. 16–31.

Gregory, Peter. "Legal Minimum Wages as an Instrument of Social Policy in Less Developed Countries, with Special Reference to Costa Rica." In *The Economics of Legal Minimum Wages*, ed. Simon Rottenberg. Washington, D.C.: American Enterprise Institute, 1981.

Heer, David M. "What Is the Annual Net Flow of Undocumented Mexican Immigrants to the United States?" *Demography*, vol. 16, no. 3 (1979), pp. 417–23.

Hernández L., Enrique, and Jorge C. Córdova. "Estructura de la distribución de ingreso en México." *Comercio exterior*, vol. 29, no. 5 (1979), pp. 505–20.

Hewitt de Alcantara, Cynthia. *Modernizing Mexican Agriculture: Socio-economic Implications of Technological Change, 1940–70*, Report no. 76.5. Geneva: United Nations Research Institute for Social Development, 1976.

Isbister, John. "Urban Employment and Wages in a Developing Economy: The Case of Mexico." *Economic Development and Cultural Change*, vol. 20, no. 1 (1971), pp. 24–46.

Keeley, Charles B. "Counting the Uncountable: Estimates of Undocumented Aliens in the United States." *Population and Development Review*, vol. 3, no. 4 (1977), pp. 473–81.

Keesing, Donald B. "Employment and Lack of Employment in Mexico, 1900–1970." In *Quantitative Latin American Studies: Methods and Findings*, ed. James W. Wilkie and Kenneth Ruddle. Los Angeles: University of California L.A., Latin American Center, 1977.

King, Jonathan. "Interstate Migration in Mexico." *Economic Development and Cultural Change*, vol. 27, no. 1 (1978), pp. 83–102.

King, Timothy. *Mexico: Industrialization and Trade Policies since 1940*. London: Oxford University Press, 1971.

Lancaster, Clarise, and Frederick J. Scheuren. "Counting the Uncountable Illegals: Some Initial Statistical Speculations Employing Capture-Recapture Techniques." *1977 Proceedings of the Social Statistical Section of the American Statistical Association*. Washington, D.C., 1978.

Lesko and Associates. "Final Report: Basic Data and Guidance Required to Implement a Major Illegal Alien Study During Fiscal Year 1976." Contract no. CO-16-75. Washington, D.C.: Office of Planning and Evaluation, U.S. Immigration and Naturalization Service, 1975.

Lewis, W. Arthur. "Economic Development with Unlimited Supplies of Labour."

Manchester School of Economic and Social Studies, no. 22 (May 1954), pp. 139–91.

Lomitz, Larissa A. *Networks and Marginality: Life in a Mexican Shantytown*. New York: Academic Press, 1977.

López Rosado, Diego G., and Juan F. Noyola Vázquez. "Los salarios reales en México, 1935–50." *El trimestre económico*, vol. 18, no. 2 (1951), pp. 201–209.

Maldonado Lee, Gabriel. *La mujer asalariada en el sector agricola*. Mexico, D.F.: Centro Nacional de Información y Estadísticas del Trabajo (CENIET), 1977.

Martínez G., Gerónimo. "El mercado de trabajo y las interrelaciones económicas entre México, los Estados Unidos, y el Canada." Paper presented at the second meeting of the Overseas Development Council's Working Group on U.S.-Mexican Border Area Issues, December 3–5, 1981, Tijuana, Mexico.

McFarland, Earl L., Jr. "Employment Growth in Services: Mexico 1950–69." Ph.D. dissertation, Columbia University, 1974.

McWilliams, Carey. *North from Mexico: The Spanish-Speaking People of the U.S.* New York: Greenwood, 1968.

Miller, Richard. "Labor Legislation and Mexican Industrial Relations." *Industrial Relations*," vol. 7, no. 2 (1968), pp. 171–82.

Muñoz, Humberto, and Orlandina de Oliveira. "Migración, oportunidades de empleo y diferencias de ingreso en la ciudad de México." *Revista Mexicana de sociología*, vol. 38, no. 1 (1976), pp. 51–83.

———. "Migraciones internas y desarrollo: Algunas consideraciones sociológicas." *Demografía y economía*, vol. 6 (1972), pp. 248–60.

Muñoz, Humberto, Orlandina de Oliveira, and Claudio Stern. *Migración y desigualdad social en la ciudad de México*. Mexico, D.F.: El Colegio de México, 1977.

———. *Migraciones internas a la ciudad de México y su impacto sobre el mercado de trabajo*. Temas de la Ciudad, no. 8. Mexico, D.F.: Delegación del D.D.F. en Venustiano Carranza, 1978.

Muñoz Izquierdo, Carlos. "Educación, estado y sociedad en México (1930–76)." *Revista de la educación superior*, no. 34 (1980), pp. 5–56.

Newman, Allen R. "Some Theoretical Considerations for Mexican Illegal Migration to the United States." Paper presented to the annual meeting of the Rocky Mountain Council for Latin American Studies, February 14, 1981, Las Cruces, New Mexico.

North, David S., and Marion F. Houstoun. *The Characteristics and Role of Illegal Aliens in the U.S. Labor Market*. Washington: Linton, 1976.

Norton, Roger D., and Leopoldo Solís M. *The Book of CHAC: Programming Studies for Mexican Agriculture*. Baltimore, Md.: Johns Hopkins University Press, 1983.

Pedrero N., Mercedes. "Corrientes migratorias internas de México (1950–60)." In *Conferencia regional latinoamericana de población (Actas I)*. Mexico, D.F.: El Colegio de México, 1972.

———. *La participación feminina en la actividad económica y su presupuesto de tiempo*. Serie Avances de Investigación no. 3. Mexico, D.F.: Centro Nacional de Información y Estadísticas de Trabajo (CENIET), 1977.

Perrakis, Stylianos. "The Surplus Labor Model and Wage Behavior in Mexico." *Industrial Relations*, vol. 11, no. 1 (1972), pp. 80–95.

Randall, Laura R. "The Process of Economic Development in Mexico from 1940 to 1959." Ph.D. dissertation, Columbia University, 1962.

Rendón, Teresa. "Utilización de mano de obra en la agricultura mexicana." *Demografía y economía*, vol. 10, no. 3 (1976), pp. 352–85.

Reyes Heroles, Jesús F. "Welfare Effects of Short-Run Macroeconomic Policies in a Dual Economy: The Case of Mexico." Ph.D. dissertation, Massachusetts Institute of Technology, 1980.

Reyes O., Sergio, Rodolfo Stavenhagen, Salomon Eckstein, and Juan Ballesteros. *Estructura agraria y desarrollo agricola en México*. Mexico, D.F.: Fondo de Cultura Económica, 1974.

Reynolds, Clark W. "Labor Market Projections for the United States and Mexico and Their Relevance to Current Migration Controversies." Food Research Institute Studies no. 17. Stanford, Calif.: Food Research Institute, 1979.

———. *The Mexican Economy*. New Haven, Conn.: Yale University Press, 1970.

Roberts, Kenneth. "Agrarian Structure and Labor Migration in Rural Mexico: The Case of Circular Migration of Undocumented Workers to the United States." Austin: Institute of Latin American Studies, University of Texas, 1980. Processed.

Robinson, J. Gregory. "Estimating the Approximate Size of the Illegal Alien Population by the Comparative Trend Analysis of Age-Specific Death Rates." *Demography*, vol. 17, no. 7 (1980), pp. 159–76.

Samora, Julian, *Los Mojados: The Wetback Story*. South Bend, Ind.: University of Notre Dame Press, 1971.

Silvers, Arthur L., and Pierre R. Crosson. *Rural Development and Urban-bound Migration in Mexico*. Washington, D.C.: Resources for the Future, 1980.

Singer, Morris. *Growth, Equality, and the Mexican Experience*. Austin: University of Texas Press, 1969.

Solís M., Leopoldo. "Reflexiones sobre el panorama general de la economía mexicana." In *El sistema económico mexicano*. Mexico, D.F.: Premia Editora, 1982.

Stavenhagen, Rodolfo. "Los jornaleros agricolas." *Revista del México agrario*, vol. 1, no. 1 (1967), pp. 164–66.

———. "Marginalidad, participación, y estructura agraria en América Latina." *Demografía y economía*, vol. 4, no. 3 (1970), pp. 267–91.

Stern, Claudio. "Migración educación y marginalidad en la ciudad de México." *Demografía y economía*, vol. 8, no. 2 (1974), pp. 171–86.

Stoltman, Joseph P., and John M. Ball. "Migration and the Local Economic Factor in Rural Mexico." *Human Organization*, vol. 30, no. 1 (1971), pp. 47–56.

Sturmthal, Adolf. "Economic Development, Income Distribution, and Capital Formation in Mexico." *Journal of Political Economy*, vol. 63, no. 3 (1955), pp. 183–201.

Thorbecke, Erik, and Everardus J. Stoutjesdijk. *Employment and Output: A Methodology Applied to Peru and Guatemala.* Paris: Organisation for Economic Co-operation and Development, 1971.

Todaro, Michael P. "A Model of Labor Migration and Urban Unemployment in Less Developed Countries." *American Economic Review*, vol. 59, no. 1 (1969), pp. 138–48.

Trejo R., Saul. "Desempleo y subocupación en México." *Comercio exterior*, vol. 22, no. 5 (1972), pp. 410–16.

———. "El desempleo en México: Caracteristicas generales." *Comercio exterior*, vol. 24, no. 7 (1974), pp. 730–38.

Unikel, Luis. *El desarrollo urbano de México*, 2d ed. Mexico, D.F.: El Colegio de México, 1978.

Urquidi, Víctor L. "Empleo y explosión demográfica." *Demografía y economía*, vol. 8, no. 2 (1974), pp. 141–53.

Urquidi, Víctor L., and José B. Morelos, eds. *Población y desarrollo en América Latina.* Mexico, D.F.: El Colegio de México, 1979.

Weaver, Thomas, and Theodore E. Downing, eds. *Mexican Migration.* Tucson: University of Arizona, Bureau of Ethnic Research, 1976.

Wilkie, James W. *The Mexican Revolution: Federal Expenditure and Social Change since 1910.* Berkeley: University of California Press, 1968.

———. "New Hypotheses for Statistical Research in Recent Mexican History." *Latin American Research Review*, vol. 6, no. 2 (1971), pp. 3–18.

———. *Statistics and National Policy.* Los Angeles: University of California at Los Angeles, Latin American Center, 1974.

Witte, Ann D. "Employment in the Manufacturing Sector of Developing Economies." Ph.D. dissertation, North Carolina State University, 1971.

Wool, Harold. "Future Labor Supply for Lower Level Occupations." *Monthly Labor Review*, vol. 99, no. 3 (1976), pp. 22–31.

Yates, P. Lamartine. *Mexico's Agricultural Dilemma.* Tucson: University of Arizona Press, 1981.

Zazueta, Carlos H. "Consideraciones acerca de los trabajadores mexicanos indocumentados en los Estados Unidos: Mitos y realidades." Mexico, D.F.: Secretaría de Trabajo y Previsión Social, Centro de Información y Estadísticas del Trabajo (CENIET), 1979. Processed.

———. "Mexican Workers in the United States: Some Initial Results and Methodological Considerations of the National Household Survey of Emigration (ENEFNEU)." Paper prepared for the Working Group on Mexican Migrants and U.S. Responsibility, Center for Philosophy and Public Policy, University of Maryland, March 1980.

Zazueta, Cesar. "Investigación reciente sobre migración mexicana indocumentada a los Estados Unidos." Secretaría de Trabajo y Previsión Social, CENIET, 1980. Processed.

———, and Simon Geluda. *Población, planta industrial y sindicatos.* Serie Estudios no. 7. Secretaría de Trabajo y Previsión Social, CENIET, 1981.

———, and Fernando Mercado. "El mercado de trabajo norteamericano y los trabajadores mexicanos: Algunos elementos teóricos y empíricos para su discusión." Paper presented at the Mexico-United States Seminar on Undocumented Migration, September 4–6, 1980, University of New Mexico, Albuquerque, New Mexico.

———, and José L. Vega, *Salarios contractuales-vs-coyuntura económica, 1977 y 1979.* Serie Estudios no. 9. Mexico, D.F.: Secretaría de Trabajo y Previsión Social, Centro de Información y Estadísticas del Trabajo (CENIET), 1981.

———, José L. Vega, and Jaime Rozenel. "Comportamiento de la negociación de salarios contractuales, México 1977 y 1979." Mexico, D.F.: Secretaría del Trabajo y Previsión Social, CENIET, 1981. Processed.

Official Documents and Publications

Banco de México. *Distribución del ingreso en México: Ensayos.* 3 vols. Mexico, D.F.: Subdirección de Investigación Económica, 1982.

———. *Indicadores económicos.* Mexico, D.F. Monthly.

———. *Informe anual.* México, D.F. Annual.

Banco Nacional de Crédito Rural, S.A. Fideicomiso para Estudios y Planes de Desarrollo Agropecuario y Programas de Credito Agricola. *Principales indicadores del estudio del empleo, subempleo y desempleo rural.* Mexico, D.F., 1983.

———. *Empleo, subempleo y desempleo en el sector rural, por subregiones económicas.* 31 vols. Mexico, D.F., 1981–83.

Banco Nacional de Comercio Exterior. *Comercio exterior.* Mexico, D.F. Monthly.

Banco Nacional de México (Banamex). *Encuesta de subempleados.* Mexico, D.F.: Estudios Sociales, 1983.

———. *Review of the Economic Situation of Mexico.* Mexico, D.F. Monthly.

Centro de Investigaciones Agrarias. *Estructura agraria y desarrollo agricola de México.* 3 vols. Mexico, D.F., 1970.

Centro de Investigaciones para el Desarrollo Rural (CIDER). *Mercado de trabajo del algodón.* Mexico, D.F., n.d..

Comisión Consultiva del Empleo. *Programa nacional de empleo 1980/82, síntesis.* Mexico, D.F.: Dirección del Empleo, November 1979.

Comisión Nacional de los Salarios Minimos. *Salarios minimos.* Mexico, D.F. Annual.

Comité Interamericano de Desarrollo Agricola. *Estructura agraria y desarrollo agricola de México.* 3 vols. Mexico, D.F., 1970.

———. *Tenencia de la tierra y desarrollo socioeconómico del sector agricola: Guatemala.* Washington, D.C.: Pan American Union, 1965.

Consejo Nacional de Población. *México demográfico: Breviario 1980–81.* Mexico, D.F., 1982.

———. Secretaría de Programación y Presupuesto and Centro Latinoamericano de Demografía. *México: Estimaciones y proyecciones de población, 1950–2000.* Mexico, D.F., 1982.

El Colegio de México. *Dinámica de la población en México.* Mexico, D.F., 1970.

Gobierno Constitucional de los Estados Unidos Mexicanos and Gobierno Constitucional del Estado de Oaxaca. *Programa de desarrollo rural integral de las Mixtecas Oaxaqueñas Alta y Baja, 1984–88.* Mexico, D.F.: Secretaría de Presupuesto y Programación, 1984.

Grupo de Estudio del Problema del Empleo. *El problema ocupacional en México: Magnitud y recomendaciones.* Versión preliminar. Mexico, D.F., n.d.

Nacional Financiera, S.A. *El mercado de valores.*

———. *50 años de revolución mexicana en cifras.* Mexico, D.F., 1963.

Organization of American States. *América en cifras.* Washington, D.C., 1977.

Programa Regional del Empleo para América Latina y el Caribe. *Dinámica del subempleo en América Latina.* Estudios e informes de la CEPAL no. 10. Santiago: United Nations/International Labour Office, 1981.

———. *Employment in Latin America.* New York: Praeger, 1978.

Secretaría de Agricultura y Recursos Hidraulicos. *Consumos aparentes de productos agricolas, 1925–78.* Mexico, D.F., 1979.

———. Centro de Estudios en Planeación (CESPA). *El desarrollo agropecuario de México.* 13 vols. Mexico, D.F., 1982.

Secretaría de Educación Publica. *Estadística basica del sistema nacional de educación tecnológica, 1979–80.* Preliminar. Mexico, D.F., August 1980.

Secretaría de Industria y Comercio, Dirección General de Estadística, *IV censos agricola-ganadero y ejidal, 1960: Resumen general.* Mexico, D.F., 1965.

———. *V Censo agricola-ganadero y ejidal, 1970.* Mexico, D.F., 1975.

———. *IV Censo comercial, 1961.* Mexico, D.F., 1965.

———. *V Censo comercial, 1966.* Mexico, D.F., 1968.

———. *VI Censo comercial, 1971.* Mexico, D.F., 1975.

———. *IV Censo de servicios, 1961.* Mexico, D.F., 1965.

———. *V Censo de servicios, 1966.* Mexico, D.F., 1967.

———. *VI Censo de servicios, 1971.* Mexico, D.F., 1974.

———. *VII Censo industrial de 1961.* Mexico, D.F., 1965.

———. *VIII Censo industrial, 1966.* Mexico, D.F., 1967.

———. *IX Censo industrial, 1971.* Mexico, D.F., 1972.

———. *VII Censo general de población, 6 de junio 1950.* Mexico, D.F., 1953.

———. *VIII Censo general de población, 1960.* Mexico, D.F., 1962.

———. *VIII Censo general de población, 1960: Población economicamente activa* (Rectificación de los cuadros 25, 26, y 27 del *Resumen general* ya publicado). Mexico, D.F., 1964.

———. *IX Censo general de población, 1970.* Mexico, D.F., 1972.

———. *Trabajo y salarios industriales.* Mexico, D.F. Various issues.

Secretaría de Programación y Presupuesto. *VII Censo de comercio, 1976.* Mexico, D.F., 1979.

———. *X Censo general de población y vivienda, 1980.* 32 vols. Mexico, D.F., 1983 and 1984.

———. *X Censo general de población y vivienda, 1980: Resultados preliminares a nivel nacional y por entidad federativa.* Mexico, D.F., n.d.

———. *VII Censo de servicios, 1976.* Mexico, D.F., 1979.

———. *X Censo industrial, 1976.* Mexico, D.F., 1979.

———. *Encuesta continua sobre ocupación.* Mexico, D.F. Quarterly.

———. *Encuesta industrial mensual.* Mexico, D.F. Monthly.

———. *Encuesta nacional de ingresos y gastos de los hogares, 1977.* Mexico, D.F., n.d.

———. *Información basica sobre estructura y caracteristicas del empleo en las areas metropolitanas de las ciudades de México, Guadalajara y Monterrey.* Mexico, D.F., n.d.

———. *Sistema de cuentas nacionales de México.* Vol. 1. *Resumen general.* Mexico, D.F., 1981.

———. Sistema de cuentas nacionales de México, 1978–1980. Mexico, D.F., 1982.

Secretaría de Programación y Presupuesto and Secretaría del Trabajo y Previsión Social. *La ocupación informal en areas urbanas, 1976.* Mexico, D.F., 1979.

Secretaría del Trabajo y Previsión Social. *Ley federal del trabajo.* Mexico, D.F., May 1978.

Secretaría del Trabajo y Previsión Social, Centro de Información y Estadísticas del Trabajo (CENIET). Análisis de algunos resultados de la primera encuesta a trabajadores mexicanos no documentados devueltos de los Estados Unidos, octubre 23–noviembre 13 de 1977," Mexico, D.F., n.d.

———. *Indicadores para el estudio de la población economicamente activa basados en la información censal de 1970.* Serie Estudios no. 4. Mexico, D.F., 1977.

Secretaría del Trabajo y Previsión Social, Dirección General del Servicio Publico del Empleo. *Cuadernos de empleo,* no. 1. Mexico, D.F., 1976.

Secretaría del Trabajo y Previsión Social, Instituto Nacional de Estudios del Trabajo. *Mercados regionales de trabajo.* Mexico, D.F., 1976.

U.S. Agency for International Development. *Spring Review of Land Reform, June 1970.* 2d ed., vol. 7. Washington, D.C., 1970.

U.S. Immigration and Naturalization Service. *Annual Report.* Washington, D.C.: Government Printing Office, various years.

U.S. Senate, Committee on the Judiciary, 96th Congress. *Temporary Worker Programs: Background and Issues*. Washington, D.C.: Government Printing Office, 1980.

World Bank. *Mexico: Manufacturing Sector, Situation, Prospects and Policies*. Washington, D.C., March 1979.

———. *Quarterly Review of Commodity Markets*. Washington, D.C.

Index

Peter Gregory is professor of economics at the University of New Mexico and a consultant to the World Bank.

The most recent World Bank publications are described in the annual spring and fall lists. The latest edition is available free of charge from Publications Sales Unit, Department B, The World Bank, Washington, D.C. 20433, U.S.A.